Compact Cities

Compact Cities:
Sustainable Urban Forms for Developing Countries

Edited by

Mike Jenks and Rod Burgess

London and New York

First Published 2000
By Spon Press
11 New Fetter Lane, London EC4P 4EE

Simultaneously published in the USA and Canada by Spon Press
29 West 35th Street, New York, NY 10001

Spon Press is an imprint of the Taylor & Francis Group

© 2000 Editorial matter and selection: Mike Jenks and Rod Burgess;
individual contributions: the contributors

The right of Mike Jenks and Rod Burgess to be identified as the Author of this
Work has been asserted by them in accordance with the Copyright, Designs and
Patents Act 1988

Printed and bound in Great Britain by
St Edmundsbury Press, Bury St Edmunds, Suffolk

British Library Cataloguing in Publication Data
A catalogue record for this book is available from the British Library

Library of Congress Cataloging in Publication Data
A catalog record for this book has been requested

ISBN 0-419-25130-8

Contents

Part Four Transport, Infrastructure and Environment

Conclusion

Contributors

Claudio Acioly Jr.
IHS – Institute of Housing and Urban Development Studies, Rotterdam, The Netherlands

Adriana Allen
Development Planning Unit, University College London, London, UK

Chang-Hee Christine Bae
Assistant Professor, Urban Design and Planning, University of Washington, Seattle, USA

Paul A. Barter
SUSTRAN Resource Centre, Kuala Lumpur, Malaysia

Murtaza Hatim Baxamusa
School of Policy, Planning and Development, University of Southern California, Los Angeles, USA

Sharon Biermann
CSIR Building and Construction Technology, Pretoria, South Africa

Peter Brand
Faculty of Architecture, National University of Colombia (at Medellín), Medellín, Columbia

Rod Burgess
Senior Lecturer and Research Fellow, Centre for Development and Emergency Practices, School of Architecture, Oxford Brookes University, Oxford, UK

Marisa Carmona
Faculty of Architecture, Housing, Urban Design and Planning, Technical University Delft, Delft, The Netherlands

Yao-Lin Chang
Doctoral Student, Department of Urban Planning, National Chen Kung University, Tainan City, Taiwan ROC

Thomas A. Clark
Professor and Chair, Department of Planning and Design, College of Architecture and Planning, University of Colorado at Denver, Denver, USA

David Dewar
Professor of Architecture and Planning and BP Chair of Urban and Regional Planning, School of Architecture and Planning, University of Cape Town, Cape Town, South Africa

Paul F. Downton
School of Architecture and Design, University of South Australia, Adelaide, Australia

Teresa Dominik
Urban Strategy Department, Durban Metro Council, Durban, South Africa

John Martin Evans
Centre for Habitat and Energy Studies, Faculty of Architecture, Design and Urbanism, University of Buenos Aires, Buenos Aires, Argentina

Giulietta Fadda
Titular Professor, School of Architecture, University of Valparaíso, Chile

Douglas Hindson
Professor, Institute for Social and Economic Research, University of Durban-Westville, Durban, South Africa

Yu-Ting Hung
Department of Urban Planning, National Chen Kung University, Tainan City, Taiwan ROC

Mike Jenks
Professor, and Director of the Oxford Centre for Sustainable Development, School of Architecture, Oxford Brookes University, Oxford, UK

Paola Jirón
Faculty of Architecture and Urbanism, University of Chile, Santiago, Chile

Ashok Kumar
Department of Physical Planning, School of Planning and Architecture, New Delhi, India

Stephen S. Y. Lau
Department of Architecture, The University of Hong Kong, Hong Kong SAR, China

Xia Li
Professor, Guangzhon Institute of Geography, Post-Doctoral Fellow, Centre of Urban Planning and Environmental Management, The University of Hong Kong, Hong Kong SAR, China

Tony Lloyd Jones
Architect and Planner, Department of Planning and Urban Design, University of Westminster, London, UK

Q. M. Mahtab-uz-Zaman
Department of Architecture, The University of Hong Kong, Hong Kong SAR, China

So Hing Mei
Doctoral Student, Department of Architecture, The University of Hong Kong, Hong Kong SAR, China

Malcolm Moor
Consultant Architect and Town Planner, Abingdon, UK

Antonio Clovis Pinto Ferraz
Department of Tranportation, São Carlos School of Engineering, University of São Paolo, São Carlos, Brazil

Archimedes Azevedo Raia Jr.
Department of Civil Engineering, Federal University of São Carlos, São Carlos, Brazil

B. Sudhakara Reddy
Indira Gandhi Institute of Development Research, Mumbai, India

Clarke Rees
Transport and Planning Consultant, Teddington, UK

Harry W. Richardson
Professor, School of Policy, Planning and Development, University of Southern California, Los Angeles, USA

Antonio Nelson Rodrigues da Silva
Department of Transportation, São Carlos School of Engineering, University of São Paolo, São Carlos, Brazil

Silvia de Schiller
Centre for Habitat and Energy Studies, Faculty of Architecture, Design and Urbanism, University of Buenos Aires, Buenos Aires, Argentina

Maria D. Schoonraad
Department of Town and Regional Planning, University of Pretoria, Pretoria, South Africa

Alison Todes
Professor, School of Architecture, Planning and Housing, University of Natal, Durban, South Africa

Te-I Albert Tsai
Doctoral Student, Department of Planning and Design, College of Architecture and Planning, University of Colorado at Denver, Denver, USA

Ko-Wan Tsou
Associate Professor, Department of Urban Planning, National Chen Kung University, Tainan City, Taiwan ROC

Anthony Gar-on Yeh
Director of GIS Research and Assistant Director, Centre of Urban Planning and Environmental Management, The University of Hong Kong, Hong Kong SAR, China

Xing Quan Zhang
Centre of Urban Planning and Environmental Management, The University of Hong Kong, Hong Kong SAR, China

Kerstin Zillman
Department of Urban Planning and Housing in Developing Countries, Technical University of Hamburg-Harburg, Escheburg, Germany

Acknowledgements

Our thanks go to all those who have helped in the writing and production of this book. We express our gratitude to all the contributors for their enthusiastic response to the project and for the production of their chapters. We also thank all those involved in the book's production: Margaret Ackrill for the sub-editing; Ian Pope for the desktop publishing; Kwamina Monney for redrawing many of the illustrations, Sarah Taylor for her assistance, and all the many staff involved at Spon Press. Thanks for their support also go to our fellow editors of the other two books in this series: Elizabeth Burton and Katie Williams. In particular our warmest thanks go to Margaret Jenks and Farida and Jazmin Burgess for their continued support during the time it took to produce this book.

Mike Jenks

Introduction:
Sustainable Urban Form in Developing Countries?

> Sustainable urban forms will only be achievable if they are underpinned by a policy background which commits to global sustainability goals, but leaves room for local formation and implementation of solutions.
> (Williams *et al.*, 2000)

The overall aim of this book is to set out some of the debate about the sustainability of cities in developing countries, and examine whether ideas about urban form and compact cities, that have evolved in developed countries, have any real relevance in the context of areas of the world subject to rapid urbanisation. This volume is the third of a trilogy of books about sustainable urban form. The first, *The Compact City: A Sustainable Urban Form?* (Jenks *et al.*, 1996), examined the claim that the compact city is a sustainable urban form (defined below). A great deal of complexity was found, and the book did not conclude with a ringing endorsement of the compact city model, at least as conceived in the context of developed countries. Questions were raised about the extent to which urban form could achieve sustainability. There were benefits in relation to the viability of public transport and saving of agricultural and other valuable land, but there were problems about environmental quality and local acceptance of more compact forms of urban living. The second book, *Achieving Sustainable Urban Form* (Williams *et al.*, 2000), building on the findings of the first, addressed two questions – what is sustainable urban form, and how can it be achieved? It was concluded that there was no single sustainable form, but rather a variety of urban forms that were 'more sustainable than typical recent development patterns' (ibid., p.355). These depended, crucially, on the characteristics of an area and the local and strategic objectives (or 'pathways') chosen for sustainability. Understanding the impacts of urban form on transport, social issues and the environment required sophisticated decision-making processes that were inclusive and adaptive.

The first two books focused almost entirely on research into and findings drawn from the experience of developed countries. This has left an obvious and significant gap in relation to knowledge about the sustainability of urban form in

1

developing countries. It is hoped that this volume will go some way towards filling that gap, presenting policies and local and strategic issues, and suggesting the extent to which there is commitment to, and success in achieving, sustainable urban forms in the developing world.

World cities, world problems?

The last decade has been remarkable for the vast array of literature, and intensity of debate, about cities and their global impact. Problems of sustainability, stemming from Brundtland (WCED, 1987) and the Rio Earth Summit (UNCED, 1992), have concentrated the minds of governments and research organisations around the world. Cities have been seen as the cause of environmental degradation and resource depletion, casting an ecological footprint across the globe, far beyond their immediate regions (e.g. Girardet, 1996; Wackernagel *et al.*, 1997). More often than not, cities are seen as problematic – congested, polluting, with poor housing, collapsing infrastructure, crime and poverty. Yet it is cities that drive economies and it is within them that innovation occurs and an increasing part of global output is produced. Soon, over half the world's population will live in cities, the majority in the developing countries.

Over the past five years the world has seen a 2.5% growth in urbanisation, but that varies between the more developed regions (0.7%) and the less developed regions where the growth has been 3.3% (UNFPA, 1999). In 1999, 47%, or 2.8 billion, of the world's population lived in cities, and this is set to increase by around 60 million people each year. The expectation is that by 2030 'nearly 5 billion (61 per cent) of the world's 8.1 billion people will live in cities' (UNFPA, 2000, p.25). Of the urban population, for every one person now living in cities in developed countries, there are two in the cities of the developing world. Within 30 years this proportion is predicted to rise to 1:4, indicating that 90% of the growth in urbanisation will be in developing countries.

In these countries the expansion of urbanisation is occurring on an unimaginable scale. Very large cities – the megacities with populations of over 10 million people – are becoming commonplace. New York and Tokyo were the only megacities in 1960, but by 1999 there were 17. In another 15 years projections suggest there will be at least 26 such cities, 22 of which will be in developing countries, and 18 of these in Asia (UNFPA, 1999). However, the most aggressive growth appears to be in the cities of between 1 and 10 million. From the 270 'million cities' in 1990, by 2015, various predictions show, there may be between 358 to 516 of these cities (UNCHS cited in Hall and Pfeiffer, 2000; WRI, 1996).

It is questionable whether these statistics necessarily represent a problem. The very size of the cities and the high proportion of the world's population living within them will inevitably concentrate problems. These will include the intensive use of resources such as land, water and energy, the over-stretching of infrastructure, poor sanitation and health, and social and economic inequalities. Yet there are wide disparities within and between them. Affluent lifestyles and profligate use of land, both in developed and developing countries, result in a disproportionate use of resources and urban forms that are often unsustainable (Jenks *et al.*, 1996, p.4). However, it is particular industries and commercial enterprises within cities or outside them such as the ubiquitous shopping mall or 'edge city' (Garreau, 1991) that are likely to cause most waste, pollution and harmful emissions. The lifestyles of those living in low-density suburban areas on the periphery will be responsible for the consumption of more resources than 'those with similar incomes living in cities' (Mitlin and Satterthwaite, 1996, p.30).

Cities may have problems, but they are not necessarily a problem in themselves. As Mitlin and Satterthwaite (1996, p.50) observe, it is the 'failure of effective governance within cities that explains the poor environmental performance of so many cities rather than an inherent characteristic of cities in general'. There are more positive perceptions, such as those conveyed in the ideas for higher-density compact cities advocated in developed countries (e.g. Williams *et al.*, 1999). The perception of these concepts in developing countries appears to be similar, with the belief that compaction will result in reductions in travel distances and thus vehicle emissions, and that the high densities can create greater viability for service provision, public transport, waste disposal, healthcare and education. The manipulation of urban form, and the provision of better forms of governance, may go some way to overcome city problems (e.g. Jenks, 2000). Despite many problems, even the densest, fastest growing cities in developing countries have positive benefits for those living there. They can provide 'enhanced opportunity for millions of people', and 'refuges from a stifling, restrictive rural life' that may no longer be economically sustainable (Seabrook, 1996, p.5). The sheer vitality and numbers of people and ideas tend to change attitudes and lifestyles, and lead to higher aspirations to improve standards of living (Pugh, 1996). How, then, does this relate to sustainable development and sustainable urban form?

Sustainable development
The most commonly cited definition of sustainable development has been drawn from the Brundtland report of well over a decade ago (WCED, 1987). Its broad concern that actions taken today should not compromise future generations still remains a valid starting point. However, it is such a broad definition that the term sustainable development has often been seen to mean different things to the different interest groups that use it. Arriving at a definition of sustainable urban form was one of the aims of the second book in this series. Sustainable development, both inter- and intra-generational, was described as development that does not require resources beyond its environmental capacity, is equitable, promotes social justice, and is created through inclusive decision-making procedures. Various components with the potential to influence the sustainability of urban form were identified by the contributors to the book, including: the size, shape, density and compactness of cities; processes of intensification and decentralisation; land use, mixed uses, layout and building type (particularly housing); and green and open spaces. These components, and the research presented in *Achieving Sustainable Urban Form*, provide a useful starting point from which the experiences of developing countries can be compared. Authors of many of the chapters in this book, implicitly and sometimes explicitly, provide perspectives on the meaning of sustainable urban form. These definitions say much about the differing contextual perceptions of sustainability. This issue is returned to in the Conclusions.

Developing countries – similarities and differences

In the face of such overwhelming statistics about developing countries, there is a danger of assuming that the problems may be much the same across different countries. There is also a danger of assuming that widely held tenets of urban planning, the signs and symbols of globalisation, or the images of modernism, mean that difference between regions and cultures is narrowing to insignificance (e.g. Gilbert and Gugler, 1992).

There is a danger inherent in categorising the world into developed and developing countries; there are many similar characteristics, as well as significant differences, in cities across this divide. It is recognised that the division is an oversimplification; nevertheless, it is useful, and there is a reasonable basis for it. This book follows the definition of developed countries as the 35 market-orientated countries belonging to the Organisation for Economic Co-operation and Development (OECD). Developing countries are the world's remaining 172, generally with a per capita GNP of below US$5,000, and which account for 70% of the world's population (Crump and Ellwood, 1998). However, there are exceptions; in this book South Africa, an OECD member, is included as a developing country, largely because of its low GNP and the characteristics of its cities.

There are clear differences between many of the countries featured, from the poor to the very rich. The poor countries, with a per capita GNP of less than US$1,500, include Bangladesh (the poorest, with US$260), China, Egypt and India. There is a middle range of countries, with a per capita GNP of US$1,500–5,000, including Brazil, Colombia, Chile, South Africa, Thailand and Venezuela. The richer or very rich countries include Argentina (US$8,380) and Taiwan, and at the extreme Hong Kong and Singapore with per capita GNP similar to the US (Instituto del Tercer Mundo, 1999; Newman and Kenworthy, 2000). There are also variations in the overall sustainability of these countries when their ecological footprint is considered (e.g. Wackernagel *et al.*, 1997).

Thus, while there are many general similarities and differences between countries, there are also specific cultural and physical differences that need to be borne in mind. The studies presented in this book go from the densest of urban development (Hong Kong) to the lowest density of urban forms in developing countries (South Africa). The cities include those with strong economies that enable investment in transport infrastructure and property, and those that have *laissez faire* controls and a dominance of market forces at one end of the spectrum. And at the other end, those cities where the informal sector is dominant, social segregation and inequalities are significant, and where self-help may be the best way to get housed. The evidence also ranges in scale from the urban metropolitan regions down to the level of the household. Despite this wide range, a number of common themes emerge, as well as distinct differences.

The structure of the book

The breadth of the debate, theories and policies, and some of the key components that affect sustainable urban form in developing countries are addressed in the four parts of the book.

The first part provides a global overview of the compact city debate, the impact of globalisation, and the need to consider the metropolitan region. Some of the key issues in relation to sustainability – density, transport, encroachment on agricultural land and urban sprawl – are examined through comparative research on cities world-wide. The more technical insights are given a theoretical context, debating, on the one hand, the potential of metaphor and symbolism to promote environmentalism and sustainability, while, on the other, demonstrating that iconic and globalised built forms designed to attract foreign investment ignore sustainable development objectives. Part one concludes with a neglected issue – the relationship of climate (that varies) to similar urban forms that occur globally, and how more climatically responsive urban design could improve sustainability.

The second part explores the tensions between high-density inner city areas and urban peripheral sprawl, and between the formal and informal sectors, and suggests some ways towards achieving compact or sustainable urban forms. Encouraging development where it is needed is shown to be possible where there is strong local government and policies for urban intensification. However, more usually the process of intensification occurs in the absence of such policies or controls. The explosive growth of urban peripheral development is characterised for the poor by local disempowerment, reduced quality of life and environmental pollution, and for the rich by a high quality of life in gated communities. Suggestions are made to overcome the unsustainability of peripheral development through the tax system in the formal sector, and inclusive processes in the informal sector.

Case studies are presented in part three showing plans and policies in response to urban compaction and sustainability objectives. Two extremes of the spectrum are demonstrated – South Africa, with some of the world's lower density urban development, and Hong Kong, with perhaps the densest. In the South African context there are questions about the viability of compaction and sustainability, but significant plans are in place to encourage denser development along transport corridors, and to give citizens equity of access to the opportunities cities provide. Plans being implemented demonstrate that some degree of success can be achieved if a pragmatic, rather than an idealistic, approach is taken. By contrast, Hong Kong demonstrates how very high densities develop. Many positive aspects are explored, such as the comprehensive provision of public transport, but there are also environmental problems, such as air pollution, that result from this extreme urban form.

The fourth part examines some of the key issues associated with sustainable urban form. The first of these is transport, and research in Asian cities points to issues of road capacity and traffic saturation, and how policies of early car restraint and public transport investment can avoid environmental disaster. Transit development zones are shown as a practical means to encourage more sustainable transport modes, and provide denser development where it is needed. Research on infrastructure provision explores the relationship between location, density and costs. It indicates that costs do not necessarily decrease as density increases, and that cost-effectiveness depends on spare infrastructure capacity. The issues examined in the final three chapters are those of ecosystems and environment, the use of sustainability indicators, and the impacts of energy use. All consider the city and its metropolitan region.

Conclusions draw out some common themes across the broad sweep of cities and regions in developing countries, and suggest the extent to which some of the compact city concepts may be successful in achieving sustainable cities.

References

Crump, A. and Ellwood, W. (eds) (1998) *The A to Z of World Development*, New Internationalist, Oxford.

Garreau, J. (1991) *Edge City: Life on the New Frontier*, Doubleday, New York.

Gilbert, A. and Gugler, J. (1992) *Cities, Poverty and Development: Urbanization in the Third World*, Oxford University Press, Oxford.

Girardet, H. (1996) *The Gaia Atlas of Cities: New Directions for Sustainable Urban Living*, Gaia, Stroud.

Hall, P. and Pfeiffer, U. (2000) *Urban Future 21: A Global Agenda for Twenty-First Century Cities*, E & FN Spon, London.

Instituto del Tercer Mundo (1999) *The World Guide 1999/2000: A View from the South*, New Internationalist, Oxford.

Jenks, M (2000) Mega-cities: a need for new paradigms for urban design and sustainability. Proceedings, *Megacities 2000*, Vol.1, Department of Architecture, The University of Hong Kong, Hong Kong.

Jenks, M., Burton, E. and Williams, K. (eds) (1996) *The Compact City: A Sustainable Urban Form?*, E & FN Spon, London.

Mitlin, D. and Satterthwaite, D. (1996) Sustainable development and cities, in *Sustainability, the Environment and Urbanization* (ed. C. Pugh), Earthscan, London.

Newman, P. and Kenworthy, J. (2000) Sustainable urban form: the big picture, in *Achieving Sustainable Urban Form* (eds K. Williams, E. Burton and M. Jenks), E & FN Spon, London.

Pugh, C. (1996) Sustainability and sustainable cities, in *Sustainability, the Environment and Urbanization* (ed. C. Pugh), Earthscan, London.

Seabrook, J. (1996) *In the Cities of the South: Scenes from a Developing World*, Verso, London.

UNCED (United Nations Conference on Environment and Development) (1992) *Earth Summit: Agenda 21 – The United Nations Programme of Action from Rio*, United Nations, New York.

United Nations Population Fund (UNFPA) (1999) *The State of World Population 1999*, United Nations, New York.

United Nations Population Fund (UNFPA) (2000) *Population Issues: Briefing Kit 2000*, United Nations, New York.

Wackernagel, M., Onisto, L., Linares, A. C., Falfan, I. S. L., Garcia, J. M., Guenero, A. I. S. and Guenero, G. S. (1997) *Ecological Footprint of Nations: How Much Nature do they Use? – How Much Nature do they Have?* Universidad Anahuac de Xalpa, Mexico.

Williams, K., Burton, E. and Jenks, M. (eds) (2000) *Achieving Sustainable Urban Form*, E & FN Spon, London.

Williams, K., Jenks, M. and Burton, E. (1999) How much is too much? Urban intensification, social capacity and sustainable development. *Open House International*, **24(1)**, pp.17–25.

World Commission on the Environment and Development (WCED) (1987) *Our Common Future*, Oxford University Press, Oxford.

World Resources Institute (WRI) (1996) *World Resources 1996–97*, Oxford University Press, Oxford.

Part One
Compact Cities in the Context of Developing Countries
Introduction

Any book about cities in developing countries faces the difficulty of tackling a vast diversity of countries and a large range of fast-growing cities and urban regions. There are cities as rich as, if not richer than, their counterparts in the West, there are middle-income cities, and cities that are extremely poor. Few of these cities will stand still, due to rapid demographic change, widespread social inequity, and the impact of globalisation on local economies. At the same time, the irony is that there is a certain uniformity of urban form, especially in the ubiquitous central business districts shaped by global markets, across the world. The key issue is how to understand and assess the sustainability of cities that will house a large proportion of a country's population. The first part of this book gives a broad context within which comparisons can begin to be made, and an understanding of the sustainability of urban form be reached. Comparisons are between cities of developed and developing countries, and consideration is given to strategic and theoretical issues of the urban region, the rapid spread of urbanisation, the impact of climate, and the meaning of environmentalism and sustainable development.

The first four chapters provide wide-ranging comparisons between developed and developing countries in some of the key issues of sustainable urban form. Burgess reviews the arguments about sustainable development and the debate about the compact city. He raises a wide range of significant issues that need to be addressed by policy-makers in developing countries. This chapter provides a critical context within which to place the evidence and research presented in this book. More detailed comparisons follow. Richardson *et al.* analyse a large sample of cities from both developed and developing countries, concentrating on issues of density and, to an extent, transport. They question the validity of some of the arguments for compaction. The higher densities in the core of developing country cities appear to have little effect on urban containment, and can lead to environmental degradation. The authors also doubt the transferability of such densities to the cities of developed countries. Lloyd Jones also compares developed and developing countries, and debates issues of decentralisation, urban sprawl and policies of containment, and introduces research into the core of cities and their metropolitan regions. He suggests a model based on travel time as a means of comparing the sustainability of different cities. Carmona takes the regional issues of centralisation and decentralisation a step further, in the context of Latin American cities. She analyses processes driven by globalisation and shows how decentralisation can be partly reversed if the global markets favour a particular urban region.

The rapid spread of urbanisation to absorb peripheral agricultural land is analysed by Clark and Tsai. Doubts are raised about the effectiveness of policies for containment, as these do not appear to improve agricultural productivity, or lead to better urban living conditions. To be effective, strict enforcement to protect land and high investment to purchase land or development rights would be needed – at present an unlikely scenario. In a case study of the Pearl River Delta, Yeh and Li show in detail the consequences of agricultural land loss and urban sprawl, and why action is necessary. They present a convincing model to help containment and achieve a measure of sustainability and compaction, demonstrating significant savings of agricultural land, and reductions in travel and fuel consumption.

In addition to the key pragmatic and technical dimensions, there is also a theoretical dimension, often left out of the debate. Brand points to the significance of the symbolism of environmental and compact city ideas. He shows how small yet significant interventions, either through the planning discourse or symbolic development on the ground, can help move public perceptions of sustainability. Symbolism and meaning can be a two-edged sword, and Lau, Zaman and Mei show its effect in Asia in a fast-growing economy. The ultra-rapid development in Shanghai takes a deliberately symbolic form – not one of environmentalism, but of modernism – attempting to attract foreign investment and achieve world city status. They demonstrate how state intervention and incentives can drive development, and point out the lack of any environmental or sustainability policies. It is a useful warning, as this type of development is a potential model to which many cities may aspire. Indeed, in a less extreme form, this type of global modernism is common to many cities. It is a phenomenon observed by de Schiller and Evans, who raise the issue of climate. While urban form world-wide may have many similarities, climates vary enormously across the world. They suggest that urban form and building design should relate to them. These authors show, for example, that compact urban form may be suitable in some climates, but not in others.

Rod Burgess
The Compact City Debate:
A Global Perspective

Introduction

One important consequence of the search for sustainable urban development has been a resurgence of interest in compact city theories and policies. The reasons offered for making cities more compact have changed in the 150 years or so since the question was first broached. In the current period the desirability – or in some views the necessity – for compaction is rooted in the sustainability imperatives of resource conservation (particularly fossil-fuelled energy) and waste-minimisation (particularly carbon emissions into the global atmospheric sink). Contemporary compact city approaches have become one form of achieving 'sustainable urban development', but that is not to say that they are coterminous with it. There are also a number of other economic, social, cultural and political justifications for compact city initiatives and different and often contradictory policies for sustainable urban development.

While there have been a number of attempts to define and clarify the concept of the compact city and its relationship to sustainable urban development, there remain questions over what should be the principal spatial point of reference in undertaking compaction. Should it be the city itself or the metropolitan region, the broader region or the urban system? Or should it be the neighbourhood, urban sub-centres, the inner city or the suburbs, or urban and regional transport corridors or nodes? Again, there is also the question of whether compaction efforts should be concentrated on the development of new settlements or on modifying existing ones. There are significant disputes over the preferred spatial models for the compact. There is also considerable debate over how cities are going to be compacted, not least because the forces determining the degree of compaction of existing settlements are far from clearly understood. In this context an adequate understanding of the particular relationship between spatial centralisation and decentralisation forces in cities in different parts of the unfolding global system is critical.

This said, it is possible to offer a tentative and composite definition of contemporary compact city approaches as: 'to increase built area and residential population densities; to intensify urban economic, social and cultural activities and to manipulate urban size, form and structure and settlement systems in pursuit of the environmental, social and global sustainability benefits derived from the concentration of urban functions'.

Compact cities and global urban sustainability

The current resurgence of interest in policies for compact cities dates from the late 1980s and has largely been propelled by the search for the global sustainability goals on climatic change and resource use embodied in the Brundtland Commission Report (WCED, 1987) and the UNCED Agenda 21 proposals (1993). In this context these theoretical and policy developments differ from earlier efforts in two ways. First, in contrast to modernism they reassert a fundamental environmental rationality for architecture, planning and design. However, in contrast to the earlier environmentalism of the Garden City and Regional Planning Movements (Howard, 1898; Geddes, 1968; Mumford, 1938), their principal preoccupation is with the environmental and socio-economic consequences of energy production and consumption for urban development – an issue never seriously considered or understood by either early compact city theorists or modernists. The second difference was the recognition of a global rationale. This ineluctably had to be considered everywhere at all spatial levels of practice and policymaking and was derived from the realities of rapid globalisation and the 'totalisation' of environmental problems. Urban architectural, planning and design practice had to be 'green and global'. It is the failure to appreciate the significance of these two dimensions that often accounts for much of the reluctance to come to terms with contemporary arguments about the compact city and sustainable urban form.

Interest in compact city policies over the last ten years has been almost exclusively limited to the experience of developed countries (US, Europe, Japan, and Australia). There are a number of reasons for encouraging interest in the compact city debate in developing countries.

Perhaps the most immediate is the global scale of the environmental problems to which the policies are addressed. What makes the current relationship between humanity and nature (Global Environmental Change) and society and space (Globalisation) different from past conditions is that they both manifest a sort of 'totalisation' of human and environmental activities. Sustainability requires that the impacts of urban development activities should not involve an uncompensated geographical or spatial displacement of environmental problems or costs onto other countries, or draw on the resource base and waste absorption capacity of the 'global commons' to levels which undermine health and which disrupt the dynamic equilibrium of the global ecosystem. Given the fact that less than a third of the world's population live in developed countries (a proportion which is set to decline further), it is clear that the success or failure of these policies will depend on their simultaneous application in developing countries. Indeed, given differences in resource use at a global level, the benefits of the successful application of compact city policies in any one part of the global economy could be wiped out by the emergence of unsustainable settlement patterns in another part. Irresponsible energy policies in the US, resistance to increases in fuel taxes in Europe, and the attempts of developed countries to maintain their energy consumption levels at the expense of developing countries using markets for carbon trading permits are currently causing great concern. In this context it is imperative to consider the implications of urban development, wherever it takes place, in a global context.

The implications of urban development

The global dimension
The first implication concerns the scale of the global urbanisation process in the contemporary period. From a global viewpoint it is somewhat sobering to remember that at the start of the twentieth century only 13% of the world's population was living in cities and at the end of it almost one half (47.5%) of its rapidly growing population was urbanised. According to recent UN estimates (UNCHS, 1996), in the 50-year period between 1975 and 2025 alone, the global level of urbanisation will have increased from 37.7% to 61.1% and the total population living in cities will have risen from 1.58 billion to 5.06 billion – an average annual urban growth rate over the period of 2.38%. Dramatic increases in the volume of global output and trade and the number and size of cities have occurred as the global economy has progressively shifted from the primary and rural to the secondary and tertiary urban sectors. This has been accompanied by an increase in the spatial scale and intensity of these environmental impacts, including now those at a global level. Cities and urban systems are part of a trade- and production-induced spatial division of labour that links them with surrounding rural areas, regions, other cities and urban systems, national markets and the global space economy. Although the nature of these myriad linkages remains widely disputed, the diminishing 'closure' of cities and urban systems in a period of rapid urbanisation and economic, social and cultural globalisation is widely accepted.

Three worlds not two
The second implication is that an adequate understanding of urban sustainability problems requires a close examination of how individual cities and regions function in terms of an increasingly integrated but differentiated global system. This structure consists of a system of different economic zones (core, semi-periphery and periphery) with multiple polities and cultures that are linked in a single trade- and production-induced spatial division of labour (Wallerstein, 1979). It should not be assumed that the way in which cities in developed countries are integrated into the global system (the core) is the same as the way cities in developing countries (semi-periphery and periphery) are integrated into it, although all are likely to experience the effects of and contribute to globalisation. Both underdevelopment and development have specific environmental consequences and the unequal rates and level of development that characterise the zones give a specific configuration of environmental issues to cities within them. These developmental differences are registered in terms of: the levels and types of renewable and non-renewable resource use; the volumes and composition of energy production and demand; the levels of production of CFCs and greenhouse gases; the levels and types of air and water pollution; the volumes and composition of solid and toxic wastes; the levels and types of soil degradation and erosion; the degree of conversion and removal of vegetation; the impacts on biodiversity and differential access to the global commons and their resources.

The relevance of compact city policies
The third implication is that the question of the relevance of compact city policies for developing countries also has to take account of the significant differences in

the levels of urbanisation and rates of urban growth between developed and developing countries and between different world regions.

In developed countries the problem is not high rates of urban growth. By the mid-twentieth century these countries had already passed through the rapid-growth, middle phase of the demographic and urban transitions and were characterised by low rates of natural increase, high levels of urbanisation and slow urban growth rates. Between 1975 and 2025 the level of urbanisation of developed countries will have increased from 69.8% to 84.0% and the total urban population from 729 million to one billion – an average urban growth rate of only 0.71% per annum over the period (UNCHS, 1996). However, economic growth, the rise in living standards and increased consumption levels have brought on dramatic increases in per capita demand for land, energy, food and fresh water and, increases of a similar magnitude in the production of wastes and pollutants. With the rapid loss of agricultural land and natural habitats (around 2% per decade in Western Europe), induced by low-density suburban sprawl, strong metropolitan decentralisation trends and the rise of the car, concern has focused on the global significance of the increase in per capita energy consumption and carbon emissions. In 1996 the US, Canada, the European Community, Japan and Australia, with 16.7% of the world's population, alone accounted for 53.6% of global carbon dioxide emissions. Over three-quarters of these emissions were derived from urban activities (energy production, industry, transport and residential use) with transport-related emissions increasing rapidly. Peter Newman (1999) has shown how the average distance travelled by US urban residents increased by over 2,000km a year between 1980 and 1990, from 9,042km to 11,133km. By 1990 the average population density of the US city had fallen to 14 persons per hectare. It was clear that if this pattern of social and urban development was to be globalised, then global ecosystem collapse looked likely.

That a rapid process of global urban growth was taking place in developing countries was indisputable. Most of these countries in the late twentieth century were still in the early or middle stages of their demographic and urban transitions, with low levels of urbanisation and rapid rates of urban growth derived from high rates of natural increase and rural to urban migration. In 1975 only 26.7% of their populations was living in cities but by 2025 the UN estimates that their level of urbanisation will reach 57.1% – an average urban growth rate of 3.21% per annum (UNCHS, 1996). In effect this means the urban population of developing countries will increase almost five times over the 50-year period – from 809 million in 1975 to 4 billion in 2025 – and it is clear that even then the urban transition process will still be far from complete. Whereas there were slightly more urban dwellers in developing countries than in developed countries in 1975, in 2025 there will be four times as many. Most of this urban growth will be concentrated in Africa and Asia, as levels of urbanisation in Latin America have approximated those of developed countries since 1975, though their rates of urban growth will still be high – at 1.61% per annum over the next 25 years.

In these cities attempts to emulate developed-country urban and social development models and trends have been largely unrestrained. However, lower levels of economic development, smaller urban budgets, shortages of environmental infrastructure, shelter and basic services and high levels of urban poverty have resulted in a different pattern of urban development and environmental degradation which looks equally as unsustainable. 'To the effluence of affluence', as one observer has put it, 'has been added the pollution of poverty'.

Quality of life and development

It is widely agreed that the basic issue of how to de-link improvements in urban living standards and the quality of life from high levels of resource use and waste production is rooted in demand factors governed by development models and modes of production and consumption. For this reason most compact city approaches have accepted the concept of 'socio-economic sustainability' based on the acceptance of an ineluctable need for economic growth and the merits of the principles of 'intra-generational equity' and 'social justice' (Haughton and Hunter, 1994). However, there are also substantial differences of opinion about how these sustainability goals can be achieved, particularly by the dominant neo-liberal development strategy.

The difference in socio-economic conditions of the urban populations of developing countries has meant that compact city approaches have focused and must continue to do so on the 'development' side of the sustainability agenda. They acknowledge that development and growth are essential for meeting existing basic human needs and those derived from population growth and rising expectations, and that this demands exploitation of natural resources, environmental services and the use of nature as a sink.

However, it is also recognised that both development and the lack of development can lead to environmental degradation and that compact city policies will have to address the problems of poverty and social inequality. The sustainable use of resources and disposal of wastes are very difficult under conditions of poverty, where survival considerations can easily outweigh those of posterity. The problem is particularly acute in cities in developing countries where the majority of the poor are now to be found and where about a quarter of urban households live in poverty. The World Bank (1990) believes that this proportion will not decrease over the next 20 years and the numbers living in urban poverty will increase substantially with urban population growth. Policies generally emphasise the commitment to meeting basic human needs through access to income-generating activities, productive assets and economic security arrangements for the old, sick, poor, disabled and unemployed. The UN Declaration of Human Rights specifies a 'development right' to a standard of living adequate for health and well-being including food, clothing, housing and medical care and the necessary physical and social services.

The impact of inadequate environmental infrastructure and services on the health and productivity of the urban poor has been recognised along with the socio-economic impacts of environmental degradation in poor neighbourhoods. The question of how to bring the urban poor (and not-so-poor) into the range of effective demand capable of improving the coverage and maintenance of urban infrastructure and services has proved to be particularly intractable. Given the significant socio-economic and environmental problems associated with poverty and low incomes, the major gains derived from improved incomes, and the improved provision and maintenance of environmental infrastructure, it is hardly surprising that these issues have dominated compact city debates in developing countries rather than the debates on transport-related carbon emissions, as in developed countries.

Requisite variety

To the substantial variations in the environmental profiles and problems of cities in the various zones of the global system must be added enormous differences in culture and in the structure of social and political systems. It follows that compact city policies must meet this requirement for variety. Although some proponents of sustainable urban development (Cohen, 1996) and global cities (Sassen, 1991) identify a tendency towards 'urban convergence' and globalisation as a homogenising force, it seems more likely that the formulation of successful compact city policies will be based on a recognition of this differentiating dynamic. The theoretical shift of the new urban environmentalism towards understanding cities as 'places' – 'spaces specified in nature' – would seem to be essential for this task. One curious thing about the reassertion of the particularity of place and environment is that it has largely been brought about by Global Climatic Change, whose effects are general and non-specific. This throws doubt on the view that globalisation can be understood merely as a homogenising force. These differences manifest themselves in all aspects of the urbanisation and urban development process and this in turn has a bearing on the applicability and viability of compact city policies in developing countries (Burgess *et al.*, 1997).

The compact city debate in developing countries
The debate on the merits of compact city policies for cities in developing countries can be discussed in relation to the various elements of the definition provided: attempts to increase built area and residential population densities; to intensify urban economic, social and cultural activities and to manipulate urban size, form and structure and settlement systems in pursuit of the environmental, social and global sustainability benefits derived from the concentration of urban functions.

Densification
The lack of empirical data on existing density levels and trends, and a lack of clarity on what are the most appropriate indicators to measure them, pose a problem for the assessment of densification policies for cities in developing countries. Resolving this problem remains a major research priority. There are substantial variations in urban densities in cities in developing countries and it is difficult to make generalisations about them in comparison with cities in developed countries. Although the level of economic and social development must be considered the most important determinant, there are other influences which also have to be taken into account but which remain poorly understood.

Cultural factors certainly influence the level of socially acceptable space consumption and proximity and these vary widely between developing countries. In general urban densities are highest in Asia; high in Europe, North Africa and the Middle East; low in Latin America and sub-Saharan Africa and lowest in North America and Australia (Acioly and Davidson, 1996). But within each of these world regions there are substantial variations that cannot be understood in cultural terms. Again, cultural attitudes to the acceptability or not of high densities cannot be regarded as fixed because the definition of what is a socially acceptable level of space consumption and proximity seems to change historically in all cultures.

Environmental factors such as scarcity of urbanisable land, the restricted availability of water and the ability of fertile hinterlands to generate large agricultural surpluses have all been important historical influences on urban densities and continue to remain influential. Cities in developing countries are often built in naturally hazardous areas, in areas of high relief, on the floodplains of major rivers, in seismically active zones, at the foot of volcanoes or in the pathways of tropical cyclones. The implications of densification for disaster mitigation and management in these contexts are considerable. The effect of densification (and global warming) on urban heat islands in tropical and subtropical climates, where so many cities are located, can be much greater than in temperate climates. With rising incomes this could generate a substantial demand for energy for cooling and diminish the desired energy savings.

However, it is the levels and rates of economic and social development which are the most important issue. The failure of the rate of economic development to match the rate of demographic growth can only lead to deterioration in all aspects of sustainability (UNDP, 1992; Satterthwaite, 1999). High demographic growth, low levels of economic development, high income inequalities, small urban budgets and shortages of environmental infrastructure, shelter and basic services have a critical effect on densification policies and the effectiveness of policy instruments. The merits of densification at a high level of development may disappear at a lower level and be counterproductive without significant improvements to this level.

What is the sense, it is frequently asked, of further densification given that densities are already high and associated with a range of problems including infrastructure overload, overcrowding, congestion, air pollution, severe health hazards, lack of public and green space and environmental degradation (Hardoy *et al.*, 1990)? The sustainability gains from further densification will be limited under conditions where densities are already high. Under these circumstances the merits of urban densification postulated for developed country cities seem far less convincing in the context of developing countries.

Infrastructure and land capacity

The argument that higher densities will lead to cheaper infrastructure costs and the absorption of spare inner city capacity is particularly contentious in developing countries. Although some inner city areas in Latin America may be de-densifying, the opposite is generally true for most cities in developing countries and there is no spare capacity to be filled. This spare capacity, if it exists anywhere, is most likely to be found in high income areas and the social implications of taking the least-cost option cannot be justified on social or sustainability grounds – which often does not prevent it from happening. The possibility of densifying empty speculative plots through the use of punitive taxes is politically constrained under current neo-liberal strategies. However, some interesting incentive schemes involving land sharing arrangements, the transfer of development rights and public/private partnerships offer some promise.

A major obstacle in recent years has been the rapid increase in land values in many cities in developing countries as the demand for urban space has soared and as large surpluses from the deregulated finance sector and the drugs trade have been ploughed into the urban land market. In 1999, for example, Mumbai had the highest commercial office rents in the world. The extent to which high densities and densification efforts have contributed to these increases remains an important question for research. However, the cost differentials between infrastructure provision in the inner city and the periphery have probably narrowed substantially.

Again, as the cost of infrastructure provision depends substantially on environmental factors and technical complexity, it is clear that the costs of densifying low-income settlements could be higher than middle-income settlements. This is because these settlements often consist of disorganised layouts built in fragile environments, on steep slopes, geologically unstable land, tidal flats or on land which is prone to flooding.

Thus the savings on infrastructure costs involved in densification may not be that substantial. The essential problem in these cities is the low level of effective demand generated by the population no matter what densities they are living at and an inadequate rate of investment in infrastructure. To densify without adequate rates of investment in infrastructure could have a highly deleterious effect on urban sustainability. Moreover, doubt has also been thrown on the ability of the privatisation and marginal cost-pricing formulae for infrastructure provision currently installed in developing countries to realise the massive investments required to extend coverage and improve maintenance and repair. The social consequences of the withdrawal of subsidies and the full commodification of services are also a major preoccupation.

Transport

Similar arguments govern the relationship between densification and the ability to generate mass thresholds for public transport – it is effective demand and higher incomes and not just 'numbers in need' that create these thresholds. The most immediate sustainability gains that can be realised are related to improvements in the fuel efficiency of public transport equipment, improved regulations and enforcement and the construction of environmentally friendly mass transit systems. The size of the investments required is immense. The sustainability gains to be derived from the reclamation of car space are limited outside Latin America and sub-Saharan Africa given the low but rapidly rising car ownership rates. Few gains are possible – at least in Asia, North Africa and the Middle East – from attempts to reclaim car space. Most cities are characterised by low road capacity per person and per hectare. This exists under conditions of low car use and emission rates per capita and high car use and emission rates per hectare. Under these circumstances there are few opportunities to diminish road capacity. The growth in incomes is accompanied by an increase in motor vehicle use – what was once a middle-class luxury increasingly becomes regarded as a universal necessity. Although densification based on transit-oriented development can help, the most effective solutions are to dampen the demand for cars through economic and social policy, and to improve mass transit systems and road capacity. The problem in developing countries is to avoid, rather than reverse, the process of public to private modal shift that characterised urban development in developed countries.

Land use

The argument that densification will allow derelict land to be brought into productive use has limited applicability for most cities in developing countries. The existence of inner city brownfield sites in developed countries is a result of the combination of the twin processes of de-industrialisation and metropolitan decentralisation. The relationship between urbanisation and industrialisation in developing countries is weak (outside the semi-periphery) and metropolitan decentralisation processes where present are only at an incipient stage in most countries.

The relationship between densification policies and the rate of loss of agricultural and rural land on the urban periphery, the incidence of urban agriculture and the availability of green and open space within the city is similarly complex (Mathey, 2000). The benefits of slowing down the rate of urban encroachment through promoting higher density settlement are particularly great in those world regions where rates of urban growth are high, arable land per capita rates are low and agricultural productivity growth rates are low. But if densification occurs using instruments that lower the availability of domestic space (e.g. reduced plot sizes, higher minimum plot/built area ratios), the effect on urban agriculture could be very serious for the poor, for whom it is a basic element in their survival strategy. How to preserve access to this strategy and to densify is a major dilemma for cities with a low level of economic development.

The same considerations govern the relationship between densification and open and green space provision. Per capita open and green space rates are often very low in cities in developing countries and where these spaces exist they are often poorly maintained, covered with waste, or are frequently squatted on. It is difficult to see how densities and green and open space rates can be increased simultaneously without using the modernist, high-rise, high-density solutions implemented in countries such as Singapore and Hong Kong and the 'radical surgery' approaches which are regarded as socially and politically unacceptable in many countries.

The advisability or not of densification has to be related to the question of how densities are distributed in cities in developing countries. In developed countries the urban poor and low-income groups live in the centre and the rich and the middle class live on the periphery. In developing countries the poor live in the centre where they are accommodated at very high densities in tenement blocks, interstitial shantytowns, and in downgraded and subdivided houses formerly belonging to the now decentralised upper income groups. But they also live in far greater numbers on the urban periphery in often-vast rings of low- and middle-density squatter settlements and illegal subdivisions. A pattern of intra-urban residential mobility has been recognised whereby rural migrants move initially to the inner city receptor areas and subsequently, with higher incomes and greater space requirements, move to the periphery where they commence an informal building process based on progressive development and self-help (Turner, 1976). This settlement pattern and process has a number of ramifications for densification policies.

First, densification of inner-city areas is not desirable given existing rates of overcrowding and can only lead to a further deterioration of already appalling social and environmental conditions. The ability to realise the gains of a more rational allocation of space within the existing building stock that are claimed for densification policies in developed countries do not apply in developing countries. This is because they are at an earlier stage in the demographic transition process. The rate of household formation is high because of high rates of natural increase and rural to urban migration; families are large (though average family sizes are falling); the number of single-parent households is high (particularly amongst the poor); the number of young people of childbearing age is high; and the numbers of the old are low. The potential sustainability gains from densification through subdivision of the existing stock are therefore modest.

Second, the low residential densities of many low-income settlements are deceptive. This is because the squatting, self-help and progressive development process consists of a slow (15–20 years) process of consolidation and densification that is finely tuned to changes in household income and space requirements. Densification efforts should therefore be aimed at assisting this process and should focus on the upgrading and guided rationalisation of urban space within these settlements.

Third, the argument that excessively high plot sizes in low-income settlements produce low densities and that densification can best be achieved by reducing the permitted maximum has to be treated with caution. This is because gross plot densities can be associated with widely different population densities depending on the type and intensity of development on each plot. Reductions in maximum plot sizes in circumstances where there is a high intensity of plot development and often 100% coverage of the plot could create serious environmental, economic and social problems and will almost certainly be politically resisted. This is because control over this space brings in income, for example, from rental units, commercial activities and workshops.

The political and social viability of densification measures has also to be considered. The acceptability of high-density urban living may be much greater in many developing countries than in developed countries. However, the globalisation of developed-country urban lifestyles based on individualism and privacy, conspicuous consumption and a low-density housing ideology is proceeding rapidly and has had a marked impact on middle-class aspirations in developing countries. A particular dilemma in these cities is that the rich have an increased propensity to consume space because of their increasing income command of it, and the poor seek to maximise their use of it for survival reasons.

A 'hands-off' approach to the process of informal densification can only lead to a worsening of existing environmental, health and social conditions. Guided densification in a planning style based on community enablement, local authority involvement and democratic 'stakeholding' arrangements would seem to offer the greatest opportunities for sustainability gains.

Intensification of activities

As with densification policies, many of the sustainability benefits that can be derived from activity intensification in cities in developing countries are bound to be limited. Cities in developing countries, as opposed to those in developed countries, are already characterised by high levels of mixed use, ease of access to a wide range of goods and services and by high levels of vitality and vibrancy. The reasons for this are the different structural characteristics of their urban economies, the more limited impact of modernist practices and the limited ability to control and regulate urban development. Amongst the structural characteristics must be included the extremely high share of employment and output accounted for by the informal sector in a vast range of production, distribution and service activities. The limited levels of industrialisation (except in some cities in the semi-periphery) has meant that artisanal production and small-scale workshops are widely dispersed throughout the city and low-income settlements. Similarly, commercial functions in the form of local markets, shops, and street stalls are widely accessible to rich and poor. The strict segregation of land uses and of work places from residences was attempted in master planning efforts between the 1950s and the 1980s, but had little effect. Thereafter, because of growing unemployment problems, the informal sector was strongly encouraged through deregulation of controls, and the extension of credit, technical assistance and training facilities, and a more flexible attitude to mixed use and street trading.

These policies have helped to generate employment but they have also created major environmental externalities including congestion, waste disposal problems, fire and health risks, as well as social and economic problems such as low wages, long work hours, the exploitation of children and the inability to collect taxes for services provided. The further stimulation of the informal sector in pursuit of the sustainability benefits claimed for intensification would therefore mark no real policy change. It is feared that further deregulation of the sector will merely add to these growing social costs and externalities, and the best strategy is now to 're-regulate' or 'formalise' it (de Soto, 1992). Whether this is possible without destroying the economic rationale for its existence is a major issue of contention.

One other concern is that in many higher income cities in the semi-periphery, a clear trend towards the centralisation of retailing and wholesaling has appeared with the development of commercial centres, shopping malls, supermarkets and commercial 'strip developments'. Informal sector opportunities in middle-class areas are therefore diminishing, and the problem of car-based accessibility has increased. Fears are growing that further economic growth and higher incomes could widen the incidence of these developments and make intensification efforts more difficult. In this context, the close integration of intensification policies with land use and spatial planning would seem to be a critical factor. Attention has focused on the merits of encouraging formal and informal activities and mixed uses along transport corridors and nodes, designated centres of concentration, inner city regeneration projects, and in satellite, dormitory and new towns previously characterised by high levels of monofunctionality.

Urban form

As in developed countries, attempts to manipulate urban form in order to achieve sustainability benefits have been limited. The reasons for this include the shift from master planning to strategic planning, and from physical planning to socio-economic planning, and a shift in the locus of urban professional practice towards urban restructuring and the neighbourhood level. In some cases urban restructuring efforts have been so profound that they have brought about a change in the urban form with a marked effect on energy consumption and emissions: over a period of 35 years Curitiba has managed to convert a radio-circular form into a linear form. Interest in linear city models, often at a very large scale, remains high particularly in South East Asia and in South Africa.

However, the main reason for the demise of holistic urban form models has been their high costs and the limited resources available to build them. The opportunities to create new cities with a sustainable urban form has been held in check by the enormous costs involved in building new settlements 'from scratch'. The high costs and limited success of the various new towns, satellite cities and capital cities that were built in many developing countries during the modernisation decades are another reason. Where sufficient capital has been available (particularly foreign investment and loans) the result has been the creation of new 'global settlements' based on finance, high-technology industries, commerce or tourism which show scant regard for sustainability concerns, particularly energy use. Many cities in search of global competitiveness have relaxed regulations governing peripheral development in order to attract economic activity and attempts at rationalising the urban form have been postponed. Nonetheless, with the strengthening of metropolitan decentralisation trends and urban sprawl there has been a resurgence of interest in urban containment instruments to control the evolution of the urban form in a sustainable way – particularly in green belts, green corridors and ecological reserve areas.

Interest, however, has generally focused on improvements to the urban fabric and attempts to rationalise the form of the historic or old city with the new in a sustainable fashion. The use of architectural, planning and design elements at the intra-urban and neighbourhood levels to reinforce urban form has often involved concerted attempts to harmonise the built environment with local and regional environmental realities.

Urban size
There has been considerable interest in the manipulation of city sizes in developing countries in recent years. The emergence of a large number of megacities (with populations of more than 10 million) has been one reason. It is estimated that 22 of the 26 global megacities in 2015 will be in developing countries and several of them will have populations of 20–30 million. The question of the economic efficiency of city size had been discussed extensively in the 'optimum city' size debates of the 1970s (Richardson, 1972, 1977; Segal, 1976), but under the impact of the environmentalist critique it was realised that this debate had to be revisited.

Debates that had focused on what was the optimum city size for achieving the best balance of agglomeration economies and diseconomies now had to consider the environmental implications of city size – particularly resource use, waste generation and disposal and the generation and displacement of environmental externalities.

Although the debate was frequently obfuscated by the failure to distinguish between the problem of primacy and the problem of size, attention focused on the scale and intensity of the environmental impacts of very large cities. It was argued that even with existing population size, consumption levels and inequalities, many megacities were already exhausting their environmental support capacity, with water consumption exceeding the replacement capacity of primary sources, the destabilisation of ecosystems, and air pollution levels that were highly injurious to human health and safety (Atkinson, 1993). Given these trends, it was highly unrealistic to believe that further market-led urban growth could continue up to the point where negative environmental externalities made it no longer profitable for producers to locate in the city. The bigger the city, and the higher its levels of consumption, the greater would be its ecological footprint. Lack of access to peripheral greenery and the effect on agricultural production were two other concerns. The issue of whether city size had a bearing on levels of energy use and carbon emission rates was less clear.

These arguments are growing in strength but action on them in developing countries has been rare, in part because of the sheer difficulty of devising effective policy instruments to control urban natural increase and the spatial mobility of rural to urban migrants. However, the principal reason for lack of action is the continued dominance of neo-liberal development strategies that argue that no causal relationship has been established between urban sustainability problems and city size: size itself is not a problem and if anything has net benefits. The key policy for solving environmental degradation should be the enhancement of urban efficiency and productivity. This requires that liberalised market forces should be left to determine spatial dynamics. The wisdom of facilitating the further growth of megacities in pursuit of urban productivity gains that do not internalise environmental externalities has been challenged.

Urban structure

Urban restructuring has become a major strategy for realising the sustainability benefits of compaction in developing countries. It has been accepted that most urban environmental problems, including excessive energy use and high carbon emission rates, can be attributed to deficiencies in the urban structure. These deficiencies can be rectified by structural changes to the built environment, by the restructuring of urban mobility systems, the closer co-ordination of land use and transport planning, and the closer harmonisation of the built environment with the natural environment.

A number of spatial models and strategies have been developed to change the urban structure to achieve the desired sustainability benefits. High-rise, high-density redevelopment that owes much to the legacy of modernism has been widely used in South East Asia. Here very high densities, short journeys to work, easy access to services, widespread mass transit use, the development of self-contained new towns and settlements and the adequate provision of public space are seen as the most environmentally and socially sustainable options. But high levels of air pollution and different cultural attitudes to spatial proximity may limit its global applicability

A second widely adopted model is the creation of 'concentrated decentralisation' within the urban structure. Here there is an attempt to shift from a monocentric to a polycentric structure based on the densification and activity intensification of selected sub-centres, connected by transport and development corridors. There have also been attempts to focus compaction efforts at the 'urban village' and neighbourhood levels and to break down their monofunctionality through design and architectural improvements and the adoption of mixed land use and intensification policies.

The third and perhaps the most widely adopted compaction model in the current period is the Curitiba linear 'transit-oriented development' model (Rabinovitch, 1992). Here the restructuring of the mobility system is used to reap major transport energy savings based on modal shift, the discouragement of the need to travel, and limited private car use. Urban growth is channelled along selected structural axes based on mass transit routes and on modal interchange nodes. This is achieved through a combination of densification, intensification and mixed land use measures that are closely integrated with transport planning and environmental policies.

The fourth urban restructuring model for compaction has been traditional infill, densification and intensification, which has been used for the regeneration of core areas, historic centres, and disused industrial and other land.

In all of these efforts emphasis has been placed on the close integration of transport and land use planning, the use of a wide a range of physical and socio-economic planning instruments to discourage car use and a range of architectural and design practices to encourage the greater harmonisation of the built environment with the natural environment.

Many of these policies have had a considerable effect in achieving transport energy savings, improved building and urban energy efficiency, better access to nature and green space, and social and aesthetic improvements. But there have also been concerns about a number of problems created or ignored by the models. These include: the effects of high-rise buildings on air pollution and the urban heat island; the effect of linear and corridor development on property values; the continued low-density suburbanisation of the middle class (often in the form of gated communities); the limited effect of these policies on rates of crime and violence in inner-city areas; the increased privatisation and commodification of public space; and the inability of public investment to keep up with urban development.

Settlement systems

It has also been increasingly accepted in developing countries that the most appropriate scale for achieving the sustainability goals associated with compaction is the regional and metropolitan region level. Interest has focused on regional development frameworks, on large scale and beaded linear cities, 'concentrated decentralisation' models, and cellular and networked systems of cities linked by transport and development corridors based on efficient and eco-friendly public transport systems. It is only at this scale that the goals of a balanced integration of settlement systems with nature (Atkinson, 1992), easy access to green environments, the conservation of rural and agricultural land, spatial equity in infrastructure and service provision and the avoidance of the spatial displacement of environmental externalities can be realised. However, the translation of these concepts into practice has rarely been achieved, for three reasons.

First, there has been the general hostility of neo-liberal development strategies to metropolitan and regional level planning. In the 1960s there were concerted interventionist attempts to check ever-widening regional inequalities through the creation of 'regional growth centres and poles' (Perroux, 1971; Friedmann, 1966) and in the 1970s the theory of 'polarisation reversal' identified regional convergence as being achievable by promoting the growth of secondary cities (Richardson, 1980). With the rise of neo-liberalism in the 1980s, however, there was a strong shift in the focus of spatial planning: now it was the 'city in itself' rather than regional or national urban systems that was identified as the locus of productive activities. This shift led to the demise of regional planning and explicit spatial decentralisation policies and the rise of urban policy narrowly defined on the single-city model. In a climate of increased international competition associated with export-oriented development, neo-liberal policymakers argued that it was unwise to disturb the market determination of the relationship between location and economic activity by government regulation. Indeed, attempts to do so could slow the rate of national growth and exacerbate regional inequalities. Planning should facilitate national economic growth and gains in inter-personal equity, rather than being concerned with misguided attempts to achieve convergence of regional incomes and service provision. Development priorities should be based on maximising competitive advantages and investments should go to those cities with the greatest advantages for the production of tradable goods and services. These cities were the large conurbations and primate cities which were seen as essential for maximising growth.

Second, there was an insistence that the relationship between cities and their regions was essentially harmonious. Cities are seen as 'engines of growth' adding value to rural products, providing services to regional markets and attracting investments. A relaxed attitude towards urban primacy has developed, rationalised by the need to seek competitive advantages and urban productivity gains. That these productivity gains have been achieved through the geographical displacement of environmental externalities to the surrounding region is a bone of contention with sustainable urban development approaches.

Third, the failure to implement sustainable regional and settlement system-level planning is also related to the contradictions of globalisation. It is clear that there has been a tendency for national space economies to fragment as cities and regions increasingly orient their economies and prioritise their investments according to the dynamics of global markets and global trade blocs (e.g. Mercosur, ASEAN, NAFTA). The new regionalism would seem to demand an emphasis on balanced regional development. However, as the globalisation process is currently driven by the need for cities and regions to compete in increasingly liberalised markets, attempts to internalise the costs of regional environmental externalities, and create equitable sustainable regional development, could diminish these competitive advantages and lead capital to pursue its interest elsewhere.

Conclusion

As the problems associated with global environmental change and globalisation deepen, so too does the need for urban policy and professional practice to respond to them. This can best be achieved through the assertion of an environmental basis for architectural, planning and design practice and the recognition of a global rationale that has to be considered everywhere and at all spatial levels. In policy terms, it involves accepting that the key issue is the relationship between social and political organisations at various scales rather than the assertion of the primacy of social organisation at one scale. The current global interest in the ability of compact city approaches to realise sustainable urban development reflects these preoccupations and the problems that create them.

References

Acioly, C. Jnr., and Davidson, F. (1996) Density in urban development. *Building Issues,* **8(3)**, Lund Centre for Habitat Studies.

Atkinson, A. (1992) The urban bioregion as a sustainable development paradigm. *Third World Planning Review,* **14 (4)**, pp.327–354.

Atkinson, A. (1993) Are third world megacities sustainable? Jabotabek as an example. *Journal of International Development,* **5(6)**, pp.605–622.

Burgess, R., Carmona, M. and Kolstee, T. (1997) *The Challenge of Sustainable Cities*, Zed Books, London.

Cohen, M. A. (1996) The hypothesis of urban convergence: are cities in the north and south becoming more alike in an age of globalisation?, in *Preparing for the Urban Future* (eds A. Cohen, B. N. Ruble, J. S. Tulchin and A. Garland), Woodrow Wilson Center Press, Washington, DC.

de Soto, H. (1992) Combating urban poverty in Latin America: the Peruvian case in urban poverty and the urban informal sector, in *Latin America,* pp.31–38, series on Poverty and Development, DGIS/Ministry of Foreign Affairs, The Hague, Netherlands.

Friedmann, J. (1966) *Regional Development Policy: A Case Study of Venezuela,* MIT Press, Cambridge, MA.

Geddes, P. (1968) *Cities in Evolution,* Benn, London.

Hardoy, J. E., Cairncross, S. and Satterthwaite, D. (eds) (1990) *The Poor Die Young: Housing and Health in Third World Cities,* Earthscan, London.

Haughton, G. and Hunter, C. (1994) *Sustainable Cities,* Jessica Kingsley, London.

Howard, E. (1898) *Garden Cities of Tomorrow,* Attic Books, Powys.

Jenks, M., Burton, E. and Williams, K. (eds) (1996) *The Compact City: A Sustainable Urban Form?,* E & FN Spon, London.

Mathey, K. (ed.) (2000) Urban agriculture, *Trialog 65: A Journal for Planning and Building in the Third World: Special Issue,* **Vol. 2,** pp.3–43.

Mumford, L. (1938) *The Culture of Cities,* Harcourt Brace Jovanovich, New York.

Newman, P. (1999) Transport: reducing automobile dependence, in *The Earthscan Reader in Sustainable Cities* (ed. D. Satterthwaite), Earthscan, London.

Perroux, F. (1971) Note on the concept of growth poles, in *Economic Policy for Development: Selected Readings* (ed. I. Livingstone), Penguin, Harmondsworth.

Porter, M. (1990) *The Competitive Advantage of Nations,* Macmillan, London.

Rabinovitch, J. (1992) Curitiba: towards sustainable development. *Environment and Urbanisation* **4(2),** pp.62–73.

Richardson, H. W. (1972) Optimality in city size, systems of cities and urban policy: a sceptic's view. *Urban Studies,* **9(1),** pp.29–48.

Richardson, H. W. (1977) *City Size and National Spatial Strategies in Developing Countries,* World Bank. Staff Working Paper 252, Washington, DC.

Richardson, H. W. (1980) Polarisation reversal in developing countries. *Papers of the Regional Science Association,* **45,** pp.67–85.

Sassen, S. (1991) *The Global City: New York, London, Tokyo,* Princeton University Press, Princeton, NJ.

Satterthwaite, D. (ed.) (1999) *The Earthscan Reader in Sustainable Cities,* Earthscan, London.

Segal, D. (1976) Are there returns to scale in city size? *Review of Economics and Statistics,* **63,** pp.339–350.

Turner, J. F. C. (1976) *Housing by People,* Marion Boyars, London.

UNCED (1993) *Earth Summit Agenda 2: The UN Programme of Action from Rio,* United Nations, New York.

UNCHS (1996) *An Urbanising World: Global Report on Human Settlements,* Oxford University Press, Oxford.

UNDP (1992) *The Urban Environment in Developing Countries,* UNDP, New York.

Wallerstein, I. (1979) *The Capitalist World Economy,* Cambridge University Press, Cambridge.

Williams, K., Burton, E. and Jenks, M. (eds) (2000) *Achieving Sustainable Urban Form,* E & FN Spon, London.

World Bank (1990) *World Development Report: Poverty,* World Bank, Washington, DC.

World Commission on Environment and Development (WCED) (1987) *Our Common Future,* Oxford University Press, Oxford.

Harry W. Richardson, Chang-Hee Christine Bae and Murtaza Hatim Baxamusa

Compact Cities in Developing Countries:
Assessment and Implications

Introduction

This chapter has four aims. The first is to collect data on densities and other correlates for a large sample of cities in developing countries.[1] The second is to evaluate the costs and benefits of compact cities in developing countries, especially with respect to transportation and environmental externalities. The third aim is to discuss the concept of sustainable urbanisation with respect to compactness in developing country contexts. Finally, the chapter explores the implications, if any, of developing country urban compactness for cities in developed countries, especially the United States.

Not only do cities of developing countries (in the sample) have much higher densities than their counterparts in developed countries, they are not becoming significantly less compact in spite of decelerating population growth and the beginnings of decentralisation. Although metropolitan boundaries are expanding in some cases, it is difficult for the increases in geographical area to keep pace with population growth. The high densities have obvious consequences in terms of the choice of transportation modes, living conditions, congestion and pollution.

This chapter does not attempt to measure the costs and benefits of urban compactness in developing countries; the data are too sparse and the underlying research has not been undertaken. Instead, the purpose is to comment on a few of the elements that might be included as a preliminary step in a costs and benefits assessment. Much of the research on this issue has focused on developed-country cities, and has examined costs and benefits in terms of city size rather than densities. As a consequence, the critical aspects of urban spatial structure have been ignored.

The question of whether there are any implications for developed-country cities is very complex. For example, mixed land uses are a major goal of compact city protagonists in the developed world, but their prevalence in the developing world reflects lax land use controls much more than explicit policy. Similarly, the strong association between densities and severe traffic congestion is less a verdict on the consequences of compactness than a by-product of street design, the minimal land use allocation for roads before the automobile age, and the resource constraints that inhibited investment in transportation infrastructure. This situation has been aggravated by rapid motorisation in recent years in many developing countries. Again, air and water pollution is not directly the result of higher densities but the product of weak environmental regulations and poor enforcement. Yet many developing country cities offer a richness of street life and vitality that the developed countries would like to emulate. It is no easy task to separate the effects of densities from those other factors such as income differentials, institutional capacity, investment, human resources and urban design, that distinguish cities in the developing world from those in the developed world.

Densities and compactness

Densities in developing country cities are much higher than in developed countries, especially in the core city. Many explanations have been given:

- Higher rates of population and urban growth explain why density gradients have, historically, shifted upwards over time rather than flattened and shifted downward as in developed country cities. However, this shift has been attenuated in recent years in many cities in developing countries as urbanisation rates have decelerated and decentralisation has begun to occur.
- Lower incomes have meant much smaller dwelling sizes and tiny lots, especially in squatter settlements. Also, household size is much larger. Data assembled by Malpezzi (1999) show a striking positive relationship between GNP per capita and housing consumption indicators (such as floor area per capita). However, the correlation between high densities and overcrowding is quite low (in core cities in our data set, the correlation coefficient was 0.18).[2] Similarly, density and household size appear to be unrelated.
- In terms of the 'modern' sector in developing countries, housing preferences have favoured high-rise apartments rather than single family housing.
- The prevalence of mixed-use structures and neighbourhoods has resulted in residential densities becoming higher the closer they are to the city centre.
- Low densities in developed country cities, especially in the United States, have been facilitated by automobiles. Automobiles have come to developing country cities very late, although very fast.
- Lax planning regulations, and either the absence or the inadequacy of building codes, have led to uncontrolled increases in densities, e.g. by subdividing existing structures to accommodate multiple families (frequently, one family per room). Although this occurs illegally in developed countries, its scale and extent are much lower than in developing countries.
- There remains considerable scope for further increases in densities in low-income settlements. For example, a study in Malaysia suggested that land use densities could be substantially increased (by almost 75%) by permitted reductions in setbacks and back alleys (Bertaud and Malpezzi, 1998a). In some cases, planning controls have resulted in high densities; for example, Seoul's greenbelt (in place since 1971) has reduced the supply of land available for urban use, raised land prices and increased densities (Kim, 1994; Bae, 1998). South Korea was certainly a developing country when its land use regulations were introduced, if no longer. On the other hand, some planning regulations have worked in the opposite direction (i.e. promoting lower densities). For

example, Ahmedabad in India has one-third of the densities of Bombay, in part a result of a very low 'floor area ratio' (FAR), that varies little over the urban area (Bertaud and Cuenco, 1996).

All this means, of course, that the compact cities of developing countries have not been planned, and they are not the result of some prescient ground design. Rather, their compactness has emerged spontaneously, if not chaotically.

Data on urban densities
The database is limited, but we compare central city densities; metropolitan area densities; the ratio of the central city area to the metropolitan area and the ratio of central city to suburban densities for a sample of cities in developing countries (Table 1). These statistics are also examined, for comparative purposes, with a sample of developed country cities (Table 2). The conclusions are not neat, largely because there are significant country-to-country variations in how both cities and metropolitan areas are defined, and some variation in the dates for which the data are available. However, the following findings are clear.

Central city densities tend to be much higher in developing countries. In this sense, their cities are more compact; the ratio of central city to suburban densities tends to be much higher in cities in developing countries, reflecting both compactness and the slower rate of suburbanisation/decentralisation. However, suburbanisation and densification are proceeding fast in some cities, e.g. Bangkok, in developing countries. In our sample, the mean ratio of central city density to suburban density was 38.5 for developing country cities compared to 11.9 for developed country cities.

In general, the areas of core cities in developing countries are not smaller. On the contrary, core cities in developing countries are larger in area overall ($882km^2$) than cities in developed countries ($449km^2$). Chinese cities are larger (in part, a definitional issue), as are Curitiba, Lima, Istanbul, Karachi and Bangkok. These are all larger than Los Angeles and Rome, the two largest-area developed country cities. Overall, the mean ratio of the central core area to the total metropolitan area was 0.23 for developing country cities, compared to 0.15 for developed country cities (however, the standard deviation was higher: 0.25 compared to 0.15). Yet there are no clear-cut differences in metropolitan area sizes between developing and developed countries. The rate of increase in suburban densities is much faster than that of central city densities because of land constraints in the central city and limited infill opportunities. This applies to both developing and developed countries.

A standardised means of comparison would be to compare density gradients. Up-to-date density gradient calculations are a major research task for developing country cities, and in any case the raw information is not even available (Mills and Tan, 1980, represents an early attempt). Also, the value of monocentric density gradient measures, while perhaps more relevant than in developed countries, will become increasingly dubious as there are also polycentric tendencies in the cities of developing countries. Bertaud and Malpezzi (1998b) present some standard density gradient results, based on data gathered in the field in each city. Although monocentricity is becoming a rarer phenomenon, even in developing country cities, the simple 2-parameter

Developing Country Cities

City	Density (persons/km²) Central City [1]	Metropolitan [2]	Rest of Metro [3]	Ratio [1]/[3] [4]	Area (km²) Central City [5]	Rest of Metro [6]	Ratio [5]/[5+6] [7]
Adana	536.5	88.1	30.9	17.37	1,952	15,301	0.11
Algiers	8,060.1	5,461.0	-	-	187	15,301	0.01
Ankara	1,533.7	120.7	13.4	114.22	1,814	15,301	0.11
Beijing	5,377.9	845.2	443.3	12.13	1,369	15,439	0.08
Bombay	22,677.4	-	-	-	438	-	-
Budapest	3,954.0	1,498.0	956.2	4.14	525	1,150	0.31
Buenos Aires	14,120.9	3,070.1	2,401.3	5.88	210	3,470	0.06
Bursa	8,488.9	125.1	39.0	217.77	1,174	9,869	0.11
Cairo	3,146.0	-	-	-	214	-	-
Calcutta	23,487.0	8164.4	5,695.6	4.12	187	1,163	0.14
Cali	3,019.0	751.8	181.1	16.67	552	2,193	0.20
Chegdu	2,123.0	732.4	566.0	3.75	1,382	11,548	0.11
Dakar	13,195.1	7,975.9	5,639.4	2.34	77	172	0.31
Delhi	4,853.0	-	-	-	1,485	-	-
Faislabad	16,271.0	919.2	-	-	91	1,111	0.08
Fuzhou	1,282.8	455.1	376.1	3.41	1,043	10,925	0.09
Guadalajara	10,286.0	9,731.0	8,798.7	1.17	188	112	0.63
Guangzhou	2,725.9	839.4	384.8	7.08	1,444	5,990	0.19
Guayaquil	4,732.0	4,582.0	3,813.3	1.24	268	52	0.84
Hanoi	23,690.4	581.1	74.9	316.39	46	2,100	0.02
Istanbul	3,824.9	1,362.8	45.3	84.42	1,991	3,721	0.35
Izmir	2,601.9	201.4	38.0	68.44	763	11,210	0.06
Jakarta	14,084.4	-	-	-	650	-	-
Jinan	1,126.9	649.1	482.5	2.34	2,127	6,100	0.26
La Habana	6,645.9	3,071.9	114.0	58.28	327	396	0.45
Lahore	1,982.0	1,333.0	-	-	1,760	455	0.79
Lima	1,534.9	1,642.1	4,325.0	0.35	3,702	148	0.96
Madras	2,207.0	-	-	-	174	-	-
Manila	45,839.0	10,872.0	8,631.4	5.31	38	598	0.06
Medan	7,203.7	-	-	-	265	-	-
Medellín	4,211.9	1,584.8	755.6	5.57	387	1,226	0.24
Mexico	5,568.4	1,914.5	1,067.5	5.22	1,479	6,381	0.19
Montevideo	6,952.0	174.0	50.7	137.20	180	9,878	0.02
Moscow	8,418.9	-	-	-	994	-	-
Pune	11,278.9	-	-	-	139	-	-
Qingdao	1,924.7	631.8	482.6	3.99	1,102	9,552	0.10
San Jose	7,020.2	239.2	177.1	39.64	45	4,915	0.01
Santiago	-	2,217.1	132.6	-	22	2,184	0.01
Seoul	16,899.1	-	-	-	605	-	-
Santafe de Bogotá	3,081.3	1,980.6	404.6	7.62	1,605	1,121	0.59
Shanghai	10,358.6	2,378.9	1,237.9	8.37	793	5,548	0.13
Shenyang	1,336.1	626.0	75.5	17.70	3,495	8,482	0.29
Tianjin	1,367.4	780.8	424.0	3.23	4,276	7,029	0.38
Warsaw	3,419.0	637.0	228.0	15.00	485	3,303	0.13
Wuhan	2,483.2	808.4	410.1	6.06	1,627	6,840	0.19
Xi'an	3,336.3	565.0	45.0	74.15	861	9,122	0.09
Mean	7,739.3	2,151.6	1,427.7	38.50	882	5,660	0.23
SD				69.48			0.25

Developed Country Cities

City	Density (persons/km²)			Ratio [1]/[3]	Area (km²)		Ratio [5]/[5+6]
	Central City [1]	Metropolitan [2]	Rest of Metro [3]	[4]	Central City [5]	Rest of Metro [6]	[7]
Barcelona	17,433.0	6,369.0	3,514.7	4.96	98	378	0.21
Chicago	4,637.9	3,186.4	2,776.7	1.67	89	2,087	0.22
Dallas	1,153.1	1,114.3	1,102.9	1.05	887	3,028	0.23
Detroit	2,763.3	2,073.3	1,959.4	1.41	359	2,176	0.14
Dublin	4,485.0	1,107.0	640.1	7.01	112	810	0.12
Hamburg	2,093.0	-	1,384.8	1.51	755	662	0.53
Houston	1,217.5	1,377.3	1,518.8	0.80	1,398	1,578	0.47
Lisbon	9,893.0	1,023.0	717.6	13.79	84	2,438	0.03
London	1,667.0	4,227.0	205.2	8.12	3	1,598	0.00
Los Angeles	2,836.0	1,166.9	996.3	2.85	1,216	11,898	0.09
Lyons	8,679.3	2,524.7	114.1	76.07	48	7,422	0.01
Madrid	5,048.0	596.0	232.9	21.68	606	7,422	0.08
Marseilles	3,334.6	1,482.9	729.8	4.57	240	590	0.29
Miami	4,054.6	2,800.0	2,697.8	1.50	92	1,125	0.08
Milan	8,227.0	2,714.0	1,717.3	4.79	182	1,005	0.15
Minneapolis	2,497.1	1,147.9	1,060.8	2.35	42	2,200	0.06
Montreal	5,749.5	891.3	633.2	0.00	177	3,332	0.05
Munich	4,192.0	421.0	199.1	21.05	310	5,194	0.06
New York	9,166.6	723.2	469.0	19.55	800	26,575	0.03
Osaka	12,430.0	2,133.0	1,850.1	6.72	221	7,534	0.03
Paris	20,647.0	838.0	663.1	31.14	105	11,907	0.01
Philadelphia	4,354.9	2,600.0	2,283.8	1.91	350	1,942	0.15
San Diego	1,373.0	1,621.7	1,887.9	0.73	839	784	0.52
Stockholm	3,051.0	293.0	165.8	18.41	216	4,684	0.04
Sydney	2,001.3	285.8	40.7	49.18	1,548	10,833	0.13
Tokyo	13,973.0	5,471.0	2,221.1	6.29	598	1,564	0.28
Washington	3,566.6	1,906.8	1,832.3	1.95	159	3,539	0.04
Mean	5,945.3	1,926.7	1,245.0	11.86	449	4,604	0.15
SD				17.08			0.15

monocentric density gradient still yields statistically significant results in almost all cases. Apart from two Chinese cities (Guangzhou and Shanghai, but not Beijing and Tianjin), all the density gradients for developing country cities had a slope of less than -0.2, with several less than -0.05 (e.g. Bombay, Curitiba, Rio de Janeiro and Tianjin). This suggests that even developing country cities tend to have substantial decentralisation.

Bertaud and Malpezzi (1998b) also constructed compactness indices for world cities (including 14 cities in developing countries). The ingenious measure they used is the average distance per person (by census tract or equivalent small area) to the central business district (CBD) as a ratio of the average distance to the centre of a circle. This measure, called a 'dispersion ratio', assumes that the city is represented by a cylinder with a height corresponding to uniform density. The higher the ratio, the more dispersed the city. Apart from problems associated with the CBD possibly being off-centre, the main difficulty is that it is a relative measure, not an absolute measure. Thus, a low-density metropolitan area, Bangkok (with 58 persons per hectare) has a dispersion ratio of 0.99, while the highest density city in the sample

Table 2. Central city and metropolitan area population densities, developed countries.
Source: Multiple data sources.²

Opposite page: *Table 1. Central city and metropolitan area population densities, developing countries.*
Source: Multiple data sources.²

(Bombay) with 389 persons per hectare has the highest dispersion ratio of 3.08. This yields the paradox of a high-density sprawling city. The truth of the matter is that the dispersion ratio is a better measure of the irregular shape of the city than of sprawl *per se*. Thus Bombay's high dispersion ratio reflects its linear rather than circular shape. Hence, it is not surprising that plausible regressions attempting to explain the degree of compactness did not generate statistically significant results. Subject to these qualifications, 10 out of 14 developing country cities and 15 out of 21 developed country cities had dispersion ratios greater than 1.0. Yet 23 of the total sample of 35 cities had dispersion ratios within the range 0.90–1.10. Thus, although two-thirds of cities had dispersion ratios greater than unity, one-half of these were within the ±10 per cent range.

Although densities in the developing country cities tended to be higher, several cities outside the developed world have densities comparable to those found in cities in developed countries, e.g. Bangkok (58 persons per hectare), Curitiba (54), Capetown (32) and Johannesburg (53), if these are counted as cities in developing countries (as they should be, applying World Bank per capita GDP criteria). In Bangkok in particular, there was significant decentralisation in the 1980s, with most housing being built in the 11–20km ring (Dowall, 1992).

Density gradients flatten, as expected, with rising incomes, population size and increasing automobile ownership rates. Cities with dispersed populations can be efficient if jobs are also dispersed. The key question for developing country cities is whether jobs can be decentralised fast enough.

Transportation
A major difference between developing and developed country cities (especially if the United States is used as the exemplar of the latter rather than Europe or Japan) is in their transport systems. Given the hypothesised relationship between densities and automobile dependence popularised most vehemently by Newman and Kenworthy (1989a and 1989b), the more diversified modal split found in developing country cities might reasonably be explained by their higher densities. However, worldwide, there is a very strong historical relationship between the growth of per capita income and the growth of vehicle ownership (Dargay and Gately, 1997; Ingram and Liu, 1999; Gomez-Ibanez, 1991; Gakenheimer, 1995). Motor vehicle ownership rates appear to be more closely associated with GDP per capita than with densities, although interpretation is complicated by the inverse correlation of income per capita and density. Motor vehicle ownership and population density appear to be positively related for high-density cities up to about 100 vehicles per 1,000 population, but the relationship is strongly negative in low-density cities (Ingram and Liu, 1999). This has strong implications for future patterns of urban growth (e.g. in Asia), given the link between motorisation and suburbanisation.

Income differentials within developing country cities account for the relatively low automobile share. The rich in developing countries have automobile ownership rates not much lower than those in developed countries. In our data set, transit use is higher in cities in countries with a lower per capita GDP, and appears less related to density (Table 3). Many developing country cities are very dependent on public transport, but some of the poorest (for example, some Chinese cities and Dhaka, Bangladesh, not in our database) rely heavily on non-motorised modes. Of course, high route densities do contribute to high public transit occupancy rates (often excessively high), but even these are not enough to make public transit agencies fiscally solvent. Because transport costs can rise to 10 per cent of household expenditures in low-income cities in developing countries, many of the poor have to walk. Hence, poverty explains more of the use of non-auto modes than does density. Nevertheless, in our data there was no strong relationship between GDP per capita and the share of non-motorised travel (including walking), although the number of sample cities was small.

Table 3. Modal split, transit and non-auto shares, developing country cities (%). Source: Multiple data sources².

City	Country	Rail [1]	Para-transit (1) [2]	Bus [3]	Car/ Auto (2) [4]	Motor Cycle [5]	Non-Motorised Vehicles [6]	Bicycle [7]	Walk [8]	Other (3) [9]	Transit [1+2+3]
Abidjan	Côte d'Ivoire	-	-	50	33	-	-	-	-	17	50
Ahmedabad	India	-	-	29	1	6	20	-	43	1	29
Ankara	Turkey	2	9	53	23					12	64
Bangalore	India	-	-	36	2	6	12	-	44	-	36
Bangkok	Thailand	-	-	58	19	5	-	-	16	2	58
Beijing	China	-	-	28.6	-	-	-	54	13.7	3.5	29
Bombay	India	-	-	58	8	1	11	-	15	7	58
Buenos Aires	Argentina	-	27	45	-	-	-	-	-	28	72
Cairo	Egypt	-	-	70	15	-	-	-	-	15	70
Chegdu	China	-	-	5	-	-	-	54.5	36	3.6	5
Delhi	India	-	-	40	-	10	18	-	29	3	40
Fuzhou	China	-	-	3.9	-	-	-	60.9	25.4	5.3	4
Guangzhou	China	-	-	23.3	-	-	-	34	39.2	3.1	23
Hong Kong	China	20.8	-	56.5	10.2	-	-	-	-	12.5	77
Jakarta	Indonesia	-	-	25	8	13	17	-	23	14	25
Jinan	China	-	-	10.5	-	-	-	63.8	23.3	1.5	11
Karachi	Pakistan	6	18	52	3	-	-	-	-	20	76
Kuala Lumpur	Malaysia	-	-	34	34	12	2	-	10	8	34
Lima	Peru	-	27	45	-	-	-	-	-	28	72
Madras	India	-	-	53	1	4	20	-	21	1	53
Manila	Philippines	-	-	65	23	-	-	-	8	-	65
Medellín	Colombia	-	5	85	6	-	-	-	-	4	90
Mexico	Mexico	15	13	51	19	-	-	-	-	-	79
Qingdao	China	-	-	27.3	-	-	-	17.9	47.1	2.9	27
Rio de Janeiro	Brazil	11	2	62	24	-	-	-	-	2	75
San Jose	Costa Rica	-	-	75	21	-	-	-	-	4	75
São Paulo	Brazil	-	10	54	32	-	-	-	-	4	64
Seoul	Korea	6.5	-	58.6	7.9	-	-	-	12	15	65
Shanghai	China	-	-	24	-	-	-	34.2	38.2	3	24
Shenyang	China	-	-	11.7	-	-	55.9	-	29.7	2.7	12
Surabaya	Indonesia	-	-	13	9	26	25	-	20	7	13
Tianjin	China	-	-	7.1	-	-	-	60.4	28	2	7
Wuhan	China	-	-	36.2	-	-	-	32.6	32.6	5	36

(1) Includes mass rapid transit
(2) Includes auto-rickshaws, shuttle vans, etc.
(3) Includes taxis

Developing country cities in general have much higher congestion levels than their developed country counterparts. This is, in part, a consequence of densities, particularly in low-income countries where animals, market stalls on the street and pedestrian overflows onto the road impede traffic. But it is also the result of inadequate allocation of land to road space (Ingram and Liu, 1999), reflecting the fact that planning and design guidelines (to the extent that they exist in developing countries) predated the introduction of the automobile there. The situation has been exacerbated by the absence of traffic management, and the absence, or very weak enforcement, of parking regulations.

Environmental externalities

The great urban economist and demographer, William Alonso (whose untimely death occurred in 1999), pointed out many years ago the fallacy of correlating densities with environmental quality variables (Alonso, 1973). Of course, traffic congestion tends to be worse in dense neighbourhoods, and because damage to human health is the main component of many environmental costs (e.g. of air pollution) total exposure (i.e. average exposure x the number of people exposed) will be higher in high-density locations. But the quality of the environment reflects many considerations that have nothing to do with density. These include industrial structure, climate, topography, water sources, institutions, regulations, the types of policy instruments and enforcement rates. The correlation between SO_2 levels and densities is -0.18 (based on the data in the master data set), hardly encouraging for those with faith in densification strategies as a pollution control device. There may be a direct relationship between the quality of water, sanitation facilities and solid waste management, and the density of squatter settlements, but again other influences, such as the presence or absence of slum upgrading programmes, may be much more important than settlement density.

Hardoy and Satterthwaite (1992) have a different view. They argue that high densities are an advantage: high population densities reduce the unit costs of infrastructure and services with obvious environmental benefits in terms of piped water, sanitation, garbage collection, drainage, etc.; high production densities generate economies in waste-handling and facilitate regulation enforcement. Even in squatter settlements, they argue that density is less important than overcrowding (where cramped conditions can contribute to transmission of infection and accident risks). However, they recognise that any benefits from high population densities can be frittered away by the lack of institutional capacities, e.g. to deliver services.

Sustainability and urbanisation

The spread of the concept of sustainability, and its application in an urban context, has been widely but not consistently discussed. Its urban aspects have focused heavily on non-automobile dependence and on ecological footprint discussions (e.g. the resource use associated with urban consumption levels), with the presumption that developing country cities are more sustainable. If this is the case, then the most convincing explanation would be the effects of lower incomes rather than compactness. However, an alternative interpretation might argue that developing country cities are unsustainable because of population growth impacts (and there has clearly been a historical correlation between city population growth rates and increasing densities in developing countries). This is the urban dimension of global doomsday population scenarios. But Drakakis-Smith (1996b) has used the population growth evidence to suggest the opposite case: the fact that developing country cities have exhibited such a strong absorptive capacity, in terms of population, demonstrates that they are indeed sustainable both now and in the long run. The difference between the two views is probably that Drakakis-Smith equates 'coping' with 'sustainable', while the more standard sustainability position identifies the urban dimension as merely a reflection of global sustainability concerns. Curiously, however, in his three review papers on sustainable urban development, Drakakis-Smith (1995, 1996a, 1997) says almost nothing about the role of intra-metropolitan space in urban sustainability, referring to the 'where' question (as distinct from the what, how, and for whom questions) only in inter-urban terms.

A key question, of course, is whether compact cities in developing countries are more sustainable. This question is almost impossible to answer. More sustainable than less compact developing country cities? More sustainable than developed country cities? What are our criteria of sustainability? How do we measure compactness? How do we separate out the effects of density from the effects of low income, an interdependence that confounded our discussion of transportation?

In the absence of the detailed research needed on this issue, a few comments are in order. More compactness at the metropolitan area level would imply economies in land consumption. However, as pointed out above, the higher core city densities in developing countries are not associated with geographically smaller metropolitan area sizes. In fact, encroachment of urban development on prime agricultural land (e.g. the Nile Delta) has been much more serious in developing countries than either the United States (where the supply of agricultural land remains elastic), or Western Europe (where greenbelts and similar land use controls constrain encroachment).

Denser living environments are associated with higher air-pollution-related human health damage, more traffic congestion and noise, more exposure to toxic releases, closer proximity to hazardous waste sites, higher risks of disease from contaminated water and overloaded sanitation systems. These negative externalities are aggravated by inadequate infrastructure and the lax enforcement of environmental laws and controls. However, the higher densities are, in part, culturally induced, and reflect traditional patterns of social organisation that are more favourable to community life and interpersonal co-operation. In other words, living in crowded developing country cities is more social and convivial, and perhaps even more fun – despite low living standards and the rigours of daily life – than living in the pleasurable suburbs of the United States. If this is the case, it is equally true that this lifestyle is not transferable, because, although high densities allow it to happen, its roots are in culture and modes of social behaviour.

A common argument is that developing country cities are much more sustainable than developed country cities because material consumption per capita levels are much lower (on average, perhaps 95 per cent lower); hence, to deploy the fashionable term, the 'ecological footprint' of developing country cities is much smaller. As Satterthwaite (1997, p.1677) points out: 'Low-income urban citizens are models of "sustainable consumption" in that they use very few non-renewable resources and generate very little waste. They are also among the most assiduous collectors and users of recycled or reclaimed materials.' The problem is that this behaviour probably has little to do with 'compactness' which may contribute little to lower levels of consumption, with the possible exception of transportation services (which explains the dominance of sustainable transportation in sustainable cities discussions). Instead, as suggested above, moderate consumption reflects low incomes; the urban rich in developing countries consume as much as, if not more than, those in developed countries as they ape their lifestyles.

Lessons and inferences

Given the strong promotion by many in the planning profession of compact city strategies in developed countries, and given the evidence that shows that developing country cities are more compact, an obvious question is whether developed countries have anything to learn from city compactness in developing countries. The short answer is probably not very much. For example, the transportation systems of developing countries (e.g. high public transit use) cannot be replicated in developed countries because income determines automobile ownership and (for the most part) automobile ownership determines low public transit use. In any event, cities in developing countries tend to have higher levels of traffic congestion (reflecting inadequate highway capacity, accelerating automobile ownership growth rates, mixed road uses and poor, and often non-existent, traffic management). Of course, a perverse prescription would be to argue in favour of creating developing country levels of congestion in developed countries (and there are a few examples in the United States of converting four-lane highways into two lanes) in an effort to make public transit trip times competitive with automobile travel, but the welfare effects of such steps would be devastating.

The compactness of cities in developing countries is the product less of strict land use planning than its absence, so the planning lessons are negligible. Compactness in developing country cities (especially in peripheral squatter settlements or central city slums) is frequently associated with high levels of environmental degradation (e.g. pressures on inadequate water supply, sanitation and solid waste management systems). Even if there is a case for densification in developed countries, it is based on relatively marginal additions to density via smaller lots for single family homes or more emphasis on condominium and townhouse development, rather than on attempts to replicate developing country central city densities.

Notes

1. The sample is those cities included in Tables 1-3, and conclusions drawn about developing countries are related to that sample. The sample was limited by data-availability, and is weighted towards cities in South America and Asia. Accordingly there is less information on cities in Africa where different trends in densities may be apparent. The sample included only cities with a population size over 1 million people.
2. For a copy of the master data set and range of sources used, please send e-mail to hrichard@usc.edu.

References

Alonso, W. (1973) Urban zero population growth. *Daedalus: Journal of the American Academy of Arts and Sciences*, **102(4)**, pp.191–206.

Bae, C.-H. C. (1998) Korea's greenbelts – impacts and options for change. *Pacific Rim Law and Policy Journal,* **7(3)**, pp.1–25.

Bertaud, A. and Cuenco, K. (1996) *Ahmedabad: Land Use Issues and Recommendations*, World Bank, Washington, DC.

Bertaud, A. and Malpezzi, S. (1998a) *Measuring the Costs and Benefits of Urban Land Regulation: A Simple Model with an Application to Malaysia*, University of Wisconsin, Centre for Urban Land Economics Research.

Bertaud, A. and Malpezzi, S. (1998b) The spatial distribution of population in 35 world cities: the role of markets, planning and topography, Working Paper, World Bank and Centre for Urban Land Economics Research, University of Wisconsin.

Dargay, J. and Gately, D. (1997) *Income's Effect on Car and Vehicle Ownership, Worldwide: 1960-2015*, New York University, C.V. Starr Centre for Applied Economics, RR No. 97–33, New York.

Dowall, D. E. (1992) A second look at the Bangkok land and housing market. *Urban Studies*, **29(1)**, pp.25–37.

Drakakis-Smith, D. (1995) Third world cities – sustainable urban development I. *Urban Studies*, **32(4-5)**, pp.659–677.

Drakakis-Smith, D. (1996a) Third world cities – sustainable urban development II – Population, labour and poverty. *Urban Studies*, **33(4-5)**, pp.673–701.

Drakakis-Smith, D. (1996b) Sustainability, urbanisation and development. *Third World Planning Review*, **18(4)**, pp.iii–x.

Drakakis-Smith, D. (1997) Third world cities – sustainable urban development III – basic needs and urban rights. *Urban Studies*, **34(5-6)**, pp.797–823.

Gakenheimer, R. (1995) *Motorisation in the Developing World*, World Bank, Washington, DC.

Gomez-Ibanez, J. A. (1991) A global view of automobile dependence. *Journal of the American Planning Association*, **57(3)**, pp.376–9.

Hardoy, J. E. and Satterthwaite, D. (1992) *Environmental Problems in Third World Cities: An Agenda for the Poor and the Planet*, International Institute for Environment and Development, London.

Ingram, G. K. and Liu, Z. (1999) Determinants of motorisation and road provision, in (eds J. A. Gomez-Ibanez, W. B. Tye and C. Winston), *Essays in Transportation Economics and Policy: A Handbook in Honour of John R. Meyer*, The Brookings Institution, Washington, DC.

Kim, K.-H. (1994) *Controlled Developments and Densification: The Case of Seoul, Korea*, United Nations Centre for Human Settlements, Nairobi.

Malpezzi, S. (1999) *The Regulation of Urban Development: Lessons from International Experience*, Department of Real Estate and Land Economics, School of Business, University of Wisconsin, Madison.

Mills, E. S. and Tan, J. P. (1980) A comparison of urban population density functions in developed and developing countries. *Urban Studies*, **17(3)**, pp.313–321.

Newman, P. and Kenworthy, J. (1989a) *Cities and Automobile Dependence: An International Sourcebook*, Gower Publishing, Aldershot.

Newman, P. and Kenworthy, J. (1989b) Gasoline consumption and cities: a comparison of US cities with a global survey. *Journal of the American Planning Association*, **55(1)**, pp.24–37.

Satterthwaite, D. (1997) Sustainable cities or cities that contribute to sustainable development? *Urban Studies*, **34(10)**, pp.1667–1691.

Tony Lloyd Jones
Compact City Policies for Megacities:
Core Areas and Metropolitan Regions

Introduction

Large cities in developing countries are following a spatial development trajectory similar to that in the developed countries. 'The largest cities are, with a few exceptions, not growing especially quickly (small ones are, and so become large ones), but their inhabitants are spreading out over much larger metropolitan regions (so as population size increases, densities decline). The region absorbs smaller cities and towns' (Harris, 1992, pp.ix–x). This pattern of development, with the growing importance of large urban regions, is similar to that found in most developed countries. However, its occurrence 50 to 100 years later means that there are important differences, in particular in relation to income structure and to the pace and scale of change. These compound the problems of the urban sprawl of developing world cities.

This chapter arose out of (and provides the context for) a research programme into urban design and management approaches for sustainable development in the core areas of megacities in developing countries.[1] The chapter first addresses the urbanisation process and policy responses at the broader metropolitan regional scale. Parallels are drawn with megacities in developed countries and the idea of travel time, as a structuring constraint, is introduced. The final section deals with inner city and core area spatial development issues. The argument is that, by addressing at source deconcentration (the relocation of the population from central areas to the periphery), one major factor contributing to the urban decentralisation and sprawl around the megacities of the developing world can be contained. The need to develop new approaches arises as a response to the development pressures on low-income communities who live and work in the core areas. Their dispersal to peripheral areas adds to growing problems of urban sprawl and lack of sustainability.

New approaches to core area development, clearly, can form only part of a package of compact city policies. Population pressures caused by continuing in-migration to the major metropolitan regions and by internally generated growth still have to be accommodated. Some relocation of inner-city economic activities and people, in response to land market forces and life stage demands, and to relieve local overcrowding, is inevitable. Thus, there should also be spatial development policies at the metropolitan regional scale that effectively contain urban sprawl. Current approaches to metropolitan planning, which follow rather mechanically the models that have previously emerged in developed countries, are, it is argued, more likely to encourage urban sprawl than moderate it.

The scale and nature of change in megacities of the developing world

Most developing countries are undergoing a major demographic transition, with economic, social and technological 'modernisation' leading to falling death rates and rapid population growth (Vaughan Williams, 1990). The experience in the developed countries has been that, eventually, birth rates also fall and rapid population growth tails off. Currently, however, many developing countries are still undergoing rapid population growth that, together with economic change (including, more recently, globalisation), fuels the urbanisation process (Bairoch, 1988). As with China and India, this demographic transformation often occurs on top of an already large population base. Primary cities, which may already have been in existence for a long time and, drawing on the population of a large rural hinterland, be quite substantial in size, rapidly become megacities.

Broadly, the largest cities in the developing countries follow a pattern of spatial development similar to that in the developed countries. However, they often contain much larger concentrations of people, and particularly of poor people including large numbers living at high densities, than cities at an equivalent stage in developed countries. In large cities in developed countries sprawl is to a large degree fuelled by middle-income homeowners. In contrast, a large part of the development on the periphery of large cities in developing countries consists of relatively isolated and poorly serviced low-income settlements. These remote neighbourhoods increasingly attract poor migrants who are unable to find affordable shelter in more central areas.

Comparing the scale of urban development at an equivalent stage of evolution is illuminating. The Greater London urban agglomeration, at the peak of its concentration in the late 1930s, contained nearly 9 million people. Greater London sixty years later contains little more than 7 million people with a wider metropolitan area of around 12 million inhabitants. The rapidly growing Delhi urban agglomeration today contains around 11.5 million people, with a metropolitan area of about 16 million. Jakarta and Cairo are similar in scale. Mexico City, Mumbai and São Paulo are larger still – agglomerations of 17 or 18 million people. Not all these cities are at an equivalent level of development but all contain large numbers of poor people.

Whether through choice or necessity, many of these people will relocate from inner city areas to the urban periphery or to other towns and cities in the urban region. Increasing development pressures will mean that many will not be able to continue to afford to live in the more central locations. Others living in illegal settlements or slums scheduled for renewal will be forced to move or be relocated by the authorities. Newly formed and growing families will move out because space is cheaper away from the centre. Households with rising incomes and whose members can afford to commute will seek more space and better living conditions in the suburbs or nearby towns and away from inner-city slums.

All cities experience a population turnover as new migrants replace those leaving the inner areas. With general economic improvement, rising land values and spatial development policies aimed at deconcentration, the experience has been that more people move away from the core areas than move in. In 1931, 71% of the UK urban population lived in the metropolitan cores. By 1966 this proportion had fallen to 60% (Cherry, 1988) and has fallen further since. At the turn of the century, the London Borough of Tower Hamlets contained nearly 600,000 people, most very poor and living in overcrowded slum conditions (Hall, 1984). Today it has a population of little more than 150,000, many still relatively poor but enjoying far higher space standards. Developing world cities are threatened by a similar scale of population shift on top of already quite massive peripheral development.

Space-time limits to the growth of large cities

While the megacities of developed countries are characterised by relatively affluent and stable populations, those in developing countries are poorer, larger and expanding more rapidly. In the 1970s and 1980s alarming population projections of 20 to 30 millions for these impoverished megacities became commonplace (Table 1). Yet the most extreme of these projections have so far failed to materialise. The growth of the largest cities and urban agglomerations in many instances has slowed, as the major urban population expansion has become focused away from the central agglomeration and its suburban periphery to secondary towns and cities within, or closely adjacent to, the major city regions.[2] As McGee (1998) notes, looking at the slowing population growth of the cities or even the larger agglomerations gives a false impression of what is happening in the wider metropolitan region, where continuing high growth threatens sprawl on a massive scale. Local decentralisation reflected in the population statistics is masking the continuing larger scale centralisation of people and capital in what McGee calls extended metropolitan regions of the major cities (EMRs) (ibid.) An outward wave of growth, of the kind identified in the London Region by Hall (1984; 1989), seems also to be happening in the megacities of developing countries.

Agglomeration	1977	1996
Tokyo-Yokohama	26.1	28.0
Mexico City	31.6	18.1
Mumbai	19.1	18.0
São Paulo	26.0	17.7
New York	22.2	16.6
Shanghai	19.2	14.2
Lagos	9.4	13.5
Los Angeles	14.8	13.1
Calcutta	19.7	12.9
Buenos Aires	14.0	12.4
Cairo*	16.4	12.3
Beijing	19.1	12.0
Karachi	15.9	11.8
Delhi	13.2	11.7

Table 1. Changing estimates of the populations (in millions) of the major urban agglomerations.
Sources: UN Department of Economics and Social Affairs (1997) Global Review of Human Settlements: Statistical Annex, pp. 77–78, New York: United Nations; UN Department of Economic and Social Affairs Population Division (1998), World Urbanization Prospects: the 1996 Revision, New York: United Nations, p.142

* Figure for Greater Cairo includes Shubra El-Khemia

What are the factors structuring the development of metropolitan regions around large cities? Some of the development factors that give rise to competition from smaller cities and towns have been mentioned. Higher costs associated with congestion, higher rents and wage costs drive basic and manufacturing industry away from the most congested areas and high land value areas. As in developed countries, cities in the wealthier developing countries such as Hong Kong and Singapore, which had grown up with a strong manufacturing base, have increasingly turned into more specialised financial and commercial centres as industry has decentralised to their regional hinterlands. Increased flows of goods, people, information and capital associated with globalisation have reinforced the pace of such physical change.

The demographic factors already mentioned play an important role. If it is increasingly difficult and expensive to find somewhere to live in a large city, and there is the promise of decent employment and cheap housing in smaller neighbouring towns and cities, then there will be outward migration, particularly of young, newly forming households. This process is occurring in the largest metropolitan centres of Latin America such as Buenos Aires, Mexico City and São Paulo. Here, outward migration to secondary centres has begun to exceed inward migration from other parts of the country (UN Centre for Human Settlements, 1996).

Why do businesses and households not simply move further out on the periphery rather than to other towns and cities? To a large extent, the latter also happens, but there are limits to this process. There are advantages to remaining in the metropolitan area of a large, primary city. Even on the periphery, where development is sparse, it is relatively easy for businesses to gain access to the transport networks that link the city to its hinterland, to draw on the huge employment base of the city, or to take advantage of the great variety of services on offer. But the further out you go, the less this is the case, and the more expensive it becomes to provide the necessary infrastructure links.

Moreover, no matter how good the transport connections, travel time places absolute constraints on how far people will travel on a regular basis. Travel time budgets are an aspect of a rather neglected area of urban science. What many studies have shown is that there is a geographical and historical constancy about the proportion of their day that people will devote to regular travel, sometimes referred to as the Anthropological Time Constant (e.g. Zahavi, 1981). There are, of course, major variations around the mean, between cities and between different income groups. Congested megacities with large poor populations living on the periphery and having to travel far to their workplace clearly have longer average commuting times. However, all people ultimately have time constraints beyond which working life is not viable.

A simplified model of distance related to travel time (Fig. 1) could be used to help explain the spatial structure of the large metropolis. Using a travel time of 45 minutes, a radius from the CBD can be drawn, which varies according to mode and efficiency of transport, but which for the purposes of this paper is defined as 40km. Within the radius is located the agglomeration; but over time, important economic functions tend to migrate to the edge of the agglomeration, utilising new infrastructure, notably orbital and radial motorways, airports, shopping malls and other 'Edge City' phenomena (Garreau, 1992).

While peripheral sub-centres do not have the variety and scale of services

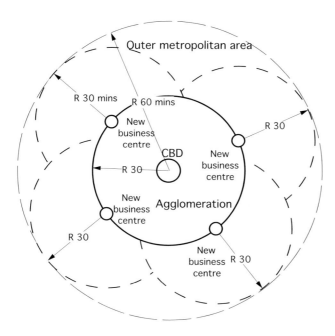

Fig. 1. Travel time and metropolitan structure.

offered by a large metropolitan centre, they may be sufficiently developed to compete effectively with secondary cities that would otherwise act as a magnet for businesses and households migrating from the main urban centre. In the model illustrated here, a ring of peripheral sub-centres can also draw on their own hinterlands (which include part of the agglomeration itself). A larger radius, some 80km out from the CBD, can be traced out; this incorporates the whole metropolitan region.

This model has been adapted slightly to take account of the fact that the outer commuter belt is extended by faster rail links and greater ease of movement in the outer areas. It remains, however, an abstraction that ignores the functional complexity of the relationship between many urban areas and their hinterlands. Many urban regions are polynuclear, with more than a single primary urban centre and large secondary centres in a close functional relationship with each other. Both within and beyond the outer suburban ring of most large metropolitan areas are small satellite towns and cities which send a significant number of commuters to the CBD or which serve as growth centres for the 'overspill' of jobs and residents from the central city.

Decentralisation and sprawl in megacities in developing and developed countries

It is to the expansion of these satellites, or the creation of new towns or cities within the same range, that regional planners in the megacities of developing countries are looking increasingly to relieve the pressures of the swollen centres (see Fig. 2). The question arises whether the most likely result of new 'growth poles' within the metropolitan regions of megacities, planned to relieve the population pressures on the central city, will be sprawl on a gigantic scale, resulting from the longer-term mobility patterns between and around the new and existing centres.

Fig. 3 compares the built areas of the largest megacities in developing and developed countries, and their surrounding urban regions, using satellite night

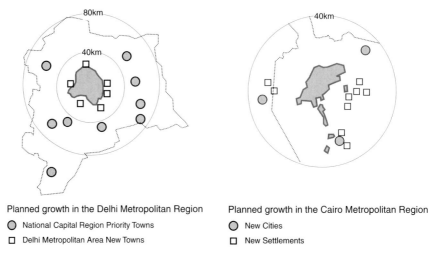

Fig. 2. Planned satellite development in Delhi and Cairo.
Sources: UNCHS, 1993 and 1996; Llewelyn-Davies, 1996; Delhi NCR Region Plan 2001, 1988.

Planned growth in the Delhi Metropolitan Region
○ National Capital Region Priority Towns
□ Delhi Metropolitan Area New Towns

Planned growth in the Cairo Metropolitan Region
○ New Cities
□ New Settlements

imaging.[3] It gives an indication, at a coarse level of resolution, of the extent of urban agglomeration and peripheral development and the development of satellite settlements within the larger region. The 'night lights' approach can provide only a crude index of the extent of urban sprawl. This is because it can underestimate built areas due to the low light emissions of informal developments and overestimate them when they include night-lit highways, without adjacent built development.[4]

Despite this, several key observations can be made. First, in the developed parts of the world in most instances megacities form part of much larger polynuclear urban areas formed by the coalescence of adjacent metropolitan areas.[5] Second, the megacities of developing countries have populations equivalent to or larger than some of those in developed countries but in much more highly concentrated urban areas at much higher densities. The outer areas of their metropolitan regions are likely to go on growing at a faster rate, as a result of the 'overspill' of internally generated population growth, planned decentralisation and in-migration. The result could be that, while 'cities' of 30 or 40 million are not likely to emerge as concentrated agglomerations, sprawling urban regions at this scale could become commonplace. The environmental impacts will become increasingly more profound with economic development and reliance on private motor transport.

A central question for spatial planners in developing countries is thus whether to reinforce urban decentralising processes through planned satellite development or whether there are better policies for achieving a more sustainable urban form. Can anything useful be learned from the experience of megacities in developed countries in dealing with these issues?

Policy lessons from megacities in developed countries
Megacities in developing countries represent the most extreme examples of urban sprawl that planners there have to deal with. They are not the only possible vehicle for compact city development policies, or necessarily the most appropriate.[6] It might even be argued that these cities have already developed beyond the stage where anything useful can be achieved by a compact city approach (e.g. Table 2).

New York – Tokyo

London – Hong Kong

LA – Jakarta

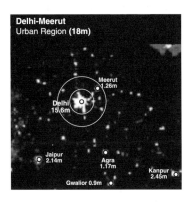

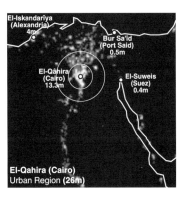

Delhi – Cairo

Fig. 3. A comparison of urban regions in developed and developing countries.
Population figures aggregated mainly from estmates for metropolitan areas and agglomerations for 1999/2000 by UNCHS 1996 and Rand McNally 1999, with additional data from other published sources.
Populations for individual urban centres are for metropolitan areas using standard definitions (Rand McNally, 1999) wherever possible.
Circles around major urban centres are shown at 40km and 80km radii.

43

	Core Area	Administrative Inner or City	Agglomeration	Metropolitan Area	Metropolitan Planning Region
Beijing (1990)	*4 inner city districts*	*Core city*	*Inner city/suburbs*	-	*Municipality, outer suburbs, 8 counties*
Population	2,336,000	5,400,000	6,325,722	-	10,819,407
Area	87	158	1,369	-	16,808
Density	26,857	34,177	4,621	-	644
Bombay (1991)	*City*	*Greater Bombay Municipal Corp.*	*Agglomeration*	-	*Bombay Metro. Region*
Population	3,159,907	9,909,547	12,851,028	-	14,425,446
Area	68	428	1,306	-	4,189
Density	46,469	22,640	9,840	-	3,444
Cairo (1986)	*Central Core*	*Cairo City/ Governate*	*Greater Cairo Metro. Region*	*Greater Cairo Region*	*3 Governates*
Population	2,870,000	6,052,836	8,761,927	10,660,000	13,097,000
Area	-	188	254	-	2,627
Density	-	32,169	34,496	-	4,986
Delhi (1991)	*Old City*	-	*Delhi Union Territory*	*Delhi Metropolitan Area*	*National Capital Region*
Population (000s)	624,184	-	9,255,000	11,000,000	25,410,000
Area	11	-	1,485	1,696	30,242
Density	55,385	-	6,232	2,646	840
London (1991)	*City of London*	*Inner London*	*Greater London Boroughs*	*Metropolitan Area (London Region)*	*South East Region*
Population	170,000	2,343,000	6,393,000	11,904,000	16,889,000
Area	27	321	1,578	11,230	27,224
Density	6,296	7,299	4,051	1,060	620
Los Angeles (1990)	-	*Los Angeles City*	-	*Los Angeles – Long Beach MSA*	*Los Angeles CMSA*
Population (000s)	-	3,485,398	-	8,863,000	14,532,000
Area	-	1,211	-	2,038	87,652
Density	-	2,878	-	4,349	166
Mexico City (1990)	-	*Central City*	*Federal District*	*Metropolitan Area/AMCM*	*Megalopolis/ Conurbation*
Population	-	1,935,708	8,621,951	14,991,281	18,000,000
Area	-	139	1,578	4,636	8,163
Density	-	13,926	5,790	3,234	2,205
New York (1990)	*CBD*	-	*Agglomeration*	-	*CMSA/Tristate New York MR*
Population	542,000	7,864,000	16,056,000	-	19,342,000
Area	22	777	12,551	-	33,483
Density	24,636	10,121	1,279	-	578
Paris (1990)	*Arondisment 1-10*	-	*Inner Agglom./ Petite Couronne*	*Region Isle de France*	-
Population (000s)	246,000	2,398,000	6,387,000	10,907,000	-
Area	23	105	750	12,007	-
Density	10,696	22,838	8,516	908	-
Shanghai (1982)	-	-	-	*Metropolitan Area*	-
Population (000s)	-	5,640,000	-	11,800,000	13,452,000
Area	-	141	-	5,000	6,000
Density	-	40,000	-	2,360	2,242
Tokyo (1990)	*6 Central Wards*	*Central City/ 23 Ward Areas*	*Agglomeration*	*Tokyo Metropolitan Area*	*National Capital Region*
Population (000s)	1,030,000	8,167,000	25,069,000	31,559,000	39,158,000
Area	87	581	11,305	13,508	36,834
Density	11,839	14,057	2,218	2,336	1,063

Notes: Areas are in km^2, and densities in persons/km^2. A number of the estimates are population projections. As far as possible, figures are given for the appropriate category, but there is local variation in the interpretation of these categories, which are intermediate in character.

However, by comparing their development with similarly sized urban centres in developed countries, it is possible to draw conclusions, both about their future development and about other cities that will soon assume megacity status.

The populations of cities like Jakarta, Cairo, Delhi and Shanghai are larger and more densely settled than those in developed countries. The peripheral suburban and satellite development around these cities sometimes stretches as far as in the cities of developed countries but, for the moment, they contain fewer people. Overall, globally, the populations of the larger metropolitan areas and regions are similar. Tokyo, with a metropolitan area of just over 30 million people, is significantly larger than the rest and this probably represents an upper limit in terms of size. Physical suburban sprawl is the greatest, predictably, in the largest US megacities illustrated in Fig. 3, New York and Los Angeles, which are the most wasteful in terms of energy use. However, Tokyo, with its denser form, represents the model that developing country megacities are more likely to follow and it is worth considering its planning and development trajectory in more detail.

Tokyo is the richest city in the world and has by far the largest population. Given its size, it works remarkably well. The impact of its vast urban sprawl is minimised by its strong reliance on public transport. Increases in capacity reduced rail congestion levels by 10% between the mid-1980s and mid-1990s, but use is still at twice the level of designed capacity (Llewelyn-Davies *et al.*, 1996). Tokyo thus has substantial planning problems, even if it has managed to persuade the rest of the world that these problems do not exist (ibid.). Decentralisation of the population from its still relatively dense inner city is likely to exacerbate these problems and threaten its hitherto commendable record in transport energy use (Newman and Kenworthy, 1989). In this respect, its attempts at controlled spatial development have not been notably successful. Early master plans followed the classic new towns policy approach and called for the construction of a ring of satellite cities at what appeared sufficient distance to prevent the development of intervening sprawl. This did not happen and the satellite towns are now linked to the central urban agglomeration by a vast suburban ring (see Fig. 4).

Opposite page: *Table 2. Populations and densities for some megacities and their associated areas.*
Sources: UNCHS, 1993 and 1996; Llewelyn-Davies, 1996; NCRPB, 1988.

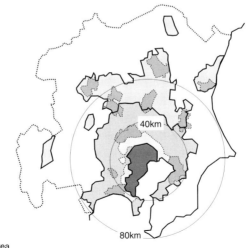

Tokyo National Capital Region - planned and actual growth

■ Central Urban Core
▫ Planned Green Belt 1965
▨ Planned Satellite Towns 1965
☐ Post 1965 Suburban development
☐ Post 1965 Satellite Town development area

Fig. 4. The decentralisation of Tokyo.
(after Hall, 1984, p.181)

The planning ideas underpinning the early Tokyo decentralisation policy were the green belt and the new and 'overspill' towns policies embodied in Abercrombie's plan for post-war London (Hall, 1984). As far as London is concerned, such policies continue to be regarded as successful in their implementation. Without a green belt, the contiguous built area of Greater London would certainly have been much larger than it is today. However, as Fig. 5 demonstrates, the 'success' in controlling outer urban development has been limited. Built development has occurred right across the outer metropolitan area, in a fragmented form, interspersed with green areas. The heavy movement of people in and between these 'towns' and 'villages' and the central conurbation creates both the impression and the reality of a continuous semi-urban area; the existence of intervening fields and woodlands does little to relieve this.

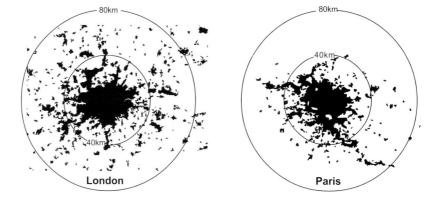

Fig. 5. Urban sprawl in London and Paris.
(after Llewlyn-Davies et al, 1996 and urban area map as defined in 1981 census)

The urban sprawl in the Paris metropolitan region is comparable to that of London. However, it could certainly be argued that the planned urban extensions along public transport-based axes that formed the basis of the plan for the Paris Region have been more successful in limiting urban sprawl across the whole metropolitan region (see Fig. 5). Linear development of this kind has been tried and tested in a number of cities well known for the effectiveness of their land use planning and public transport systems, such as Stockholm, Singapore and Curitiba in Brazil.

Development changes in the inner zones of megacities
The problems of urban decentralisation and sprawl cannot be resolved without the rapid implementation of targeted compact city-oriented policies, combining carefully thought-through strategic spatial development frameworks at the urban regional scale with flexible, 'fine-grain' planning tools at the local scale. This implies a radical re-think of many present spatial planning policies targeted towards planned relocation of economic activities and deconcentration of the population from inner-city areas.

Such policies need to take account of the urban structure that has evolved in megacities in developing countries. The development zones that have accreted around the historical core are broadly similar in megacities around the world, but with some important differences relating to the colonial legacy and 'structural' socio-economic differences. Broadly, these zones are as follows:

- The historic core and central business district;
- The inner-city districts;
- The outer suburban ring;
- The outer metropolitan or peri-urban area, and
- The outer planning zone which contains some satellite cities and other cities with good transport and close economic links to the central city.

The focus, here, is primarily on the first two zones, and the impact of conventional spatial planning approaches both on them and on the city region as a whole.

The historic core and central business district is usually the financial, commercial and cultural core of a city. In some cities, the colonial power built a new administrative centre alongside the old 'native quarters'. The 'new city' then developed as the political and business centre, with the old city remaining a mixed use area. The old city combined very high densities with traditional craft and small-scale manufacturing activities and low-cost wholesaling, retailing and commercial services (e.g. Delhi/New Delhi).

The inner-city districts form the ring around the historic core and are also characterised by service and manufacturing activities, but have the highest concentration of high-density residential development. The residents tend to be either relatively poor or relatively affluent. The inner city developed in the nineteenth and early part of the twentieth century in developed countries. In the megacities of developing countries, this type of development continued up to the 1960s, and in some places is still continuing as empty spaces are developed, and lower density or illegally developed areas have been redeveloped or consolidated.

Because cities developed as industrial or commercial centres, a large proportion of manufacturing and transport-related activity (railways, docks, warehousing) was concentrated in these areas. A significant proportion of this activity in cities in developed countries has since been dispersed to the periphery or secondary cities. This has led to inner-city decline and depopulation, and opportunities or pressures for regeneration and revitalisation. Many cities in developing countries are increasingly facing similar problems, with heavy concentrations of traditional manufacturing and transport-related activities in the inner cities now being decentralised through planned relocation or in response to economic changes. Some of these activities will be replaced by new developments in the outer suburban ring of the central city. The rest will disperse to nearby towns and cities that can benefit from their proximity to the infrastructure grown up around the central megacity.

Pressure of rising rents and costs, the attraction of new employment centres, and planned inner-city slum and squatter resettlement projects on the periphery are also leading directly to an net outflow of people from the inner city areas.[7] This process follows the logic of the land market but challenges the logic of sustainable development based on the need to reduce distances between place of residence and place of employment.

Socio-economic impacts of depopulation

The immediate issue is not inner-city decline, but the planned depopulation of the historic core and the expansion and sprawl of the outer city which is absorbing migrants from rural areas, other cities, the inner city and historic core alike.

The historic core houses large numbers of people (e.g. 2 million in Old Cairo), usually at very high residential densities (e.g. up to 100,000 people per km² in the Sharabiah district of Cairo) (UN Centre for Human Settlements, 1993). Overcrowding results from extended households forming within single living quarters and the subdivision of dwellings to accommodate newly forming households. The traditional networks of family and community tend to be strong, as is the link with the traditional economic activities of the area.

In Shanghai, for example, the tradition of newly married women moving in with their in-laws has led to cramped living conditions and high residential densities.[8] Shanghai has followed Beijing in its policy of wholesale redevelopment of the old urban quarters and the relocation of the residential population in new mid-rise apartment blocks on site and in the periphery. This results not only in an unrecoverable loss of built cultural heritage, but also in the break-up of communities, loss of 'social capital', loss of important traditional and 'informal' low-income services and manufacturing activities, and the destruction of livelihood patterns which are highly sustainable.

Because of their high population densities and mixed uses, the historic cores (and many inner-city districts) are normally characterised by a high level of street activity and vitality. Their historic street patterns may make vehicular access difficult and in some cases impossible. The high concentration of poverty in these areas, and the decline of traditional economic activities result in the deterioration of the physical fabric, threatening the cultural heritage.

Traditional solutions to these problems, like the planned relocation of important primary economic activities such as in the wholesale markets of Old Delhi, or the comprehensive redevelopment of traditional residential quarters in Beijing and Shanghai, are often inappropriate if sustainability is to be regarded as a priority. Other revitalisation approaches, such as the extension of cultural tourism, or upgrading the best areas for new commercial and service activities, also have their dangers. The most important of these is gentrification, which may well preserve and revitalise the existing physical fabric but which can undermine and destroy the existing social fabric. Any upgrading and revitalisation efforts will almost certainly lead to increased land and property values and bring some degree of gentrification. On its own, this is not a bad thing and will be a necessary element of any revitalisation or conservation plan. The concern, however, should be to avoid a wholesale uprooting and dispersal of the existing low-income communities, whether through planned relocation or through the unintended action of economic forces. Poor people should be able to continue to live in the central areas in healthy environments, with security of tenure where they perform vital economic functions in the service industries.

Maintaining the delicate balance between entrenched poverty and economic stagnation on the one hand, and total gentrification on the other, is the immediate challenge of core area planning. This requires thoughtful interventions and fine-tuning at the local scale, with the nurturing of partnerships between local authorities and other public development agencies, private investors and local businesses and communities.

Planning tools for sustainable core-area development
Blanket policies of comprehensive redevelopment, wholesale decentralisation and 'overspill' relocation of low-income residents and 'low-value' activities to

monofunctional peripheral zones or new satellite centres should be avoided. Monofunctional land use zones in inner cities and core areas (such as commercial office zones) should also be avoided. Zones for cultural preservation should be set up with care since they bring attendant dangers of creating tourism-dominated museum-like areas, with little room for economic or income diversity.

Achieving compaction in the megacities of developing countries requires appropriate policies of planned higher density, mixed-use development in central areas and in urban extensions along corridors well served with public transport.[9] The planning approach to core-area development should be more sensitive to the existing urban fabric, which can accommodate a whole range of economic activities.[10] It will require a change in the traditional attitude of planners towards poor inner-city neighbourhoods, for example the view that they are overcrowded slums that need to be eliminated. The value of their social networks and economic diversity should be recognised and, rather than being swept away, they should undergo environmental improvement.

There are a number of planning tools for achieving and maintaining sustainable urban form in the core areas. All need to be combined with a more flexible local planning approach. The public ownership of building land is potentially the most powerful tool for sustainable development. It can allow the municipality to bank and release land for development in response to market forces. It can also allow it to reserve areas for 'social' development, cross-financed through revenues from commercial land development. First, however, it needs to be coupled with mixed-use zoning policies and a fine-grained approach to the mixing of uses, incomes and tenures at the local scale. In Delhi, for example, the land is in public ownership and development rights are vested in the Delhi Development Authority. However, the master plan for the city is largely based on single-use zoning and encourages the resettling of low-income residents from the core areas in vast new residential estates on the urban periphery (Max Lock Centre, 2000; Sringagan, 2000).

Second, local development taxes can be used for cross-subsidising low-income housing and community provision through commercial development, but conditions similarly need local fine-tuning. Third, the use of 'floor space bonuses' combined with plot ratio planning requirements limiting the allowable built floor space per unit of site area have been widely used for planning gain and public benefit in North America and Asia. In Mumbai, the municipal government instituted a city-wide floor space bonus scheme which rewards developers who make provision for low-income housing in commercial site developments. This ensures that the issue is dealt with at the site level and encourages developers to form partnerships with low-income communities for the redevelopment of squatter settlements. It provides a formal and institutional framework for the land-sharing approaches that have been practised on an *ad hoc* basis in many cities in Asia (Winarso, forthcoming; Povey and Lloyd Jones, 2000).

More flexible and responsive planning tools than those currently in use are required to manage these new development interventions. Most of these tools rely on an urban design approach – for example, site development briefs which set out guidelines for built form and spatial configuration, or more general area-based or use-based urban design guidelines. The Core Areas research project has developed simple modelling tools. These can allow all the potential stakeholders involved in an area or site-based development to explore the feasibility of a range of design options addressing both social and economic concerns at an early stage, prior to the preparation of full architectural proposals.

These tools can form an important element in a reinvigoration of the planning infrastructure of developing country cities. Planning authorities in too many cities have been overwhelmed by rapid urban growth and have demonstrated an inability to manage the formal land supply system. They have often been hamstrung by policies inherited from the developed world where they have demonstrably failed. But many cities have accepted that large-scale informal development is inevitable and adopted policies, such as those based on upgrading, which make the best of the situation.[11] The current costs of servicing ever-growing, low-income informal sprawl, combined with the growing environmental costs of more general urban sprawl on a regional scale, however, present huge hurdles which better spatial planning, based on the compact city approach, could go some way to avoid.

Notes

1. The research project was entitled 'A Guide to Good Practice in Core Areas Development', funded by the Department for International Development – see *Urbanisation*, 7, November 1998, WEDC/DFID. The case studies in the 'Core Areas' research programme were located in Delhi, Jakarta, Cairo and Recife and evidence from some of these cities is used to illustrate the points made in this chapter. This research has tended to confirm the relevance of the arguments for other cities in developing countries.

2. UN Centre for Human Settlements, 1996, pp.17–18. Among the largest urban agglomerations, a few, like Tokyo, Bombay, Jakarta and Lagos, showed relatively large increases in population in recent years, but a great part of this can be put down to extensions in the boundaries of the urban area. The current population figure for Lagos is regarded as an over-estimate.

3. Satellite image capture by Dr Mike Theis of the Max Lock Centre in November and December 1999, using John Walker's excellent *Earthviewer* software (http://www.fourmilab.ch/earthview/cities.html). All of the largest megacities are illustrated. With about the population of Cairo, several other cities could have been included – such as Calcutta, Manila, Karachi, Buenos Aires and Moscow.

4. Visible light, however, may provide quite a good indicator of overall energy use and lack of environmental sustainability.

5. The original 'megalopolis' of the eastern seaboard of the United States has around 46 million people. Complexes of similar or even larger extent have been identified on the eastern coast of Honshû, Japan, Southern Florida, in the Ruhr and Low Countries in Europe, in north central and south eastern England. Emerging urban regions include Bombay–Pune in India and Rio–São Paulo in Brazil. A number of urban regions on a similar scale exist in China, Taiwan and South Korea (see Fig. 3). The rapidly growing urban area of the Pearl River Delta linking Hong Kong with Guandong is expected to grow to 40 million in 20 years. Some Western enthusiasts of Asian megacities have described this as a new type of 'super city', though space-time geography prevents it from acting as a single socio-economic entity.

6. Megacities represent just 3% of the world's population. A much larger and more rapidly growing population lives in large cities of between 1 and 10 million. It represents 30% of the total urban population (compared to 10% for megacities over 10 million and 60% for towns and cities of less than 1 million (UN, 1998, p.179).

7. Given the present population structure with its predominance of the young, this outflow is unlikely to lead to population decline in these areas – rather a slowdown in population increase. In the longer term, however, as family sizes decline, and the population becomes older, absolute population decline may be possible.

8. In 1982, the residential densities in some sub-districts of the Shanghai core area reached 150,000–160,000 per km^2 (Li, 1999).

9. The significant hurdles to effective spatial planning that arise from the fragmented character of local government administration in most metropolitan regions are recognised. Institutional reforms which provide the necessary powers for strategic planning authorities on a city or region-wide scale may be a necessary prerequisite of some of the larger scale planning policies suggested here.

10. Preserving a range of accommodation of various sizes and conditions that can provide low-rental space for small enterprises in central areas is one of the arguments used by Jane Jacobs (1994) in her classic statement on the value of high-density, mixed-use urban design.

11. See Burgess, Carmona and Kolstee (1997), Chapter 7: Contemporary spatial strategies and urban policies in developing countries: a critical review, for a historical review of these policies.

References

Adusumille, U. (1999) Partnership approaches in India, in *Making Common Ground – Public–Private Partnerships in Land for Housing* (ed. G. K. Payne), Intermediate Technology Publications, London.

Bairoch, P. (1988) *Cities and Economic Development*, Mansell Publishing, London.

Burgess, R., Carmona, M. and Kolstee, T. (1997) *The Challenge of Sustainable Cities: Neoliberalism and Urban Strategies in Developing Countries*, Zed Books, London.

Cherry, G. (1988) *Cities and Plans*, Edward Arnold, London.

Garreau, J. (1992) *Edge City*, Anchor Books, New York.

Gilbert, A. G. and Gugler, J. (1982) *Cities, Poverty and Development: Urbanization in the Third World*, Oxford University Press, Oxford.

Hall, P. (1984) *The World Cities*, Weidenfeld & Nicolson, London.

Hall, P. (1989) *London 2001*, Unwin Hyman, London.

Harris, N. (ed.) (1992) *Cities in the 1990s: The Challenge for Developing Countries*, UCL Press, London.

Jacobs, J. (1994) *The Death and Life of Great American Cities: The Failure of Town Planning*, Penguin Books (first published 1961), Harmondsworth.

Li, J. (1999) Sustainable development of megacity Shanghai, unpublished MA Dissertation, University of Westminster, London.

Llewelyn-Davies, UCL Bartlett School of Planning and Comedia (1996) *Four World Cities: A Comparative Study of London, Paris, New York and Tokyo*, Llewelyn-Davies, London.

Max Lock Centre (2000) Guide to good practice in core area development: Delhi Field Study, Working Paper, University of Westminster, London.

McGee, T. G. (1998) Globalization and rural–urban relations in the developing world, in *Globalization and the World of Large Cities* (eds Fu-chen Lo and Yue-man Yeung), United Nations University Press, Tokyo.

NCRPB (National Capital Region Planning Board) (1988) *Regional Plan 2000: National Capital Region*, Ministry of Urban Development, Government of India.

Newman, P. and Kenworthy, J. (1989) *Cities and Automobile Dependence*, Gower, Aldershot.

Povey, M. and Lloyd Jones, T. (2000) Mixed use development: mechanisms for sustaining the livelihoods and social capital of the urban poor in core areas, paper presented at the *17th Inter-Schools Conference on Sustainable Cities: Sustainable Development*, Oxford Brookes University, April 2000, Oxford.

Rand McNally (1999) *Millennium World Atlas*, Rand McNally, Illinois.

Sringagan, K. (2000) *Public Land, Property Development and Cross Subsidisation for Low Income Housing*, Max Lock Centre Working Paper, University of Westminster, London.

UN Centre for Human Settlements (1993) *Metropolitan Planning and Management in the Developing World: Spatial Decentralisation in Bombay and Cairo*, UN Centre for

Human Settlements, Nairobi.

UN Centre for Human Settlements (1996) *An Urbanising World: Global Report on Human Settlements 1996*, UNCHS, Oxford University Press, Oxford.

UN Department of Economic and Social Affairs Population Division (1998) *World Urbanization Prospects: The 1996 Revision*, United Nations, World Bank/UNCHS, New York.

Vaughan Williams, P. (1990) *Brazil: A Thematic Geography*, Unwin Hyman, London.

Winarso, H. (forthcoming) 'Innercity redevelopment strategy: a lesson from two case studies in Indonesia', *Third World Planning Review*.

Zahavi, Y. (1981) The UMOT–Urban Interactions, DOT–RSPA–DPB 10/7, US Department of Transportation, Washington, DC.

Marisa Carmona
The Regional Dimension of the Compact City Debate:
Latin America

Introduction

The spatial structure of most Latin American metropolitan areas has changed considerably in the last two decades as result of the impact of globalisation. Most governments have opened up national economies to the international market and sought to enhance the competitive advantages of urban agglomerations through infrastructure upgrading and the development of services and financial activities.

Although substantial differences exist between countries and regions in Latin America, similar trends have been identified in many large cities. These trends include: a decline in manufacturing employment and its relocation to the periphery or metropolitan region; high rates of urban growth transforming many cities into metropolitan regions; the transformation of the traditional monocentric structure of radial development towards a polycentric model; the transformation of monofunctional residential suburbs to multifunctional urban areas; and the turn around in the fortunes of many downgraded inner-city areas, through a process of gentrification and intensification. Transport developments have improved the accessibility and centrality of places. Increases in car ownership have led to new commercial 'strip development' along road arteries, and to gated communities along metropolitan corridors. Many centrally located derelict industrial areas have been redeveloped and restructured. The modernisation and commercialisation of public places, including streets, parks and squares, has meant that many public spaces have lost their meaning as places for community contact, and many have been privatised in the form of closed commercial malls and residential areas.

The urban social structure has also changed substantially in the last twenty years. The concentration of wealth and income in fewer hands, the pauperisation of middle and lower middle-income groups and an increase in the population living in illegal settlements and poor communities have been the dominant trends. In terms of the urban economy, there have been drastic changes in production away from manufacturing towards services, a dramatic reduction in industrial and public sector employment and the continued growth of the informal economy.

This chapter discusses some of the challenges to achieving compact city goals in contemporary Latin America, where urban planning and policymaking now operates within a broader development strategy, based on the forces of global neoliberalism. These new forces have polarised some metropolitan regions and urban centres, increasing the tendency towards the spatial segregation of communities. It is argued that integration and spatial consolidation depend on the urban–regional dynamics, and that consequently the metropolitan region should be the conceptual focus for policymaking. The chapter concludes that, under such circumstances, the achievement of compact city goals seems unlikely.

Regional dimensions of spatial change

In most Latin American countries a process of industrial concentration and urbanisation occurred during the 1960s and 1970s. This was followed in the 1980s by a process, sometimes called 'polarisation reversal', of the emergence of separated industrial areas and the rapid growth of secondary and small cities. A regional process of industrial de-concentration has been driven by a number of factors, including the development of infrastructure, and the role of public investment and tax incentives. More recently, the growth of investment from overseas – Foreign Direct Investment (FDI) – has stimulated the development of national economic groupings and productive restructuring. This has led to a new type of spatial polarisation in large metropolitan regions through the development of new industrial areas, and modern service and financial centres.

In the search for competitiveness in the world economy, national and transnational firms operating in Latin America have formed new strategic alliances that have created integrated production systems, greater efficiency and access to national and regional markets. Deregulated and privatised economies have opened up new investment opportunities in sectors previously operated by the public sector. The acquisition of local public and private firms by foreign transnational firms has been the principal form of penetration of FDI in Latin American countries. The growth of transnational firms has meant a proliferation of medium and small firms searching for locational proximity to facilitate direct contact and exchange of information, and for ease of transportation for goods and labour (Sassen, 1988; Diniz and Crocco, 1998). The spatial effect has been a new type of polarisation, enhancing large metropolitan regions that have a global competitive advantage, and depressing other regions and cities.

The international expansion of transnational firms was fuelled by FDI, and formed one of the central elements of the globalisation of Latin American economies during the 1990s (Table 1).[1] Since 1997, the principal dynamic has been the transfer of public and private assets into foreign hands, especially in the larger economies such as Brazil, Mexico, Argentina, Colombia, Venezuela and Chile.

Globalisation has favoured metropolitan regions that have the competitive advantages of labour flexibility required for dynamic industrialisation, and has disadvantaged those regions where the technical and social infrastructure is poor. A process of selection and exclusion of regions and localities from the global economy is thus taking place in Latin America. The result is that spatial changes occurring in metropolitan regions are different from the changes

Country	1990–1994	1995–1997	1996	1997	1998 (estimated)
Argentina	2,931	5,400	5,000	6,326	5,800
Bolivia	107	489	474	601	660
Brazil	1,703	11,904	11,200	19,652	24,000
Chile	1,207	4,373	4,724	5,417	4,700
Colombia	860	3,828	3,276	5,982	6,000
Ecuador	293	498	447	577	580
Mexico	5,409	10,396	9,185	12,477	8,000
Peru	785	2,419	3,226	2,030	3,000
Uruguay	69	151	137	160	160
Venezuela	836	2,752	2,183	5,087	5,000

Table 1. Foreign Direct Investment flows to ALADE countries 1990–1998 (in US$ millions). Source: CEPAL,1998b.

occurring in traditional economies and rural communities. In the latter, similar economic pressures have been devastating, since global markets appear to produce goods and services at lower prices than can be achieved in subsistence economies in Latin America. In these areas, the lack of material resources, training and technology pushes their populations to other regions, exacerbating inter-rural and rural–urban migration flows. This process accelerates inter-regional migration towards the large metropolitan regions.

Urban–regional dynamics

In recent decades, these socio-economic transformations have dramatically changed the relative rates of metropolitan centralisation and decentralisation processes, and rates of de-industrialisation and service development. Recently, de Mattos (1998) has challenged the dominant view that there is a slowdown in the process of centralisation towards primary cities, and that development is spreading instead to medium and smaller sized secondary cities (e.g. Richardson, 1980). Rather, it is argued, there has been a resurgence of the trend towards territorial concentration and urbanisation – a phenomenon which de Mattos (1998) has called 'polarisation inversion'. Four main reasons to substantiate this view have been identified.

First, the shift from public to private capital has meant that profit-making imperatives have dominated decision making on the location of investment. The productivity of the enterprise has become the main criterion for seeking competitive advantage in the capital markets. In particular an increasing number of enterprises have made investment decisions more in relation to the geographical distribution of differences in inter-sectorial and inter-regional productivity than in relation to any other factor.

Second, the growing power of private managerial structures has weakened the sectorial, regional and local roots of capital. Locational decisions have favoured the more profitable sectors and territories, in a context of weak regulatory capacity and limited public control over local capital accumulation and growth.

Third, the progressive de-territorialisation of capital has meant that the different regional, provincial and local communities have lost control over the management of their own capital accumulation and growth processes. Under the new criteria of efficiency and productivity, the public sector is no longer allowed to create local artificial advantages as in former decades.

Fourth, it is clear that what Reich has called 'the creative potential of proximity' (Reich, 1991) has played an important role in the decision-making process of investors. The advantages of proximity to advanced services, highly qualified human resources and managerial capacity have undoubtedly stimulated the growth of large metropolitan regions.

The studies have also shown how uneven the process of spatial restructuring has been in Latin America (de Mattos, 1998). Most small cities suffer from a lack of locational and managerial leadership and are having great difficulty in transforming traditional development patterns. The cities that have gained the most are within the area of influence of large metropolitan regions (e.g. Mexico City, Greater Buenos Aires and São Paulo). Despite major urban, social and environmental problems, these have progressively been able to restructure on the basis of a long-term economic model.

Demography and metropolitan polarisation

Despite demographic growth, many cities have found it difficult to restructure and to modernise (Hiernaux, 1998; Cuenya, 1999). The metropolitan area of Greater Buenos Aires grew from 6 to 10 million between 1980 and 1998. In the same period the population of Buenos Aires city remained static at 3 million. This pattern of lower rates of demographic growth of the central districts and a relative population loss in favour of the rest of the metropolitan region and the country is also typical of Montevideo and Santiago.

Table 2 shows the reduction in the urban growth rates, indicating a 'polarisation reversal' process during the 1970s and 1980s (Richardson, 1980; Gilbert, 1993; Davila, 1996). In all metropolitan areas, with the exception of La Paz, a reduction in population growth rate occurred between the 1970s and the 1980s. Nevertheless, most major cities maintained their primacy with high concentrations of their country's total population.

Country	Metropolitan Area*	% of Total Population			Growth Rates p.a. (%)	
		1970	1980	1990	1970–1980	1980–1990
Argentina	Greater Buenos Aires	35.6	35.7	34.5	1.6	1.1
Bolivia	La Paz	13.0	13.8	17.4	2.6	3.6
Brazil	São Paulo	8.4	10.2	10.6	4.4	2.0
Chile	Santiago	32.3	34.8	35.4	2.7	1.8
Ecuador	Guayaquil	13.0	14.9	15.6	4.6	2.9
Salvador	San Salvador	13.9	-	11.5	-	-
Peru	Lima	24.4	25.9	27.9	3.7	2.6
Uruguay	Montevideo	48.2	49.5	41.6	0.7	0.6

Table 2. The population and population growth rates of metropolitan areas.
Source: CEPAL, 1998a.

* The metropolitan area comprises the city plus adjoining high-density areas

A dynamic combination of both centralisation and decentralisation – 'polarisation inversion' – began in the 1990s (de Mattos, 1994). A trend towards the reconcentration of economic activity in the metropolitan region was observed – particularly of those businesses involved in high technology and modern service provision, characteristic of the global economy. This trend strengthened the argument that, in emergent territories, the maintenance of liberalisation and deregulation policies would lead to a polarisation tendency (de Mattos, 1998). Such polarisation tendencies are to be found even in the smaller economies such as Chile and Colombia. These have failed to produce the scale of technological innovation, high technology firms and specialised services found in the metropolitan regions of São Paulo, Buenos Aires and the Mexico City (Diniz and Crocco, 1998).

Mexico City has increased its primacy, not only in terms of population and the development of modern services and industrial employment, but also in terms of its financial and political activities. The spatial dynamics here have been characterised as 'recentralisation with de-concentration' (Hiernaux, 1998). It is clear that any compact city policy must consider space as an element that articulates complex local, regional and global processes. Policies will have to address the tendencies for agglomeration and dispersion that produce metropolitan de-concentration and polarisation, and the intensification of inter- and intra-urban mobility if they are to be successful.

New patterns of urbanisation
A new pattern of urbanisation has emerged which embraces both inter-regional growth (the territorial dimension of the globalisation process), and intra-urban mobility (the local expression of social processes). The metropolitan regions have reacted more quickly to the shifts in the world economy than have smaller agglomerations. There are two distinct aspects of this process. First, they have benefited from greater foreign and national investment, and investment in infrastructure; they have a pool of skilled labour, and access to advanced technology and global markets. Second, they express the contradictions of globalisation, inasmuch as these megacities are socially and spatially fragmented, with high levels of unemployment and a wide range of informal activities with significant social, economic and spatial side-effects.

In the main metropolitan areas, the decentralisation process has meant the transference of manufacturing, commercial and retail facilities from the inner city to the periphery, and led to free-standing towns in the metropolitan region. This has resulted in the development of new urban centres for services, shopping and tourist activities, often accompanied by a substantial modernisation of agriculture in the surrounding rural areas. At the same time the global cities of Latin America have attracted specialised and technologically advanced activities, including financial activities, business events, sophisticated shopping facilities and diversified leisure and cultural activities. Despite the decentralisation of some manufacturing and service facilities, the headquarters of the larger corporations have remained in city centres (Valenzuela,1994). The complex and emerging new patterns of urbanisation seem to embody, at the same time, processes of centralisation and decentralisation and the polarisation of regions. These patterns reflect the impact of globalisation on employment, income distribution, mobility and systems of social support.

Changes in employment structure
The variations in the structure of the economically active population by economic sector from the 1970s to the 1990s shows the shift from agricultural and industrial employment towards service sector employment in almost all countries (Table 3). All countries show a reduction in the share of industrial employment except Brazil, where it increased by 6% between 1970 and 1990.

Country	Agriculture				Industrial				Services			
	1970	1980	1990	Variation 1970–90	1970	1980	1990	Variation 1970–90	1970	1980	1990	Variation 1970–90
Argentina	16.0	13.0	11.0	-5.0	34.3	33.8	25.3	-9.0	49.7	53.2	62.7	+13.0
Bolivia	52.1	45.5	39.3	-12.8	20.0	19.7	16.8	-3.2	27.9	33.8	42.2	+14.3
Brazil	44.9	31.2	22.7	-22.2	21.8	26.6	27.8	+ 6.0	33.3	42.2	49.5	+16.2
Chile	23.2	16.5	15.8	-7.4	28.7	25.2	27.4	-1.3	48.1	58.3	55.8	+7.7
Ecuador	50.6	38.6	30.8	-19.8	20.5	19.8	17.9	-2.6	28.9	41.6	48.3	+19.4
Peru	47.1	40	26.7	-20.4	17.6	18.3	15.9	-1.7	35.3	41.7	50.3	+15.0
Uruguay	18.6	18.8	11.9	-6.7	29.1	29.2	25.2	-3.9	52.3	55.0	63.0	+10.7

Table 3. Percentage of the economically active population (EAP) employed by industrial sector.
Source: CEPAL, 1998c.

Agriculture – includes forestry, hunting and fishing.
Industrial – includes mining and quarrying, manufacturing, construction, electricity, gas, water and sanitary services.
Services – includes commerce, transport, storage, communications and services.

Table 4 reveals employment trends in the non-agricultural (and hence predominantly urban) sectors during the period 1980 to 1992. Latin America's informal urban sector grew from 40.2% to 54.4% of total non-agricultural employment while employment in the formal sector was reduced from 59.8% to 45.6%. There were, however, some exceptions. In Chile the relative size of the formal and informal sectors remained the same. The growth of urban informal sector employment was particularly strong in Mexico and Brazil, taking advantage of low wages. Some observers argue that the flexible employment practices pursued in the name of productivity gains do not help local development or local markets, because wages will always remain low as there will always be cheaper labour available somewhere else in the global market (Pradilla, 1990).

	Informal Sector				Formal Sector		
	Total	Independent Worker	Domestic Service	Small Enterprise	Total	Public Sector	Large Enterprise
Latin America							
1980	40.2	19.2	6.4	14.6	59.8	15.7	44.1
1992	54.4	25.0	6.9	22.5	45.7	14.9	30.8
Chile							
1980	50.4	27.8	8.3	14.3	49.6	11.9	37.7
1992	49.5	23.0	7.5	19.0	50.4	8.1	42.3
Mexico							
1980	49.1	18.0	6.2	24.9	50.9	21.8	29.1
1992	56.0	30.5	5.5	20.0	44.0	22.5	19.5
Brazil							
1980	33.7	17.3	6.7	9.7	66.3	11.1	55.2
1992	54.1	22.5	7.8	23.8	45.8	10.4	35.4

Table 4. Percentages employed in the non-agricultural sector in Latin America (%).
Source: Sunkel, O. (1994).

Inequalities of income distribution
Income inequalities have widened, particularly in those countries such as Argentina and Chile, which have been under neoliberal policy regimes for a long period (Table 5). In Brazil in 1996, the share of national income of the richest 20% was 60.9%, whilst the poorest 20% received only 3.4%. In Argentina income inequalities grew rapidly, with the richest 20% increasing their share of national income from 45.3% to 52% between 1980 and 1997. In general, the rich got richer and the poor poorer, particularly in Argentina, Brazil and Ecuador, though there were slight

improvements in the distribution of income in Bolivia, Chile and Uruguay. The data also show that the situation of middle-income groups worsened in most countries. A significant number of public sector employees in education, preventative health care and government were removed from the employment market, whilst in the private sector job growth has been slow, because of technological developments. A new sector has appeared – the so-called 'new poor', made up of former middle-class sectors. Cuts in social security payments and coverage, the privatisation of services, education, health, housing and of retirement funds have also taken their toll on the middle classes.

Country	Year	Quintile 1 (poorest)	Quintile 2	Quintile 3	Quintile 4	Quintile 5 (richest)
Argentina	1980	6.8	10.6	15.7	21.7	45.3
	1997	5.4	9.5	13.4	19.9	52.0
Bolivia	1989	3.4	8.7	13.1	20.6	54.3
	1997	4.7	9.0	13.6	20.5	52.3
Brazil	1979	3.9	7.9	12.2	20.0	56.0
	1996	3.4	7.2	10.4	18.2	60.9
Chile	1987	4.4	8.3	12.8	19.4	56.1
	1996	4.7	8.7	12.6	19.2	54.8
Ecuador	1990	5.9	11.3	15.5	21.5	45.8
	1997	5.8	11.2	15.1	21.6	46.3
Uruguay	1981	6.8	10.9	14.7	21.2	46.4
	1997	9.0	12.9	16.5	21.1	40.4

Table 5. Distribution of income in urban households: percentage of national income per quintile.
Source: CEPAL, 1998c.

Mobility and social disparities

The increase in land prices, transport tariffs and service and utility charges has also changed the pattern of inter-urban mobility. Many poor households with limited mobility are forced to live with relatives in overcrowded conditions on the low-income periphery. Other poor households have moved from the urban periphery to decaying rental housing in central areas in order to reduce costs. The impoverished middle class has also moved from residential suburbs to the periphery, in search of locational advantages for informal activities. At the same time, the counter-urbanisation of high-income groups has proceeded, motivated by the search for healthy and safe environments in suburbs which bring together retail outlets, schools, leisure and commercial activities. If accessibility improvements and infrastructure modernisation have become the means to achieve polycentric consolidation, the privatisation of firms, infrastructure and services has acted to oppose it.

Research on the privatisation of urban utilities (Silva, 1992; 1997; 1999) revealed that the expectation that regulatory bodies would guarantee generalised access to urban services has not been realised. Rather, the networked utilities have operated more as profit-making enterprises than as public services. The transfer of service operations and many controls from the public to the private domain has created new forms of monopoly (Silva, 1999). These new monopolies will have major implications for urban compaction, regional urban systems, and for inter-governmental relationships. The lack of adequate regulations at the national scale, particularly in relation to the environment and public utilities management and pricing, has weakened local and regional structures of public power, social participation and citizenship in general. Their absence has become a major restraint on reaping benefits of polynuclear structures and on attempts to reduce social and spatial disparities. Privatisation of public utilities is associated with the search for improvements to the coverage and quality of services, and urban management and administration. But investment by the privatised utilities has been relatively modest in Latin America, in contrast to that by privatised companies in developed countries. In advanced industrial economies regional disparities are smaller, and privatised companies have taken control of social and physical systems whose initial costs have been paid off by society over several decades through taxation. The opposite is the case in Latin America, where large differences exist between regions and rural and urban areas in coverage of basic services, and where there is a large deficit of central production and distribution systems, despite a substantial growth in demand.

Conclusions

In developing countries, the attempt to create more sustainable and compact cities will have to deal with the contradictions that exist between the nature of spatial transformations and the sort of regulations and resources available. The development of large-scale real estate investment has proceeded faster than the ability of public works to provide the infrastructure to service it.

Public investment has not been able to cope with the rapid growth of private investment in some central locations in large Latin American cities, nor to meet the needs arising from population growth and the extension of the built area caused by counter-urbanisation. Some have maintained that rapid social and spatial transformations have been achieved only by increasing the deficit of the public goods, resulting in a general deterioration of cities as a whole. Rapid economic growth and a significant expansion of the private economy have occurred without corresponding public investment in public space, residential infrastructure and public services, leading to the downgrading of services elsewhere. In Latin American cities, there is no clear urban policy to reorient development towards better living conditions for all citizens. The issues of what kind of city was wanted, how to plan the city and how compact or dispersed it should be, were debated several decades ago. Structural adjustment policies of the 1970s and 1980s have made the problem more complex. In most cases, municipalities have been empowered, regional powers have emerged and the metropolitan power has disappeared. In most cities, urban management practices have been oriented towards concrete daily problems and, often, the interests of particular groups. Problems such as air pollution, street vendors and public space shortages are on many political agendas. Sectoral issues such as a car-free inner city, vehicular restrictions, the privatisation of services and the improvement of the public transport system are the basis of much political discourse and increasingly capture the public's attention. The growing significance of public opinion for city governance and demands for the adoption of coherent, simple and strict urban policies, capable of achieving concrete rapid results, is challenging institutional inertia. Often urban demands have transcended the ideological agenda of the political parties. There is a general consensus about the need to adopt strategic visions, to implement urgent measures, the need to co-ordinate and the need to involve the user in financing goods and services. Many believe that the search for compact city goals, for modernity, efficiency, competitiveness, adaptability and flexibility do not necessarily conflict with goals based on ethics, solidarity and social justice.

Achieving integration and spatial consolidation depends on the urban–regional dynamics, and in this regard many believe that the metropolitan region should be the conceptual focus for policymaking. Population mobility has reinforced the urbanisation process, increasing the options available for residence and work within a dispersed and polycentric metropolitan environment. Within this spatial configuration, the patterns of inter-urban mobility and the formation of polycentric urban forms should constitute the principal elements for the consolidation of more compact and liveable urban spaces. This implies approaching the decentralisation issue not simply as a political distribution of power but as a real component of territorial planning and management. Planning should be based on the different scales at which the metropolitan government becomes a regulator of the urban development process, and new instruments should be developed, based on negotiation, consultation and consensus.

However, it can be concluded that globalisation is reducing the levels of autonomy of cities and regions. Nation states still play a decisive role in urban and regional development, even if they have no explicit urban policy at a national level. Silva (1999) has argued that the degree of deregulation of financial markets and public infrastructure will determine the degree of inclusion or exclusion of particular regions and cities in global markets. The question remains: can these urban–regional and spatial processes be redirected, within the context of global neoliberalism, towards reduction of internal socio-economic and spatial disparities? If not, then these global forces will act as a powerful counter to the desirable goals of compact cities and urban sustainability.

Notes

1. During the decade of the 1990s, the FDI at world level grew from an annual average of US$245,000 million between 1991 and 1996 to nearly US$400,000 millions in 1997, increasing the significance of transnational firms in the majority of developed and developing national economies. Although inflows and outflows concentrated in developed countries, the participation of developing countries as receptors of FDI grew to 38% in 1997. Of this, Latin America receives 44% (CEPAL, 1998b).
2. ALADI (Asociación Latinoamericana de Integración) is the Latin American Association for Integration, which includes: Argentina, Bolivia, Brazil, Chile, Colombia, Ecuador, Mexico, Peru, Uruguay and Venezuela.

References

CEPAL-ECLAC (1998a) *Panorama social de América Latina*, Naciones Unidas CEPAL, Santiago de Chile.

CEPAL-ECLAC (1998b) *La inversion extranjera en America Latina y el Caribe*, Naciones Unidas CEPAL, Santiago de Chile.

CEPAL-ECLAC (1998c) *Statistical Yearbook for Latin America and the Caribbean*, Naciones Unidas CEPAL, Santiago de Chile.

Cuenya, B. (1999) Urban policy in the framework of globalisation, in *Globalisation, Urban Form and Governance* (ed. M. Carmona), Conference Book, IBIS Network, Bouwkunde Publication Buro, Delft.

Davila, J. (1996) Bogota, Colombia: restructuring with continued growth, in *Cities and Structural Adjustment* (eds N. Harris and I. Fabricius), UCL Press, London.

de Mattos, C. (1994) Capital, poblacion y territorio, seminar Distribucion y Mobilidad Territorial de la Poblacion y Desarrollo Humano, Fundación

Bariloche/CENEP/PROLAP, Bariloche, Argentina.

de Mattos, C. (1998) Reestructuración, globalización, nuevo poder económico y territorio en el Chile de los Noventa, in *Globalización y territorio* (eds C. de Mattos, N. D. Hiernaux and D. Restrepo Botero), PUCE Instituto de Estudios Urbanos, Santiago.

Diniz, C. and Crocco, M. (1998) Reestructuración económica e impacto regional el nuevo mapa de la industria brasilera, in *Globalización y territorio*, (eds C. de Mattos, N. D. Hiernaux and D. Restrepo Botero), PUCE Instituto de Estudios Urbanos, Santiago.

Gilbert, A. (1993) Third world cities: the changing national settlement system. *Urban Studies*, **30(4/5)**, pp.721–740.

Hiernaux, N. D. (1998) Reestructuración económica y cambios territoriales en Mexico: un balance 1982-1995, in *Globalización y territorio* (eds C. de Mattos, N. D. Hiernaux and D. Restrepo Botero), PUCE Instituto de Estudios Urbanos, Santiago.

Pradilla, E. (1990) Las politicas neoliberales y la cuestion territorial. *Revista Interamericana de Planificacion*, **22**, April–June, pp.77–107.

Reich, R. (1991) *The Work of Nations*, Vintage Books, New York.

Richardson, H. (1980) *Economía regional, teoria da localizcao, estructura urbana e crescimiento regional*, Zahar Editores, Rio de Janeiro.

Sassen, S. (1988) *The Mobility of Labor and Capital*, Cambridge University Press, Cambridge.

Silva, Toledo R. (1992) Urban infrastructure, privatisation and public regulation: the limit of the market, in *Urban Restructuring in Latin America* (ed. M. Carmona), Publicatie Buro Bouwkunde, Delft.

Silva, Toledo R. (1997) The environment and infrastructure supply in Brazil, in *The Challenge of Sustainable Cities* (eds R. Burgess, M. Carmona and T. Kolstee), Zed Books, London.

Silva, Toledo R. (1999) Multi-utilities and horizontal monopolies in the provision of urban infrastructure, in *Globalisation, Urban Form and Governance* (ed. M. Carmona), Conference Book, IBIS Network, Bouwkunde Publication Buro, Delft, pp.171–175.

Sunkel, Osvaldo (1994) La crisis social de America Latina: una perspectiva neoestructuralista, in *Pobreza y modelos de desarrollo en America Latina*, Ediciones FICONG and Economic Development Institute of the World Bank, Buenos Aires.

Valenzuela, J. (1994) Urban decay and local management strategies for the metropolitan centre: the experience of the municipality of Santiago, Chile, in *Latin American Regional Development in an Era of Transition*, UN Centre for Regional Development, Nagoya, Japan.

Thomas A. Clark and Te-I Albert Tsai

The Agricultural Consequences of Compact Urban Development:
The Case of Asian Cities

Introduction

Asia's urban population has tripled in size and increased by over one-half a billion people over the last three decades. Three decades from now Asia's population will have tripled once more, increasing by over one billion people. Most of the new population will reside in the cities and on their fringes (Angel *et al.*, 1993). In developed countries a variety of urban policy measures have been put forward to accommodate natural increase and net in-migration to metropolitan areas (Geyer and Kontuly, 1996). One of these is to slow or stop metropolitan sprawl by confining development to contiguous areas adjoining built-up spaces (Downs, 1994). Containment, of course, necessitates higher internal densities and the eventual diversion of the overflow as growth occurs to other similarly constrained spaces within the larger region. As such, *containment* is but one formulation of a broader array of approaches for *compact development* examined in this book. But how well would this approach – containment – fit the very different circumstances of cities in the developing countries of Asia? The consequences of this approach for agriculture in and around these urban regions are the subject of this chapter.

The urban–rural divide has already begun to dissipate in the extended metropolitan regions of Asia (Wang, 1997), as it has in the United States and other developed countries (Clark, 1990). Urban functions now extend into non-metropolitan spaces (Yeh and Li, 1999) and agriculture is now a vital fixture within urban landscapes, especially domestic agriculture in low-income settlements (Yeung, 1993). Both spaces are now more interwoven with global markets than ever before (Gilbert and Gugler, 1992). In Asia there is a critical relationship between agriculture and urbanisation, with flows of goods and services, capital and labour between country and city, and between both of these spaces and distant markets (Bhaduri and Skarstein, 1997). Understanding this dual role – urban/rural and local/global – is essential for establishing efficient and effective policies for the use of agricultural land inside and adjoining metropolitan regions.

This is not an easy task. Domestic agriculture, lodged within the informal sector, provides direct sustenance and barter possibilities for both urban and rural residents.

Specialised agriculture addresses regional demands while, at times, producing exports that generate the income needed to procure foodstuffs for local consumption as well as other commodities and services. These two types of agriculture differ in form, product, and effect. Both, however, consume land, labour, and capital, and so are linked to the markets for each of these, and swayed in varying degrees and ways by factor prices (rents, wages, and interest rates), and by prices for foodstuffs and other agricultural outputs.

Much has been made of the assertion that containment spares agricultural land from urban encroachment (Ewing, 1995). It is argued that where these lands are scarce, and their potential for food production is high in relation to domestic and export demand, there is reason to suppose that their preservation will have significant and largely favourable consequences. But is the case compelling? Or are there countervailing arguments that may tilt the balance against preservation and away from this form of compact development? This chapter examines these questions in the context of cities in developing countries in Asia.

Two propositions

Two general propositions are singled out for consideration. The first is that the preservation of open spaces increases agricultural productivity on the urban fringe when the urban edge is firm and rural values are protected. Protecting agriculture, in turn, bolsters the sale of exports and secures foreign capital for other development activities, while increasing agricultural output for domestic consumption. It appears that this effect is magnified further in those cities situated where rivers meet oceans, and where soils are particularly rich, and marginal rural-to-urban land conversions exact a heavy toll.

However, in Asian cities, land management practices on the metropolitan periphery may inhibit the use of adjoining lands for farming and ranching. As a result, rival uses often capture these spaces before agriculture secures its footing. Moreover, when rural densities are high, and individual holdings are small, the sort of farming that takes hold may compromise productivity potential, while at the same time supporting many who might otherwise migrate to the cities.

The second proposition is that the net marginal social benefit of urban containment in these countries will be positive because it enables cities to function more efficiently. These effects will be positively reinforced as a result of the preservation of agricultural land that such containment allows, and of the increase in agricultural productivity on the urban fringe, when the urban edge is defined and rural values are protected. In Asian cities, however, we find that containment, leading eventually to higher interior densities, does not necessarily yield efficiencies in public service provision, and it also carries risks that accompany poverty at higher densities.

Of course, a high degree of interior densification can occur even when the peripheral edge is poorly defined, and less intensive uses are scattered across the countryside. But, even here, there is the risk that interior densification may elevate urban squalor while doing little *per se* to increase agricultural productivity, or slow down hyper-urbanisation.[1] The chapter concludes with a summary of the urban–rural trade-offs that surround containment, and the ramifications of compaction policies for Asian cities.

Compact development

The proponents of compact urban development argue that certain spatial forms are particularly advantageous for metropolitan regions. Metropolitan regions would be more liveable, efficient and sustainable, they claim, if peripheral sprawl was contained and if higher densities within metropolitan regions and satellite settlements were promoted (Calthorpe, 1993). Higher densities would mean less space is consumed per capita, and more land is saved for agriculture and for open space. Bus and rail better serve denser settlements, and there could be less reliance on the automobile. Higher densities reduce society's environmental footprint and slow the consumption of non-renewable resources (Ewing, 1995).

Gordon and Richardson (1997) outline these various arguments – only to dispute them all. They dwell in particular upon the claims made by proponents of compaction about the favourable effects derived from preserving open space and agricultural land, and fostering efficient energy usage. Urban encroachment, they claim, is not a threat to prime agricultural land, nor will it diminish agricultural capacity in the United States. Owing to major productivity advances in recent years, less space is needed for agriculture. In any case, even at today's average suburban densities only a small share of that nation's land is consumed by urban growth. Moreover, they argue that compaction does not guarantee reduced travel or energy consumption. And even if it did, the savings would be slight, since energy prices remain low. The costs of the large public infrastructural investments designed to enable higher densities could easily exceed the savings in energy expenditures they would purportedly engender.

Clearly the subject of compact urban development in developed countries is complex. This is no less true for developing countries. The benefits of compact development seem to be at least in part dependent on local conditions and global prices, especially of food, energy and environmental devastation. If these parameters vary over time, then so too may the conception of what is the optimal urban form. Clearly conditions do vary between cities in developed and developing countries and we should be prepared to question the utility of compact development for Asian cities. In these cities, it is argued, poverty is extreme (Doebele, 1987); public resources are no match for the problems faced (Kasarda and Parnell, 1993); land markets are inefficient (ESCAP, 1985, 1995); mass transit is the only mechanical alternative to the bike for travel for most people; property management practices are highly politicised (Dowell, 1991); essential infrastructure is in short supply (Rodwin, 1987); urban agriculture is on the rise (Yeung, 1993); and rural agriculture is torn between national subsistence and export valorisation (Tacoli, 1998).

Western experience in growth management

In the United States a number of strategies have been tried to slow sprawl and preserve farmland and open space (Gale, 1992). Fiscal policies attempt to bolster farming so that it can resist urban encroachment. Impact fees increase the cost of housing and foster the substitution of non-land for land inputs in the production of housing and hence promote higher densities in more built-up areas.[2] Urban service areas are designated beyond which no services are allowed that might promote development. Urban growth boundaries and policies that limit growth to areas with sufficient infrastructure capacity achieve similar effects. Farmland and other peripheral open spaces are preserved through outright acquisition in fee simple, or through the purchase of easements. Underpinning these efforts are questions about property rights and local control. The two are linked (Clark, 1994). Development interests tend to favour local control because local regulation of land does not generally take account of inter-local concerns, and is thus more permissive and less likely to infringe upon the supposed 'rights' of property owners.

Growth management, as practised in the United States, aims to contain peripheral sprawl, preserve agricultural land, and maintain the interstitial spaces that separate free-standing municipalities. It also aims to foster higher densities to ensure the full utilisation of existing infrastructure, to promote the use of urban mass transit, and to secure lower public service costs.

Success in growth management requires general acceptance, not only of the plan, but also of the means for its implementation. It also requires a high level of co-ordination amongst disparate public and private actors, played out within the rubric of fiscal and regulatory policy. This in turn requires the sustained support of a political base, without which these plans cannot succeed. In developing countries the capacity for effective collective action is necessarily doubtful where the market for land and real estate is often inefficient, the institutions for planning vulnerable and the steadiness of political support suspect.

The impact of containment on agriculture

Proposition one: Preservation of open spaces on the urban periphery increases agricultural productivity. Protecting agriculture on peripheral lands in turn, increases the capacity to generate food and forest products for export, while increasing agricultural output for domestic consumption.

Both commercial and informal agriculture exist within the extended metropolitan regions of Asia. Each is found on the metropolitan periphery (Wang, 1997) and in the, often ephemeral, interstitial spaces scattered amongst and around the built-up areas of cities (Yeung, 1993). Cash crops produced for local consumption and export influence land use in proportion to the yield per hectare and the unit prices of farm output. Where market demand is substantial and the prices are favourable relative to the costs of production, more resources are available to farmers and farming industries for the acquisition of land, and the procurement of public and private infrastructure (Archer, 1991).

The mechanisms by which users are assigned to sites determine exactly how land-using activities vie for location in urban regions. Where land is traded, there exists a land market. How markets guide these competitive transactions varies between commercial capitalist forms at one extreme, and informal markets at the other (Dunkerley, 1983). In commercial land markets, lesser net profits, excluding rent paid for land, mean that fewer monetary and political resources are available for site acquisition (Billand, 1993; Mougeot, 1994). Activities which have a lower rent-paying ability are thus both economically and geographically marginalised (ESCAP, 1995). These activities are driven to more remote sites that are less well served by infrastructure (ESCAP, 1993 and 1994). The least profitable commercial activities, and much urban farming within the informal sector, fall within this category. Over time, these activities are displaced as more competitive urban and agricultural land-using activities capture the best locations. Informal market institutions thus tend to be located in the most marginal of all these spaces. The poor are most likely to be found there, mainly, but not exclusively, on the urban periphery. These spaces include slums, illegal subdivisions and squatter settlements. If containment policies were to densify interior spaces and bring these marginalised spaces into the domain of market competition, the poor might find that domestic agriculture within the informal sector is no longer an option. And while food grown on the urban periphery or at greater distances might fill the void left by the demise of local production, such commercially produced food carries a price that many would be unable to pay in the absence of alternative income sources.

The issues posed in this proposition beg two questions: first, will the preservation of open space on the urban periphery ensure a stronger agricultural presence there? Second, by what means are the scale and nature of agricultural output in these areas to be determined?

On the question of the relationship between the preservation of open space and the role of agriculture, it is clear that if the land preserved for open space is unsuited for agriculture, then open space preservation will not boost agricultural output. However, if preserved open spaces are prime agricultural land, but there are abundant supplies of equally good agricultural land elsewhere within the country, then there may be no compelling case to support agriculture there. Of course, if there is a burgeoning demand for the country's agricultural output, then there will be a greater likelihood that all available lands will be drawn into production unless rival economic pursuits take up agricultural land.

On the question of the means used to determine the nature and scale of agricultural output, the following considerations are important. If parcels are fragmented, if supporting infrastructure is in short supply, or if the rights of owners are not supported by government institutions, then farming activities may be marginalised (Farvacque and McAuslan, 1992). Under these circumstances family plots using less efficient farming methods may capture much of the space. These tend to achieve relatively low productivity levels, but do produce food and provide a livelihood for the households involved. More capital-intensive and chemical-intensive farming regimes can, at times, achieve superior results. But these employ less labour per unit of farm output, and their technologies may compromise the long-term potential for farming.

Whether more intensive farming in these peripheral areas is advantageous depends very much on the institutional means by which outputs are priced and marketed, and the manner in which profits are redeployed within the regional economy. Subsistence farming may benefit the relatively few it employs, while denying non-farming urban residents the benefits of abundant output at lower prices. Peripheral land is also by definition near to major markets for agricultural output. In this sense peripheral lands are different from non-peripheral lands, since farm produce must be hauled over longer distances when farm sites are remote from major urban markets. Perishable outputs may be the most seriously affected here.

Calculation of urban–rural trade-offs

Proposition two: The net marginal social benefit of urban containment in developing countries will be positive because compaction enables cities to function more efficiently. These effects will be positively reinforced as a result of the preservation of agricultural land that containment facilitates, and of the increase in agricultural productivity on the urban fringe, when the urban edge is defined and rural values are protected.

In the developing countries of Asia we find that containment does not necessarily yield efficiencies in public service provision and it also carries risks that accompany poverty at higher densities (Murphy, 1993). In the United States there is considerable evidence that unit public service costs vary inversely with density, at least up to a point (Clark, 1994). But are those findings pertinent for Asian cities? The answer in all likelihood is *no* (Parnwell and Turner, 1998).

In most of these cities, public services fall considerably short of those in comparable areas of cities in developed countries (Choguill, 1994). Water supplies are insufficient, wastes are improperly managed, air pollution is intolerable, and social order is in extreme disrepair (Setchell, 1995). Public resources are simply insufficient (Baker, 1991). So the real question is not whether public services might be more efficiently delivered at less cost if there were higher densities rather than lower densities. It is rather whether living conditions are better or worse at higher densities when public services are inadequate (see also Dowell and Giles, 1991). True, if higher densities enable greater service efficiencies, then government might be able to serve more people more effectively, with fewer resources. Such an outcome in a narrow mathematical sense is possible. Higher densities, however, may also magnify various urban problems and add new ones to the list as well. So marginal gains in service efficiency may be more than offset by declines in overall living quality (Brennan, 1993).

Higher densities also, by their nature, place greater numbers of people and urban activities on the available land. The inevitable result is that the price of land increases with growing land scarcity. Small parcels are squeezed into use (Islam and Yap, 1989). Developed parcels may be used all the more intensively. Squatters may find less land on which to reside, and the alternative, high-rise residential structures, tends to entail higher levels of social organisation and control, greater exclusiveness, and the rationing of access through the imposition of prices.

Urban farming is also a loser under rising densities, since the ground rents will become too high for agricultural uses. Indeed, higher densities in the built-up areas of cities diminish the intra-urban capacity for agricultural output and heighten the dependence of urban residents on rural food supplies. Where urban food demands must be satisfied on relatively limited quantities of rural land, rising rural land prices, coupled with the relatively high price-elasticity of demand, will compel farmers to cut the non-land components of their costs of production. This may mean greater capital intensiveness, and that in turn could drive farm workers away from farming and into cities, if there is no other rural economic alternative.

Urban containment and other forms of compaction, in sum, will tend eventually to drive up land prices within urban areas, with consequences for every category of land-using activity. Housing prices will rise, leading to ever more intensive development and higher and higher densities (Yap, 1992; Skinner *et al.*, 1987). Urban farming will find it increasingly hard to compete for turf. Some larger, but less competitive, industrial enterprises may be forced to the countryside or beyond, in search of lower ground rents (Kelly, 1998). And marginal family-run enterprises may find it hard to remain competitive.

If metropolitan areas are squeezed too hard by containment policies, users of urban land may exercise both economic and political influence to secure footholds in the very rural areas that containment was meant to protect. Furthermore, denial of rural access to marginal non-farming enterprises can restrict their capacity to incubate, innovate, and increase market share and elevate their competitiveness. The transport corridors that radiate out of Asian metropolitan centres and into the countryside are one venue where farm and city collide, and where marginal and progressive economic enterprises vie for position. It would be difficult to undo development along these corridors where major enterprises are already in place. Moreover, containment policies could accelerate development along these linear spaces, since they will be seen as an antidote to land shortages in contained urban spaces.

Containment may ultimately produce a double negative. Outside urban areas, efforts to maintain agricultural open space may result in inefficient subsistence farming to the detriment of urban residents. Inside urban areas, compaction may elevate environmental woes, complicate efforts to achieve affordable housing solutions, frustrate efforts to promote more efficient transit and achieve higher densities but with no commensurate gain in the supply or quality of public services. The result could be density without efficiency, and congestion without corresponding improvements in quality of life.

Of course, a high degree of compaction can occur, even when the peripheral edge is less defined and less intensive uses are to be found in the countryside. Here too, densification may elevate urban squalor while doing little to increase agricultural productivity or slow hyper-urbanisation. In this scenario we have a single negative – intra-urban conditions deteriorate while peripheral conditions remain unchanged.

Policy options: facing the prospect of the double negative
The prospect that containment and other forms of compaction will have negative impacts, both urban and rural, is cause for reconsideration. In general, the pay-offs of the policy should more than offset the immediate costs of implementation and the negative externalities that accompany it. The impacts of containment on agriculture seem to be highly favourable, but this chapter suggests that this may not be so in some, and possibly most, cities in developing countries in Asia. This conclusion, however, is contingent on certain assumptions that may be amenable to strategic manipulation. Whether they are or not, in the end, will depend both upon the availability of plausible policy interventions and upon the political marketability of these approaches. Where implementation is a drama played out over decades, a consensus in support of the policies has to be sustainable for the duration.

In summary, this chapter has argued that containment will often do little to improve national agricultural productivity and output, and that compaction is also unlikely to improve urban living conditions. Poor land management practices mean that peripheral lands will seldom be captured for more productive forms of agriculture. In fact, social benefits accrue to peripheral areas that permit a mixture of land uses, including marginal farming enterprises. Containment and other forms of compaction can at times produce discernible gains in the form of transit compatibility, and energy and urban public service efficiencies in cities in developed countries. However, in the cities of the developing countries of Asia, there is a lack of resources with which to respond to the opportunities that higher densities can offer. Moreover, where population and employment densities are already rather high, progressive incremental gains in density may produce progressive declines in net positive social benefit.

Can policy deflect the course of change and tilt the balance back in favour of urban compaction in these Asian cities? We believe pragmatic interventions do offer some hope. But whether these can win political support, given the very considerable momentum of the status quo, is in doubt. For containment to yield agricultural productivity gains, it is essential that peripheral lands be preserved for both larger-scale, but not necessarily more capital-intensive, production units and for smaller-scale but reasonably efficient farms. Efforts to elevate farming's rent-paying ability, to allow it to withstand competition with urban uses encroaching on rural areas, will fail when urban land-using activities are well endowed and highly competitive. Precluding urban land-using activities from competing at all for space in designated farming domains would clearly succeed. This, however, would require either a very strong political capacity to enforce a strict regulatory zoning of peripheral land-using functions, or massive public resources with which to purchase agricultural land or development rights. Strategic placement of road, rail, energy, water and waste-related infrastructures can also deflect development away from agricultural domains and towards places having sufficient carrying capacity.

Within the built-up areas of metropolitan regions, governments will need to do more to muster the resources needed to fund public improvements that would respond favourably to higher densities, while mitigating the negative consequences arising from the impact of the increase in land prices brought about by higher densities. Basic public infrastructure needs should be a first priority to elevate living standards, reduce burdens on private businesses, and help move private capital into socially advantageous uses. Property would need to be properly registered (Larsson, 1991), tax policies reformed, and capital gains provisions instituted to discourage rampant speculation and land reservation (Dillinger, 1991). There would need to be plans to harmonise all elements of the built environment, including land use and transportation and other infrastructure, with renewed efforts to create an economic base that can employ the less skilled urban workers in export and local industries.

Governments could consider taxation to capture the monetary gains of containment and other forms of compaction, including those arising from growth in agricultural exports. Such funds could be made available to mitigate the negative effects of compaction, and to enable cities to secure the various benefits that compaction might engender. Only with firm policy and enriched fiscal interventions can we find a compelling case for containment and other forms of compaction, and for agricultural land preservation in the extended metropolitan regions of the developing countries of Asia.

Notes

1. Hyper-urbanisation denotes the population numbers surpassing the urban carrying capacity. Hyper-urbanisation tends to coexist with the increasing concentration of population in a region's most populous cities. Demographic dominance is often accompanied by the depletion of capital in adjoining areas.

2. Impact fees are charges against land development for the social burdens that such development evokes. Where low-density development elevates the unit costs of public services, for example, some argue that the increment beyond average unit costs should be compensated through a fee charged to the developer. Of course, developers will always pass on the burden of the charge to the final consumer of the developed land. In the longer run, the higher prices witnessed by final consumers may lead them to shift consumption away from more costly parcels of land, or towards other forms of consumption entirely. The upshot might be higher density development.

References

Angel, S., Archer, R. W., Tanphiphat, S. and Wegelin, E. A. (eds) (1993) *Land for Housing the Poor*, Select Books, Singapore.

Archer, R. W. (1991) Provision of urban infrastructure through land subdivision control in Thailand. HSD Research Paper No. 26, Asian Institute Technology, Bangkok.

Baker, L. (1991) *India: Private/Public Partnership in Land Development.* Washington, DC., Office of Housing and Urban Programs, USAID.

Bhaduri, A. and Skarstein, R.(1997) *Economic Development and Agricultural Productivity*, Edward Elgar, Cheltenham, United Kingdom.

Billand, C. J. (1993) Private sector participation in land development: guidelines for increasing co-operation between local government and developers. *Habitat International*, **17(2)**, pp.53–62.

Brennan, E. M. (1993) Urban land and housing issues, in *Third World Cities: Problems, Policies and Prospects* (eds J. D. Kasarda and A. M. Parnell), Sage, Newbury Park, California.

Calthorpe, P. G. (1993) *The Next American Metropolis*, Princeton, New Jersey, Princeton University Press.

Choguill, C. L.(1994) Crisis, chaos, crunch? Planning for urban growth in the developing world. *Urban Studies*, **31(6)**, pp.935–946.

Clark, T. A. (1990) Capital constraints on non metropolitan accumulation: rural process in the United States since the sixties. *Journal of Rural Studies*, **7**,3, pp.169–190.

Clark, T. A. (1994) The state–local regulatory nexus in US growth management: claims of property and participation in the localist resistance. *Environment and Planning C: Government and Policy*, **12**, pp.425–447.

Dillinger, W. (1991) Urban property tax reform: guidelines recommendations. Urban Management Program Discussion Paper No. 11, World Bank, Washington, DC.

Doebele, W. A. (1987) Land policy, in *Shelter, Settlement and Development* (ed. L. Rodwin), Allen and Unwin, Boston, Massachusetts.

Dowell, D. E.(1991) The land market assessment: a new tool for management. Urban Management Programme Discussion Paper No. 4, World Bank, Washington, DC.

Dowell, D. E. and Giles, C. (1991) A framework for reforming urban policies in developing countries. Urban Management Programme Discussion Paper No. 7, The World Bank, Washington, DC.

Downs, A. (1994) *New Visions for Metropolitan America.* Island Press, Washington, DC.

Dunkerley, H. B. (ed.) (1983) *Urban Land Policy: Issues and Opportunities*, Oxford University Press, New York.

Economic and Social Commission for Asia and the Pacific, ESCAP/UNCHS Joint Section on Human Settlements, Population, Rural and Urban Development Division (1985) *Land Policies in Human Settlements: A Regional Overview on Current Practice Towards More Effective Utilisation of Urban Land*, United Nations, Bangkok.

Economic and Social Commission for Asia and the Pacific, ESCAP/UNCHS Joint Section on Human Settlements, Population, Rural and Urban Development Division (1993) *State of*

Urbanisation in Asia and the Pacific, ST/ESCAP/1300, United Nations, Bangkok.

Economic and Social Commission for Asia and the Pacific, ESCAP/UNCHS Joint Section on Human Settlements, Population, Rural and Urban Development Division (1994) *Urbanisation in Asia and the Pacific*, ST/ESCAP/1334. United Nations, Bangkok.

Economic and Social Commission for Asia and the Pacific, ESCAP/UNCHS Joint Section on Human Settlements, Population, Rural and Urban Development Division (CITYNET) (1995) *Municipal Land Management in Asia: A Comparative Study*, ST/ESCAP/1539, United Nations, Bangkok.

Ewing, R. H.(1995) Characteristics, causes, and effects of sprawl: a literature review. *Environmental and Urban Issues*, **Spring**, pp.1–15.

Farvacque, C. and McAuslan, P. (1992) Reforming urban land policies and institutions in developing countries. Urban Management Programme Discussion Paper No. 5, The World Bank, Washington, DC.

Gale, D. E. (1992) Eight state-sponsored growth management programs: comparative analysis. *Journal of the American Planning Association*, **58**, pp.425–439.

Geyer, H. S. and Kontuly, T. M. (eds) (1996) *Differential Urbanisation: Integrating Spatial Models*, Arnold, New York.

Gilbert, A. and Gugler, J. (1992) *Cities, Poverty and Development Urbanisation in the Third World* (2nd edn.), Oxford University Press, New York.

Gordon, P. and Richardson, H. W. (1997) Alternative views of sprawl: are compact cities a desirable planning goal? *Journal of the American Planning Association*, **63(1)**, pp.95–106.

Islam, P. and Yap, K. S. (1989) Land-sharing as low-income housing policy: an analysis of its potential. *Habitat International*, **13(1)**, pp.117–126.

Kasarda, J. D. and Parnell, A. M. (1993) *Third World Cities: Problems, Policies and Prospects,* Sage, Newbury Park, California.

Kelly, P. F. (1998) The politics of urban-rural relations: land use conversion in the Philippines. *Environment and Urbanisation*, **10(1)**, pp.35–54.

Larsson, G. (1991) *Land Registration and Cadastral Systems: Tools of Information and Management*, Longman Scientific & Technical, New York.

Mougeot, L. J. A. (1994) Urban food production. Cities feeding people, *CFP Report Series*, **Report 8**. International Development Research Centre, Ottawa, Ontario.

Murphy, D. (1993) *The Urban Poor: Land and Housing*, Claretian Publications, Quezon City, Philippines.

Parnwell, M. and Turner, S. (1998) Sustaining the unsustainable? City and society in Indonesia. *Third World Planning Review*, **20(2)**, pp.147–163.

Rodwin, L. (ed.) (1987) *Shelter, Settlement and Development*, Allen and Unwin, Boston, Massachusetts.

Setchell, C. A. (1995) The growing environmental crisis in the world's megacities: the case of Bangkok. *Third World Planning Review*, **17(1)**, pp.1–18.

Skinner, R. J., Taylor, J. L. and Wegelin, E. A. (1987) *Upgrading for the Urban Poor: Evaluation of Third World Experience*, Island Publishing House Inc., Manila.

Tacoli, C.(1998) Rural–urban interactions: a guide to the literature. *Environment and Urbanisation*, **10(1)**, pp.147–166.

Wang, M. Y. L. (1997) The disappearing rural–urban boundary. *Third World Planning Review*, **23(3)**, pp.373–390.

Yap, K. S. (ed.) (1992). Low-income housing in Bangkok: a review of some housing sub-markets. *HSD Monograph 25*, Asian Institute of Technology, Bangkok.

Yeh, A. G. O. and Li, X. (1999) Economic development and agricultural land loss in the Pearl River Delta, China. *Habitat International*, **23(3)**, pp.373–390.

Yeung, Y. (1993) Urban agriculture research in East and Southeast Asia: record, capacities and opportunities, in *Cities Feeding People*, CFP Report Series, Report 6. International Development Research Centre, Hong Kong.

Anthony Gar-on Yeh and Xia Li

The Need for Compact Development in the Fast-Growing Areas of China:
The Pearl River Delta

Introduction

Urban forms in the West are under scrutiny after a century of dispersed urban development. It is often advocated that urban form should be more compact and humane, in contrast to the increasingly dispersed forms of metropolitan development (Bourne, 1992). There is evidence of a strong but complex link between urban form and sustainable development. Significant relationships have been found between energy use in transport and the physical characteristics of cities, such as density, size, and amount of open space (Banister *et al.*, 1997). It has been argued that land development will bring about a series of costs that are related to the consumption of capital, resources and energy. It is also claimed that compact development will reduce development costs in providing infrastructure to new development sites as well as transportation costs. Compact urban form can be a major means of guiding urban development to sustainability, especially in reducing the negative effects of the present dispersed pattern of development in Western cities (Jenks *et al.*, 1996).

Cities in developing countries are expanding very rapidly. Most of the development is in the form of urban sprawl at the fringe of the urban areas (Ginsburg *et al.*, 1991). This urban sprawl has led to many environmental and transport problems and the loss of valuable agricultural land. The promotion of compact development could help to protect the loss of prime agricultural land, reduce development costs, save energy and promote more sustainable urban development.

The promotion of compact development has more important implications in China because of rapid rates of urbanisation as a result of its fast-growing economic development. Since the adoption of an open door policy and economic reforms in 1978, China has achieved spectacular progress in its economic development. However, rapid economic development and urbanisation have had significant impacts on China's land resources, energy, environment and agricultural production, and have led to many resource and environmental problems (Muldavin, 1997; Ash and Edmonds, 1998). One of the most severe problems is the acceleration of agricultural land loss since 1978, especially in the late 1980s and early 1990s. China has an inherent land-use problem because the per capita arable land is far below the world's average. Unfortunately, China's arable land base has continued to be reduced as a result of recent rapid industrialisation and urbanisation (Ash and Edmonds, 1998). The shrinkage of arable land has resulted in a decrease in food production in some coastal regions. For example, paddy production in Dongguan in the Pearl River Delta in southern China dropped by an astonishing 63% between 1979 and 1994.

The Pearl River Delta in Guangdong Province in southern China is the fastest growing region in China (Vogel, 1989; Yeung and Chu, 1994). Urbanisation is very rapid as a result of its very high rate of economic development (Xu, 1990; Xu and Li, 1990), and takes the form of urban sprawl around the small cities and towns. The Pearl River Delta was an important food production area in the past, but now there are concerns about encroachment on valuable agricultural land and the deterioration of the environment. As the Pearl River Delta is developing ahead of other areas in China (Vogel, 1989), any solution for it could be a solution for other areas in China. This chapter will examine urban sprawl and agricultural land loss in the Pearl River Delta, using Dongguan as a case study. It will attempt to develop a sustainable compact development model using GIS. The agricultural land, development costs, and energy consumption that can be saved by using this model compared with highly dispersed development are investigated. The model will help to guide planners and policymakers towards more sustainable urban development.

Rapid economic development and urbanisation

Dongguan is located north of Hong Kong and Shenzhen and south of Guangzhou in the eastern part of the Pearl River Delta in the Guangdong Province of Southern China (Fig. 1). It was upgraded from a rural county to a city in 1985, with a total area of 2,465km², consisting of a city (Guancheng) and 29 towns. The growth of industry has outstripped that of agriculture. The average annual industrial growth rate was 37% between 1985 and 1992, and in some years it was over 45%, compared with 8.5% for agriculture. Together with Shunde, Nanhai and Zhongshan, Dongguan is considered to be one of the 'Four Little Tigers' of the Pearl River Delta.

Rapid economic development has led to rapid urbanisation (Yeh and Li, 1999). There has been a quick transition of the labour force from agricultural activities to non-agricultural activities. In 1978, prior to economic reform, only 16% of Dongguan's labour force was engaged in non-agricultural activities. By 1993, the proportion of the labour force engaged in non-agricultural activities had risen to 64%. The labour force engaged in non-agricultural activities was 77,172 and 406,341 respectively in 1978 and 1993. The rate of increase was as high as 28.4% per annum in this period. Since 1986, more than half of the labour force has been engaged in non-agricultural activities due to a process of rapid rural industrialisation. Although urbanisation levels are still low compared to those of Western countries, it has one of the highest levels in the nation.

The greatest economic stimulus in the 1980s came from labour-intensive processing industries. Hong Kong's partners subcontracted their manufacturing work to Chinese partners with the provision of the necessary raw materials,

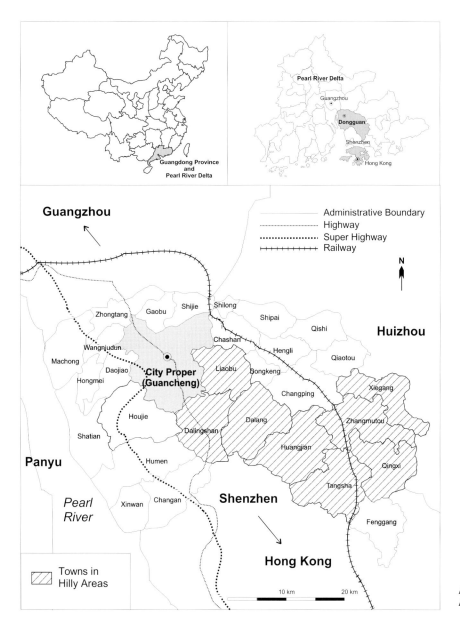

Fig. 1. The location of Dongguan and its towns.

equipment and techniques for production. The Chinese partners earned processing fees by finishing the required production and shipping back the processed products to Hong Kong for export. In 1990, according to China's Customs Statistics, Guangdong's export earnings were US$18.7 billion, 30% of the national total. Nearly half of these earnings came from subcontracted processing industries (Liu *et al.*, 1992), many of which were located as village enterprises in the townships of the Pearl River Delta. These village enterprises have taken up agricultural land, but not on a very large scale.

In the 1990s there has been rapid development of the property market and tertiary sector in the Pearl River Delta, fuelled by the property boom in Hong

Kong. Land speculation has been severe and geared towards Hong Kong's buyers because house prices in the Pearl River Delta are only one-tenth of those in Hong Kong. Investors and local governments can obtain a much quicker return from the development of Pearl River real estate. It is reported that 40–50% of the revenues of some local governments is derived from real estate (Pan, 1994). Even the Guangdong Province earned 44.8% of its revenue from land sales in 1993. In the early 1990s, which was the peak period for property development, the rate of return from investment in real estate could be as high as 50–100%, whereas the rate of return from investment in manufacturing was only 10% (Pan, 1994). This drove a lot of foreign and domestic investors into land and property speculation although some of them had not worked in the real estate industry before. Land speculation in many cities and towns, not surprisingly, is characterised by an inappropriate allocation of land resources and capital.

Urban sprawl and agricultural land loss

Although it is easy to observe the rapid land-use changes to urban sprawl and the agricultural land loss in the region, detailed and up-to-date information is not available from official sources. This can be overcome by the use of remote sensing and GIS which can provide a fast and efficient method to carry out a land-use inventory and detect changes, and analyse the environmental impacts of land development. Remote sensing data are capable of detecting and measuring a variety of elements relating to the morphology of cities, such as the amount, shape, density, textural form and spread of urban areas (Webster, 1995; Mesev et al., 1995). Remote sensing data are especially important in the areas of rapid land-use changes where the updating of information is tedious and time-consuming. The monitoring of urban development is mainly to find out the type, amount and location of land conversion. There are numerous studies in using remote sensing to monitor land-use change (Fung and LeDrew, 1987; Eastman and Fulk, 1993; Jensen et al., 1995). Satellite images can be used to help planners and government officials to monitor and control rampant development patterns.

Land-use change and urban development analysis in Dongguan were carried out by the use of three temporal Landsat TM multi-spectral images of 30m resolution dated 10 December 1988, 13 October 1990 and 22 November 1993. Principal component analysis of stacked multi-temporal images method was used in analysing the images (Li and Yeh, 1998). The results of the analysis of the three images showed that between 1990 and 1993, the whole city experienced a fast expansion of urban areas at the expense of agricultural land. The area for urban land use rapidly expanded from 18,351 hectares in 1988 to 19,604 hectares in 1990 and to 39,636 hectares in 1993. Major urban expansion appeared in the early 1990s. The annual growth rate of the urban area was only 3.4% in 1988–90, but rose to 34% in 1990–93.

Compared with other cities in developing countries, the land-use changes in Dongguan in 1988≠93 were focused on the surrounding towns rather than the city. Taking advantage of cheap labour and land, and more relaxed environmental and development controls, the towns in Dongguan developed as fast as the city, resulting in a more dispersed pattern of urban development

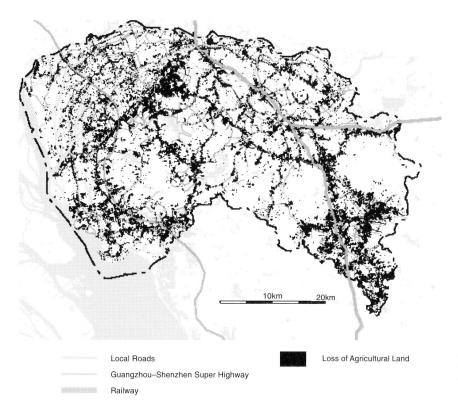

Local Roads

Guangzhou–Shenzhen Super Highway

Railway

Loss of Agricultural Land

Fig. 2. Urban sprawl and agricultural land loss in Dongguan 1988–93.

(Fig. 2). Much of the development was sporadically located and unplanned, and mainly occurred in Guancheng and towns along the railroad and super-highway from Hong Kong to Guangzhou. These are the areas that are most accessible to Hong Kong by rail and road and are therefore more attractive for building housing and factories oriented towards the Hong Kong market. Land consumption per capita increased substantially from 128.4m^2 to 295.8m^2 between 1988 and 1993, both much higher than the national standard of 100m^2. Urban expansion has resulted in the loss of 21,286 hectares of agricultural land, made up of cropland and orchard, constituting 13.2% of the total (Fig. 2).

Rapid land-use changes can be explained by analysing the average net annual income from various kinds of agricultural activities (Table 1). Growth of cash crops, such as bananas and oranges, has the highest net income. But this is insignificant compared to the sale of land for urban development, which has a price of about US$80,000,000 per km^2. The price of a square kilometre deposited in a bank at an interest rate of 6% would be US$4,800,000, which is about 20 times the annual income from the highest return in growing cash crops. Furthermore, the large amount of capital gained from the sale of land can be further invested in property or industrial development which can easily have a yield of 20% per annum. Some of the money from land sales was channelled into Hong Kong's property market, and at the peak of its property boom in the early 1990s yielded an annual return of 50%.

Agricultural Production (km^2)	Net Income (US$)
Growth of paddies	19,000
Growth of sugar cane	38,000
Growth of bananas	151,000
Growth of oranges	203,000

Table 1. The net annual income from various types of activities produced in agricultural land.

Land-use planning has also contributed to the loss of valuable agricultural land through an over-estimation of future population growth and land demand (Table 2). Although many towns in Dongguan have a current population of only about 20,000–30,000, urban planning is usually based on bold assumptions that they will reach a population of 150,000–300,000 by 2005. The nation has a fixed standard of land consumption per capita – 100m^2 for cities and 150m^2 for rural towns. With a high population projection, a town gets a larger land consumption quota from the provincial government. The average natural population growth of Dongguan was only 1.5% per annum in 1978–1993, and it is unlikely to reach the projected population through natural increase. For example, the population of Qingxi was 22,856 and 25,651 in 1953 and 1978 respectively, with an annual growth rate of only 0.46% in 1953-78 (Xiao *et al.*, 1994). With this growth rate, Qingxi would have a population of 36,814 by 2005. Yet the town has been planned to become a middle-rank city with a population of 300,000 by 2005, about eight times higher than the natural growth rate. This is very high even taking into account the large temporary population working in the factories, which is often two to three times that of the permanent population.

Table 2. Over-planned development (1993–2005) in the towns of Dalingshan and Qingxi.
Source: Compiled from remote sensing data and reports of the Xiao et al. (1994)

Town	1993 (actual)		2005 (planned)	
	Population	Urban Areas (km^2)	Population	Urban Areas (km^2)
Dalingshan	34,253	15	100,000	20
Qingxi	29,365	19	300,000	50

Land consumption per capita in Dongguan is much higher than the national standard. It is 226m^2 for the city, Guancheng, and in some towns, such as Fenggang, it can be over 1,000m^2. This is considerably higher than Guangzhou, the provincial capital of the Pearl River Delta, adjacent to Dongguan. In 1992, the built-up areas of Guangzhou had an area of 245km^2, a registered population of 3.05 million and a floating population of 500,000 (Yao, 1992). The land consumption per capita is thus only 69m^2, giving a density of around 14,500 persons/km^2.

Compact development with substantially reduced per capita land consumption can be found in many international cities. For example, 6 million people are living in a radius of 14km around Paris, giving a density of 30,612 persons/km^2. In Seoul 6 million people live within 10km of the city centre, giving a density of 60,000 persons/km^2 (World Bank, 1993). Hong Kong is an extreme case of compact development, with the density of the inner city as high as 116,531 persons/km^2. Apart from needing less land, compact development has other significant advantages, such as easier collection of solid waste, and efficient maintenance of sewers and roads. Compact development can limit urban sprawl and reduce servicing costs. Urban planners and local governments in the Pearl River Delta should carefully consider the experience of other cities in China and Western countries to reduce urban sprawl in the Pearl River Delta. Some regulations and policies should be drawn up to encourage more compact land development to reduce land consumption. Otherwise, future generations of the city will suffer from the problems caused by the present urban sprawl.

Causes of urban sprawl and agricultural land loss

Urban development is very dispersed in Dongguan, leading to a great loss of valuable agricultural land. The analysis of agricultural land loss shows this trend is continuing in some towns. Such a highly dispersed pattern of urban development is not uncommon in cities that were formerly rural counties in China, especially those in the fast-growing provinces along the coast. This is caused by rural industrialisation, the rise of localism, land reform, the influence of Hong Kong, road development, and the lack of a good land-management and monitoring system (Yeh and Li, 1999).

Rural industrialisation

Rural industrialisation is a common phenomenon in China, especially in the Pearl River Delta. The introduction of a 'fiscal responsibility system' in the economic reforms of 1978 has had a great impact on the economy and spatial organisation in China. Under this system, local government had to pay a proportion of its profits to the central state and the remaining profit could be kept by local government for other uses (Cheung, 1994). The system allowed a great deal of local autonomy to develop. As a result, many township–village enterprises (TVEs), owned by township and village communities and controlled by their respective local government, flourished in the rural areas of China (Byrd and Lin, 1990; Chang and Wang, 1994; Nee and Su, 1990). In 1993, TVEs produced 30% of the total industrial output in China. These rural industries transformed the rural landscape, and drove a process of rural urbanisation (Chang and Kwok, 1990). Small towns are especially important in the industrialisation and the transformation of the rural economy and landscape of the Pearl River Delta (Johnson, 1992; Xu and Li, 1990). Much of the development was located next to the villages, and dormitories were constructed for workers from other parts of China (Lin, 1997; Ma and Lin, 1993). By building a factory within the jurisdiction of the village, factory owners were able to save a considerable amount of land rent. These factories are often close to roads for the easy transport of raw materials and products. This has led to the scattered development in the towns, blurring the rural–urban distinction.

The rise of localism

Local autonomy and the fiscal responsibility system have given local governments the freedom and incentive to develop their economies, and are among the principal reasons for the economic success of China (Montinola, Qian and Weingast, 1995). But the system also has its negative effects. It has developed into what has been called the 'local state corporation' (Oi, 1995) or the 'Duke Economy' (Jiang, 1990; Shen and Dai, 1990), in which local interest prevails over the national interest. It has introduced competition at all levels of local government–provinces are competing against provinces, cities against cities, and towns against towns. One of the results of this competition is the relaxation of development and environmental controls, for a local government that imposes tight controls within its jurisdiction will face a competitive disadvantage against those that have not tightened their controls. Another result is competition to provide a hospitable environment for investment, such as the development of infrastructure. The provision of a favourable environment in the form of 'five connections and one levelling' (roads, telecommunications, water, electricity, ports, and the levelling of sites) is the main method of providing incentives to develop the special economic zones in China (Yeh, 1985). Roads are built in the towns to increase accessibility and land is levelled to provide an instant start for development projects. Agricultural land and hillsides have been levelled, and developed into Economic and Technological Development Zones (ETDZs) to attract projects (Yeh and Wu, 1995). Some of these ETDZs are speculative, in the hope that investment will come through the provision of serviced land. The proliferation of construction sites in Dongguan is one result of rising localism in the Pearl River Delta.

Land reform

Variations in land development patterns have been observed in Dongguan. Land-development monitoring reveals that some towns have a disproportionately higher rate of land loss. The establishment of the property market in China was important in triggering rapid agricultural land loss. The use of land in China was virtually free from 1954 to 1984. Since the land reform of 1987 which allowed the paid transfer of land-use rights, land now has a value and has had a very significant impact on urban development. The reintroduction of land value through land leasing and the charging of land-use fees has created a property market and increased the rate of housing construction.

Experiments with land leasing and charging were first tried in the early 1980s within the special economic zones (SEZ) on land involving foreign investment (Yeh, 1985). Further land reform was carried out in the Shenzhen SEZ in 1987, when a 'Land Management Reform in the Special Economic Zone' proposed to lease state-owned land to developers through open auctions or competitive bidding. The maximum term of lease was 50 years, renewable through negotiation when the lease expired. Lessees were allowed to sell, assign, or transfer land-use rights. The paid transfer of land-use rights was made official in the First Session of the Seventh People's Congress in 1987.

Local officers began to realise that the sale of land was an easy and effective way to increase income. In the past, there were major difficulties for local governments in raising funds to improve their infrastructure and to attract investment. With land reform, local governments became willing to invest in infrastructure to improve the environment and accessibility in order to increase land values. They could use the money generated from land sales to fund further infrastructure projects and start a virtuous circle of using income from land to promote development further. This is commonly called 'using land to breed land development'. With better accessibility and infrastructure, land commanded a higher price in the market. Revenue from land could now be used to fund infrastructure projects such as roads and telecommunications that were not possible before the introduction of the land market (Yeh and Wu, 1996).

Before the second stage of economic development in the Pearl River Delta, land development was mainly restricted to the development of factories, ETDZs, workers' dormitories, and housing projects. Land development was much related to industrial production. But after the property boom in the Pearl River Delta, induced by the property boom in Hong Kong in 1991, there was a massive levelling of land for development and speculation in residential development, aimed at the housing market for Hong Kong residents. House prices in Dongguan were 10% of those in Hong Kong. In 1992, 69,561 housing units were being marketed and about 30,000 of them were sold in Hong Kong. This is a huge amount compared to the 26,222 private domestic units completed in Hong Kong in the same year (Rating and Valuation Department, 1993). People in Hong Kong, who could not join the property speculation there, could afford to buy property for themselves, their families or for speculation in Dongguan.

Local government at the town level has a great deal of freedom in the disposal of collectively owned land. Government in the Pearl River Delta found it more profitable to sell land to developers, or engage in property development, than to grow crops and fruit trees. Some of the towns located in the relatively hilly areas away from the delta, near the Hong Kong–Guangzhou railway, were not doing well from agricultural production. They quickly capitalised on the property boom by developing housing and factories on flat agricultural land, generating a large agricultural land loss. They were able to do so because of their autonomy over land management and the lack of urban planning and strict development control. A large amount of agricultural land was levelled into construction sites for property development, disregarding the impacts on the environment and on future generations.

A lot of this development was fuelled by speculation, leading to a wasteful use of land resources. A developer could acquire a large piece of land beyond the needs of his normal business and sell all or part of it at a much higher price several years later. The largest increase in land use took the form of construction sites. Satellite images show that the total number of these sites had increased by an astonishing rate of 969% between 1988 and 1993, much higher than the 14% increase within built-up areas.

The influence of Hong Kong

Development in Dongguan is highly influenced by investment from Hong Kong, which provides over 60% of foreign investment in China. Guangdong takes full advantage of its proximity to Hong Kong. Central government has enabled Guangdong to attract foreign investment by designating special economic zones, coastal open cities, and an open economic region that offer preferential treatment to foreign investment within its jurisdiction. Central government gave the province three out of the four Special Economic Zones (Shenzhen, Zhuhai, and Shantou) created in 1979, and two of the fourteen Open Coastal Cities (Guangzhou and Zhanjiang) in 1984. The Pearl River Delta Open Economic Region was designated in 1985 specifically to attract foreign investment. Over 87% of its direct foreign investment is from Hong Kong. In addition to direct foreign investment for joint-venture factories and enterprises, co-operatives or sole-foreign investment, many Hong Kong manufacturers have established subcontracting arrangements with Chinese enterprises in the Pearl River Delta and the Shenzhen SEZ, to take advantage of the cheap labour and land, and loose environmental legislation. Chinese partners provide the land, plant, labour, water, electricity and other basic facilities, whereas the foreign investors supply machinery, materials, product design, and are responsible for the marketing. The links with Hong Kong are very important for the development of the Pearl River Delta, especially personal contacts between friends and villagers who migrated to Hong Kong and who later went back to their villages to invest (Leung, 1993; Smart and Smart, 1991). Hong Kong was very important for industrial development in the first stage of economic development and has become even more important in the second stage of property development.

Road development

Accessibility, especially to Hong Kong, is very important for attracting investment. Like other cities in the Pearl River Delta, Dongguan has given a high priority to improving its existing road systems by constructing more major roads across the city. In 1992 alone, there was an increase in major highway construction from only 5.5km to 151km. The improved transport system, however, allows many rural areas to be exposed to non-agricultural activities. The result is the occurrence of faster land loss along most of the main roads.

Lack of land-management and monitoring systems

Unlike large cities which have a long tradition and history of urban planning and land management, many new county-level cities which were upgraded from former rural counties in the Pearl River Delta have neither a good urban planning management system nor sufficiently trained staff. Central and provincial government have to rely on local government to report to them the amount of land development and agricultural land loss. This is often under-reported because some land may have been used or 'sold' illegally. Under-reporting is also due to a poor land-administration and monitoring system. Although remote sensing and GIS can provide an effective means of monitoring land development (Yeh and Li, 1997), these have not been used in the Pearl River Delta. When the agricultural land loss obtained from the analysis of remote sensing images was compared with that reported in official statistical data, it was found that the loss of agricultural land was under-reported by 61.3% in government statistics. The reported figure was only 38.7% of the total 21,286 hectares of cropland and orchard that was converted into construction sites in 1988–93. As the property boom came very quickly, much agricultural land had been lost before government officials could react to the situation.

Modelling sustainable compact development

One of the problems frequently cited in the compact city debate is the lack of proper tools to ensure successful implementation of compact development, because of its complexity (Burton *et al.*, 1996). To help overcome this problem, a cellular automata model for land-use simulation has been developed to minimise agricultural land loss and create compact development that will be sustainable (Li and Yeh, 2000).

Based on the concept of sustainable development in *Our Common Future* (World Commission on Environment and Development, 1987), sustainable land use is defined here as land use that satisfies the needs of the current generation and maintains the opportunities for the needs of future generations. The main issue is to search for sustainable urban forms that can help to minimise unnecessary agricultural land loss and promote compact development to minimise infrastructure and energy costs. Four operational criteria for sustainable urban form can be used in the context of urban development in the Pearl River Delta:

- not to convert too much agricultural land at the early stages of development;
- to decide the amount of land consumption based on available land resources and population growth;
- to guide urban development to sites which are of less importance for food production; and
- to maintain compact development patterns.

These criteria can be implemented in a sustainable compact land-development model, using constrained cellular automata.

The use of cellular automata for modelling

Cellular automata (CA) were developed by Ulam in the 1940s and soon used by Von Neumann to investigate the logical nature of self-reproducible systems (White and Engelen, 1993). A CA system usually consists of four elements – cells, states, neighbourhood and rules. Cells are the smallest units which must manifest some adjacency or proximity. The state of a cell can change according to transition rules which are defined in terms of neighbourhood functions (Couclelis, 1997). CA have become a useful tool for modelling urban spatial dynamics and structures (Batty and Xie, 1994a, 1994b, 1997; White and Engelen, 1997; Deadman *et al.*, 1993). The essence of cellular automata is that the states of the neighbouring cells influence the state of the central cell. A simple model is to project the state of central cell using a 3 x 3 window to count the distribution of states in its neighbouring cells. Cells developed in the neighbourhood cells can add some probability for development in the central cell (Fig. 3).

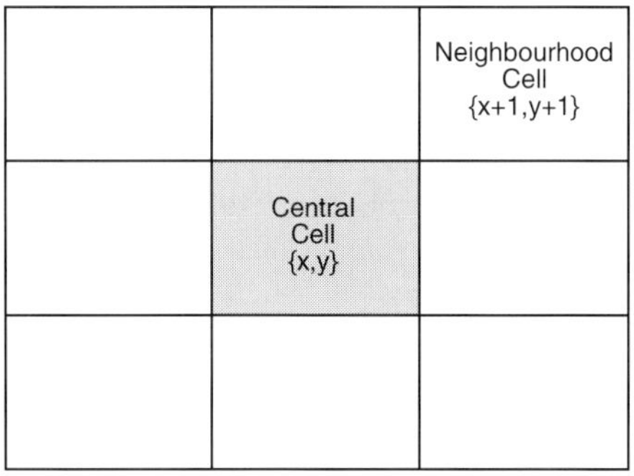

		Neighbourhood Cell {x+1,y+1}
	Central Cell {x,y}	

IF any neighbourhood cell {x±1, y±1} is already developed
THEN $p\{x,y\}=\Sigma_{ij \in \Omega}\,p\{i,j\}/8$
&
IF $p\{x,y\}$ > some threshold value
THEN central cell {x,y} is developed where $p\{x,y\}$ is the development probability for the central cell {x,y}, and cells {i,j} are all the cells which form the Moore neighbourhood Ω including the central cell {x,y} itself.

Fig. 3. The basic principle of cellular automata.
Source: Modified from Batty (1997)

CA is a good tool for modelling compact development because it is fundamentally neighbourhood-based. A more compact development can be achieved by taking into consideration the state of development of the neighbouring land parcels. The minimisation of agricultural land loss can be achieved by extending a simple CA model to a constrained cellular automata model. Agricultural land loss can be dealt with in the constrained CA model by restricting the development of land most suitable for agriculture and by, initially, allocating development to land most unsuitable for agriculture. Thus, land consumption over different periods of time can be allocated to avoid the early depletion of land resources.

The constrained CA model for sustainable land development in the Pearl River Delta was implemented in ARC/INFO GRID environment using the AML language. The development of the CA model, within GIS, can facilitate convenient access to information in the GIS database which contains land-use maps, soil maps, economic data and land-use changes detected from remote sensing. The basic data were mainly obtained from TM satellite data with 30m resolution on the ground. The data set was converted into a resolution of 50m on the ground using 619 x 889 pixels. The transition rules of the CA model were based on the calculation of the 'grey' state of each cell which was subject to an assessment of development probability and a series of constraints. A circular neighbourhood was used to count the development probability for a cell. The following is a brief description of the operation of the model, further details of which can be found in Li and Yeh (2000).

An operational model for sustainable compact development

Three sets of constraints that correspond to the needs of sustainable compact development are applied to the model. The first is the local constraint, which is agricultural suitability. Agricultural suitability of a cell is obtained by interpreting the soil and slope maps. Each land parcel is given a development suitability score that is inversely related to its agricultural suitability, to protect agricultural land from development. Development suitability scores range from 0 to 1, with good-quality agricultural land having low development suitability scores. The conversion criterion is that land parcels (cells) with high scores of development suitability, i.e. low agricultural suitability score, will be selected for development first.

The second is the regional constraint, which is based on the percentage of land resources available around towns. The percentage of land for conversion available to towns was calculated using satellite remote sensing data. As a result of this constraint, towns with a higher percentage of available land were allowed to grow faster in the CA model. In contrast, growth in towns with a lower percentage of available land was restricted by applying lower growth rates.

The third is the global constraint, which is the amount of land consumption for different planning periods. The essence of this constraint is to control land consumption across time. The amounts of optimal land consumption for different planning periods were obtained by using an 'equity' model according to the criteria of sustainable development (Yeh and Li, 1998). In the CA modelling, a global constraint score of 0 was applied and the simulation stopped when urban growth reached its optimal land consumption.

Fig. 4 is the result for 1988–93 when the products of local, regional and global constraints were modelled to derive optimal development patterns for the city compared with the same amount of actual land consumption in Dongguan during the same time period. When compared with the actual development in 1988–93 in Fig. 2, land development in the model is more compact with much less loss of agricultural land. Table 3 shows the comparison between the actual development and the modelled development. Only about one-fifth of the actual land conversion occurs on the exact locations expected by the model. This means that a large proportion (80.7%) of the actual land conversion falls outside the criteria for compact development.

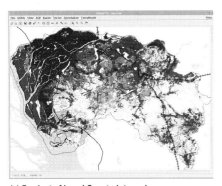  

Combined Constraint Scores

0 - Highest Constraint

1 - No Constraint

(a) Product of Local Constraints and Regional Constraints

(b) Urban Growth Based on Local, Regional and Global Constraints (k=3; t=22)

Fig. 4. The simulation of sustainable compact development in Dongguan 1988–93 with the constrained CA model.

Sustainable Compact Development	Actual Development		
	Converted	Not Converted	Total
Should Be Converted	4,098.7 (19.3%)	17,187.0 (9.4%)	21,285.7
Should Not Be Converted	17,187.0 (80.7%)	204,882.5 (90.6%)	222,069.5
Total	21,285.7 (100.0%)	222,069.5 (100.0%)	

Table 3. Comparison of actual and modelled sustainable compact development with the same amount of land consumption in 1988–1993 (in hectares).

Comparison of compact and non-compact development

The evaluation of actual development, and modelled development, was carried out by measuring compactness and agricultural suitability loss. The compactness index (*CI*) is used to identify whether development is concentrated or dispersed. *CI* can be calculated by the equation:

$$CI = \sqrt{A/P} \qquad (1)$$

where *A* is the total area and *P* is the perimeter of development sites.

The index of suitability loss measures the impact of land development on land that is suitable for agriculture. It represents the amount of agricultural land of the best quality consumed by urban development. It is calculated by:

$$TSL = \sum_{\{ij\} \in \Omega k} \sum S_{k\{ij\}} \qquad (2)$$

where *TSL* is the total suitability loss, $S_{k\{ij\}}$ is the agricultural suitability score for agricultural type *k* in location *ij*, and Ω is the set of all cells of land loss. The agricultural suitability score ranges from 1 to 7 for the two main types of agriculture – crop and orchard – 7 being most suitable and 1 being most unsuitable.

The index of total suitability loss can be standardised by finding the average suitability loss to remove the effects of the sizes of regions. This enables comparison with other areas of different sizes. As for the agricultural suitability score, the average suitability loss ranges from 1 to 7. A higher value indicates that urban

85

development has encroached on more fertile agricultural land. The average suitability loss index (*AvSL*) is calculated by:

$$AvSL = \sum_{\{ij\} \in \Omega k} \sum S_{k\{ij\}}/nn_k \qquad (3)$$

where *n* is the total number of cells of land loss and n_k is number of agricultural types.

	Compactness Index	Suitability Loss	Standardised Suitability Loss
	(CI)	(TSL)	(AvSL)
Actual Development	1.78	5,537	6.2
Sustainable Compact Development	9.79	3,878	4.8

Table 4. Comparison of the compactness and suitability loss between actual development and sustainable compact development.

Table 4 shows that the modelled development has much better performance than the actual development in terms of compactness and agricultural land loss. The model is able to provide a compact urban form that is 5.5 times more compact than that of the actual development. Sustainable compact development also has a smaller amount of agricultural suitability loss, with a lower value of total suitability loss (*TSL*) and average suitability loss (*AvSL*).

There could be substantial savings in development and infrastructure costs with the implementation of the sustainable compact development model. Infrastructure includes the supply of water, electricity, gas, telecommunications, and the construction of roads. A rough estimation of various kinds of infrastructure costs is presented in Table 5. It is assumed that the basic infrastructure has already been built along the main transport networks. The infrastructure development costs of each developed land parcel are the costs for connecting the land parcel to the main provider along the main transport network. The development costs (*DC*) of each land parcel can be calculated by the following equation:

$$DC = \sum_{\{i\} \in \Omega k} \sum C_k D_{i(N)} A_i \qquad (4)$$

where C_k is the unit price for each type of infrastructure *k*, $D_{i(N)}$ is the distance between the developed land parcel *i* and its closest network *N*, A_i is the area of the developed land parcel, and Ω is the set of all development parcels.

Items	Unit price (US$/km)	Actual Development (in million US$)	Sustainable Compact Development (in million US$)
Electricity	770,000	528.31	339.31
Water	130,000	89.20	57.29
Gas	520,000	356.78	229.15
Telecommunications	520,000	356.78	229.15
Roads	2,580,000	1,770.18	1,136.92
TOTAL		3,101.25	1,991.82

Table 5. Comparison of infrastructure costs between actual development and sustainable compact development (in million US$).

Buffer analysis in GIS was conducted for calculating the development costs. It can be seen that the development cost of sustainable compact development is only about 64.3% of that of the actual development. Thus, very substantial savings can be achieved by sustainable compact development, and this has not taken into account the annual savings likely to be achieved in transport costs and resultant savings in energy. As dispersed patterns will increase the average length of each trip, the total consumption of fuels will be greater. For example, the gasoline consumption is 120,700kl per year for the existing dispersed pattern according to statistical data. However, the estimated gasoline consumption would be reduced to only 79,813kl per year for the compact pattern, as average distances were significantly reduced. This would represent a substantial saving of 34% of gasoline consumption.

Conclusions
The protection of valuable agricultural land is important in China, where cities have been growing rapidly since the economic reform of 1978. The Pearl River Delta has pioneered the urbanisation process with tremendous changes in recent years that have caused a significant loss of valuable agricultural land. Excessive agricultural land has been consumed in the early 1990s as a result of the property boom in southern China, leading to excessive land conversion and urban sprawl (Yeh and Li, 1999). Rapid land development and agricultural land losses are taking place in Dongguan. Of the total area of Dongguan, 23.7% had undergone changes between 1988 and 1993, much higher, for example, than the 3.2% land-use change in Hong Kong over a similar period between 1987 and 1995 (Yeh and Li, 1997; Yeh and Chan, 1996).

Rapid urban expansion remains inevitable in the Pearl River Delta, but the patterns of urban sprawl should be controlled to conserve land resources. Urban sprawl, which takes no consideration of urban form and valuable agricultural land use, has produced severe impacts on agricultural production and sustainable urban development. Some towns have an unusually high degree of urban dispersal with excessive per capita land consumption, because of poor urban planning and management. In many rural towns, the over-estimation of population growth has led to the allocation of excessive land resources, resulting in much larger per capita land consumption than the nation's standards. There is an urgent need to control such development patterns so that further development in the region can be sustained.

There has been worldwide concern for sustainable development, especially after the 1992 Rio Summit (United Nations, 1993). Many countries have prepared Agenda 21 strategies for the formulation and the implementation of sustainable development policies. As food supply is one main component of sustainable development, it is important to make sure that unnecessary urban development on valuable agricultural land can be prevented as far as possible. The modelling of sustainable compact development, using constrained cellular automata with a geographic information system, shows that substantial reductions in the loss of good agricultural land can be achieved. In addition, the model can also demonstrate substantial savings in development, transport and energy costs, further achieving the objectives of sustainable development. It can help achieve savings as high as 35.7% for land-development and infrastructure costs, and 34% for gasoline consumption. Thus the model can be used to formulate sustainable strategies for protecting valuable agricultural land from development, for reducing costs, and for co-ordinating the timing and location of land development.

An operational model for sustainable land development exists, but its implementation now depends on the will of planners and local governments to use it to achieve sustainable development for the benefit of the future generations. The present study has only analysed the advantages of sustainable compact development compared with the actual amount of land consumption. However, further studies are needed to examine the land-development process in the Pearl River Delta to see whether the amount of land consumption is really necessary and whether its impact on the environment can be further minimised. A better development control process and planning system with sustainable development objectives may need to be formulated and implemented in these studies. Higher development intensity may also be needed to minimise land consumption.

The problems of agricultural land loss present in Dongguan are not unique in China. Indeed, they are commonly found in many cities in China, but especially in those new county-level coastal cities that are surrounded by fertile agricultural land. If a solution for Dongguan can be found, then it should be possible to apply it to other cities in China and in other parts of the world, thus helping to make cities more sustainable in the future.

Acknowledgement
We would like to acknowledge the financial support of the Croucher Foundation for funding this study.

References
Ash, R. F. and Edmonds, R. L. (1998) China's land resources, environment and agricultural production. *The China Quarterly*, **156**, pp.836–879.

Banister, D., Watson, S. and Wood, C. (1997) Sustainable cities: transport, energy, and urban form. *Environment and Planning B*, **24**, pp.125–143.

Batty, M. (1997) Growing cities, Working Paper, Centre for Advanced Spatial Analysis, University College London.

Batty, M. and Xie, Y. (1994a) From cells to cities. *Environment and Planning B: Planning and Design*, **21**, pp.531–548.

Batty, M. and Xie, Y. (1994b) Urban analysis in a GIS environment: population density modelling using ARC/INFO, in *GIS and Spatial Analysis* (eds S. Fotheringham and P. Rogerson), Taylor and Francis, London, pp.189–219.

Batty, M. and Xie, Y. (1997) Possible urban automata. *Environment and Planning B: Planning and Design*, **24**, pp.175–192.

Burton, E., Williams, K. and Jenks, M. (1996) The compact city and urban sustainability: conflicts and complexities, in *The Compact City: A Sustainable Urban Form?* (eds M. Jenks, E. Burton and K. Williams), E & FN Spon, London, pp.231–247.

Bourne, L. S. (1992) Self-fulfilling prophecies? Decentralization, inner city decline, and the quality of urban life. *Journal of the American Planning Association*, **58(4)**, pp.509–513.

Byrd, W. and Lin, Q. S. (eds) (1990) *China's Rural Industry: Structure, Development and Reform*, Oxford University Press, Oxford.

Chang, C. and Wang, Y. J. (1994) The nature of the township enterprise. *Journal of Comparative Economics*, **19**: pp.434–452.

Chang, S. D. and Kwok, R. Y. W. (1990) The urbanization of rural China, in *Chinese Urban Reform: What Model Now?* (eds R. Y. W. Kwok, W. Parish and A. G. O. Yeh), M. E. Sharpe, New York, pp.140–157.

Cheung, P. T. (1994) The case of Guangdong in central–provincial relations, in *Changing Central–Local Relations in China* (eds H. Jia and Z. Lin), Westview Press, Boulder, CO, pp.207–38.

Couclelis, H. (1997) From cellular automata to urban models: new principles for model development and implementation. *Environment and Planning B: Planning and Design*, **24**, pp.165–174.

Deadman, P. D., Brown, R. D. and Gimblett, H. R. (1993) Modelling rural residential settlement patterns with cellular automata. *Journal of Environmental Management*, **37**, pp.147–160.

Eastman, J. R. and Fulk, M. (1993) Long sequence time series evaluation using standardized principle components. *Photogrammetric Engineering and Remote Sensing*, **59(6)**, pp. 991–996.

Fung, T. and LeDrew, E. (1987) Application of principal components analysis change detection, *Photogrammetric Engineering and Remote Sensing*, **53(12)**, pp.1649-1658.

Ginsburg, N. S., Koppel, B. and McGee, T. G. (eds) (1991) *The Extended Metropolis: Settlement Transition in Asia*, University of Hawaii Press, Honolulu.

Jenks, M., Burton, E. and Williams, K. (1996) Compact cities and sustainability: an introduction, in *The Compact City: A Sustainable Urban Form?* (eds M. Jenks, E. Burton, and K. Williams), E&FN Spon, London, pp.11–12.

Jensen, J. R., Rutchey, K., Koch, M. S. and Narumalani, S. (1995) Inland wetland change detection in the Everglades water conservation area 2A using a time series of normalized remotely sensed data. *Photogrammetric Engineering and Remote Sensing*, **61(2)**, pp.199–209.

Jiang, C. (1990) On duke economies *(Lunzhuhou Jingji)*. *Inquiry on Economic Issues* (*Jingji Wenti Tansuo*), **5**, pp.10–14 (in Chinese).

Johnson, G. E. (1992) The political economy of Chinese urbanization: Guangdong and the Pearl River Delta Region, in *Urbanizing China* (ed. G. Guldin), Greenwood Press, Westport, CO, pp.185–220.

Leung, C. K. (1993) Personal contacts, subcontracting linkages, and development in the Hong Kong-Zhujiang Delta Region. *Annals of the Association of American Geographers*, **83**(2), pp.272–302.

Li, X. and Yeh, A. G. O. (1998) Principal component analysis of stacked multi-temporal images for monitoring of rapid urban expansion in the Pearl River Delta. *International Journal of Remote Sensing*, **19(8)**, pp.1501–1518.

Li, X. and Yeh, A. G. O. (2000) Modelling sustainable urban development by the integration of constrained cellular automata and GIS. *International Journal of Geographical Information Science*, **14(2)**, pp.131–152

Lin, G. C. S. (1997) *Red Captalism in South China – Growth and Development of the Pearl River Delta,* UBC Press, Vancouver.

Liu, P. W., Wong, R. Y. C., Sung, Y. W. and Lau, P. K. (1992) *China's Economic Reform and Development Strategy of the Pearl River Delta*, Research Report, Nanyang Commercial Bank, Ltd, Hong Kong.

Ma, L. J. C. and Lin, G. C. S. (1993) Development of towns in China: a case study of Guangdong Province. *Population and Development Review*, **19(3)**, pp.583–606.

Mesev, T. V., Longley, P. A., Batty, M. and Xie, Y. (1995) Morphology from imagery: detecting and measuring the density of urban land use. *Environment and Planning A*, **27**, pp.759–780.

Montinola, G., Qian, Y. Y. and Weingast, B. R. (1995) Federalism, Chinese style: the political basis for economic success in China. *World Politics*, **48**, pp.50–81.

Muldavin, J. S. S. (1997) Environmental degradation in Heilongjiang: policy reform and agrarian dynamics in China's new hybrid economy. *Annals of the American Geographers*, **87(4)**, pp.579–613.

Nee, V. and Su, S. J. (1990) Institutional change and economic growth in China: the view from the villages. *Journal of Asian Studies*, **49(1)**, pp.3–25.

Oi, J. (1995) The role of the local state in China's transitional economy. *The China Quarterly*, **144**, pp.1132–49.

Pan, X. Q. (1994) The reviews and prospects of the development of real estate in China in 1992, in *Dongguan's Economy: 1988–1993* (ed. Economic Department of Dongguan Government), Economic Department Investigation Report, Dongguan, pp.196–212. (in Chinese).

Rating and Valuation Department (1993) *Hong Kong Property Review,* Rating and Valuation Department, Hong Kong Government, Hong Kong.

Shen, L. R. and Dai, Y. C. (1990) Formation, problems, and origins of duke economies in our country (*Woguo Zhuhou Jingji de Xingcheng Jichi Biduan Hegenyuan). Economic Research (Jingji Yanjiu)*, **3**, pp.12–19. (in Chinese).

Smart, J. and Smart, A. (1991) Personal relations and divergent economies: a case study of Hong Kong investment in China. *International Journal of Urban and Regional Research*, **15**(2), pp.216–233.

United Nations (1993) *Earth Summit Agenda 21: The UN Programme of Action from Rio,* United Nations, New York.

Vogel, E. F. (1989) *One Step Ahead in China: Guangdong Under Reform,* Harvard University Press, Cambridge.

Webster, C. J. (1995) Urban morphological fingerprints. *Environment and Planning B*, **22**, pp.279–297.

White, R. and Engelen, G. (1993) Cellular automata and fractal urban form: a cellular modelling approach to the evolution of urban land-use patterns. *Environment and Planning A*, **25**, pp.1175–1199.

White, R. and Engelen, G. (1997) Cellular automata as the basis of integrated dynamic regional modelling. *Environment and Planning B: Planning and Design*, **24**, pp.235-246.

World Bank (1993) *China: Urban Land Management in an Emerging Market Economy,* The World Bank, Washington, DC.

World Commission on Environment and Development (1987) *Our Common Future,* Oxford University Press, Oxford

Xiao, X. T., Mo, O. D. and Dai, B. Y. (1994) The Growth of Population in Qingxi, in *The Strategies for the 21st Century,* (ed. Economic Department of Dongguan Government), Huachen Press, Guangzhou, pp.166–185. (in Chinese).

Xu, X. Q. (1990) Urban development issues in the Pearl River Delta, in *Chinese Urban Reform: What Model Now?* (eds R. Y. W. Kwok, W. Parish, and A. G. O. Yeh), M. E. Sharpe, New York, pp.183–196.

Xu, X. Q. and Li, S. M. (1990) China's open door policy and urbanization in the Pearl River Delta region. *International Journal of Urban and Regional Research*, **14(1)**, pp.49–69.

Yao, S. M. (1992) *The Urban Agglomerations of China.* Chinese Scientific Technology Press, Beijing. (in Chinese).

Yeh, A. G. O. (1985) Physical planning of Shenzhen Special Economic Zone, in *Modernization in China: The Case of the Shenzhen Special Economic Zone,* (eds K. Y. Wong and D. K. Y. Chu), Oxford University Press, Hong Kong, pp.108–30.

Yeh, A. G. O. and Chan, J. C. W. (1996) Territorial development strategy and land use changes in Hong Kong, in *Hong Kong and the Pearl River Delta As Seen from Space,* (eds K. N. Au and M. Lulla), GeoCarto International, Hong Kong, pp.63–74.

Yeh, A. G. O. and Li, X. (1997) An integrated remote sensing and GIS approach in the monitoring and evaluation of rapid urban growth for sustainable development in the Pearl Rive Delta, China, *International Planning Studies*, **2(2)**, pp.193–210.

Yeh, A. G. O. and Li, X. (1998) Sustainable land development model for rapid growth areas using GIS. *International Journal of Geographical Information Science*, **12(2)**, pp.169–189.

Yeh, A. G. O. and Li, X. (1999) Economic development and agricultural land loss in the Pearl River Delta, China. *Habitat International,* **23(3)**, pp.373–390

Yeh, A. G. O. and Wu, F. (1995) Internal structure of Chinese cities in the midst of economic reform, *Urban Geography*, **16**(6), pp.521–554.

Yeh, A. G. O. and Wu, F. (1996) The new land development process and urban development in Chinese cities, *International Journal of Urban and Regional Research*, **20(2)**, pp.330–353.

Yeung, Y. M. and Chu, D. K. Y. (eds) (1994) *Guangdong: Survey of a Province Undergoing Rapid Change*, Chinese University Press, Hong Kong, pp.449–468.

Peter Brand

The Sustainable City as Metaphor:
Urban Environmentalism in Medellín, Colombia

Introduction

The application of environmental concerns to the city has brought with it tantalising new questions for both urbanists and environmentalists. Given the environmental crisis facing humanity as a whole, and the high urban content of that crisis, was there a settlement pattern and built form that was somehow intrinsically suited to fostering a sustainable future? Could a particular urban configuration be devised with spatial properties sufficient in themselves to overcome the substantial economic, social, political and technological obstacles to urban sustainability? In short, sustainability has opened up the possibility, substantiated on environmental grounds, for a new idealisation of urban form. The 'compact city', though not restricted to exclusively environmental concerns, is one of the most compelling propositions in this direction.

In the brief period since the debate was formally opened in Europe with the publication of the Commission of the European Community's (1990) *Green Paper on the Urban Environment*, the internal logical contradictions of the compact city first signalled by Breheny (1992) have been either largely ignored, or identified as a practical challenge to the technical and social organisation of cities. This emphasis on sustainable practice was confirmed at the Istanbul Habitat 2 Conference (United Nations, 1996) and now dominates most urban research and management efforts. Although it would be foolish to underestimate the substantial innovations achieved in the search for urban sustainability, it would be equally unwise to ignore their modest impact in solving global environmental problems (see UNEP, 1999; Low *et al.*, 2000). Nevertheless, sustainability is now a universally established urban development goal, despite a continued lack of clarity about its implications for urban form and lifestyles and its implications for the production and consumption of urban space.

The focus of this contribution is on the sustainable city as an idea rather than on a technical agenda for improving objective environmental conditions. More specifically, the sustainable city can be understood as an ideal – a particular fixation of social aspirations and spatial meaning, with the power to reorganise urban purpose and legitimate public action in the name of the common good. In this sense, the measurement of achievement is not concerned with such things as levels of contamination and urban biodiversity, or even quality of life issues or social justice, but the degree to which the idea achieves public recognition and support, thereby contributing to the question of social cohesion and urban governability. The sustainable city is thus apprehended in its metaphorical purity: as a way of conveying meaning and rephrasing socio-spatial problems in a politically manageable form. As a consequence, analysis passes from the technical to the discursive, from natural resource systems to the social mobilisation of meaning through discourse and urban form.

This particular angle on the compact city idea will be explored in relation to the city of Medellín, Colombia. This extraordinarily dynamic city is an appropriate case study since its energetic pursuit of the sustainable development agendas since the mid-1980s has been undertaken in the midst of a severe social crisis. Acute social conflict associated with drugs cartels has been complemented by political violence and crises of public order, as well as the normal Latin American problems of escalating crime and violence. The need for the reconstruction of a sense of unity of purpose has never been more acute in Medellín and the opportunity to use the environment to further that end has been eagerly and successfully taken up.

The metaphor and its context: the case of Medellín
Whilst there has been some recent critical discussion of the notion of urban sustainability (see Dragsbaek Schmid, 1998; Parnwell and Turner, 1998; Marcuse, 1998), in general the terms sustainable urban development and the compact city have been largely taken in a literal sense. On the basis of the internal conditions of cities and their contribution to global environmental problems, an urban environmental agenda has emerged, grouped around the issues of energy consumption, pollution, transport, nature, lifestyle and management (Brand, 1998). The challenge of sustainable cities has been framed in essentially technical terms – the reduction or elimination of objectively defined problems. This, in turn, has largely defined the socio-spatial agenda for the environmental management of urban change. The approach has been pragmatic and piecemeal, doing what is possible in each particular place – and the scale of achievement is measured precisely in terms of sustainability indicators.

The idea of the compact city, with its emphasis on form, reflects this overall trend. Interestingly, the debate has not been restricted to any particular spatial scale – the sustainable city debate is not limited to the city as the defining spatial unit. The pragmatic and incremental approach to urban sustainability has focused attention on the individual building and on the neighbourhood, whilst the recognition of urban systems has turned attention to regional settlement patterns. The defining element appears to be the environmental impact of this set of spatial forms and activity patterns. In this way, the compact city idea reveals itself in a figurative as opposed to a literal sense. Furthermore, it can be argued, following Castells (1996), that the more economic and social space has exploded, the more the urban environmental agenda attempts to anchor the consequences of this movement to geographical space, in an environmental referencing of place creation.

When seen in this light – the control over space and the management of place – the logical-technical inconsistencies of sustainable development and the persistent ecological limitations of sustainable urban practice cease being problematic in the orthodox sense. The challenge of the sustainable city becomes less an ecological problem and more a means of spatial administration. It becomes, in other words, an expressly political project aimed at re-framing urban problems and predefining socio-spatial goals. The compact city may thus be seen as a metaphorical device for condensing these goals, for encapsulating a new set of social meanings and for captivating the intellectual and social imagination in the management of place.

The nature of metaphor

Metaphors have a long and honourable tradition in urbanism, from the garden city of the late nineteenth and early twentieth centuries, through the streets-in-the-sky proposed by modernism, to today's new urban villages. In the current period of postmodernism, planning metaphors have proliferated with proposals for the liveable city, the healthy city, the educating city and so on. Whilst visual metaphors are part of the everyday diet of architecture (see Jencks, 1977), the use of literary metaphors in urban planning is equally pervasive yet, perhaps, less studied. Indeed, it might be suggested that metaphors are more pertinent to planning than architecture as a form of communicating meaning, in that planning communicates not just aesthetic pleasure but also social purpose. The way in which metaphors communicate is of key importance. Planning in general, and the natural/scientific basis of the sustainable urban development ideal in particular, are socially legitimised on the basis of expert knowledge and rational explanation, yet planning makes permanent recourse to rhetoric. Metaphors are a powerful part of those rhetorical resources and, in contrast to rational analysis, metaphors are direct, appealing and suggestive – they stir the emotions and motivate. They are not analytical in the sense of disaggregating problems and uncovering causal relations – they condense meaning and symbolise aspirations (see Harré *et al.*, 1999).

The general movement of the idea of sustainability over the last ten years tends to support this metaphorical understanding of the term. Whilst initially referring to the objective condition of natural resource systems, sustainable urban development is now increasingly associated with a certain social subjectivity concerning the quality of life, interdependency, welfare, inclusion and cohesion. The sustainable city may thus be seen as a vital metaphor for re-animating social aspirations in the context of postmodern individuality and the privatisation of life, whilst at the same time insistently profiling the future in counterpoint to the mesmerising uncertainties of an ever-changing present (Brand, 1999). For its part, the compact city is an even more powerful metaphor, more resonant and connected to today's consumer culture. It is, after all, a contemporary of the compact disc – it feeds off the latter's connotations of leading edge technology, the latest in lifestyle, and push-button efficiency. The compact city places itself in tacit opposition to the tawdriness of sprawl (of cities, or cathode tubes, or overweight bodies and ill-focused lives).

The metaphor has no precise meaning – it evokes rather than denotes. Meaning is not determined by the metaphor itself, but is established through an interplay with context and the way it reverberates in particular circumstances. As a corollary, there is always an intentional manipulation of meaning, and a social metaphor such as sustainable urban development is never an objective goal but, rather, an open-ended range of possibilities whose priorities are determined by the urgencies of the present. The following section outlines that context and those priorities in the case of Medellín.

The case of Medellín

Medellín is a city of 2 million inhabitants and the centre of a metropolitan area, comprising nine other adjacent municipalities, with a total population of approximately 3 million. In 1930 it was a town of around 100,000 people resting in a rich upland valley in the central cordillera of the Colombian Andes. Now it claws its way ever higher up the steep valley sides, and is bursting at the seams (Fig. 1). It is a bustling, dynamic industrial centre boasting some of the highest rates of utility provision of any Latin American city – 99% of households have electricity, 98% water and sewerage connections and 82% have domestic telephones – and enjoys a strong sense of regional identity and leadership (Alcaldía de Medellín, 1998).

Fig. 1. The city of Medellín set in a narrow steep-sided valley in the Andes.

However, in the 1980s things started to go wrong. Accumulated urban problems and industrial recession combined to produce economic stagnation, widespread impoverishment and spatial segregation (Departamento Administrativo de Planeación Metropolitana, 1985). Latent social tensions rose to the surface and then exploded with the emergence of the local drugs cartels (Jaramillo, 1996). A culture of violence began to set in and the number of homicides in the metropolitan area reached 6,644 in 1991 (1 in 400 people being murdered per annum). Violence reached epidemic proportions and murder has continued to be the principal cause of death amongst 15–40-year-olds throughout the 1990s, and remains the everyday obsession of all social groups (Jaramillo, 1995; Veeduría Plan de Desarrollo, 1997).

Two major policy areas were designed to re-establish public order and local state control. The first, most obvious and most widely recognised was overtly political. In an unprecedented move a Presidential Commission was set up to address the critical social problems of the city directly, particularly those associated with the high levels of generalised crime and violence and the drugs cartels. The strategy involved a policy of political negotiation with illegal organisations (drugs cartels, urban guerrilla movements and criminal gangs) and the establishment of non-violence pacts between warring factions in the popular sectors of the city (Programa Presidencial, 1992; Jaramillo *et al.*, 1998).

The second policy area was explicitly spatial and aimed at improving living conditions in the poorer areas of the city. It focused on people's everyday lives within the context of escalating violence, disorder and desperation. Given the exceptionally high level of public service provision, and generally decent physical housing conditions, spatial improvement was largely (though not exclusively) a qualitative challenge. The rest of this chapter will examine how, in the face of an acute urban social crisis, the environment and the idea of sustainability played a key role in the symbolic reconstruction of a sense of unity and common purpose. In focusing attention on the environment, it is not suggested that the environment in itself was an effective medium for re-establishing social order in the city, or that it has innate qualities which somehow determine socio-spatial welfare.[1] Indeed, it is precisely the social construction and exploitation of meanings of the environment in relation to the overall set of urban problems which, it is argued, constitute the potency of the sustainability ideal.

The sustainability metaphor and the mobilisation of meaning in Medellín

The implicit challenge of urban environmentalism in Medellín was to mobilise meanings of the value of life, harmony and peaceful coexistence in and through nature, and to use the construction of those values to re-think a future overcast by violence. The environmental problem lay not so much in the objective conditions of the city's natural resource systems, but in how to insert the environment in the deployment of formal urban development resources (both discursive and physical) in order to provide coherence and direction to urban social life and to legitimise public authority. The exercise was by no means merely academic – disasters caused by floods and landslides ensured that the environment was a socially potent concern. However, for the sustainability metaphor to acquire social acceptance, meaning had to be mobilised and materialised in the symbolic forms within which people played out their everyday existence. The following sections will outline how discourse and spatial form provided the symbolic meaning, and how specialised institutions ensured its effective transmission.

Planning discourse

The environment was first seriously considered in the city's 1986 development plan, and the social context was crucial to the way in which it was presented. Economic recession and the impact of the drugs cartels were accentuating acute social problems, and the city's prestigious Metro project, initiated in 1984, was submerged in corruption scandals and financial difficulties which would temporarily suspend construction (Acevedo *et al.*, 1993). As a consequence the credibility of the local administration was severely weakened, public confidence in local institutions was low, and a sense of vulnerability pervaded the city. The environment emerged as a vector of that vulnerability, which could be usefully exploited to deflect the complicity, or impotence, of the local state with regard to the generalised and critical decline in the city's fortunes. The following extract (Departamento Administrativo de Planeación Metropolitana, 1986, p.39) illustrates the way in which this effect was achieved:

> A vital concern is citizen security, without which the panorama will remain overshadowed by anxiety and fear. This security must be founded on state

initiatives for the prevention and suppression of crime in all its forms. However, these measures will be ineffective unless accompanied by the efforts of all citizens in the fight against crime: collaboration in the vigilance and protection of public space and private property, the reporting of crime to the police and, above all, a change in social behaviour which has become lax and complacent on many fronts. Also of fundamental importance will be those measures designed to prevent tragedies caused by landslides and floods in the high-risk zones already identified in the city, improved disaster management procedures should such events occur, a reduction in road accidents, and better fire prevention and control. To the extent that the community manages to recover a sense of tranquillity and become co-author of its own security, it will in turn be able to devote greater energy to building progress in the city and to consolidate confidence in the future.

A year later, a landslide in the Villa Tina sector of the city caused the loss of 300 homes and 500 lives, thrusting the environment tragically to the forefront of public attention. The vulnerability/environment equation was consolidated, as illustrated in the post-Brundtland spirit of the following announcement from the leader of the city council, in a public forum on the environment and urban development (Concejo de Medellín, 1989):

> Together with violence, hunger and social decomposition, the twentieth century citizen is witnessing the painful spectacle of the extinction of his natural environment and his own life, in a future scenario which to many seems irremediable ... This forum will suggest priorities for action. State initiatives must be backed up through education and community awareness. Solutions are urgently needed and there is no time to lose.

By the early 1990s the association of the environment with the quality of life and liveability of the city had been consolidated in discourse, along with a technical agenda based on disaster prevention and management, water pollution and urban forestry. However, social conflict continued to escalate. National proposals for constitutional reform included the highly controversial issue of extradition, solicited by the USA and fiercely opposed by the Medellín drugs cartels. The latter waged a campaign of intimidation and terror. A war raged on the streets between the Mafia and the police and bombings and shootings were a daily occurrence (Jaramillo, 1996). The Presidential programmes, mentioned earlier, were introduced with some success, and a city development plan produced in 1993 argued that the city was beginning to emerge from the worst of the violence and bloodshed. A sense of relief permeated the city, along with an urgent awareness of the need to re-establish social harmony, rebuild social structures and restore urban self-confidence. Sustainable development was introduced for the first time, as one of the eight general principles of the plan. The definition of the meaning of the term (Concejo de Medellín, 1993, p.97) resulted in an adaptation of the Brundtland definition to the city's context of violence:

> Planning in Medellín will be undertaken from a human perspective and with a sense of responsibility for future generations, through the adoption of the criterion

of sustainable development. In meeting present needs, deficiencies arising from the past will also be addressed, along with the setting of conditions which guarantee peace and prosperity for the future citizens of Medellín. The governance of the city will be ruled by the principles of respect for human life and all other forms of life and the integral development of the city's inhabitants, and therefore of the city itself. It will be realised through harmonising the activities between human beings and between human beings and the ecosystem which surrounds us.

The Rio de Janeiro Summit of 1992 provided international recognition of the environment as an integrated urban development issue. It gave additional authority to the city's use of the environment as a device for conceptually reconstituting a sense of wholeness and harmony in a socially fractured and violent society, and as a means of solidifying optimism in the future. The environment became intimately associated with notions of equality, security, peaceful coexistence, rationality and harmony – all those qualities so notoriously absent from the world of social relations in the city at that time. This unwritten strategy continues today. More recently the technical agenda has been consolidated (especially for air pollution and solid waste management) and much emphasis has been given to environmental education. However, the environment continues to be associated and discursively articulated with social cohesion and the quality of life. The hard edge of urban living is increasingly discussed in terms of competition with other cities in a global economy and the environment is now the privileged arena for reason, harmony and healthy good living.

Institutions

Development plans have established the contours of the urban environmental discourse and staked out the set of meanings of the environment in relation to the overall urban problematic. However, this formal discourse on urban development has occurred only within a limited technical and political realm. New institutions were required for meaning to be transmitted to the larger public audience and to extend the discourse beyond the limited scope of public participation exercises. Above all, institutions with specific environmental responsibilities were required to convert discourse into practical action, and to ground symbolic meaning in the everyday experience of urban reality.

In the case of Medellín there were two institutions of special importance. The first of these was the Instituto Mi Río (My River Institute), created in 1992 with the purpose of protecting the metropolitan river system. This function was quickly expanded to include the integrated management of the river Medellín basin, which coincides almost exactly with the boundaries of the metropolitan area. As both an executive and co-ordinating body, its governing board was made up of the city mayor, the chief executive and head of planning of the metropolitan authority, the general and technical directors of the public utilities company, and the executive director of the chamber of commerce. A community representative was later added to the board.

The initial emphasis was on the landscape improvement of the immediate environs of the river Medellín in the central area of the city, but this was rapidly expanded to the management of the tributary streams which flow down the mountain slopes, especially in the popular sectors of the city. In the period between 1995 and 1996, the Institute implemented some 600 projects involving civil engineering works, river bed maintenance, and revegetation and landscaping involving an area of 1,688,000m^2 and the planting of 90,000 trees (Instituto Mi Río, 1996). More recently, the Institute has strengthened its social development programme, and half of its 1999 budget of US\$7.5 million is devoted to environmental education and employment generation (Instituto Mi Río, 1999). Although the control of the Institute is traditionally political and its management structure somewhat vertical, the Institute has developed vigorous participation strategy. It quickly reached a wide body of community organisations through its direct work in the neighbourhood improvements, campaigns, competitions, workshops and festivals, as well as developing an energetic public relations policy through publications, promotional brochures, videos and media campaigns. The Instituto Mi Río was quickly developed as a modern, efficient, high-profile organisation working closely with both the media and the community. Its works have had a high visual impact on the city and it enjoys widespread public support. Above all, it was able to demonstrate 'sustainability' in action (Fig. 2).

Fig. 2. Environmental symbols through architecture – the cultural centre of the Instituto Mi Río, the first and only building to occupy the river environs.

The second institutional innovation resulted not from a local initiative but from national policy. The creation of the Environment Ministry in 1993 led to the setting up of regional corporations with responsibility for environmental protection. As regional environmental authorities, their functions include environmental approval for development projects and local development plans. Financed through a special rate on land tax, they have quickly acquired financial muscle and technical expertise, and have become powerful actors in the development process. A curiosity of the system is that large cities such as Medellín are controlled by two such regional corporations, one for the rural area and another for the built area.

The interesting thing about the regional corporations is that they exercise authority through legislation and technical knowledge. Whilst the Instituto Mi Río mobilises meaning through concrete action and urban projects, the corporations act as arbiters in the event of disputes over those meanings. Through their legal powers, their scientific knowledge base and technical expertise, they control the discursive limits of urban environmentalism and ensure that the social content remains within the institutionalised limits of the state. Furthermore, these new environmental institutions were installed at the same time as housing, health and social security institutions were being dismantled, reformed or privatised, thereby consolidating a shift in the idea of welfare away from traditional areas and on to the environment.

Spatial form

Sustainable urban development, understood as the mobilisation of meaning through symbolic form, leads to a substantially different spatial agenda from that normally associated with the compact city. The functional dimension of spatial organisation (such as energy consumption, pollution, environmental and health issues) cedes to an alternative social rationality. Whilst the general objective might be the same, sustainable urban development, the means to achieve it is posited in the aesthetic rather than the technical realm. The systematic mobilisation of meaning is achieved not through the objective organisation of spatial activity, but through the systematic articulation of visually significant events in the urban landscape. In other words, even though ecological and environmental improvements are almost inevitably involved, there is an implicit aestheticisation of the urban sustainability ideal.

The Medellín experience can be described in terms of three major aspects which, it might be observed, are characteristic of urban environmentalism in general: the elevation of natural elements to key status in spatial organisation, the greening of built form, and the redirection of socially significant urban events to 'natural' space. In Medellín, the first aspect was most clearly pursued in relation to the tributary streams which descend, at times ferociously, from the steep valley slopes. These streams had traditionally acted as dividing lines between neighbourhoods and as dumping grounds for domestic waste. The potential risks and dangers have increased with the gradual settlement of stream beds through invasion. Once the main river environment had been landscaped, the Instituto Mi Río quickly turned its attention to these tributary streams and ably exploited the aesthetic potential of the river system for the improvement of the popular sectors of the city (Fig. 3).

The second aspect concerns urban greening, or the generalised distribution of nature in urban green space. The tree in particular symbolises and simplifies the idea of nature and its associated values of peace and harmony. Urban greening can, of course, be rationalised on the basis of the ecological function of urban forestry in relation to decontamination, micro-climatic control, soil stabilisation and the conservation of urban wildlife habitats. However, in Medellín the 'Green Mayor' was particularly influential in promoting the planting of socially useful fruit trees and the sheer pleasure of a green environment. The potential of greening in a moist tropical climate was enormous, and through the actions of the Instituto Mi Río and other organisations, an estimated 650,000 trees have been planted over the last fifteen years (Departamento Administrativo de Planeación Metropolitana, 1999). The appearance of the city has been radically transformed. Tree planting was concentrated in flow spaces such as river courses and highways, as well as in parks and open green spaces.

The third aspect is perhaps the most radical and innovative in terms of spatial reorganisation, and concerns the extension (and perhaps eventual displacement) of symbolic space from the historic centre to the main river (Viviescas, 1998; Plan

Estratégico, 1997). The geographical distance is 1 to 5 kilometres, but the cultural and spatial obstacles are enormous. The cultural significance of the historic centre remains very strong in the city, despite a recent shift of the financial and business sectors to an intermediate location and widespread concern over the social deterioration of the city centre. More important still are the spatial difficulties. The river presents a harsh and hostile environment; it was channelled in the 1950s and its immediate environs converted into the main artery for road and rail transport, electricity distribution lines, oil and gas ducts – an efficient monument to civil engineering and modernist rational planning. Despite the sewage collection and water treatment programme which has been underway since the early 1980s, it remains a noisy, polluted, and highly constrained linear space with few redeeming architectural features. However, since the landscape works undertaken in 1993–4, the city authorities have successfully transferred major festivals such as the Christmas celebrations to the river and invented numerous sports and recreational events around it (Fig. 4).

Left: *Fig. 3. Environmental symbols through residential improvement – stream management engineers the spatial organisation of low-income areas.*
Source: photograph courtesy of Instituto Mi Río.

Right: *Fig. 4. Environmental symbols through activity – the annual boat race.*
Source: photograph courtesy of El Mundo newspaper.

The conversion of the riverbanks, something similar to the central reservation of a motorway, into the city's principal urban space denies all the traditional logic of planning and urban design. It can only be explained by the elevation and mobilisation of environmental values through discourse and institutions, and the aestheticisation of the environment above and beyond all functional considerations.

Conclusions

This chapter has focused on the symbolic content of the urban sustainability agenda and illustrated the means and possibilities of the mobilisation of meaning through a case study of Medellín. It is important to clarify that this symbolic content is not divorced from the technical rationality of environmental systems management, but simply acts at a different level. Technological rationality consists of an analytic explanation of external reality, whilst the symbolic aspect condenses and internalises its meaning. In the process, the objects of the technical agenda undergo a kind of metamorphosis – they become, as it were, ethereal, representations of something other than themselves, objects of collective desire.

Medellín may be seen as an energetic and enterprising example of the systematic exploitation of the symbolic power of the environment to address social ills – an inwardly directed and unpremeditated strategy to materialise the representational rather than the functional sustainable city through discourse and spatial form.

However, if Medellín is an exaggerated case of social decomposition being held in check through urban environmentalism, it is far from unique in its overall urban problematic, whether in developing or developed countries. Something similar is going on in all cities. The Medellín example shows that meaning must be permanently reconstructed in line with the evolution of social and political conditions. It remains to be seen how this symbolic, relational exploitation of the environment will develop over time and in different places.

The perspective developed in this chapter is perhaps at odds with more conventional, technical approaches to the sustainable or compact city. On the other hand, it helps remove the debate from the constraints of the natural sciences, and repositions the discussion within the mainstream tradition of architectural and urban studies, which understand urban form as the spatial configuration of social structure, meaning, power and control. The idea of the compact city (or neighbourhood or region) ceases to be a concern limited to spatial organisation and activity patterns. It begins to embrace the idea of the compaction of meaning through symbols consisting of words, actions/institutions and objects, and the systematic articulation of the signifying power of the environment.

Note

1. The widespread association of the objective conditions of the natural and built environment with the 'quality of life' tends to reify the environment and suggest a return to environmental determinism. Whilst the individual experience of the physical conditions of cities is obviously important, it should not overshadow the social processes of environmental production. This chapter shares the perspective of recent developments in critical theory that emphasise the embeddedness of the environment in cultural dynamics and social practices (see Macnaughten and Urry, 1998; Fischer and Hajer, 1999) and the view that arguments about nature/environment are 'necessarily and simultaneously proposals for social change' (Harvey, 1996, p.119).

References

Acevedo, J., Salazar, J. and Case, W. (1993) *El Metro de Medellín: Una ilusion costeada por todos los colombianos*, Fonade/Instituto Ser, Bogotá.

Alcaldía de Medellín (1998) *Por una Ciudad más Humana: Plan de Desarrollo de Medellín 1998–2000*, Alcaldía de Medellín, Medellín.

Brand, P. (1998) Environmentalism and the configuration of urban space: contemporary city development in Medellín, Colombia (unpublished Ph.D. thesis), Joint Centre for Urban Design, Oxford Brookes University, Oxford.

Brand, P. (1999) The environment and postmodern spatial consciousness: a sociology of urban environmental agendas. *Journal of Environmental Planning and Management*, **42(5)**, pp.631– 648.

Breheny, M. (1992) The contradictions of the compact city, in *The Compact City*, (ed. M. Breheny), Pion, London.

Castells, M. (1996) *The Information Age: Economy, Society and Culture, Vol. I: The Rise of the Network Society*, Blackwell, Oxford.

Commission of the European Communities (1990) *Green Paper on the Urban Environment*, European Commission, Brussels.

Concejo de Medellín (1989) *Problemática Ambiental del Valle de Aburrá*, Concejo de Medellín, Medellín.

Concejo de Medellín (1993) *Plan General de Desarrollo para Medellín*, Consejo de Medellín, Medellín.

Departamento Administrativo de Planeación Metropolitana (1985) *Plan de Desarrollo Metropolitano del Valle de Aburrá*, Area Metropolitana del Valle de Aburrá, Medellín.

Departamento Administrativo de Planeación Metropolitana (1986) *Plan de Desarrollo de Medellín*, Municipio de Medellín, Medellín.

Departamento Administrativo de Planeación Metropolitana (1999) *Plan de Ordenamiento Territorial* (Technical support document vol.1), Municipio de Medellín, Medellín.

Dragsbaek Schmid, J. (1998) Globalisation and inequality in urban South-east Asia. *Third World Planning Review*, **20(2)**, pp.127- 145.

Fischer, F. and Hajer, M. (1999) *Living with Nature: Environmental Politics as Cultural Discourse*, Oxford University Press, Oxford.

Harré, R., Brockmeier, J. and Mülhäusler, P. (1999) *Greenspeak: A Study of Environmental Discourse*, Sage, London.

Harvey, D. (1996) *Justice, Nature and the Geography of Difference*, Blackwell, Oxford.

Instituto Mi Río (1996) *Balance de Gestión 1995–1996*, Instituto Mi Río, Medellín.

Instituto Mi Río (1999) *Instituto Mi Río para el Manejo Integral de la Cuenca del Río Medellín*, (bulletin), Instituto Mi Río, Medellín.

Jaramillo, A. (1995) Control social y criminalidad en el Medellín del siglo XX. *Desde la Region*, Bulletin No.19, Corporacion Region, Medellín.

Jaramillo, A. (1996) No era culpa de Pablo Escobar: Medellín sigue entre la vida y la muerte. *Desde la Region*, Bulletin No.21, Corporacion Region, Medellín.

Jaramillo, A., Ceballos, R. and Villa, M. (1998) *En la Encrucijada: conflicto y cultura política en el Medellín de los noventa*, Corpración Región, Medellín.

Jencks, C. (1977) *The Language of Post-modern Architecture*, Academy, London.

Low, N., Gleeson, B., Elander, I. and Lidskog, R. (2000) *Consuming Cities: The Urban Environment in the Global Economy after the Rio Declaration*, Routledge, London.

Macnaughten, P. and Urry, J. (1998) *Contested Natures*, Sage, London.

Marcuse, P. (1998) Sustainability is not enough. *Environment and Urbanization*, **10(2)**, pp.103–111.

Parnwell, M. and Turner, S. (1998) Sustaining the unsustainable? City and society in Indonesia. *Third World Planning Review*, **20(2)**, pp.147–163.

Plan Estratégico (1997) *El Futuro de la Ciudad Metropolitana 2015*, Alcaldia de Medellín, Medellín.

Programa Presidencial para Medellín y su Area Metropolitana (1992) *Medellín: En el camino a la concertación: Informe de gestión 1990–1992*, Presidencia de la República, Medellín.

United Nations (1996) How cities will look in the 21st century, *United Nations Conference on Human Settlements*, 2nd, Istanbul, Proceedings of Habitat II, Dialogue, Nagoya, Japan.

United Nations Environment Programme (1999) *Global Environment Outlook 2000*, http://www.grida.no/geo2000/

Veeduría Plan de Desarrollo (1997) *Evaluacion del Plan de Desarrollo de Medellín: La Seguridad y la Convivencia*, Veeduría Plan de Desarrollo, Medellín.

Viviescas, F. (1998) El Plan Estratégico y la Imaginación de la Ciudad: El caso del Tren-Bulevard-Medellín, in *La Ciudad Observada: Violencia, Cultura y Política* (eds Y. Campos and I. Ortiz), Tercer Mundo Editores/Observatorio de Cultura Urbana, Bogotá.

Stephen S. Y. Lau, Q. M. Mahtab-uz-Zaman and So Hing Mei

A High-Density 'Instant' City: *Pudong in Shanghai*

Introduction

The visible change to many Chinese cities over the past two decades has been the ultra-rapid emergence of high-density, high-rise built forms, a phenomenon that has led to the term 'instant' cities. This chapter discusses the process of forming the 'instant' city of Pudong, a large area within Shanghai, and analyses the present environmental, economic, social and cultural impact of its phenomenal pace of development. It is argued that 'instant' cities in China do not reflect regionalism, but are a product of intense competition to reach world city status. This chapter suggests that while these forms of rapid development seem to be becoming a model for future development, the process of urban growth occurs with apparent disregard for sustainability.

Shanghai has a favoured geographic location at the mid-point of the Asian economic corridor, which encompasses global cities such as Tokyo, Hong Kong, and Singapore (Fig. 1). It has a total land area of 6,219km², nearly 3,250km² are urbanised, and by 1998 it had a population of 13 million. Historically, Shanghai has been an important city to China since it was designated as a Treaty Port in the early 1840s. By1949, Shanghai's financial market was the third largest in the world after London and New York, surpassing Tokyo, Zurich and Hong Kong (Li, 1998). During the period 1949–1984, China's anti-development strategy drained 87% of Shanghai's total revenue through taxation, leaving little money to improve the city, especially its infrastructure (MacPherson, 1994). In 1984 Shanghai, together with 13 other coastal cities, was opened up to foreign investment as a result of China's Open Door Policy (Li, 1991). Now, Shanghai is shifting from being an economic powerhouse in East Asia towards world city status. The state's intention of turning Shanghai into a world city led the government to adopt a high-density, vertical city form, with eye-catching skyscrapers, setting a new standard for China's overall development. A foreign-led, and high-density-driven, urban development strategy has become the acceptable norm in Shanghai. This strategy is supported by the Chinese government and private developers and will be used for the 'national reconstruction' for the whole of China.

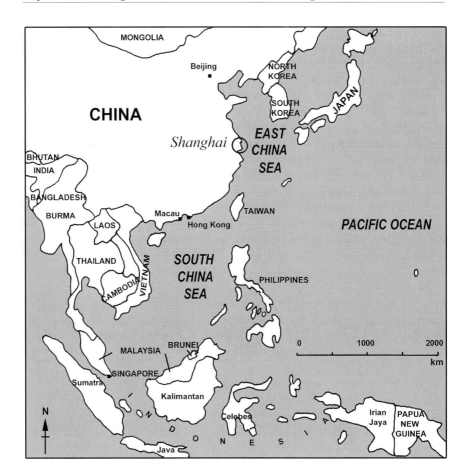

Fig. 1. Shanghai located in the Asian economic corridor.

For many provincial and state authorities, Pudong is seen as the land of promise. The ambitious vision which created it grew from the recognition that China is gradually emerging from the world trade embargo imposed by the International Trade Organisation (ITO) in 1950. Alongside access to the world economy, the Chinese government adopted Open Door and Economic Reform Policies in 1978. This change was reflected in the growth of GDP (Gross Domestic Product) by an average annual rate of 9.8% during 1979 to 1997, the highest growth in the world for that period (Zhao, 1999). China's market-oriented economic reforms triggered the rise in living standards, enhanced economic freedom, and considerably reduced state control over most aspects of the individual lives of the Chinese people. These reforms also brought with them a fundamental social transformation, rapid urban growth, and large-scale population migration from rural to urban areas, mainly for construction-related jobs.

The formation of an 'instant' city
Traditionally, cities such as Paris, Calcutta, Tokyo and New York have grown out of a long process of human intervention that has shaped their form (e.g. Mumford, 1961; Lynch, 1981; Braunfels, 1988). Nevertheless, there have been examples of a different process, which could be described as 'instant' cities. For instance, in the mid-nineteenth century, it took only a few months for San Francisco to grow

from a small village of 400 people to an eclectic habitat and bustling sea-port of several thousand inhabitants, following the discovery of gold. The concept became a unique aspect of California's development. In the late 1850s, a group of German idealists arrived in Orange County with a plan for a Utopian town. They created Anaheim overnight, with a grand plan for common ownership of land, and vast tracts dedicated to agriculture (Lavoie, 1998). Arguably, Pudong falls into the 'instant' city category as, since 1990, it has become the focal point for rapid development resulting from the government's development policies of attracting overseas investment.

The growth of Pudong

Rivers have strongly influenced the spatial development of Shanghai. Historically, its development has taken place on the Bund on the west bank of the Huangpu River. Pudong is located across the river, opposite to the Bund, and it comprises a triangular area of 523km^2 bounded to the north and east by the Yangtze River estuary (Fig. 2).

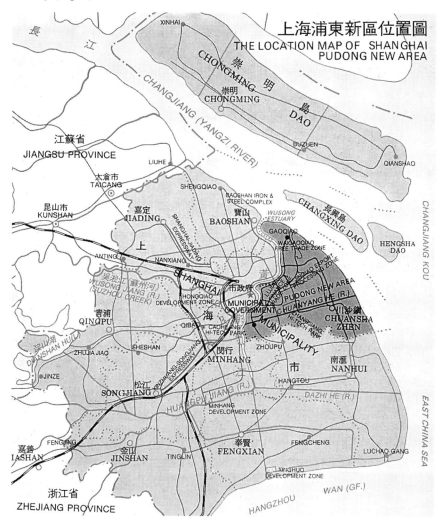

Fig. 2. Pudong New Area.

In the early days, before Shanghai and the Pudong area were opened to foreign trade in 1843, there had been foreign settlers along the Bund Area of Puxi (Fig. 3). Shanghai was first 'officially opened' by the British military on 17 November 1842, as result of an agreement made at the Ching Court, when the British Consul selected an area of about 100 acres[1] east of the Huangpu River. The British recognised the geographic importance of the site (later named as 'Settlement'), because of the link between the Huangpu and Yangtze rivers, giving access to other parts of inland China.

Fig. 3. Old Pudong Area 1990.

The first buildings in the Bund were very simple, aligned along the Huangpu River, and designed by foreign architects. The first public project was improvement of the Bund shore with an 18m wide road forming a 'boulevard'. During its early development, the architecture of the Bund was a mixture of the 'colonial' and Chinese styles, leading to a distinct individual identity, yet retaining a coherence of form. Nevertheless, the overall construction and development of Shanghai was haphazard (Shanghai Pudong New Area Administration, 1993), and concentrated along the Bund Area, leaving Pudong as an under-developed low-density residential area.

By the late twentieth century, to release urban pressure from the Bund Area, Pudong's development was necessary. Yet, despite its favourable location, the development of Pudong was not approved until the drawing up of the Comprehensive Plan of Shanghai by the State Council in 1988 (MacPherson, 1994). On 18 April 1990, the Pudong New Area Administration was established, to take charge of its development (You, 1995; Zhang and Xie, 1998). The intention was to rejuvenate Shanghai as an international finance and trade centre, and to link China with the outside world, by raising its profile to 'World City' status, with foreign investment fuelling development.

Stages of Pudong's development

The central government planned for Pudong to become a regional development centre for the eastern part of China. The intention was to attract investors and advanced technology industries, as a base from which to expand to other regions. The Shanghai Pudong New Area Administration (1993) scheduled development in three major stages:

- Stage 1 (1991–1995): During this stage, the focus was on planning and improving the environment, and completing a river-crossing and avenue-building projects, to pave the way for foreign investors. Concentration was on the construction of four development zones to attract both domestic and foreign investment, and to exploit the advantages of these special areas;
- Stage 2 (1996–2000): This stage comprises further infrastructure projects for avenues and public utilities to form a backbone for the Pudong New Area; and
- Stage 3 (the first two decades of the twenty-first century): This will be the final stage to transform Pudong into a modern symbol of the twenty-first century, primarily as an export-oriented international metropolis, but with the Bund and neighbouring Pudong area developed as Shanghai's central business district (CBD) (Shanghai Pudong New Area Administration, 1993).

Key development zones in Pudong
There are four key development zones with their own specifically designed functions and distinctive characteristics.

Lujiazui Finance and Trade Zone
Lujiazui is located at the heart of Pudong New Area (Figs. 4 and 5), and is close to the traditional CBD (the Bund). The Lujiazui Finance and Trade Zone Development Company, a quasi-government corporation, was established in September 1990, to supervise the development and management of land parcels in the zone (Chen *et al.*, 1994). Lujiazui has a total area of 28km^2 with 5 km^2 already developed for municipal administration, financial business, trading, and commercial purposes. By the end of 1998, there were 170 high-rise buildings of which 24 were occupied by financial institutions.

Jinqiao Export Processing Zone
This zone has a total area of 20km^2 and is mainly for high-tech manufacturing industries such as microelectronics and telecommunications. About 16km^2 are used

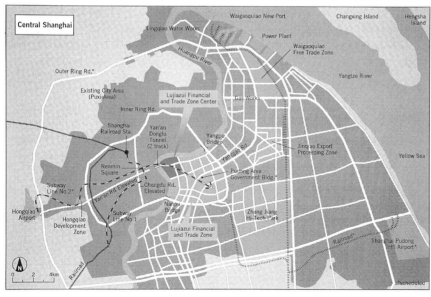

Fig. 4. Four major development zones in the Pudong New Area.

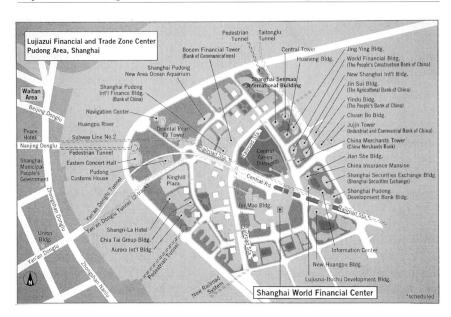

Fig. 5. High-density mixed land use in Pudong: Lujiazui Financial and Trade Zone.

for industrial parks and 4km² for new residential development. By 1998, there were 320 foreign (or partnership) projects, for example the Shanghai Huahong NEC Microelectronics Project, involving a total investment of US$1.2 billion, for producing computer chips.

Zhangjiang Hi-Tech Park

The Hi-Tech Park covers an area of 17km² for manufacturing industry with high-investment, technology-intensive products. The park is divided into six zones: a hi-tech industrialisation zone; a commercial and residential zone; a manufacturing zone; a research and education zone; the town area; and living quarters.

Waigaoquiao Free Trade Zone

This is located at the northeastern part of Pudong New Area and close to the estuary of Yangtze River, with an area of 10km². It is an integrated multi-function free trade zone for warehousing and international trading. The handling capacity of the Waigaoquiao has reached 4.76 million tons and 491,000 standard-size containers were loaded and unloaded in this harbour in 1997.

Joint-investment and city restructuring

The Shanghai Pudong New Area Administration (1993) embarked on a process of the 'making of a world city' by initiating a number of policies, including infrastructure construction together with a strategy of mixed-use development to accommodate industrial, commercial and residential zones (Fig. 5) (Zhang and Xie, 1998). Up to 1998, Pudong had received a total investment of US$ 20 billion from 60 countries and regions for more than 4,600 projects (Li, 1998).

Policies to reinforce state-owned enterprises (SOEs) operate in parallel to the private sector, and encourage further amalgamation of private and foreign investment to fund the technical transformation of SOEs. The reform of SOEs is one of the ten tasks set for the next three years in overall planning policy. This and the remaining nine tasks shape the main direction of development in Pudong New Area (Chen, 1998):

- Reinforcing Shanghai's role in serving the whole of China;
- Developing high-technology industries and upgrading key industries;
- Further opening of the Pudong Area to the world;
- Completing the city's urban improvement programme;
- Completing key municipal projects and reinforcing urban management within the city;
- Applying science and technology to stimulate the whole economy;
- Improving Shanghai's social insurance and employment systems;
- Ensuring citizens live by a proper code of morals; and
- Strengthening legislation to achieve efficient administration.

The implementation of these policies has, to an extent, been predicated on the image given to Pudong's development. Skyscrapers have become one of the key strategies to make Shanghai's skyline a new tourist (and investor) attraction, reflecting an intensity of investment and presenting an image of Shanghai as a 'window to the world' (Zhang and Xie, 1998) (Fig. 6). Landscape is being designed as corporate art. New condominiums with their plexi-glass-screened sunrooms and window-mounted air conditioners are becoming models for privately initiated residential buildings. Most of the developments are produced with the intention of creating symbiotic effects on the growth of the property market by capturing foreign investors' attention.

Fig. 6. Pudong's eclecticism – the foreign-imported building boom.

Instruments for creating the 'instant' city of Pudong

Residential and office building

Sixty per cent of the old area of Pudong has been razed to make room for new office building and housing. As a result, 25,000 households have been moved to new residential buildings and, in addition, high-class residential projects have been erected for foreign investors (Xiao, 1998). About 73% of the 8.5 million m² of residential space completed in the past eight years has been sold or rented. Most of these new residential projects are on redeveloped old residential sites, for instance at Jiuyuan, the largest old urban area in Pudong, which housed about 6,000 families and enterprises before demolition. At the time of completion, this site will have 450,000m² of medium to high-class buildings. The Pudong authorities have demolished 940,000m² of dilapidated houses since 1995 to spur urban developments in the new area, making the local government's task of resettling almost 52,700 families an arduous one. Priority is placed on affordable housing for residents looking to buy their own homes, and reforms are being put in place to abolish welfare housing and introduce a funding system to assist purchase. This ongoing process of demolition and rebuilding new residential areas has redistributed the population over the whole Pudong Area.

Between 1990 and 1997, about 2.4 million m² of office buildings were completed in Pudong, 75% of which were in the Lujiazui subdistrict, and about 60% have been bought or rented by companies from both home and abroad (Wei, 1998c). In addition to the four key zones, a new development zone, named the Pudong New Century Economic City, was set up in the last three years to serve private enterprises, especially to support investment from East China. It is expected to attract even more foreign investors (Shao, 1998).

Iconic structures

Table 1. Iconic structures in Pudong New Area.
Source: adapted from Li, 1998 with updated data.

In 1998, around 240 modern high-rise structures were being planned to make Lujiazui Financial and Trade Zone in Pudong China's largest commercial centre (Li, 1998). Some of the projects were planned as iconic structures to attract foreign investment (Table 1).

Structure	Characteristics	World Comparison
The Oriental Pearl TV Tower	468m tall; weighing 120,000 tons	As contrasted with the Eiffel Tower's 7,000 tons
Yangpu Bridge	Cable-stayed bridge; 7,658m long; 602m main span	The longest (main span) in the world (1999)
Shanghai Grand Theatre	French design	Asia's largest concert hall (1998)
Jinmao Mansion	420.5m tall; 88 storeys above ground and 3 storeys under ground; 23,611m² (site area); 287,359m² (GFA)	World's 3rd tallest building (1998)
World Financial Centre	460 metres high (under construction); 94 storeys above ground and 3 storeys under ground; 30,000m² (site area); 335,700m² (GFA)	It would have been the world's tallest building if completed to the original schedule of 2001, but it has been postponed to 2004. It may still be the world's tallest building with a revised height (under consideration) to exceed South Dearborn (468.5m tall) in Chicago (1999).
Cross-straits bridge linking Shanghai with Zhoushan and Ningbo	Under construction	World's largest planned port facilities at Zhoushan (1998)

Infrastructure: joint-venture projects

Pudong's infrastructure is improving rapidly. During the initial period of 1991 to 1995, about RMB¥25 billion (US$3 billion)[2] has been invested in ten infrastructure projects including bridges, road projects and port facilities (Xinhua, 1998). From 1996 to 2000, the investment is expected to reach a total of RMB¥100 billion (US$ 12 billion) in infrastructure projects including: Pudong International Airport, a river-crossing project, metro line, and a light railway transit system (Li, 1995). These projects are supported by preferential policies sanctioned by the central government. The policies for overseas investment are based on the nature of projects and the amount of export value for the trading companies. Foreign investors engaged in energy and transportation projects including airports, harbours, railway, and roads will enjoy the benefits of a 'five-year exemption and five-year half-deduction' tax plan. Foreign-funded manufacturing projects will pay income tax at a rate of 15% and enjoy a 'two-year exemption and three-year half-deduction' tax plan. For foreign wholly-owned and joint-venture banks, financial companies and other financial institutions, the rate of enterprise income tax is set at 15% if the amount of investment exceeds US$10 million and the contract period exceeds 10 years (Pudong New Area Administration, 1998).

The impact of the 'instant' city

Pudong development has needed a huge amount of capital and resources to shape its physical environment as it had not been developed as a commercial and trade area before 1990. Due to the high investment in Pudong, its GDP has increased tenfold, and the household consumption rate tripled, over the last decade. The changes in the economic infrastructure indicate two significant intentions of central government: ambitious economic growth, and the search for joint-venture economic activities. These joint-ventures are supposed to yield foreign-led urban development, in a context of few controls and a non-interventionist government stance. However, it has been argued that the government should be very cautious about such superficial and foreign investment-led strategies for growth (Thong, 1995).

Problems of foreign-led development

The great emphasis on attracting foreign investment to yield commercial and economic benefits by building eye-catching skyscrapers has meant that the proportion of expenditure on households or individuals has been relatively small, and may have led to polarisation of wealth distribution. It is difficult to determine whether or not there has been a betterment of the overall socio-economic and environmental conditions for people living in Shanghai.[3] In 1997, the proportion of schools and hospitals accounted for only 1.3% and 0.3% of the total floor space respectively (Statistical Bureau of Shanghai Pudong New Area, 1998). According to Rees and Roseland (1998), the pain and gain should be shared fairly by the citizens during the growth of the city.

Another uncertainty is the over-supply, especially of office space, in property markets. Vacancy rates for office space in some areas were recently as high as 70%, in part due to the local authorities' power in allocating resources and directing the developments irrespective of market forces (Associated Press, 1999; Washburn and Allen, 1999). In addition, the Asian economic crisis added to the structural problems, for example the World Financial Centre, with a planned height of 460 metres, was started in 1997 and building was suspended in 1998 (Associated Press, 1999). The suspension of the World Financial Centre poses a question – is the Pudong development over-dependent on overseas capital? By the end of 1998 there were 5,405 foreign-funded projects in Pudong with a total contractual foreign investment of US$10.36 billion during the period 1995–1998. The vulnerability of this development to economic recession is clearly evident.

Environmental control

The rapid rate of infrastructure construction has led the Pudong New Area Administration to set up a 'one-stop service' to simplify the procedures for the examination and approval process of investment projects. The government promises that this process will be completed in no more than 10 days for all applications, provided that its requirements for industrial policy, pre-planning and environmental protection are met. Despite the requirements, there is doubt whether a 'sound natural ecological environment' can be attained within this fast-track decision-making process (MacPherson, 1994). Table 2 shows the environmental indicators for Pudong New Area. They include: the types of pollutants in the 'industrial waste gas emissions'; the pollutant emissions from other sectors; and other environmental indicators such as noise.

Indicators	Unit	1993	1994	1995	1996	1997
Discharge of industrial waste water	1,000 tons/ day average	677.1	615	619	636.6	523.8
Water discharge up to standard	1,000 tons/ day average	549.1	517	512	594.2	496
Industrial wasted gas emission	1 million standard m^3/day average	93.5	98.5	116.8	148.9	188.8
Gas purified	1 million standard m^3/day average	24.5	29.3	79.9	119.5	155.7
Industrial dust produced	1,000 tons/year	43.1	171.7	155.6	100.8	108
Volume discharged	1,000 tons/year	7.1	61.9	12.4	5.8	15.6
Volume retrieved	1,000 tons/year	36	164.9	143.2	95	92.4
Retrieval rate of industrial dust	%	83.5	96	92	94.2	85.5
Steam boilers	Number	711	641	680	364	263
Comprehensive utilisation of industrial solid wastes	1,000 tons	581.9	742.5	755.8	1,059.5	1,325.3

Table 2. Environmental indicators of Pudong New Area (1993–1997).
Source: Statistical Yearbook of Shanghai Pudong New Area (for various years).

Most of the development in Pudong appears to have been undertaken without any environmental impact assessment, as evidenced from a questionnaire survey carried out by the authors. Although there are significant changes in the environment expressed in terms of land use, land topography, building density, household mobility and more room for vehicular traffic in the area, there are virtually no environmental studies.

Environmental impact of small-scale activities

Small-scale economic activities are not welcomed by the Pudong New Area Administration, as it is claimed that these do not assist the globalisation process, and are believed to be a source of environmental degradation. As part of the administration, the Pudong Urban Working Commission (PUWC) has aims to control illegal buildings, with the objective of improving the social facilities in the area. At present, there are more than 340,000m² of illegal buildings such as housing for news-stands, stalls or small groceries that have built businesses on streets without permits. They are mainly scattered around the area's residential quarters. However, property developers, or property management companies, in some areas have established more than one-third of the so-called illegal businesses, which are then resold to migrant workers for a profit. Furthermore, some government institutions, such as schools or hospitals, have also engaged in setting up illegal business buildings in order to cover welfare payments to their employees. The unauthorised business buildings established by government authorities are often in the best locations.

In response to local residents' complaints, the government authorities have designated the illegal business buildings set up by government institutions as their first target in a demolition drive. In 1998, the authorities demolished 140,000m² of illegal buildings, representing 40% of the total. The PUWC has spent RMB¥4 million (US$482,000) in dismantling the illegal buildings, and will spend another several million Chinese yuan to construct green areas, roads and other maintenance works (Wei, 1998b).

Spatial and demographic remodelling
Since Pudong has developed into a financial and trade centre, there is a high net movement rate of population, which shows the natural pulling force of this metropolis (Fig. 7).

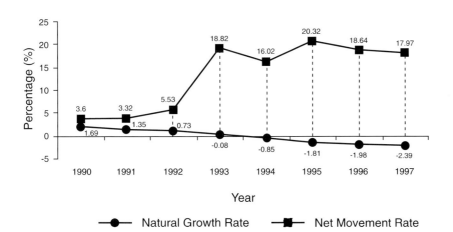

Fig. 7. The natural growth rate and net movement rate of population in Pudong 1990–1997.
Source: Statistical Bureau of Shanghai Pudong New Area, 1998.

The reshaping of its spatial pattern has inevitably led to large-scale displacement. In the process of urban reconstruction up to 1995, 11,813 households and 264 enterprises had been resettled to give room for new development, 0.91 million m² of existing structures have been demolished and 2.2 million m² of site have been created (Xiao, 1995). The process has not slowed: for example in 1998, 3,859 households were displaced just for projects related to the construction of one avenue in the Lujiazui Finance and Trade Zone.

Nevertheless, there still remain more than 2,300 villages in Pudong, although nearly 500 of the so-called villages house just two or three families. Such low densities have led the local authorities, in order to save land for future development, to plan the renovation of some existing villages, or to build residential sites which can house thousands of families. This is accomplished through the housing subsidy policy and gives a comparatively better living environment (Wei, 1998a). For example, since 1978 per capita living space has increased from 4.5 to 9.3m², and the bulk of this residential development has been through investment from the Chinese Mainland (Xu, 1998).

Conclusion

China's economy has been predicted to grow at around 5% to 7% a year for the next 20 years, moderating to 3 to 5% in the following 30 years (Shao, 1999). With such aggressive growth, China may become home to many large, 'instant' and intensified cities, of which Pudong in Shanghai is an example. The challenge facing urban decision-makers is whether such cities will become poorly planned and haphazardly juxtaposed city forms, or efficiently restructured urban developments with a sustainable future.

The new high-density development symbolises the state's intention of shifting the focus away from other major Asian cities towards Shanghai, making it a 'Global City' (e.g. Friedmann, 1997). The most readily available tool for the state to reinstate Shanghai as a key financial centre in the world with foreign-led investment is the manipulation of built form that is vivid and has a language that is easily communicated globally. Built form is a powerful symbol, as it can express the socio-economic viability and vitality of the city. This is an emerging notion in many Asian cities, like the Petronas Towers of Kuala Lumpur, Malaysia. The danger of this 'instant' globalised urbanity is the lack of cohesiveness with its local economic system. This may be manifested in a localised concentration of its economic cycle compared to other global cities such as London, New York and Los Angeles, which behave as a 'central place' in the global economic network (Sassen, 1991; Castells, 1989).

In Pudong, the process has taken only one decade, and the term 'instant' city appears to have some relevance. However, it is still too early to assess whether the strategy of state incentives for foreign investment and ultra-rapid growth is a successful and appropriate direction for achieving an economic–environmental balance. Yet the process of globalisation seems successful and undeniably true in the case of Pudong. The spatial perception of many traditional Chinese cities has dissolved under a mirage of modernism in Pudong. A new locale for socio-economic development and culture is emerging, undoubtedly driven by the power of real estate embedded in globalisation. High-density urban development successfully generates the image of a globalised order of urban space, urban syntax and form. While high densities and a global image do not necessarily make either a compact city or one that is sustainable, these 'instant' cities may still become exemplars for rest of China, and, perhaps, for rest of the world.

Notes

1. 100 acres are equivalent to 404,700m².
2. The RMB¥ is the yuan, the Chinese unit of currency (1 RMB¥ = 0.121 US$).

3. The authors' views on the social reactions to the Pudong new development are incomplete, due to the difficulties of conducting a public survey. About 100 questionnaires were distributed to organisations in Pudong to gather information on the social implications of Pudong developments, but only one completed questionnaire was recovered. This reflects the reluctance to reveal any true opinions on Pudong development. For the majority of people, Pudong is a surprise and a source of hope (verbal discussions with some Pudong inhabitants show a positive reaction).

References

Associated Press (1999) Builder revives plan for world-record tower in China, *Chicago Tribune*, 20 September.

Braunfels, W. (1988) *Urban Design in Western Europe – Regime and Architecture, 900–1900*, University of Chicago Press, Chicago.

Castells, M. (1989) *The Informational City*, Blackwell, Oxford.

Chen, Q. (1998) Mayor gives congress blueprint for Shanghai, *China Daily*, 13 February.

Chen, S. N., Shao, Y. D. and Yu, S. K. (eds) (1994) *Pudong New Area Almanac 1994* (in Chinese), Shanghai Joint Publishing Company, Shanghai.

Friedmann, J. (1986) The world city hypothesis, *Development and Change*, 17, pp.69–83.

Friedmann, J. (1997) World city futures – the role of urban and regional policies in the Asia–Pacific Region, Occasional Paper No. 56, Hong Kong Institute of Asia–Pacific Studies, The Chinese University of Hong Kong, Hong Kong.

Lavoie, S. (1998) *Instant City, More Tales from the Mines, California's Untold Stories, Gold Rush!*, Oakland Museum of California, California.

Li, C. T. (ed.) (1991), *Construction in Shanghai 1986–1990* (in Chinese), Shanghai Science Popularisation Press, Shanghai.

Li, J. G. (1998) Shanghai and the next century, *China Today*, **XLVII(1)**, pp.10–13.

Li, N. (1995) Pudong-full of hope, *Beijing Review*, **38(18)**, pp.10–14.

Lynch, K. (1981) *A Theory of Good City Form*, MIT Press, Cambridge, Massachusetts.

MacPherson, K. L. (1994) The head of the dragon: the Pudong New Area and Shanghai's urban development, *Planning Perspectives*, 9, pp.61–85.

Mumford, L. (1961) *The City in History*, Secker & Warburg, London.

Pudong New Area Administration (1998) *Guidelines for Investment in Pudong*, Pudong New Area Administration, Shanghai.

Rees, W. E. and Roseland, M. (1998) Sustainable communities: planning for the 21st century, in *Sustainable Development and the Future of Cities* (eds B. Hamm and P. K. Muttagi), Centre for European Studies, Intermediate Technology Publications Ltd, London.

Sassen, S. (1991) *The Global City – New York, London, Tokyo*, Princeton University Press, Princeton, NJ.

Shanghai Pudong New Area Administration (1993) *Shanghai Pudong New Area Handbook*, Shanghai Pudong New Area Administration, Shanghai.

Shao, S. (1998) Development zone woos private capital, *China Daily*, 3 November.

Shao, Z. W. (1999) China set to be Asia's top economy in 2040, *China Daily*, 30 September.

Statistical Bureau of Shanghai Pudong New Area (1998) *98 Statistical Yearbook of Shanghai Pudong New Area*, China Statistical Publishing House, China.

Thong, L. B. (1995) Challenges of superinduced development; the mega-urban region of Kuala Lumpur–Klang Valley, in *The Mega-Urban Regions of Southeast Asia* (eds T. G. McGee and I. M. Robinson), University of British Columbia Press, Vancouver.

Washburn, G. and Allen, J. L. (1999) 'Tallest' building gets OK and some rivals, *Chicago Tribune*, 29 September.

Wei, L. L. (1998a) Pudong farmers on the move, *China Daily*, 14 July.

Wei, L. L. (1998b) Illegal buildings get the push in Pudong, *China Daily*, 8 June.

Wei L. L. (1998c) Pudong focuses on residential buildings, *China Daily*, 27 April.

Xiao, W. (1998) DBS Land joins renovation drive, *China Daily*, 11 May.

Xiao, X. P. (1995) The emerging charm of urban infrastructural development in Pudong (in Chinese), *Pudong Development*, 1, pp.22–23.

Xinhua (1998) Pudong projects, *China Daily*, 13 August.

Xu, B. (1998) Pudong's real estate to improve, *China Daily*, 19 January.
You, Y. W. (1995) Pudong and new developments in Shanghai, *China Today*, **XLIV(10)**, pp.10–12.
Zhang, C. J. and Xie, J. H. (1998) Pudong – the head of the dragon, *China Today*, **XLVII(11)**, pp.10–13.
Zhao, Q. Z. (1999) Economic giants gather in China, *China Today*, **XLVIII(9)**, pp.11–18.

Silvia de Schiller and John Martin Evans
Urban Climate and Compact Cities in Developing Countries

Introduction

The compactness of urban form affects energy demand and environmental quality. A significant part of the environmental impact of urban activities is related to energy consumption. In most cases, the amount of energy consumed by industrial production is similar to that consumed by transport and by buildings, although energy use in buildings is now increasing to become the most important sector of energy demand. Energy use in buildings is related principally to heating and cooling, ventilation and lighting, with a very much smaller proportion for other building-related uses such as vertical circulation, water pumps, and non building-related uses such as domestic and office equipment, TVs, refrigerators.

It should be emphasised that much of the energy used in buildings is in part dependent on building design at the urban, architectural and construction scales. Factors such as access to direct winter sun and daylight, building form that reduces heat loss and construction materials that control heat transmission through the building envelope, all affect the energy demand of the built environment. At the city scale, spaces between buildings are as important as the building form to ensure appropriate levels of air movement, daylight and solar access in urban spaces, and the availability of natural energy resources on building facades. The design of urban space also helps to control pollution, favour ventilation of the urban fabric and moderate thermal conditions. There is a counter-argument that low-density development allows better access to renewable energies, especially solar radiation.

Proponents of compact cities mention energy efficiency and favourable environmental benefits as important positive advantages of compactness. It is argued that there are three converging factors that produce this result:

- Compact cities allow more efficient transport as travel distances are shorter and public transport is encouraged – reducing energy consumption, especially of fossil fuels that are responsible for a major part of CO_2 emissions and other forms of air pollution (e.g. Vale and Vale, 1991).
- Compact buildings, and the compact grouping of buildings, reduce heating

117

loads in winter, without affecting the energy demand for other services such as lighting, ventilation and refrigeration. Increased densities and compact building forms also help to minimise heat loss and have other energy benefits (e.g. Knowles, 2000; Olgyay, 1963; Department of Trade and Industry, 1998).

- Compact urban design also improves the environment of outdoor space within the city, providing wind protection, reducing outgoing radiation to the night sky and storing heat absorbed in the building surfaces during the day to reduce the temperature drop at night. These modified external conditions can improve outdoor comfort as well as reduce energy demand for the control of environmental conditions within buildings (Givoni, 1989; Yannas, 1994).

These environmental benefits are related to the complementary social and economic advantages of compactness, not discussed directly in this chapter. The energy savings of an efficient transport system also relate to the social and economic benefits of shorter travel times and more direct links between home, work, commerce and recreation.

However, the three environmental advantages mentioned above are related to specific climatic conditions and systems of urban management; they are not necessarily applicable to all climatic regions (e.g. Figs 1 and 2). Therefore, before analysing the advantages of compact cities in the developing world, their specific climatic conditions and characteristics will be considered as well as the impact of climate and urban microclimate on thermal comfort.

Left: *Fig. 1. Similar forms of 'first world' urban development are found in many different countries, despite variations of climate and latitude (Sydney, Australia)*

Right: *Fig. 2. Dense centres of large cities in emerging countries in subtropical climates incorporate building forms, planning controls and urban townscapes similar to those found in colder climates at higher latitudes (Buenos Aires, Argentina).*

Climates of the developing world

Most of the countries of the developing world are found at low latitudes with generally higher annual average temperatures than those found in the developed world. They also show very important contrasts between different types of hot climate affecting both comfort and energy use in diversified ways. The desert climates of North Africa and the Middle East are very different from the warm humid equatorial climates of West Africa or the Amazon Basin. Even within countries, there are important climatic differences. The warm humid coast of Kenya is totally different from the cool and cold uplands, while the desert of northern Chile is a total contrast to the cold rain forest found in the south.

The hot climates of the equatorial and tropical regions may be divided into three main groups, with a large number of intermediate and composite climates in the transitions between them, and some in combination with cooler conditions found in the subtropical regions at higher latitudes (Olgyay, 1963).

The *warm humid climates* found in the low latitudes of the equatorial belt are characterised by high but not excessive temperatures, high humidity, low daily and seasonal temperature swings, extensive cloud cover and high rainfall. The traditional measures to provide relief include shading from overhead direct sunlight, use of cooling breezes and light materials that cool down at night to provide acceptable conditions for sleeping.

The *hot dry climates* of the equatorial belt have completely different characteristics, with very high peak daytime temperatures, low humidity, large daily temperature swings, low cloud cover, and low rainfall. The differences between summer and winter can be marked, with cooler conditions and some rainfall in the winter season. The traditional measures for comfort in this climate include protection from hot dusty winds, heavy-weight building materials that delay and reduce the transmission of temperature peaks to the interior of buildings. Enclosed patios with vegetation also provide natural cooling, using water evaporation, and provide shade, conserving the cooled air within controlled and enclosed outdoor spaces.

The *composite or monsoon climates* such as those of India and West Africa combine the characteristics of the warm humid and hot dry climates in different seasons of the year, sometimes with the addition of a cool season. The monsoon climate derives its name from the Arabic word for change. The combination of strategies for cooling in the different seasons presents a special challenge for the appropriate design of buildings and urban spaces, combining cross-ventilation with control of hot winds, and the use of thermal mass without the disadvantages of heat storage in the warm humid season.

The impact of height above sea level, latitude and large expanses of water produce specific climatic conditions. These variations are found in the tropical islands of the Caribbean and the Pacific; the cool tropical uplands of Central Africa, the Atlas, and the Andes; and the maritime desert climates of the Arabian Gulf, where the uncomfortable climate of the desert is exacerbated by high humidity.

Many of the traditional cities in low latitudes incorporate urban design features that improve comfort conditions. The narrow streets of the cities of the Middle East and North Africa provide shade and protection from the hot dusty winds, while retaining the cool night air. The enclosed patios and gardens also encourage shade and evaporation of water, using fountains and irrigation channels. Finally, the large open treeless squares, excessively hot by day, provide comfortable conditions in the evening, attracting large crowds to the market stalls where the temperature cools down rapidly.

In warm humid equatorial climates, wide spaces between buildings and the use of vegetation are designed to provide shade without interrupting cooling breezes. The verandas and covered circulation also provide shade and exposure to the breeze without increasing the heat retention of the building.

Even in the subtropical climates, traditional buildings incorporated many design features to improve comfort in the days before air conditioning. These include controlled window size, extensive use of thermal mass, building zoning to reduce overheating, adjustable shading elements and even sliding glazed covers over internal patios. At the urban scale, comfort is improved by tree planting, colonnades at street level, and proportions of streets for enclosure and shade (e.g. Figs 3 and 4).

Urban microclimate

All cities produce significant changes in the local climate, including those found

Left: *Fig. 3. Traditional low-rise buildings set among palm trees are giving way to high-rise development with little shade in outdoor spaces (Haikou, Hainan, China).*

Right: *Fig. 4. New high-rise buildings, blocking favourable onshore breezes, replace low-rise buildings with vegetation (Fortaleza, Brazil).*

in equatorial, tropical and subtropical city microclimates. However, the degree of change and its impact may be more severe than in cooler climates at higher latitudes. Global warming may produce a slight rise in the average annual temperature of about 0.5°K in the next half century. But it is already possible to measure an increase in evening temperatures within urban areas, which can exceed 3°K in large dense cities compared with the surrounding rural area. This temperature increase is clearly related to city size and urban density (WMO, 1994).

While the urban heat island is a potentially favourable phenomenon in colder climates, it increases discomfort and energy demand in warmer climates. This may initiate a vicious circle. Higher outdoor temperatures increase the demand for air conditioning, while the increase in air conditioning contributes to urban warming through the increase in heat dumped in the urban air by air-conditioning cooling towers, and produced by additional electricity generation and distribution.

A study of the heat island in Buenos Aires shows that the central area can exceed the temperature of the suburban area by 3°K in the evenings when the temperature difference tends to increase. The spatial extent of the heat island coincides with the areas of highest building density, whilst temperature differences are reduced in park areas and near the coast where the influence of the River Plate moderates the temperature (de Schiller, 1999).

The evening and night increase in urban temperature has important implications for the use of air conditioning. Traditionally, cooler evening air could be used to ventilate the hot building interiors, reducing the indoor temperature to provide improved comfort, especially for uninterrupted sleep. However, the higher evening air temperatures produced by the urban heat island may limit effective night cooling, leading to an increase in the demand for air conditioning in the residential sector, especially amongst higher income groups. This tendency is disturbing since the penetration of air conditioning in the residential sector is fairly limited in most developing countries. A steep increase in demand could have a critical impact on energy use with an increase in the peak demand in residential areas, which will require significant investment to increase the capacity of the electrical distribution infrastructure.

Air conditioning and other forms of energy use in buildings are not the only causes of the urban heat island. Energy use in transport also produces large quantities of waste heat, from both internal combustion engines and electrical traction. The other effect is the heat received in the form of solar radiation during the day and absorbed in the high heat capacity surfaces of the city, especially pavements and building facades. Higher buildings and narrower streets tend to trap larger quantities of solar heat and cool down more slowly as they are less exposed to the cooler night sky. Increasingly high-density urban development will therefore increase the heat island in the evening, especially in summer.

Air conditioning

Despite the wide climatic differences between different types of hot climates and the traditional use of natural cooling strategies at the urban and building scale, the conventional solution to improve comfort conditions within buildings has been the introduction of air conditioning. First in prestige offices, then in factories where the production process may be affected by adverse environmental conditions, and finally, in other buildings such as conventional offices, housing and commerce. Air-conditioning installations can provide comfortable and productive indoor conditions whatever the variation in external conditions.

However, the universal incorporation of air conditioning to achieve thermal comfort has created new environmental problems at the global, regional, urban and building scale. The extensive use of refrigerants such as CFC has been a major factor in the reduction of the ozone layer and the resulting increase of harmful ultraviolet radiation. At the same time, the rapid increase in energy use for air conditioning has contributed to the greenhouse effect at the global scale. At the regional scale, increased energy use has produced acid rain and increased pollution. Within the urban area, the exhaust heat removed from the interior of buildings by artificial conditioning is dumped into the urban atmosphere, contributing to the harmful rise in urban air temperatures in the warmer regions of the world. Even within buildings, the use of air conditioning can give rise to deterioration in the indoor air quality as a result of insufficient ventilation, defective air filters and even poor control of air temperature, leading to excessive temperature gradients and local conditions of discomfort.

The avoidance or reduction of air conditioning in the buildings of the developing world can make a major contribution to the reduction of harmful environmental impacts. Despite the higher average temperatures found at lower latitudes, outdoor temperatures in these regions are usually within favourable comfort limits for sedentary activity during much of the day, in most seasons of the year. The traditional cooling strategies used at the urban and architectural scale show the possibilities of improving conditions by natural means without resorting to energy-intensive artificial conditioning. The design of cities, proposals for urban development and planning controls can play an important part in this strategy.

In this connection, a number of factors that have led to the introduction of air conditioning must be recognised:

- *Prestige*: Air conditioning is associated with high-cost buildings and is often offered as an essential part of a new office building;
- *Air quality*: The increase of traffic pollution in central urban areas prevents the use of natural ventilation for cooling buildings;
- *Noise*: Natural ventilation may not be possible with high and increasing levels of traffic;
- *Temperatures*: Energy consumed and building materials used in central and dense urban areas lead to an increase in external air temperatures, and to the urban heat island, which may require artificial cooling, even when the temperatures in surrounding rural areas are acceptable and comfortable;

- *Conservation*: In some situations, such as supermarkets, hospitals and museums, low and controlled temperatures are required for the conservation of products or artefacts, as well as human thermal comfort; and
- *Internal gains*: The increased use of computers, artificial lighting, and higher density of occupation all lead to increased internal heat gains, especially in deep-plan offices.

The prestige aspect is also related to an argument that may be raised at the political level in developing countries. If air conditioning is used extensively in cooler developed countries, why should developing countries forgo the benefits of this equipment that makes conditions more comfortable? An imposed policy of avoidance of air conditioning may be seen as an attempt by developed countries, responsible for the majority of the environmental impacts at the global scale, to prevent developing countries from achieving an improvement in their quality of life. The environmental responsibilities of the developed world must be faced, and a reduction in energy use in buildings in these countries would be an important step in this direction.

Urban and architectural bioclimatic design strategies

The strategies to improve thermal comfort at the urban scale have a favourable impact on both air-conditioned and naturally conditioned buildings. The avoidance or reduction of air conditioning has important environmental, economic and social benefits, if appropriate measures are taken to promote thermal comfort in indoor spaces. The economic advantages include the reduction in the capital cost of buildings, in addition to lower energy bills. The environmental benefits include reduced thermal and air pollution, as well as greater occupant satisfaction in naturally conditioned buildings. For this reason, policies to promote natural conditioning are needed at the urban, architectural and building scale. The following section analyses some of the possible measures at the urban scale and their relation to the promotion of compact cities.

Warm humid climates

In warm humid climates, shade and air movement are the principal measures used to improve thermal comfort, in both outdoor areas and indoors. At the same time, natural breezes may be relatively weak and unreliable. Within buildings, fans may be used to improve air movement, but in outdoor spaces the disposition of building forms has a major impact on urban air movement. Typically, a space between buildings that exceeds its height by five times is required to ensure that air movement returns to ground level after deviation over the roof or round the edges of a building. This distance may be decreased by a careful disposition of buildings, using some higher buildings to deflect high-level wind to ground level and staggering the gaps between buildings.

At the urban scale, care must be taken to utilise favourable aspects of the wind regime, such as on-shore breezes, and the topography that channels the breeze and creates local accelerations. Continuous lines of high-rise buildings along the coast may provide attractive views for the occupants, but can also block favourable breezes for large distances inland. Although tree planting contributes to the already high humidities, the combined effect of evaporation and shade will always improve comfort conditions when temperatures are above the comfort limit. Avenues of trees in the streets, public urban parks and the conservation of green areas within private plots can all contribute to improved conditions in the urban area.

The orientation of buildings is always a significant factor in the resulting energy demand in all climates and urban conditions, with a very strong impact at low latitudes. In these regions, afternoon sun from the west increases discomfort in all seasons, while building orientation and form to catch cooling breezes will improve comfort throughout the year.

Finally, the difference between design for air-conditioned and that for naturally conditioned buildings should be stressed. The use of air conditioning allows the use of deep-plan compact buildings, though in many situations the possibility of extended power cuts or 'brownouts'[1] may preclude totally sealed buildings. Naturally conditioned buildings should allow air movement at body level with inlets on one side of the building and outlets on the opposite side.

The bioclimatic design recommendations at the urban as well as the building scale do not favour the increase of urban densities in warm humid climates. The promotion of compact cities in these climates should consider the possible disadvantages of high-density development on the urban thermal environment and the possible increase in energy use to overcome these conditions.

Hot dry climates

In hot dry climates, urban comfort strategies are different. Provision of shade and evaporation are effective strategies, though preferably in partially enclosed spaces such as patios and walled gardens where the cool air can be 'trapped'. Closely clustered low development using patios and courtyards is found in most hot dry climates, allowing high-density low-rise urban development. Night cooling is most effective in spaces open to the night sky. Flat roofs and open squares are the most comfortable spaces in the evenings. The cool air that forms on the flat surfaces exposed to the clear sky can descend into patios and courtyards, as well as urban squares, conserving the cool air in a protected and shaded space till the next day. Enclosed and narrow pedestrian streets also provide shade and protection from hot dusty winds.

Modern high-capacity traffic streets in dense urban areas can present difficult environmental problems due to the large areas of dark paving, lack of shade and wind protection, and increased heat and pollution. Open-air parking areas also require shade, as cars become extremely hot when left in the sun. Air conditioning of vehicles increases fuel consumption and the hot air added to the urban atmosphere by a significant amount.

Lower densities with wider spaces between buildings have been proposed for hot dry desert climates with extensive vegetation in the spaces around buildings. In these climates, water may be at a premium. Careful use of irrigation is needed to achieve maximum benefit with minimum use of scarce water resources. Shade trees are more effective than low vegetation, while grass consumes large quantities of water without providing shade or effective evaporative cooling.

Conclusions

In both hot, dry and warm, humid climates, the desirable bioclimatic solutions to promote comfort through natural conditioning do not necessarily reflect the global architectural tendencies in mainstream architectural publications. Indeed, many commentators in these journals object to architectural images that tend to reflect traditional forms of urban development or recall motifs from the past.

Environmental and cultural differences in the developing world require differentiated solutions to the promotion of compact cities, while globalising trends favour universal solutions. The planning of compact cities and the design of urban developments within these cities must respond to these differences. The concept of modernity is related to global images, but truly modern compact cities of the developing world must be conceived as a form of urban development that promotes and contributes to the development process. Urban growth is not only a result of development but is also a motor of development. Urban development that promotes improved environmental conditions and reduces energy demand will favour economic development and improve the quality of life.

Note

1. Brownouts are like power cuts, but with low voltage that can be harmful to electric equipment and motors. Incandescent light bulbs glow a flickering orange.

References

DTI (Department of Trade and Industry) (1998) *Planning for Passive Solar Design*, BRECSU, Watford.

de Schiller, S. (1999) *Impacto de la Forma Edilicia en el Confort de Espacios Urbanos (Impact of Building Form on Comfort in Urban Spaces)*, Anais, ANTAC, Fortaleza.

de Schiller, S. and Evans, J. M. (1998) Sustainable urban development: design guidelines for warm humid cities, *Urban Design International*, **3(4)**, pp.165–184, Taylor & Francis.

Foley, G. (1981) *The Energy Question*, Penguin Books, Harmondsworth.

Givoni, B. (1989) *Urban Design in Different Climates*, WCAP-10, WMO/TD-N°346, World Meteorological Organization, Geneva.

Knowles, R. (2000) The solar envelope: its meaning for urban growth and form, *Architecture – City – Environment, Proceedings of PLEA 2000* (eds K. Steemers and S. Yannas), James & James, London.

Olgyay, V. (1963) *Design with Climate*, Princeton University Press, Princeton, N.J.

Vale, B. and Vale, R. (1991) *Green Architecture: Design for a Sustainable Future*, Thames and Hudson, London.

WMO (1994), *Report on the Technical Conference on Tropical Urban Climates*, WCASP-30, World Meteorological Organization, Geneva.

Yannas, S. (1994) *Solar Energy House Design, Volume 1: Principles, Objectives, Guidelines*, Architectural Association, London.

Part Two
Intensification, Urban Sprawl and the Peripheries
Introduction

Setting the global context and raising strategic issues were the focus of the first part of the book. The second part concentrates on a number of the key aspects that affect the sustainability of urban form. The intensification of built form, also called densification, is an important strategy for increasing densities in existing urban areas. However, it can be a questionable policy where inner-city core areas are already very dense. But scope exists on vacant land, along transport corridors and at transport interchanges, and on the periphery. It is characteristic that the fastest growth occurs on the periphery, and low-density urban sprawl is the result, causing many environmental problems and unsustainable development. These areas are also most likely to be the location for illegal and squatter settlements.

In the first chapter, Acioly compares the informal development of Egyptian cities with policies in Brazil (Curitiba) to manage the process of intensification. He analyses the advantages and disadvantages of compact development and low-density areas, showing the significance of managing the process and use of incentives for developers such as the transfer of development rights. He concludes that empowered local government is the key to success, and touches on the idea of decentralised networks of compact cities as a way forward. Zaman and Lau show how the process of intensification happens in Dhaka. Lax regulation allows the private sector to drive the intensification process through conversion of residential areas to mixed uses with higher densities, and the increase in density (and crowding) through plot subdivisions. This process is contrasted with formal plans for the peripheral expansion of the city, which have singularly failed through lack of adequate investment in infrastructure and transport. Kumar contrasts low- and high-density development and points to the importance of considering the quality of life. He notes that the process of urban intensification will be limited by the capacity of the infrastructure needed to support it.

The consequences of peripheral expansion policies are examined by Fadda *et al.* in a detailed study of development on the periphery of Santiago, Chile. The quality of life of residents was examined, and shown to be affected by environmental pollution, social exclusion and high levels of crime. Although home ownership was seen as empowering, the remote locations on the periphery were found to be disempowering, with residents feeling they could do little to effect improvements. Developer greed is shown by da Silva *et al.* to be one of the reasons for 'leapfrogging', leading to remotely located development, with vacant land left between city and periphery – a greater profit is made once the public sector provides the infrastructure. They propose a method to achieve more equity through taxation, designed to encourage development of vacant plots and prevent 'leapfrogging' development of the outer peripheries. However, not all development on the periphery is low-density or provided through the formal sector. Zillmann shows how the informal sector intensifies and consolidates development to become a densely developed part of the city. She shows how precariously established dwellings are extended, and become sources of income as well as homes. In the difficult terrain around Caracas, she demonstrates the skills and knowledge needed to build these informal settlements, and argues that this process should be a legitimate part of urban planning and development.

The juxtaposition in this part of accounts of high-density and low-density peripheral development, in both the formal and informal sectors, is revealing. Where the political will exists, as in Curitiba, then sustainability benefits begin to accrue. High density, when uncontrolled, can lead to problems, through overcrowding, pollution, and lack of open space. Yet the effectiveness of the investment of human capital and self-regulation is apparent in the informal sector barrios of Caracas, despite the problems and disadvantages. The low-density developments, provided through the formal sector, show no improvement in quality of life, and appear rife with social and economic problems. Remoteness, extended journey times, and social exclusion seem no compensation for less crowded living space.

Claudio C. Acioly Jr.

Can Urban Management Deliver the Sustainable City?
Guided Densification in Brazil versus Informal Compactness in Egypt

Introduction

A recent study of urban densities in developing countries, conducted for the 1996 United Nations Conference on Human Settlements (Acioly and Davidson, 1996), concluded that there is no universal recipe for urban densities in terms of an ideal, or most appropriate density, particularly for residential development. Several case studies have shown that what is regarded as a high or a low density, and what is an acceptable density, differ between continents and countries, and even within cities and neighbourhoods. However, there was evidence that a general process of change was leading to more compact cities, though often in the face of considerable resistance. The study revealed that costs of low-density solutions are increasingly recognised. Case studies in Brazil and India showed that government policies, plans and development control instruments can shape cities and densities in a way which optimises infrastructure, municipal services, land and public resources (Acioly and Davidson, 1996; 1998).

Subsequent research in Cairo triggered the idea for this chapter – a comparative analysis of the process of compaction in Egyptian cities and the process of densification found in selected Brazilian cities. The main objectives of the chapter are to analyse the different modes of densification, to highlight the advantages and disadvantages of densely occupied urban environments, and to assess their outcomes from the point of view of sustainable urban development.

In Egypt, informal urbanisation and the illegal extension of buildings exacerbate the positive and negative effects of extreme compaction. This phenomenon is normally the result of a spontaneous process coupled with inadequate housing and urban policies. By contrast, the process in Brazil is steered by active and enabled local governments using a range of urban management instruments that result in physical compactness and the optimal use of infrastructure and land.

In the first part of this chapter the problems and opportunities presented by compact urban environments in Cairo and Giza are analysed. This reveals the particular ways in which informal development in Egypt leads to compactness, and attention is focused on various aspects of urban development such as urban

127

vitality, social interaction, local economic development, transportation, air quality, congestion and spatial management. It is argued that the sustainability benefits of a compact city environment cannot be attained in the absence of guiding policies, urban management tools and a capable local government.

The second part of this chapter focuses on the experience of those Brazilian cities whose local governments are actively engaged in policies of urban intensification (guided densification) that lead to more compact urban environments (e.g. São Paulo, Curitiba, Porto Alegre). This is attained through the transfer of development rights to and from parcels situated in the existing built-up area, via shifts in land-use zoning and floor area ratio (FAR), based on the principles of enablement and public–private negotiations. At times the transfer of development rights (TDR) is used to preserve and reuse buildings with a recognised heritage importance. The densification policies are also used to generate public revenues targeted on infrastructure improvement programmes in poorer areas and social housing programmes. Physical compactness measures are also mechanisms for social justice. The chapter shows how this approach is becoming increasingly popular as a source of revenue generation and as a tool for redistribution, since it produces a financial surplus available for investment in needy areas of the city. The chapter suggests that an encouragement of compact city environments can provide an impulse to a different path of urban development from that of the dominant urban sprawl model.

Spontaneous compactness in Egyptian cities

Most Egyptian settlements are situated in a strip of land along the river Nile. A total population of approximately 62.5 million inhabitants (in 1999) is living on only 5% of total national territory. The remaining 95% of the land is desert. The demand for urban land is enormous, yet the only available land is the scarce, privately owned fertile agricultural land which the country needs to feed a rapidly growing population. The process of transformation of agricultural land to urban use is currently under military jurisdiction – a regime that imposes severe sanctions in order to halt urban expansion. On the other hand, ownership of outlying desert land is a state monopoly and the land is not immediately available for development. Given the military decrees against building on agricultural land, the only options for growth for cities like Cairo and Giza are the peripheral desert areas, or the in-fill of available and increasingly scarce vacant land within the urban fabric. This results in a tremendous pressure on the land and building stock, causing market distortions and the exclusion of poorer families from housing opportunities in these cities.

The consequences for urban growth are twofold: first, the replacement of villas by high-rise buildings and high-density developments, often through informal roof-top building extensions, and second, a continuous and vigorous process of informal subdivision of agricultural land. In some cases, informal urbanisation accounts for nearly 90% of total urban growth, and is based on an annual rate of consumption of arable land that is even more striking, given the restrictions of military legislation. In 1993 the annual consumption of land in the Greater Cairo Region was 900 hectares, of which 340 hectares was agricultural land (UNCHS, 1993). The demographic and building changes that have taken place during the last 30 years in Giza city have converted a rural area into dense urban environments, largely as a result of the dynamic informal urbanisation process.

Informal neighbourhoods in Giza currently have gross densities above 750 inhabitants per hectare and in some cases above 1,000 inhabitants per hectare (Governorate of Giza, 1998a). Data collected by the GTZ (German Technical Cooperation Agency) and the Governorate of Giza for the informal neighbourhood of Boulaq El-Dakrour indicate a population of 650,000 inhabitants living in an area of merely 300 hectares at a density of more than 2,000 inhabitants per hectare (Governorate of Giza and GTZ, 1995). Another report indicates gross densities of 500 inhabitants per hectare (Governorate of Giza, 1998b) for the same area. Whatever the true figure, Giza's informal settlements are characterised by profound overcrowding and physical compactness.

Gross densities in Cairo have been estimated at an average of 400 inhabitants per hectare (UNCHS, 1993). This is higher than New York and Bangkok and similar to places like Hong Kong. Centrally located neighbourhoods in Cairo such as El Atouf (El Gamalia), Souk El Selah (El Darb El Ahmar) and El Kabsh (Said Zienb) have gross densities of 1,569, 1,433 and 1,725 inhabitants per hectare respectively (UNDP and SCA, 1997). These figures are extremely high and are the result of a process of urban intensification.

The high level of compactness of the built area is an overall characteristic of Egyptian cities. The traditional *medina*, or inner-city core, has a peculiar built form and structure, characterised by narrow roads and alleys, compact building blocks and mixed land uses and activities that result in very dense urban environments. In informal areas, this pattern is exacerbated by the subdivision of agricultural land by private owners in pursuit of the maximisation of profit and the minimisation of vacant land. The land development process produces little space for amenities and open public space and allows only for very narrow roads, which in some cases have a width of only 3m. The residents for their part fully occupy the land parcels and develop high-rise buildings on the plots. It is common to find six-storey informal buildings with 100% plot coverage, resulting in a residential space that is unhealthy, and which lacks basic lighting and ventilation. The most striking negative features of the informal settlements of Cairo and Giza are overcrowding, inadequate housing, poverty and poor environmental conditions. Compact housing blocks coupled with narrow roads result in inadequate accessibility and traffic congestion. High levels of congestion in street canyons produce air pollution levels (particularly of particulates and lead) far above those set by international health standards, and present severe health hazards (Governorate of Giza, 1998a; Kolb, 1998; MacDonald, 1999).

The physical features mentioned above also hinder solid waste collection, resulting in the accumulation of garbage on vacant plots and street alleys that further contributes to worsening environmental conditions. For example, the pollution caused by garbage dumping was identified as the most serious problem by the residents of Boulaq El-Dakrour (Governorate of Giza and GTZ, 1995; RTEC, 1996). Furthermore, the lack of open public space and social amenities forces children to play on the street and women to stay inside the house. The situation is worsened by the weak capacity of local government to provide municipal services such as solid waste collection, community development services, road paving and the upgrading of infrastructure. There is a very low capacity to enforce basic urban planning standards and minimum development controls. The absence of means and resources, coupled with a lack of political and administrative autonomy, exacerbates the local government's inability to cope with these problems.

Despite these adverse effects, derived from densely occupied environments, it is also possible to identify some favourable features. Compact urban settlements like Boulaq El-Dakrour and Imbaba do provide a significant volume of employment in formal and informal small-scale enterprises in the service and manufacturing sectors (Governorate of Giza, 1998a). In Boulaq El-Dakrour, where one-third of the residents find employment within the area, there are 2,500 small manufacturing businesses with an average of 3.9 jobs per unit (Governorate of Giza, 1998b). Local economic development and the possibilities for income generation are associated positively with the level of population density in these neighbourhoods. These high levels of vitality and urbanity are also to be found in other formal and informal parts of the city.

Actions to cope with the adverse effects of urban compactness
The Egyptian government has embarked on a programme of urban restructuring in Cairo and Giza, and has pursued policies of spatial decentralisation and de-concentration of population in recognition of the adverse effects of densely occupied urban environments. The goal has been to ease those forces producing the congestion, and the concentration of population, jobs and economic activity that result in a high demand for fertile agricultural land in the Greater Cairo Region and the Delta Region (Cairo, Giza and Qalyabia). A programme of new towns was drawn up and several were built in the desert. Industrial developments and job creation programmes linked to state-supported housing development programmes were undertaken to attract and consolidate human settlement. Land-development schemes were assigned to private-sector developers at attractive land prices. However, these cities faced serious difficulties. They did not manage to attract the levels of population and private investment required to achieve self-sustained development and consolidation. Public transport and accessibility remain inadequate, and the level of service provision and employment opportunities cannot, as yet, compete with those of Cairo and Giza.

The urban configuration of these cities also created sustainability problems since they were based on low-density modernist city models, such as Brasilia and Abuja, that consolidated urban sprawl and imposed the rigid separation of functions, land use and urban activities. These features diminished social interaction, public security and the economic viability of local shops and businesses. This model contrasted sharply with the realities of most Egyptian cities (Zaghloul, 1998).

The government also pursued policies to deal directly with the congestion problem and the scarcity of land within the city fabric. It did this by changing the FAR of land parcels situated along the main artery roads, allowing high-rise developments up to 1.5 times the width of the road. It also built a ring road, extended the metro lines, and constructed a series of bridges and flyovers to alleviate traffic congestion and to facilitate accessibility.

Lessons learned from Egypt
The new towns have not managed to attract population away from Cairo and Giza, or to ease congestion in these cities. The reasons for this include:

• the lack of appropriate public transport facilities;

- the lack of a sound urban economic base;
- the scattered morphology of the urban environment;
- the functional segregation of land uses and the monofunctionality of neighbourhoods;
- high land and house prices; and
- insufficient incentives for the population to move into these new locations.

Similarly, land-use and traffic-management interventions have done little to lessen serious congestion problems and the deterioration of air quality in Cairo and Giza. Informal densification through roof-top extensions has remained a key feature of Cairo's intra-urban growth. Government agencies have not developed the means to halt the process or to tax the considerable number of households involved. Informal densification and urban intensification are increasing the demand for more road lanes and parking space throughout the city as more vehicles appear. The problem is aggravated by the poor condition of the pavements, and their obstruction by vehicles and goods, by street vendors and drivers, which force large numbers of pedestrians on to the street. The government has failed to enforce the regulations governing the use of public space.

Buses and the metro are greatly overcrowded, and there has been a mushrooming of microbuses and vans that offer alternative transport (Negus, 1997). Air quality is deteriorating rapidly in the Greater Cairo area and despite the expansion of the metro network, the ring road and peripheral new town developments, the number of vehicles in circulation is increasing rapidly (currently more than 1 million).

The restrictions on urban land supply, an inappropriate regulatory system and the incapacity of local government to play an active role in monitoring, planning and managing city growth can be considered as some of the deeply rooted causes that amplify the adverse effects of high-density and compact urban settings. An obsolete rent control act prevents owners from updating house rental values and grants inheritance rights of the lease. This results in a situation where flats are rented at ridiculous prices (US$10.00 per month for a 3-bedroom flat), whilst thousands of others remain vacant, as landlords tend to keep their dwellings vacant for fear of not being able to raise the rent and to recover flats for their own use. In 1986 it was estimated that there were 350,000 vacant flats in Cairo (UNCHS, 1993). This supply-side obstacle has led to a skyrocketing of land, housing and rent prices. An artificial housing shortage has encouraged informality in land-use occupation, land subdivision, sub-renting and overcrowding that has increased urban compactness and its adverse effects, without any direct participation of the local government.

Urban operations: a Brazilian urban management tool
Policies of liberalisation of zoning and land use are becoming increasingly popular amongst urban managers and city planning authorities in Brazil. Cities like Rio de Janeiro, São Paulo, Curitiba, Campinas, Porto Alegre and Santo André, amongst others, are relaxing land-use restrictions and speeding up decisions on densification measures. This is commonly achieved by negotiated increases in floor area in exchange for a financial contribution from developers and landowners (Acioly, 1999; Corrêa Oliveira, 1999; Klink, 1995). Very often it results in the transfer of development rights from one location in the city to another (Giordano, 1988; Johnston and Madison, 1997).

The transfer of development rights (TDR) is now widely used by Brazilian cities and is being incorporated into municipal legislation, utilising the concept of *solo criado* which separates property rights from the right to build (Acioly, 1999). The legislation allows owners of properties preserved by government acts – for their heritage values for example – to sell to third parties the development rights or building potential that has been restricted by zoning and conservation legislation. In spatial terms, the development right covers an area (m^2) equal to the difference between the total built area of the existing building and the area permitted by the zoning codes where it is situated (Polis, 1996). TDR compensates the losses incurred by a property owner whose rights to build have been subject to restrictions imposed by zoning ordinances, or another higher public interest. The *solo criado* is also associated with urban operations (*operações urbanas*) or inter-linked operations (*operações interligadas*). These complex operations regulate the purchase and exchange of development rights in the city, as well as the release of land-use restrictions, through negotiations between local governments and the private sector. One must bear in mind that local government in Brazil possesses one of the highest degrees of political, administrative and fiscal autonomy in the world.

Guided densification and urban intensification in Curitiba

Curitiba is internationally acclaimed as an environmentally friendly city. However, not much is known about the role of the local government in shaping urban form through densification policies that have been applied since 1965, when the first master plan was drawn up. The plan encouraged the decongestion and revitalisation of the inner city, and the shift from a radial concentric to a linear urban growth pattern. This was accomplished through the creation of a north–south axis of traffic and transportation, tangential to the inner city, the Structural Axis. This created a core street layout that allowed for the subsequent expansion of the public transport network and the construction of other structural axes (Lerner, 1989; IPPUC, 1991; 1993). This innovation has allowed the local government to implement one of the continent's most successful and efficient public transport systems based on buses. The system transports 1.3 million passengers a day out of a population of 1.6 million people, giving an energy-saving ratio 30% higher than in other large Brazilian cities. This has been achieved in a city that has the second highest level of car ownership in Brazil (Acioly and Davidson, 1996; 1998).

Land-use planning measures in the city promote mixed uses and higher population densities along the various structural axes, in order to secure an economically viable public transport system and to encourage the location of new developments out of the inner city (see Fig. 1). A policy of land acquisition was a *sine qua non* condition for expanding the bus network, and for consolidating the densification process that gave the city a particular urban form and skyline. The principle applied has been to link urban intensification with the availability of public transport and mixed land use by promoting housing developments at a higher FAR in the plots situated alongside the structural axis. The maximisation and optimisation of land, infrastructure and public investments was a cornerstone of the policy. In the land parcels situated within one block from the structural axis, the value of FAR has been increased to 6, permitting buildings that can reach a volume of construction six times the area of the land parcels, at gross population densities of up to 600 inhabitants per hectare. The FAR of land parcels decreases with distance from the public transport network, resulting in an interesting symbiosis between high-rise and high-density built areas and low-rise low-density environments within a continuous urban fabric provided with a network of urban parks containing public services and amenities. The final result is a city that contains one of the world s highest rates of green area per capita (50m²/inhabitant).

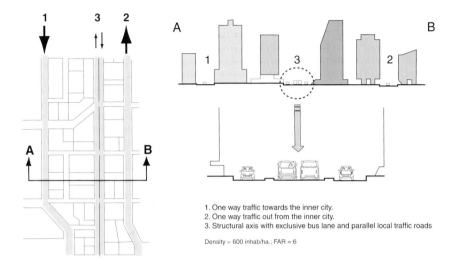

1. One way traffic towards the inner city.
2. One way traffic out from the inner city.
3. Structural axis with exclusive bus lane and parallel local traffic roads

Density = 600 inhab/ha.; FAR = 6

Fig. 1. The trinary system in Curitiba.

Local government has applied the transfer of development rights or building potential (the principle of *solo criado*) in order to preserve buildings of architectural and historical value and to achieve inner-city revitalisation. Development rights were transferred from the original sites to elsewhere in the city, provided that the infrastructure and services were in place to absorb the increase of densities and the FAR in the receiving land parcels. Decisions to increase the FAR were based on a careful study of the impacts of densification, e.g. absorption capacity of infrastructure, impact on transit and public-service provision. Densification could only take place if no negative impacts were identified.

Local government's right to expropriation was abandoned in favour of a swap. The owners of those properties benefit from additional FAR, and a relaxation of zoning restrictions on other land parcels owned by them elsewhere in the city (see Fig. 2). In this way, local government simultaneously embarked on a systematic process of densification whilst safeguarding the building heritage and creating different uses and activities that recaptured the vitality and urbanity of the city centre. An automated *cadastre* and a land-information system, established in the early 1980s, have provided the municipality with very precise information about the building coefficients, densities and development potentials of every single plot in the city. These systems permit a careful assessment of the physical transformation and compactness of the city in its various sectors.

So successful has been TDR that the municipality of Curitiba has followed the example of São Paulo by linking the financial surplus generated from these transactions with a municipal housing fund, established in 1991. This linkage gave the owners the option of exchanging their benefits from the new FAR for a land

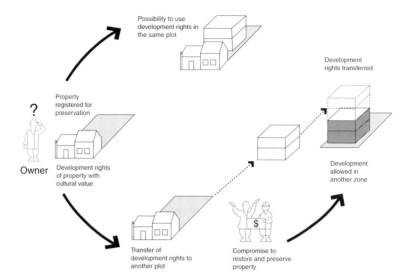

Fig. 2. Transfer of development rights for preservation of architectural heritage in Curitiba, Brazil.
Source: IPPUC, 1999.

parcel where social housing could be constructed by the municipality. Thus, instead of paying a financial contribution, the private sector delivers land parcels for local government-sponsored social housing projects. The new municipal law also allows owners to pay counterpart contributions in cash. The land parcel to be donated to the municipal housing fund must correspond in development rights to 75% of the market value of the total area, this being an incentive for multifamily residential development. The law also allows for vertical extension that does not imply an alteration in the FAR of the parcel. In this case, the land parcel donated in exchange for this increase in the number of floors must be equivalent to 15% of the market price of a land parcel of equivalent size in the zone where it is situated (PMC, 1991). From 1990 to July 1999, transactions with development rights generated nearly US$8.4 million (at 1999 exchange rates) which have been transferred to the social housing development fund.

Densification and social housing in São Paulo
The municipality of São Paulo applied TDR in 1969 when it expropriated land needed to restructure the city's most famous road – the Avenida Paulista. At the end of the 1980s, legislation was enacted to facilitate social housing production by the private sector in exchange for FAR increases and the modification of zoning of land parcels through the application of TDR. This was subsequently regulated through a municipal law that linked the financial revenue derived from TDR to the accumulation of a municipal social housing fund (FUNAPS). This framework was articulated within a densification strategy that was spelt out in the 1991 urban development plan (PMSP, 1991; 1992b). One of the goals was to constitute an integrated urban management system that would allow the municipality to optimise the infrastructure and services, through a guided densification process coupled with the occupation of available vacant land.

The planners developed a series of indicators in order to determine the absorption capacity of the infrastructure and services in place, and the potential of the built area to assimilate higher densities and urban intensification. A meticulous analysis and inventory of the city resulted in the identification of 15 zones where guided densification could occur. The areas subject to densification were divided into three main regions. The first was where the available space was almost overburdened, but where there was a high concentration of public transport and other infrastructure. The second was a non-critical region where the absorption capacity of the infrastructure was at the limit, and a third region was where the highest potential for densification was found. The planners' main concern was to monitor closely the use of the additional built space derived from densification strategies and the adverse effects of urban compactness. This was to allow the municipality to stimulate the diversification of land uses, and to tackle the loss of urbanity that had emerged in inner-city areas. Here the problem was one of fluctuating densities: a variation of 400% in the population density in the inner city between daytime and night-time converted it into an urban desert where economic inefficiency, criminality and insecurity reigned (Acioly and Davidson, 1996; 1998).

The most innovative aspect of the policy was the linkage between densification and social housing production, financed by revenues generated through inter-linked operations. Fifty-four proposals generated 4,088 social housing units. In 37 cases, the municipality received 1m^2 of social housing for each 2.44m^2 of residential space provided as an additional development right. In 16 other operations involving commercial service uses, the exchange ratio was 2.29m^2 of TDR to 1m^2 of social housing (Acioly and Davidson, 1996; 1998; PMSP, 1992a; 1992b). Camargo's analysis shows that since 1986 the municipality has sponsored 58 of these operations, resulting in 4,314 housing units as a counterpart contribution by the private sector. In total, 321 inter-linked operations were registered by the urban operations management unit (Camargo, 1994).

Nevertheless, densification strategies were continuously confronted with backward legislation. A pioneering study undertaken in 1991 by an inner city-based NGO, the Associação o Viva o Centro, showed that São Paulo's inner city had high levels of economic vitality and was well-connected with the metropolitan area, but its development was constrained by obsolete legislation that indirectly stimulated peripheral growth. This legislation was based on the assumption that the inner city was saturated, and resulted in building constraints beyond the FAR=4 level. It prohibited the building of garages, and embodied a series of limits on housing, businesses and firms, which subsequently preferred to migrate to other areas of the city (Barreto, 1997; Longareri, 1997; Guimarães, 1998).

A large-scale urban operation called Anhangabaú was initiated to realise an increase of 150,000m^2 of built area through TDR at the heart of the inner city, approved by the municipal law 11.090, 16 September 1991. However, the high costs assigned to private-sector developers – the counterpart contribution was fixed at 60% of the market value of the land parcel – did not attract the expected amount of investment. In 1997 a municipal law renamed the operation the City Centre Operation (Operação Centro), allowing a FAR of up to 12. Original estimates anticipated that this operation would raise US$30 million through regularisation of existing construction and nearly US$32 million through the sale of development rights (Camargo, 1993; Junior, 1994). Recent figures indicate that the municipality approved six transactions in the period 1991–94 involving changes in FAR, and the regularisation of the illegal excess of built areas has generated nearly US$8.7 million at today's prices (EMURB, 1999a; 1999b).

The pressure exercised by Viva o Centro over seven years (1991–98) resulted in positive changes towards compactness, urban vitality, more inner-city housing and amenities, a higher FAR and increased private-sector participation in land readjustment mechanisms and transactions involving TDR. There is no doubt that the implementation of this operation will lead to the materialisation of the goals of the compact city.

Lessons learned from Brazil

The experience with guided densification in Brazilian cities like Curitiba and São Paulo reveals the potential for modifying existing urban areas, creating even more compact urban environments that optimise public investment in infrastructure and transport. Even in cities that are apparently as saturated as São Paulo, there is still room for the maximisation of development opportunities within the urban fabric. The Brazilian cities examined in this chapter show that proper management and accurate knowledge of the built environment are essential conditions for pursuing densification policies. These may help to reduce urban sprawl and the loss of rural land, and recapture urban vitality, diversity and intra-urban economic development.

The actual trend towards residential expansion within the inner city provides additional support to the current densification policies and the advocacy of the compact city. However, if this is not accompanied by an efficient transit and public transport management system, one can expect the exacerbation of congestion, the deterioration of quality of life and decreasing air quality, as is currently experienced by São Paulo. Curitiba, by contrast, links public transport, land use and housing development in an intelligent densification strategy that helps the city to save energy, ease congestion, maximise population mobility and promote private-sector participation in urban development. The high performance standards of Curitiba's public transportation system, as well as its reliability and economic efficiency, cannot be divorced from the densification policy and urban intensification strategies undertaken by the municipal government. These are the main reasons why many people choose to leave their private vehicles at home.

Both cities show innovative ways in which a compact city strategy can be implemented through the land rent and land development potential attached to private real estate properties. These can be appropriated by the city, and socialised by providing funds for low-income housing programmes. Proper urban governance and increased public participation give sufficient transparency and political support to urban management practices in both Curitiba and São Paulo. It is unlikely that complex urban operations of this type can be accomplished without the municipalities taking the driving seat in the process. The examples in Brazil show that an enabled local government, accountable to its population, is a key prerequisite to resolving urban equity issues and to maximising the benefits of the compact city approach.

Comparing the Egyptian and Brazilian experiences

The guided densification in Curitiba and São Paulo provides clear examples of how an active and enabled municipal government is capable of generating resources from within the city's stock of space – resources that are not immediately visible through the implementation and management of complex urban operations. A thorough analysis of intra-urban potential for growth and urban intensification provides a sound basis for pursuing the maximisation of available land, infrastructure and public services, enhancing housing opportunities and local economic development. The final result is cities that tackle urban equity issues, and which contain the key elements of the compact city – social and economic diversity, urbanity, vitality, high densities and mixed land use. Furthermore, current policies to reintroduce housing in inner-city locations will help to increase both the population and investment in the city core necessary to mitigate the process of inner-city decay. These densification strategies place the question of sustainable urban development at the forefront, but they do not provide evidence that they will be sufficient in themselves for reversing the trend of peripheral development and urban expansion towards greenfield sites.

The case studies in Egypt and Brazil provide concrete evidence of the critical obstacles to be overcome by compact city policies. Fig. 3 attempts to summarise the problems and advantages of compact cities on the basis of this evidence.

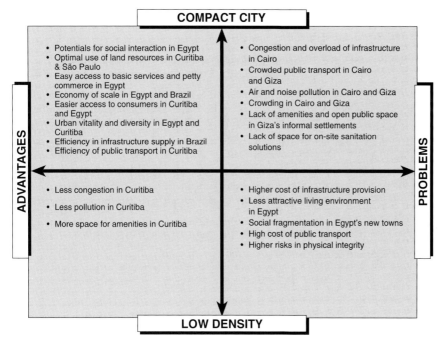

Fig. 3. Problems and opportunities in compact city environments.
Based on Acioly and Davidson, 1996; 1998.

There are clear benefits in Curitiba of physical compactness along the structural development axis of the city where public transport provision is maximised and optimised by high population densities and mixed land use. The benefits include economic vitality, revenue generation and energy saving, all of which have impacts on the performance of the city as a whole. In São Paulo, many studies extol the positive impacts from intra-urban growth, densification and urban intensification within the city core (Acioly, 1999). These benefits are supported by public organisations and powerful private-sector actors. But it is not clear if these strategies will have positive effects on the functioning of a city of the size of São Paulo, or whether they will exacerbate the adverse effects of urban compaction that are already visible in parts of the city (e.g. congestion and air pollution). The Brazilian cases highlight the difficulties involved in comparing the results of similar policies of densification when cities differ in structure, internal organisation, form, size and population.

In comparing compact city policies in Brazil and Egypt, difficulties arise from differences in urban governance and the legitimacy and autonomy of local government. The active role of municipalities in Brazil in guiding urban development processes is facilitated by their constitutional autonomy, which paves the way for sustainable urban management practices. Potentially there is an institutional, organisational and political environment conducive to policies that are socially equitable, economically efficient and environmentally sustainable. This may sustain compact city policies and assure their social acceptability, whilst simultaneously creating mechanisms to manage and mitigate their adverse effects.

In Egypt, informality in city building and urban densification are the result of social and economic forces with a dynamic that is difficult to tame. In the absence of good local governance, the environmental impacts from extremely dense urban environments – air pollution, noise, traffic congestion, health risks and lack of open public space – are exacerbated and constitute a clear threat to sustainable urban development. This is aggravated by equivocal urban policies that lose sight of the guiding and facilitating role that local governments must play. Indeed, the municipalities are currently incapable of playing this role because of their lack of capacity and autonomy. Any adequate theory of the relationship between the compact city and its adverse effects in Cairo and Giza will have to take into consideration governance, local capacities, and land and housing market instruments. The results of central government policies, geared to spatial decentralisation, indicate that there is a great need for further research into the benefits and effectiveness of spatial decentralisation as an anti-congestion remedy. A network of compact cities, inter-linked by an efficient transportation system, could become a viable alternative given Egypt's peculiar geography and the current level of compactness of the cities situated in the Nile Delta. Cultural acceptability and urban diversity do not seem to be an obstacle to achieving this.

The diversity and level of urbanity in Egypt's informal settlements seem to be a function of the viability of small-scale businesses, and the type of neighbourhood-based services and petty employment opportunities. However, there is need to investigate further the linkages between compact cities and local economic development and between social cohesion and compact cities. The inner-city neighbourhoods of Cairo show a certain degree of social cohesion, but in peripheral informal settlements, like Boulaq El-Dakrour, this is less evident.

Finally, the more entrepreneurial approaches pursued by Brazilian local governments and the experiences with TDR reveal the opportunities for public–private collaboration and partnership in compact city policy-making and implementation. Despite the world trend towards enabling the market to work and private-sector participation in city building, these experiences indicate that an empowered local government is the key to sustainable urban development.

References

Acioly, C. C. Jr., (1999) *Institutional and Urban Management Instruments for Inner City Revitalisation: A Brief Review with a Special Focus on Brazilian Experiences*, IHS Occasional Paper, Institute for Housing and Urban Development Studies – IHS, Rotterdam.

Acioly, C. C. Jr. and Davidson, F. (1996) Density in urban development. *Building Issues*, **3(8)**, Lund Centre for Habitat Studies, Lund University, Sweden.

Acioly, C. C. Jr. and Davidson, F. (1998) *Densidade Urbana e Gestão Urbana*, Mauad Editora, Rio de Janeiro, Brazil.

Barreto, J. (1997) Uma ONG para o centro. *URBS*, Ano **I**, October 1997, pp.8–13.

Camargo, M. I. (1993). Fracasso de Bilheteria, *Revista Construção*, **2371**, São Paulo. pp.8–11.

Camargo, M. I. (1994) Emenda da ruptura: disputa de competência leva operaçoes interligadas para a Justiça. *Revista Construção*, **2413**, May 1994, pp.11–13.

Corrêa Oliveira, M. T. (1999) *Partnership-Based Instruments for Urban Policy in Brazil*. IHS Occasional Paper Series no. 7, Institute for Housing and Urban Development Studies – IHS, Rotterdam.

EMURB – Empresa Municipal de Urbanização (1999a) Relatório Sept 91 – Sept 94 Operacão Urbana Anhangabaú, 2pp. Mimeo, Prefeitura Municipal de São Paulo, São Paulo.

EMURB-Empresa Municipal de Urbanização (1999b). NG Comunicado 001/99. Relatório Semestral de Acompanhamento da Operação Centro UCL, 4pp. Mimeo, Prefeitura Municipal de São Paulo, São Paulo.

Giordano, M. (1988) Over-stuffing the envelope: the problem with creative transfer of development rights, *Fordham Urban Law Journal*, **16**, pp.43–66.

Governorate of Giza and GTZ – German Technical Cooperation Agency (1995) Participatory urban upgrading Boulaq Dakrour. Draft project design report, project appraisal mission report for GTZ. Governorate of Giza, Egypt and GTZ (Deutsche Gesellschaft für Technische Zusammenarbeit).

Governorate of Giza (1998a) Giza City, environmental profile, Presentation Document, Governorate of Giza, Egypt.

Governorate of Giza (1998b) Giza City, environmental profile, Technical Document, Governorate of Giza, Egypt.

Guimarães, Paula (1998) Ancoras do capital, *URBS*, April/May 1998, pp.9–14. Associação Viva o Centro, São Paulo, Brazil.

IPPUC – Instituto de Pesquisa e Planejamento Urbano de Curitiba (1991) *Curitiba em Dados 80/90*, IPPUC, Curitiba.

IPPUC – Instituto de Pesquisa e Planejamento Urbano de Curitiba (1993) *Zoneamento e Uso do Solo*, IPPUC, Curitiba.

IPPUC – Instituto de Pesquisa e Planejamento Urbano de Curitiba (1999) *Curitiba's Planning Process: 33 Years of New Ideas*, A CDROM Presentation, IPPUC, Curitiba.

Johnston, R. A. and Madison, M. E. (1997). From Landmarks to landscapes: a review of current practices in the transfer of development rights, *American Planning Association Journal*, **63(3)**, pp.365–377.

Junior, O. (1994) Melhor do que ontem: entrevista Marco Antonio Ramos de Almeida, *Revista Construação, São Paulo*, **2407**, pp.8–10.

Klink, J. (1995) Negotiated land use changes. An advance in planning practices or a second best instrument? *Trialog*, **46**, pp.34–39.

Kolb, J. (1998) Gasping for breath, *Cairo Times*, 30 April–13 May, Cairo, Egypt.

Lerner, J. (1989) Um sistema de transporte urbano integrado, *Revista Oficial del Colegio de Arquitectos de Chile*, Oct–Dec, pp.44–51.

Longareri, T. (1997) A comunidade em aço, *URBS*, ano **I**, October 1997, pp.22–25.

MacDonald, N. (1999) Knowledge is the key, *Cairo Times*, 18 February–3 March, Cairo, Egypt.

Negus, S. (1997) Can order be imposed on Cairo's chaos? *Cairo Times*, 17–10 April, Cairo, Egypt.

PMC – Prefeitura Municipal de Curitiba (1991) *Lei Nº 781*, 19 December 1991, Prefeitura Municipal de Curitiba, Curitiba.

PMSP – Prefeitura Municipal de São Paulo (1991) *O Plano Diretor de São Paulo ao alcance de todos*, DEMPLN – Departamento Municipal de Planejamento da Secretaria Municipal de Planejamento, São Paulo.

PMSP – Prefeitura Municipal de São Paulo (1992a) Participação da Iniciativa Privada na Construção da Cidade, *Suplemento do DOM – Diario Oficial do Município de São Paulo*, **243(37)**, 24 December.

PMSP – Prefeitura Municipal de São Paulo (1992b) Infra-estrutura urbana e potencial de adensamento, *Suplemento do DOM – Diario Oficial do Município de São Paulo*, **243(37)**, 24 December.

Polis (1996) Políticas públicas para o manejo do solo urbano: experiências e possibilidades. *Anais do Seminário*, Número especial, **27**, Instituto Polis, São Paulo.

RTEC – Research Training and Experimental Center (1996) *Identifying Problems and Order of Priority for the Needs of Bolaq El-Darour Area*, A study prepared for GTZ, Cairo, Egypt.

UNCHS – United Nations Centre for Human Settlements/HABITAT (1993) *Metropolitan Planning and Management in the Developing World: Spatial Decentralisation Policy in Bombay and Cairo*, UNCHS, Nairobi.

UNDP – United Nations Development Program and SCA – Supreme Council for Antiquities (1997) *Rehabilitation of Historic Cairo*, Final Report by the Technical Cooperation Office, UNDP/SCA. Cairo.

Zaghloul, Khaled (1998) Neither a paradise nor a waste land, *Al Ahram Weekly*, 13–19 August, Cairo, Egypt.

Q. M. Mahtab-uz-Zaman and Stephen S. Y. Lau

City Expansion Policy versus Compact City Demand:
The Case of Dhaka

Introduction

Dhaka, the capital city of Bangladesh, is in a continuous process of urban expansion. This is a common phenomenon in many developing countries, where cities lose control over urban growth patterns. The need to cater for high population growth and inward migration from rural areas theoretically reinforces governmental policy towards city expansion. In support of this policy, the Dhaka Metropolitan Development Plan 1995–2015 (DMDP) proposed new urban development guidelines for development in the twenty-first century. The DMDP recommends the outward expansion of the city by encroachment on suburban and agricultural land. More roads and highways are recommended to link with the sprawling new developments, leading to a vision of a low-rise, low-density city form, with long journeys-to-work. However, this planning proposal lacks any comprehensive study of the reality of Dhaka's inner city, and fails to take account of the cost of developing infrastructure on the fringe (Rodger, 1991).

Examination of the inner-city core reveals a tendency towards high-density built form, giving close proximity between place of residence and place of work. Transportation is of a poor quality; there is insufficient provision of appropriate transport modes and inadequate infrastructure. As a result, there are questions about the built form most appropriate for Dhaka city – a future megacity with a population growth of more than 2.2% per annum (*Weekly Independent*, 1996).

At present, suburban and agricultural land is being transformed and prepared for vast new towns. However, these new towns are like ghost towns, driven by the false hope of attracting real-estate developers and buyers who may need to wait for several decades to recoup their investment on these barren lands. As Dhaka city restructures towards high-density built form through private initiatives, there appears to be an imbalance between the demand for high-density central development and the new policy for Greater Metropolitan Dhaka. Imbalance between economic transformation and institutional response seems to exist in most Asian cities (McGee and Robinson, 1995).

This chapter examines the rapid restructuring of the inner city towards high-rise high-density built form, and argues against the policy for outward growth of the city in the absence of infrastructure upgrading. It justifies a compact form for cities where there is poor infrastructure provision, and supports the underlying principle of short journeys-to-work. The issue of urban management is important in developing countries, and is discussed as an important factor if a compact city is to achieve a sustainable urban form for the future.

The city of Dhaka

Bangladesh is primarily an agrarian country and this has been reflected in its slow rate of urbanisation. It is only in the past two decades that rapid urbanisation has occurred led by a 'skill transfer' from primary sector production to secondary semi-skilled industries, which has pulled people into the cities from the low-wage agricultural sectors (Mahtab-uz-Zaman, 1999). Over the past 20 years, the country has experienced a rapid growth of urban population and the subsequent urbanisation has led to drastic urban morphological changes.

Dhaka (Fig. 1) has a population of about 9.3 million in the metropolitan region. The present area of Dhaka city is 360km^2, with a population of about 3.8 million. The metropolitan or RAJUK[1] area (Rajdhani Unnayan Kartipakha) is about 1,528km^2, and consists of the city, four municipal areas, one cantonment board, and a few urban centres and rural areas. This entire area has suffered from a process of mismanaged urban expansion.

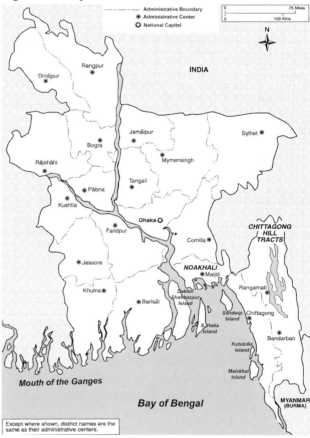

Fig. 1. Bangladesh: district boundaries and administrative centres.
Source: The Moschovitis Group, 1996.

Dhaka has been an important city since the seventh century AD. Dhaka's growth has mainly been attributed to its regional importance, or what is known as its 'Power and Authority' (Friedmann, 1975). The constant growth (Table 1) has led to the intensification of land uses and urban functions within the central city, causing stress on transport and services.

Year	Period	Approximate Area (km²)	Population	Density (per km²)
1600	Pre-Mughal	2.6	-	-
1700	Mughal Capital	12.6	900,000	7,149
1800	British Town	20.7	200,000	9,653
1867	British Town	20.7	51,600	2,491
1911	British Town	15.7	125,700	8,012
1947	Provincial Capital	31.1	250,000	8,044
1961	Provincial Capital	72.5	550,100	7,586
1971	National Capital	103.6	1,500,000	14,479
1981	National Capital	-	2,200,000	-
1991	National Capital	256	3,500,000	13,672
1998	National Capital	300	7,000,000	23,333

Table 1. Urban growth and the densification of Dhaka 1600–1998.
Source: Mohit, 1998.

Various administrations have attempted to control development and urban restructuring, but with little consistency. Changes appear to be more influenced by market forces. Virtually all land can be sold in the free market under a 99-year lease. The lease can be renewed for generations, and land can be resold and redeveloped with the permission of the Dhaka Municipality Authority and the RAJUK.

The first master plan for Dhaka

The first formal planning effort began with the preparation of the Dhaka Master Plan (DMP) in 1958 (Dhaka Metropolitan Development Planning, 1997a). It covered an area of 518km² with a population of over 1 million. The plan followed the principle of segregated and discrete land-use planning for all new development, with the provision of civic facilities and amenities. Emphasis was given to spatial planning. Urban expansion tended to be to the north of the city centre (Fig. 2), and therefore the plan predicted major urbanisation towards the northern region, with an estimated population growth of 1.75% per annum.

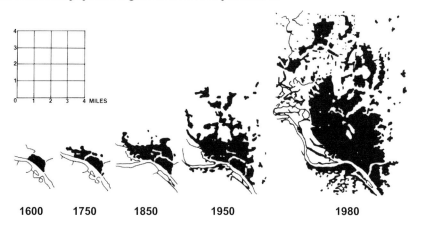

1600   1750   1850   1950   1980

Fig. 2. The urban expansion of Dhaka 1600–1998.
Source: Shankland Cox Partnership, 1981

143

An integrated urban development plan

In 1981, the Shankland Cox Partnership was commissioned by the government to prepare the Dhaka Metropolitan Area Integrated Urban Development Plan (DMAIUDP). This evolved from the serious storm water drainage and flood problems of Dhaka metropolitan area, and its purpose was to provide a long-term growth strategy for urban expansion. Three alternatives were formulated from a long list of growth options, and included: comprehensive flood protection, peripheral growth, and northward expansion. Northward expansion to accommodate an urbanised population of 9 million by 2000 was finally recommended as the most feasible of the physical and economic options. However, the plan's proposals could not be implemented because of the need for reorganisation and the consequent lack of commitment. Nevertheless, many of the assumptions of the plan proved to be accurate, and later these provided a comprehensive basis for the future urban growth of Dhaka.

Dhaka Metropolitan Development Plan

The Dhaka Metropolitan Development Plan (DMDP) of 1995 (Dhaka Metropolitan Development Planning, 1997a) was a development plan in the British 'style', which addressed planning issues at three geographic levels: sub-regional, urban, and suburban. Fig. 3 shows the proposed areas under the long-term development plan up to the year 2025. The DMDP consisted of the following three components:

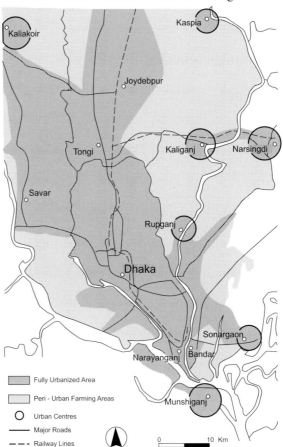

Fig. 3. Dhaka Metropolitan Development Plan 1995.
Source: Hasan, 1991.

144

- *A Structure Plan*: a long-term strategy for 20 years (until the year 2015) for the development of the metro-politan Dhaka sub-region. The plan identified the order of magnitude and direction of anticipated urban growth, and it formulated a broad set of policies to achieve the overall plan objectives.
- *An Urban Area Plan:* an interim mid-term strategy for 10 years (until the year 2005) for the development of urban areas within RAJUK's administrative area.
- *Detailed Area Plans:* more detailed planning proposals for specific sub-areas of Dhaka. The selected sub-areas were those with a high priority because of urgent problems, or in a process of rapid change.

Institutional framework

Urban planning and development management in Dhaka is fragmented and uncoordinated. There are 42 agencies belonging to 22 ministries that guide and control development of metropolitan Dhaka. On the one hand, RAJUK, the capital development authority, has both urban planning and development responsibilities for the Dhaka metropolitan area. On the other hand, citizen services are provided and maintained by Dhaka City Corporation (DCC) and other municipalities. This arrangement has led to conflicts and misunderstandings among different authorities.

Planning laws and regulation to control overall urban development

At present, the procedures for land use and development control in metropolitan Dhaka are found in:

- *The Building Construction Act of 1952,* which applies nationally. The Act requires approval for construction of buildings, excavation of tanks and cutting of hills. This Act also provides for enforcement and penalties, preparation of rules, and the designation of authorised officers.
- *The Town Improvement Act of 1953* for Metro Dhaka. This Act gave the Dhaka Improvement Trust (DIT, now RAJUK) a mandate to undertake development schemes; to provide infrastructure; to acquire, lease, sell or exchange land; to provide public transport, and to levy fees and raise loans. The Act also required the DIT to prepare a master plan, although this was not clearly defined.
- *The Dhaka Master Plan of 1959* is still the tool for judging planning applications, despite being clearly outdated, and it covers part of the current extent of the metropolis (Dhaka Metropolitan Development Planning, 1997a).
- *The Building Construction Rules 1996* have replaced earlier versions. These rules seek to control development by imposing conditions on set-back, site coverage, construction of garages and verandas, and the provision of lifts and industrial use (Mohit, 1998).

There are many other subsidiary rules through which planning and development control of metropolitan Dhaka are effected.[2]

Weak regulation and control

All the above building regulations are not particularly effective in controlling building development, since there are numerous administrative loopholes that allow much building malpractice. There is no strict control on implementing the building regulations. As the city grows with increasing demand for high-rise and high-density development, building regulations on building height have been revised several times. Despite the demand for greater building heights and denser forms of city planning, this has been neither analysed nor understood by RAJUK, the building authority.

Infrastructure policy and urban sprawl

Dhaka has a very low level of motorisation within the city, and almost half of the movement is in non-motorised human-powered vehicles. Because the majority of the city's population is low-income, and because of the poor condition of the city's transit system, the non-motorised rickshaw[3] has proved a popular mode of transport. This slow and low-capacity carrier has contributed little to urban expansion, as its slowness ensures that people commute less, and confine their journeys to locations in close proximity.

The automobile is usually a prime agent for decentralisation and it reinforces other strong pressures that lead to a more dispersed pattern of land use. However, in Dhaka, this does not seem to be the case. The ambitious plans for expansion of Dhaka city have been diluted. Despite most developers using rural areas for new town development, they appear to have little idea of its potential drawbacks. Such sprawling development has not been supported by the urban dwellers of Dhaka. The need for large-scale infrastructure provision for utilities and transportation has never been met by either the public or private sectors, and thus has left tracts of unused land on the urban fringes. Indeed, this is a common phenomenon where infrastructure provision is slow to cope with the pace of development (Rodger, 1991). As a result, urban dwellers tend to concentrate in small areas within the metropolitan area.

At present, the average journey to work takes only eleven minutes in Dhaka. Without major transport changes, most of the population will continue to live near to the source of their employment for the foreseeable future (Dhaka Metropolitan Development Planning, 1997a). The road hierarchy is poorly established, and development is taking place without any coherent plans for the road system. The DMDP predicts that, to bring a reasonable size of population into the peripheral areas of urban sprawl, it will take at least 20 years, provided there is steady economic development as well as the administrative commitment.

Urban intensification and residential area restructuring

Despite peripheral low-density development to the north of Dhaka, the preference of urban dwellers is to remain close to their work, and live, perhaps at higher densities, in the city. The poor infrastructure for services and transport helps to favour modes of travel such as the rickshaw, which in turn reinforces trends towards short travel distances, urban intensification and compact city forms. Two case studies illustrate some of the processes through which the city is developing to higher densities through urban intensification.

Case 1: Dhanmondi Residential Area – consolidation by private initiatives

The Dhanmondi Residential Area (Fig. 4) illustrates a self-regulated restructuring of residential areas towards compact and high-density development. It was the DIT's first planned residential area, of about 472.6 acres,[4] created from barren paddy fields in 1950. The average plot size was 1,296m^2, which derived from the space requirements for higher income groups[5]. Initially, more than 810 plots were allocated for residential use and the residential area was mainly inhabited by higher income groups and politicians (Fig. 4). In 1986, an average of 40% of the land was built up, with the remaining 60% left as a lake and open space. The gross density of the whole area was about 2.4 plots per acre, and most of the residential buildings were no more than two storeys high (Table 2).

Height (in Storeys)	Percentage of the Total Area (%)
Single storey	24.8
2 storeys	51.3
3 storeys	20.3
4 storeys and above	3.5

Table 2. Building heights in the Dhanmondi Residential Area (1984).
Source: Alam et al, 1986

Post-1970 transformation

After Dhaka became the capital of Bangladesh, various proposals were formulated to restructure and redistribute land ownership. At the time, building regulations were inadequate for regulating city growth. Individual landowners exploited their plot-holdings by attracting foreign institutes and private companies on short-term leases, turning many residential areas into mixed-use zones. This phenomenon appeared mostly on the edges of the residential areas due to the ease of access from highways. Figs 5 and 6 illustrate graphically the typical transformation of the residential plots into high-density mixed-use development.

The present practice of converting large plots in Dhanmondi into smaller subdivisions, and constructing taller residential buildings, was neither expected nor planned. A field survey conducted by Alam *et al.* (1986) revealed that many private owners used the front part of their residential plot either for their own private business or for other shops that served the area. Although the whole area was initially planned solely for residential use, there was a gradual transformation of its land use. By 1984, about 70% of the Dhanmondi Residential Area was in residential use, with around 30% of the area already transformed into non-residential and combined land uses (Table 3). Residential use now coexists with

Fig. 4. Dhanmondi Residential Area: present land use.
Source: Alam et al, 1986

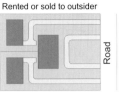

Fig. 5. Plot division.
Source: Mahtab-uz-Zaman, 1993

Plot area: 14,440sq.ft. In 1960   Divided into 3 plots in 1990

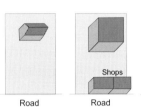
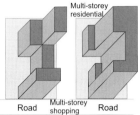

Fig. 6. Transformation in built form (from low-density to high-density mixed-use development).
Source: Mahtab-uz-Zaman, 1993

other non-residential uses in such a way as to maximise revenue on investment. The transformation of the Dhanmondi Residential Area is one of the many privately initiated exercises that are now a common scene in many parts of the city.

Type of Use	Number of Plots	Percentage (%)
Residential	*810*	*71.6*
Non-residential	*218*	*19.3*
Commercial	69	
Social Organisation	36	
Commercial/Social	1	
Educational	24	
Government Office	12	
Autonomous Organisation	35	
Political Organisation	2	
Diplomatic Office	22	
Cultural Organisation	7	
Unspecified	10	
Combined Use	*96*	*8.5*
Residential/ Commercial	64	
Residential/ Social	12	
Residential/ Education	6	
Residential/ Commercial/Social	1	
Residential/ Political	2	
Residential/ Government office	1	
Residential/ Autonomous	5	
Residential/ Diplomatic	1	
Residential/ Unspecified	4	
Vacant	*7*	*0.6*
Total	*1,418*	*100*

Table 3. Different land uses in the Dhanmondi Residential Area 1984.
Source: Alam et al., 1986

Change of building regulations in response to self-regulated transformation
The building authority (RAJUK) has revised the building regulations several times, in response to the process of self-regulated development from residential to mixed uses that Dhanmondi typifies. The revised regulations now encourage

mixed-use development. For example, all plots facing the main road (Mirpur Road, Fig. 4) will be allowed to have commercial uses with buildings up to 20 storeys high, provided a conversion fee is paid to the authority. Permission also extends to other wider roads such as the Satmasjid Road (Fig. 4) where similar mixed uses will be allowed.

Case 2: Sukrabad Residential Area – consolidation by land lease subdivision

Sukrabad is another residential area close to the Dhanmondi Residential Area, less than 1km² in area, with a population density of about 50,000 per km² (Iqbal, 1992). The successive subdivision of plots has been accelerating since 1965 (15 years after the official plot allocation). According to Iqbal (1992) the pressure of population growth and widely available housing finance were the two major reasons for the land subdivision. This phenomenon is symbiotic in nature, as subdivisions in one plot trigger adjacent plots to restructure into a higher plot ratio (Fig. 7).

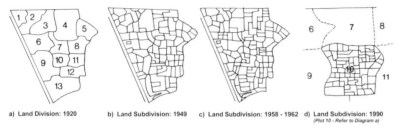

a) Land Division: 1920   b) Land Subdivision: 1949   c) Land Subdivision: 1958 - 1962   d) Land Subdivision: 1990
(Plot 10 - Refer to Diagram a)

Fig. 7. Land subdivision – towards compactness in urban fabric.
Source: Iqbal, 1992.

Determinants for the intensification of the city fabric are found mainly in land and plot subdivision, initiated by landowners. The case of Sukrabad suggests the following key factors:

- high concentration of economic activities,
- diversification of job opportunities,
- rising income levels encouraging real-estate investment, and
- changes in land use with little or no control from government.

Both the case studies demonstrate a process of intensification through privately initiated higher density development on individual plots, or through a process of successive plot subdivision. It is a process that, *de facto*, leads to a more 'compact' city form. These two cases are indicative of a process that is occurring throughout the city of Dhaka.

Real estate and high-density city forms

Real-estate activities are a common secondary economic activity in the city, and take the form of major restructuring from low- and medium-density residential areas into high-density high-rise buildings. Seraj and Alam (1991) have established that the growth of high-rise apartments (shown as black spots in Fig. 8) is due to the influx of population into the city, and the lack of buildable land within the city centre. Due to the rapid growth of the city, land value has greatly increased, and consequently raised residential prices and rents. The cost of living in Dhaka has increased fourfold during the period of 1969 to 1979, while the price of high-class residential land has increased by 25 to 35 times. For instance, the price of land in

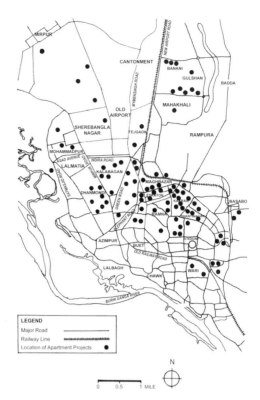

Fig. 8. High-rise residential development.
Source: Seraj and Alam, 1991.

the Dhanmondi Residential Area increased from US$14 per m² in 1974 to US$278 in 1989 (Seraj and Alam, 1991). The high land price makes economies of scale necessary, and this leads to more compact forms of high-rise development.

Conclusion

One fundamental problem of the planning and development of Dhaka lies in its institutional framework, which is fragmented, and this affects the performance of other sectors as well. The implementation of the 1995 Dhaka Metropolitan Development Plan has been handicapped because of its new type of planning approach; it requires new institutional arrangements that have not yet been implemented. Institutional reorganisation is a contentious issue, which is bound up in relationships between central and local government, and in arguments about the division of power. The fragmentation and weak controls have meant that violation of the city master plan is found even in the formal sector, for example there is malpractice in distributing plots and green land to influential individuals for development (Khan, 1998).

An active real-estate market also exerts pressure on government. Many private plots coexist with RAJUK-allocated plots, due to the land ownership system that has prevailed for several decades. This makes land readjustment for the implementation of planned development a difficult task. The market also means that environmental criteria usually have the lowest priority in development. For example, the Urban Area Development Plan (DMDP, 1997b) recommends adequate measures to prevent the filling-up and reduction of one of Dhaka's important open spaces, the Gulshan Lake,[6] to create new residential plots. Yet RAJUK is under considerable pressure to fill it up, and its shortfall of manpower for development control, and inability to update its plans, have resulted in lakeside plots being allocated to influential individuals.

Transportation and infrastructure are two major areas which suffer in Dhaka. The city has about 436km of primary roads, 1,207km of secondary roads, and 324km of lanes (*Weekly Independent*, 1996). There are about 300,000 rickshaws plying the city's roads. The planning goal of reducing the journey-to-work trips and distances by bringing employment nearer to the place of residence is a challenge. To achieve this, it is necessary to change the direction of transport planning towards mass transit provision. But before this can be achieved, the present growth pattern for high-rise, high-density compact development should be allowed, albeit with stricter control through building regulations. Quium (1994) identified the integration of the non-motorised transport system with the motorised transport system as the means to enhance mobility of people within a compact city form. However, an integrated planning strategy for the whole metropolitan area with proper traffic management would be needed. The non-motorised transport system will greatly reduce localised pollution, if it is coherently distributed through effective land-use planning aimed at sustainable urban development. Mixed land use, with compact urban development, which is currently the emerging pattern, should be encouraged as a means to reduce journey-to-work trips and the traffic-related environmental problems (Nijkamp and Rienstra, 1996; McLaren, 1992; Rickaby, 1987).

The experience of Dhaka suggests that there is a long way to go to achieve a compact city that embraces environmental considerations and sustainability. It is clear that through unregulated activity in the real-estate market a process of intensification is taking place. It is also apparent that the existing controls and regulations are too weak, and are overwhelmed by the pressures for development and population growth. The lack of infrastructure, and particularly of public transport, means that there is a reliance on non-motorised transport with limited range and capacity. All these have encouraged an increasingly compact city, but it is one that may be over-crowded, unplanned and environmentally unfriendly. At the same time as the city is intensifying, the growth on the periphery, through lack of infrastructure, is not prospering. For it to succeed, the development of polycentric urban nodes could be one of the long-term sustainable planning strategies for Dhaka City. This would, however, depend on well-developed transport infrastructure and efficient mass transit systems. This scenario is equally suitable for other developing countries that are striving to achieve a sustainable urban environment.

Notes

1. RAJUK: Rajdhani Unnayan Kartipakha is a government body responsible for regulating building development and overall urban growth, and formerly was the Dhaka Improvement Trust (DIT).
2. Other planning and development control rules include: Private Housing Approval Rules and Standards of 1991 (TI Act section 102(1)); Acquisition and Requisition of Immovable Property (Amendment) Act, 1994 (ACT No. XX of 1994); Dhaka City Corporation Ordinance, 1988; Bangladesh National Building Code, 1993; and Dhaka Metropolitan Development Planning, 1997b.
3. It is a man-powered or manual public transport mode.
4. 472.6 acres is equivalent to 1.913 million m² (1 acre = 4,047 square metres).
5. The basis of this derivation is unknown. However, this reflects the per capita space needs in Dhaka, which in turn reflects the lack of constraints on developing land.
6. Gulshan is a northern part of Dhaka City, and has a foreign consulate enclave, as well as housing for higher-income groups and government officials.

References

Alam, K. N., Karim, M. R. and Ullah, M. S. (1986) Residential scheme for high and middle income groups in Dhaka City, Bangladesh, Paper presented at the World Congress on Land Policy, July 1986, London.

Dhaka Metropolitan Development Planning (1997a) *Dhaka Metropolitan Development Plan (1995–2015): Dhaka Structure Plan (1995–2015)*, Dhaka Metropolitan Development Planning (DMDP) and Rajdhani Unnayan Kartipakha (RAJUK), Government of the People's Republic of Bangladesh, Dhaka.

Dhaka Metropolitan Development Planning (1997b) *Dhaka Metropolitan Development Plan (1995–2015): Urban Area Plan (1995–2015)*, Dhaka Metropolitan Development Planning (DMDP) and Rajdhani Unnayan Kartipakha (RAJUK), Government of the People's Republic of Bangladesh, Dhaka.

Friedmann, J. (1975) The spatial organization of power in the development of urban systems, in *Regional Policy – Readings in Theory and Applications* (eds J. Friedmann and W. Alonso), MIT Press, New York.

Hasan, S. R. (1991) Historical Dhaka: a market for tourism, in *Dhaka – Past Present Future* (ed. S. U. Ahmed), The Asiatic Society of Bangladesh, Dhaka.

Iqbal, M. (1992) A geographical analysis of residential land subdivision and resubdivision processes in Dhaka city: a case study of Sukrabad, *Bangladesh Urban Studies*, **1(1)**, pp.89–100.

Khan, M. A. (1998) Rajuk 'secretly' allotting plots to high-ups, *Daily Star*, 30 April, Dhaka, Bangladesh.

McGee, T. G. and Robinson, I. M. (1995) ASEAN mega-urbanization: a synthesis, in *The Mega-Urban Regions of Southeast Asia* (eds T. G. McGee and I. M. Robinson), University of British Columbia Press, Vancouver, Canada.

McLaren, D. (1992) Compact or dispersed? Dilution is no solution, *Built Environment*, **18(4)**, pp.268–284.

Mahtab-uz-Zaman, Q. M. (1993) Consolidation as a response to urban growth – a case in Dhaka, unpublished Master of Urban Design Dissertation, The University of Hong Kong, Hong Kong.

Mahtab-uz-Zaman, Q. M. (1999) Accumulated negligence, *Daily Star*, 4 September, Dhaka, Bangladesh.

Mohit, M. A. (1998) Dhaka – planning and development problems, unpublished Paper, Urban and Rural Planning, Bangladesh University of Engineering and Technology, Dhaka.

The Moschovitis Group (1996) Asia on file, Facts on File, New York.

Nijkamp, P. and Rienstra, S. A. (1996) Sustainable transport in a compact city, in *The Compact City: A Sustainable Urban Form?* (eds M. Jenks, E. Burton and K. Williams), E & FN Spon, London.

Quium, A. S. M. A. (1994) Integration of motorized and non-motorized transport modes: an alternative strategy for creating a sustainable urban transport system for Dhaka, Bangladesh, *Proceedings of the International Seminar on Urban Development, Transport and Environment*, 4–8 June, United Nations Centre for Regional Development, Sagamihara, Japan.

Rickaby, P. A. (1987) Six settlement patterns compared, *Environment and Planning B: Planning and Design*, **14**, pp.192–223.

Rodger, A. (1991) Urban consolidation in the context of sustainable development, *Urban Consolidation – Myths and Realities*, Proceedings of Division Annual Conference Seminar held at Belmont, WA, 6–7 June, Australian Institute of Urban Studies, Australia, pp.120–132.

Seraj, T. M. and Alam, M. S. (1991) Housing problem and apartment development in Dhaka city, in *Dhaka - Past Present Future* (ed. S. U. Ahmed), The Asiatic Society of Bangladesh, Dhaka.

Shankland Cox Partnership (1981), Dhaka Metropolitan Area integrated urban development project, Report for the Government of Bangladesh, Bangladesh.

Weekly Independent (1996) Dhaka City and Bangladesh statistics – a source: Dhaka City Corporation (DCC), 9 February.

Ashok Kumar
The Inverted Compact City of Delhi

Introduction: urbanisation and compaction

The compact city offers various claimed benefits (Elkin *et al.*, 1991). First, the high intensity of development reduces geographical spread and thus permits consumption of less land and other resources. Second, the planned higher residential densities offer opportunities for accommodating more people on the same land area and also contribute to greater social interaction. Third, average journey trips become shorter, leading to lower fuel consumption and lower harmful emissions. This makes compact cities more energy efficient (McLaren, 1992; Hillman, 1996). Fourth, governments are able to provide basic services more efficiently as transmission wastes are minimised. Ultimately, the compact city planning approach can contribute to the attainment of sustainable cities (Jenks *et al.*, 1996).

This chapter demonstrates that the city of Delhi does not enjoy any of these benefits. One reason is that its form is the opposite of that of the compact city, i.e. it is an inverted compact city, which has low gross residential densities in the inner areas and high gross densities in the outer areas. Gross densities are at least four times higher in outer areas than in the inner city. Intensity of development is also low. For instance, there are single- or double-storey residential buildings in most of its inner-city areas, whilst four- to eight-storey residential buildings are quite common in the outer areas. Sometimes these outer areas lie outside the urban area boundary. High-rise residential apartments in the southern parts of Delhi are one such example.

How did this urban form happen? It can be explained by looking at the political events of the first decade of the twentieth century, which led to the unique process of urbanisation of the city of Delhi. At this time a statement of imperial grandeur, order and authority was made through the construction of New Delhi. Vast low-density residential areas were developed in New Delhi when the British Government of India constructed its new capital. Lutyens' Delhi was planned to contain merely 140 bungalows (Mehra, 1999). No bungalow would rise above a single storey in the heart of the city (King, 1976). Furthermore, large spaces are occupied by even less dense land uses, such as Second World War military barracks now used as central government offices, and low-rise commercial areas, such as Connaught Place, which occasionally rise up to two storeys high.

The process of urbanisation in India, including Delhi, took on another characteristic after the country became independent in 1947. Over the last 50 years the free movement of people in a democratic context has resulted in an accelerated rate of rural to urban migration, primarily the result of the search for employment. Rural to urban migration contributed about 30% to urban growth between 1981 and 1991 in India (Visaria, 1997). However, this figure was more than 50 per cent for the four Indian megacities (United Nations, 1986a; 1986b; 1987). It is estimated that on average 1,000 people migrated to Delhi every day between 1981 and 1991 (Kumar, 1996). Consequently, the squatter population increased from 493,545 in 1981 to 1,296,720 in 1991, almost 263% growth in a decade (Singh, 1999). As most of these people did not have jobs, they could not afford to buy a house. In the desperate search for survival, migrants squatted on whatever land came their way. Having repeated this process year after year, cities have become crowded with squatters and littered with slums. The squatters, particularly, have built low-rise and less compact residential developments in various parts of the city. Most of these settlements contain thatched huts (*jhuggies*). In fact, unauthorised residential developments have slowed down the compact character of the megacities.

Another feature of Indian urbanisation is the illegal sub-division of undeveloped land into residential plots. These kinds of development act as attachments to planned urban areas where vacant undeveloped land is divided into plots and sold to individuals, who in turn construct medium to high-rise buildings. As these developments are neither planned nor authorised, infrastructure is provided at a later stage, leading to the interim use of rudimentary techniques for the provision of infrastructure and the inefficient use of energy. Thus intense development leads to slum-like development, rather than beneficial compact development, as the high intensity of development does not lead to the optimum use of social and physical infrastructure (Kumar, 1999).

The compact city policies of the Delhi government

Compact city policy became part of Delhi's city planning in 1990 when the Delhi Development Authority (DDA) made various proposals, including the densification of the existing built form, in the modified master plan. Total land requirement by 2001 was estimated to be a maximum of 24,000 hectares. The DDA formulated five major strategies to achieve this target.

First, it contended that additional land for residential purposes would have to be found beyond the existing city structure. Accordingly, it expanded the Delhi Urban Area (1981) with an additional 4,000 hectares of land for residential purposes.

Second, it proposed that another 14,000 hectares of land required would be met through the densification of the census towns[1] of Najafgarh, Nangloi, Bawana and Alipur, and the construction of the new township of Narela. Planning and design work on Narela Township has been finished and implementation has begun in earnest. However, no intensification mechanisms have been devised for densification in the census towns.

Third, it was argued that developed urban land would always remain limited when compared with the requirements of the exploding population's housing and other land-related needs. The DDA thus proposed that the remaining land requirement of 6,000 hectares would be met by increasing what it called the 'holding capacity' of the Delhi Urban Area of 1981 (Government of India, 1990). This meant that the DDA had inadvertently given the go-ahead to property owners selectively to increase densities by intensification without securing planning permissions. The public knew that the DDA would subsequently legalise these illegal developments. With hindsight, the public got it right.

Fourth, the DDA proposed that in future it would primarily encourage group housing rather than plot development, in order to accommodate more households on the same amount of land. To some extent this policy has been pursued successfully. It is expected that 350–400 persons per hectare gross density will be achieved (Government of India, 1990).

The fifth policy was popularly known as the 'containment policy'. The DDA argued that it would strive to create self-contained planning divisions. It was expected that people would not need to make inter-division trips for a majority of purposes including, work, education, leisure and recreation.

A further step was taken in the direction of the compact city when a commission, popularly known as the Malhotra Committee, recently submitted a report to the government. One of the main recommendations of the Committee was that individual owners of plots should be allowed to construct three-storey residential buildings instead of the previous provision of two and a half-storey development, and four-storey residential buildings instead of the previous provision of three and a half-storey development (Government of the National Capital Territory of Delhi, 1997). Most of the Committee's recommendations have been accepted by central government and are awaiting the approval of the President of India. But this policy, in effect, only legalised what had already taken place, and the policy was nothing more than a reaction that legitimated planning violations.

The Prime Minister (Atal Behari Vajpayee) recently became the most ardent supporter of the compact city planning approach when in 1998 he argued in the media for a densification of the New Delhi Municipal Council (NDMC) area. He noted that 'the Lutyens' Bungalow Zone could not continue to exist without basic change in a city where space and affordable housing are scarce' (Mehra, 1999, p.56). The Prime Minister's comments immediately led to the establishment of the M. N. Buch Committee. This Committee has recently submitted its report to the central Ministry of Urban Development (Ministry of Urban Affairs and Employment, 1999). The report argued that densification of Lutyens' Delhi should not be carried out for a number of reasons. First, no matter what type of intense development is carried out, it will not substantially contribute to Delhi's housing supply. Second, densification would eat away all the green spaces that the city has. Third, since Lutyens' Delhi occupies a strategic location, it would create housing for the rich and elite only, and would not benefit the poor who require most housing. Fourth, permission to build residential flats and apartments would benefit only speculative property dealers and builders, who would be able to earn enormous profits.

Nevertheless, the Committee's findings can be faulted on many counts. First, the Prime Minister's comments should not be taken literally. The basic idea that the Prime Minister conveyed was that intensification of the Lutyens' Bungalow Zone is necessary because of the scarcity of prime developed urban land. Why should residential development led by the private sector be considered as the only possibility? Why not other alternative forms of development such as mixed land use or commercial development? Why have partnerships, or even government-led urban development, been ruled out? It is not entirely out of the question to consider residential development for politicians and bureaucrats in this place, which is so near to Parliament House. This would indirectly help the general public, as it would reduce road blockages resulting from the motorcades carrying politicians from the outer areas to Parliament House. Eating away the green spaces is not an issue, as only the intensification of the existing built areas is being considered.

In the second half of 1999 the DDA concluded a design competition. The entries selected for implementation in three proposed residential sites, at Tehkhand, Dwarka and Vasant Kunj, are path-breaking. The DDA seems to have accepted the idea of multi-storey housing complexes, which will include the use of state-of-the-art technologies to provide some of the basic facilities in common areas at each floor. The DDA expects that this change in design will minimise the need to make frequent outdoor (other-floor) trips by people living on higher floors. The acceptance of these design ideas should gather further support for high-rise living concepts. At present, preparations are underway to put together the new master plan for the city for 2021. In a seminar held in the middle of October 1999, the DDA once again committed itself to high-rise residential development.

Overall, compact city policies have been reactive. While the creation of two sub-cities (Dwarka and Rohini) could be counted as a success, in general compact city policies have lagged behind actual developments. However, it is also expected that the Malhotra Committee recommendations will further encourage the process of illegal compaction beyond three and half-storey residential development. This is contrary to the spirit of compact city development: a coherently thought-out city structure based on higher densities and the efficient use of energy, land and other resources. The only hope for the compact city planning approach lies in the fact that DDA continues to support strongly the idea of high-rise, high-quality life in the city.

Densities in Delhi

Densities in Delhi increase with distance from the central area and continue to do so even at the urban fringes (Fig. 1). The area covered by the New Delhi Municipal Council (NDMC) has one of lowest densities, at 50 to 100 persons per hectare. Even lower densities, less than 25 persons per hectare, are found in the Delhi Cantonment area (see Table 1). New Delhi was created by Edwin Landseer Lutyens as a huge single-storey 'bungalow zone' to house the British civil servants. After Indian independence, Indian politicians and senior civil servants continued to occupy these spaces. Change to this built form was thought to be 'anti-aesthetic'.

Table 1. Gross densities in urban Delhi, 1991.
Source: Government of India (1991, pp.282–292); Government of the National Capital Territory of Delhi (1996, p.3).

Name of the Area	Population, 1991	Area, 1991 (ha)	Density (pph)
NCT* Urban	8,471,625	68,534	124
NCT Rural	949,019	79,766	12
NCT Total	9,420,644	148,300	64
New Delhi Municipal Council	301,297	4,274	71
Delhi Cantonment	94,393	4,297	22
Delhi Municipal Corporation	7,206,704	43,109	167

* NCT (National Capital Territory of Delhi)

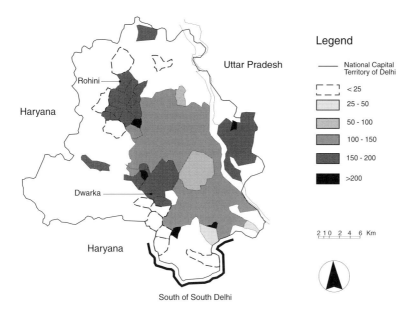

Fig. 1. Gross densities in urban Delhi, 1991.

The Delhi Cantonment was exclusively created as a secluded area for the military. A major part of the Cantonment contains low-rise development, and huge plots, similar to those in the NDMC area, house senior military officers. A large area of land is used for the golf course and other recreational activities. An equally large area has been left vacant for future residential development, and at present is used to grow vegetables and grain. However, about one-fifth of the Cantonment area has moderately intense development consisting of three- to four-storey apartments. Because of these uses, Delhi Cantonment area shows the lowest gross densities. In the early parts of this century this area was located outside urban Delhi, but the subsequent rapid expansion of urban Delhi has encompassed both the Cantonment and the NDMC area within central Delhi. Lower densities are also to be found to the west of the Cantonment area, where high-value land is put to extensive land use in the form of the central prison, the Tihar Jail. To the southeast and east of the Cantonment area, there are a few villages with a very low density, sometimes even less than one person per hectare (Government of India, 1991).

Delhi Municipal Corporation (DMC) has slightly higher densities, ranging between 100 and 150 persons per hectare. This is because this area contains some of most densely populated areas such as Old Delhi and Karol Bagh, with densities as high as 900 persons per hectare. But lower densities in other parts of the DMC area moderate this extra ordinarily high density. On the other hand, outer areas in southwestern and northern parts of the DMC show densities as high as 150–200 persons per hectare.

High densities are also to be found on the periphery of urban Delhi. They include the census towns of Tigri, Babar Pur, Nasir Pur, Sultanpur Majra, and Sultan Pur (see Table 2). Although only low-rise development was initially permitted in these areas, over time people violated the building by-laws in order to accommodate more and more people on the same land area. Today these areas are characterised by intense development.

Name of the Area	Population, 1991	Area, 1991 (ha)	Density (pph)
Alipur Development Block			
Alipur	9,256	855	10.83
Pooth Khurd	8,293	998	8.31
Pehlad Pur Banger	4,832	467	10.35
Bhalswa Jahangirpur	95,065	670	141.89
Kanjhawala Development Block			
Bawana	18,999	1,697	11.20
Kanjhawala	6,100	894	6.82
Mundka	17,380	1,189	14.62
Sultan Pur Majra	111,567	277	402.77
Nangloi Jat	76,063	667	114.04
Najafgarh Development Block			
Roshan Pura	13,870	276	50.25
Binda Pur	36,148	249	145.17
Nasir Pur	81,366	285	285.49
Palam	11,766	849	13.86
Mehrauli Development Block			
Asola	5,061	1,195	4.24
Nangal Dewat	7,657	720	10.63
Malik Pur Kohi	3,251	750	4.33
Rajokri	11,766	864	13.62
Ghitorni	6,254	427	14.65
Yahya Nagar	4,405	822	5.36
Sultan Pur	8,365	286	29.25
Tigri	34,416	105	327.77
Deoli	33,214	1,012	32.82
Pul Pehlad	14,343	216	66.40
Taj Pul	5,882	122	48.21
Molar Band	19,629	412	47.64
Shahdara Development Block			
Gokal Pur	49,186	232	212.01
Babar Pur	47,451	79	600.65
Jaffarabad	17,492	90	194.36
Patpar Ganj	22,945	149	153.99

Table 2. Gross densities in census towns of Delhi, 1991.
Source: Government of India (1991, pp.282–292); Government of the National Capital Territory of Delhi (1996, p.3).

The Delhi Development Authority in some of the eastern Delhi areas planned higher densities. Patparganj, with densities in the range of 150 to 200 persons per hectare, is the prime example of this type of development. Of the development blocks, Shahdara Development Block has the highest density of around 600 persons per hectare. All the census towns of this area have densities of more than 150 persons per hectare, most of which is caused by unplanned development.

More than 10 census towns show the lowest densities – with less than 25 persons per hectare. This is because they were only recently recognised (in the 1991 census) as urban settlements (see Table 2). These settlements are likely to become intensely developed, and could house many more people in same area. The acquisition of urban status means more funds for infrastructure and development, and multiplier effects bring about intense development and higher population densities.

Emerging density patterns
The density patterns of Delhi emerged as a result of the interplay of planning policies and various other political, social and economic factors. These are discussed below.

Planned low-rise Imperial developments

The lowest population densities and low-intensity residential developments can be found in Lutyens' New Delhi, Delhi Development Authority areas in southern Delhi such as Green Park, and in Model Town in the eastern parts of Delhi.

The Imperial town planning movement, which gave birth to New Delhi, Model Town and Civil Lines, advocated low-rise orderly development, with large plot sizes and single-storey buildings, with a maximum ground coverage of as little as 25% of the entire plot area. Lutyens' Delhi is located adjacent to the low-rise planned commercial centre of Connaught Place. In complete contrast to theories that highly accessible areas are densely built and used primarily for commercial purposes, New Delhi is primarily residential, with some sectors having low-rise commercial and office buildings. Model Town and Civil Lines are also relatively centrally located, not more than 8km from the city centre.

Planned high-rise developments

Dwarka, Rohini and Narela in the southwest and west of Delhi have been planned to accommodate higher gross densities. Since the late 1970s, the Delhi Development Authority has justifiably felt that Delhi has no more land to accommodate the exploding population, and maintains that densification can resolve the problem of scarcity of developed urban land. Dwarka is particularly important because it is planned to accommodate 1 million people on 5,645 hectares of land – a gross density of 177 persons per hectare. The DDA has cautiously decided that the private co-operative housing societies, various government and other organisations, and the DDA itself will build housing in Dwarka in the form of high-rise apartments. As much as half of the net residential area will be developed by co-operative group housing societies (Office of the Commissioner of Planning, 1992). Most co-operative group housing is built as high as six to ten storeys. Plot development will be negligible, with only 38 hectares of land earmarked for residential plots. Private-sector development in the neighbouring states of Haryana and Uttar Pradesh have further reinforced the trend for increasing densities and high-rise developments even beyond the administrative boundaries of the National Capital Territory of Delhi (NCT Delhi). Housing in Gurgoan in Haryana and Gaziabad in Uttar Pradesh is provided in the form of 18- to 20-storey-high apartment blocks.

Illegal high-rise developments

The new phenomenon of illegal high-rise developments on legally allotted plots has recently been observed. Private builders have generated a great demand for residential plots of between 165 and 420m². What has happened is quite innovative. An agreement is struck between the owner of the plot and the builder to intensify the development on a plot where low-rise residential development generally already exists. Despite regulations limiting development to three and a half storeys high, or 12.5m, builders construct up to four or more storeys. The plot owner does not pay any money to the builder. The builder gets one floor in exchange for constructing three to four floors for the owner. This process of illegal apartment building has generated additional dwelling units for the growing middle class of Delhi. This phenomenon is by no means sporadic, and can be found over all plotted developments in Delhi.

Unplanned high-rise urban villages
Delhi has 369 villages, 170 of which have been incorporated into the urban area (Curtis, 1998). The total population of all urban villages is 600,000, with an area of 1,500 hectares. This makes the gross density of population 400 persons per hectare, which is closer to the higher densities found in Old Delhi, rather than those of New Delhi. Villages have higher densities because no planning controls have ever been formulated and implemented in these areas. People have built as high as they could and use has been targeted at those activities which were most profitable. Planned development was never more than a ground floor plus one in the resettlement colonies, but over time these areas have also become on average a ground floor plus five storeys.

High-rise flatted developments
Since local planning authorities have failed to provide adequate housing in Delhi, people have adopted their own ingenious intensification methods. As families expanded and split into separate households, most people living in flats added one or two more rooms to their existing flats by covering whatever open spaces were provided in the front and rear of the apartment blocks. In the case of plot development, the majority of owners have exceeded the permitted two and a half-storey development within the given height of 12.5m. Those who violated these planning norms have built up to at least three and a half storeys high. In the 1990s the government set up a committee to investigate the matter and recommend appropriate changes in the building by-laws. Almost all members of the committee and its various sub-committees came from 'urban landed aristocracy'. Therefore it was not surprising when this committee accepted the violations without any penal action, and recommended others to build three and a half storeys high. This committee, however, did not look into development in the New Delhi Municipal Council area, which primarily houses Lutyens' Bungalow Zone.

Low-rise squatter settlements
There are 1,100 squatter settlements in Delhi, which are more or less evenly distributed over the city. Notable examples of squatter clusters are the Katputli Colony in western Delhi, and the Kalkaji squatter settlement in southern Delhi. With increasing distance from the central area of the city, the number of squatter clusters significantly declines. All squatter settlements are characterised by low-rise development, as *jhuggies* and other precarious structures cannot be erected at more than a single storey. In spite of the fact that the population has large household sizes, densities are quite low. It was estimated that a total 1,609,609 people lived in squatter settlements in 1997 on an area of 74,800 hectares (Singh, 1999, p.12), giving a gross density of 22 persons per hectare.

High-rise slums
In 1989 the Delhi Municipal Corporation recognised 22 notified slums. They covered an area of 1,966 hectares and had a population of 1,800,000, giving a gross density of 900 persons per hectare, the highest anywhere in the city (Government of India, 1991). These notified slums accommodated 21% of Delhi's total population.

Unplanned development on undeveloped land

As the city expanded, rural areas were incorporated in the DMC area. Before the authorities could act, farmers subdivided agricultural land into plots of varying sizes and sold them at cheap rates to poor people. Since no development work was undertaken to provide on-site services, the lower prices attracted those who could not afford developed urban land. However, the process allowed for the provision of services such as water, sewerage, drainage, and solid waste collection at a later date when the development has already taken place. This process has proved a hindrance to the implementation of more compact development in the city.

The characteristics of the inverted compact city

From all this it is clear that Delhi is not a compact city; it has few pockets of high density and intense development. Urban Delhi is spread over an area of 68,534 hectares and accommodates only 8,471,625 (Government of India, 1991). Its gross residential density comes to a little more than 123 persons per hectare, yet it still suffers from all the ills of urban sprawl including the wasteful use of energy, resources and time.

Travel characteristics

Delhi has 2,245,681 vehicles, including 1,467,182 motorcycles and scooters (Government of the National Capital Territory of Delhi, 1995), which is equal to the total number of vehicles found in Mumbai, Calcutta and Chennai. As vehicle ownership has increased, people have tended to live further away from the city centre and to make longer and more frequent trips, creating many problems.

To begin with, the average trip length in Delhi has increased over time. The average trip length, which was 5.4km in 1970, had increased to 8.5km in 1993 (Table 3). It has been noted that people wanting to travel from Delhi can take as much time to travel from the airport to the central business district as to fly from Delhi to Mumbai (D'Monte, 1999). The problem is further compounded by the fact that average trip length by public transport buses has more than doubled from 6.2km in 1971–72 to 14km in 1988–89 (Sahoo, 1995). More than half the commuters who still use buses from home to work now make longer trips.

Name of the City	Trip Length (Kilometres)	Travel Time (Minutes)	Travel Speed (Minutes/kilometre)
Delhi	08.50	44.34	5.10
Mumbai (Bombay)	12.40	33.37	2.70
Chennai (Madras)	07.30	21.62	3.00
Bangalore	06.70	17.60	3.30

Table 3. Travel characteristics of the major metropolitan cities, 1993. Source: National Steering Committee: India (1996, p.48).

The large number and variety of vehicles as well as narrow roads have caused extreme congestion leading to long en-route delays. Average travel time in Delhi was 30 minutes in 1985 but had increased to three-quarters of an hour in 1993. Thus Delhi's commuters spent almost double the amount of time on the road to travel a kilometre than in other megacities. Furthermore, as a result of the increased number of vehicles and almost the same length of roads as in 1985, journey speeds have come down. The future is not very promising. It is expected that the average vehicle speed on the roads of Delhi will be reduced to 5km per hour in the next decade (Chakraborty, 1999). This clearly suggests that average trip length and travel time must be reduced. Among the various options, one is to reduce the need to make longer trips, particularly for work. A compact city, with high-density mixed land use, could reduce the need to make longer trips.

Geographical size
Delhi has grown in terms of both its geographical extent and its population (see Table 4). Between 1951 and 1991, Delhi's area increased by more than three and half times while its population grew by eight times. As a result, densities have increased considerably. Urban Delhi's extremely low gross density of 73 persons per hectare in 1951 rose to 124 persons per hectare by 1991. While the city's area increased more than three times between 1951 and 1991, the average trip length doubled between 1970 and 1993. This shows that there is a direct and positive relationship between the geographical area and the average trip length. The larger the geographical area, the longer the average trip length.

Table 4. Delhi's urban population, area and density, 1951–91.
Source: Government of India (1991)

Year	Population	Area (ha)	Density (pph)
1951	1,437,134	19,600	73.32
1961	2,359,408	32,600	72.37
1971	3,647,023	44,600	81.77
1981	5,770,000	59,200	97.47
1991	8,471,625	68,534	123.61

Note: pph stands for persons per hectare.

Furthermore, as the geographical area of Delhi has increased, it has also led to ever-longer networks of physical infrastructure and greater wastage of precious resources such as water and power. The current rates of wastage of water and power seriously challenge the sustainability of the city. For example, power transmission losses in Delhi rose to an unprecedented 50.2% in January 1996. These far exceeded the 7% maximum transmission losses permitted by the Central Electricity Authority for intra-city distribution (Raj, 1996).

The difficulty of saving energy is one outcome of urban sprawl over a large geographical area. Energy savings may have been negligible in the case of cities in the developed world; but these savings could be substantial in the cities of developing countries if existing trip lengths were shortened. If a majority of trips in Delhi could be restricted to within planning divisions, the average trip length could be reduced from the existing 8.5km to 5km. This would result in the reduction of average travel time from 45 to 25 minutes.

Energy consumption and containment
Vehicular traffic is the largest energy consumer in the metropolis. In order to use energy efficiently, the DDA has advocated a policy of containment at the planning division level. 'Thus the Plan's objective ... has been to provide efficient land use and transportation relationships so as to effectuate containment within the divisions, in order to reduce work and education trips by vehicular modes' (Government of India, 1990, p.146).

To achieve the goal of containment at the planning division level, the DDA divided Delhi into 15 planning divisions. Urban Delhi was divided into eight and Rural Delhi into seven (National Institute of Urban Affairs, 1994). While the policy-makers wanted to create a multi-nodal city organised around commercial district centres as major employment areas, the DDA has not implemented many of these important projects. Out of 15 proposed commercial district centres, only three have been completed so far. This has led to more passenger and vehicular trips from other divisions to those which have commercial district centres. Similarly, the policy of dispersal of those offices which generate a large number of inter-division trips has failed to take off.

After 30 years of dithering, the Ministry of Surface Transport of the Government of India has started construction work on the first phase of a rapid mass transit system. This will be a good starting point for an efficient public transport system. The government expects that the mass rapid transit system will help to reduce the energy consumed by vehicles, because it will consume only 10% of that consumed by individual transport modes. While national and state governments officially stress the significance of public transport to save energy, and thereby reduce harmful emissions, their actions seem to achieve exactly the opposite. One recent example has been the doubling of bus fares by the state government after a 30% increase in diesel prices by the central government. The issue of energy savings is therefore much more complex than just reducing the number of vehicles on the roads and minimising trip lengths. It must also include efficient transport technologies and fuel pricing policies.

Not a matter of preference

In the cities of most of the developing countries, including India, the issue is not whether people want to live in houses constructed on plots or in apartments. The issue rather is that people want to live in a house at an affordable cost, no matter whether it is a detached or semi-detached house, or an apartment in a high-rise residential block. India, or for that matter Delhi, is no different. According to the National Building Organisation, urban India alone had a massive housing shortage of 9.6 million dwelling units in 1991 (quoted in Visaria, 1997, p.280). Likewise, Delhi has a housing shortage of 300,000 dwelling units, which means 1.5 million people do not have a house to live in (Government of India, 1990; Central Statistical Organisation, 1998). Others have calculated the housing shortage in Delhi at 825,000 dwelling units for 1997 (Gupta, 1995). In this situation it is obvious that people would be likely to move to any kind of dwelling unit.

Most of the flatted development constructed and offered by the DDA is fully occupied. Even these properties command a high price. As developed land in Delhi has become increasingly scarce, the private sector has provided a large number of high-rise apartments for the middle classes in and around Delhi. Entire blocks of apartments are sold out even before construction is completed. Clearly in Delhi's housing market there is a segment of the population that prefers high-rise housing because the alternative is no housing at all.

Quality of life

Few could dispute that the quality of life needs to be improved in the cities of developing countries. In Delhi, the significant quality of life issues include pollution

163

levels and safety levels, particularly in terms of crime. Delhi is the fourth most polluted city in the world. Most recent estimates reveal that 'at current air pollution levels, one person dies every hour in Delhi because of respiratory and other pollution-related diseases' (Narain, 1999, p.9). The primary reason for respiratory diseases is the pollution created by vehicle emissions. Therefore, every possible step should be taken to reduce this unacceptable pollution. The reduction in the need to travel, or the reduction in the need to make longer trips in the city, would greatly contribute to lowering emissions and thus pollution levels.

Delhi has also become one of the most unsafe cities in Asia. The number of crimes and the crime rates have gone up considerably. A total of 30,441 crimes were reported in 1997. This number increased to 35,101 in 1998, an increase of 11% (Sharma, 1998). One reason is that the proportionally smaller number of police officers who have to police a larger area and population reduces their effectiveness in combating and controlling crime.

It is clear that the quality of life could hardly get worse than that experienced by the residents of the slums and squatter settlements of Delhi and other cities in the developing countries. The dignity of these people has been stolen in a context of floating human and animal excreta in open drains that contaminate drinking water, and piles of solid wastes breeding flies that cause death and disease. If the effort is made, the quality of life can only improve. Therefore, the central quality of life issue is the provision of housing and physical and social infrastructure. The quality of goods and services is a secondary issue at the moment.

Conclusions: some guidelines for the future

This chapter has argued that urban Delhi is an inverted compact city. A policy of 'decentralised concentration' was pursued by the DDA only halfheartedly and led to no major gains. But many policy initiatives can be taken to contain urban sprawl and to bring compaction to the city of Delhi.

First, it should be accepted that the compact city planning approach is not merely about attaining high population densities and high-intensity development. It is also about attaining a higher quality of life for its present and future residents. Alexander Maller calls it *structured accidentalness*: 'a congested, livable urban environment' (Maller, 1999, p.131). This is significant because unplanned settlements, like slums, can also achieve higher densities and intensities of development, but could merely lead to undesirable congestion. To make compact city policy operative, high-rise private-sector development could be permitted only in planned residential areas. This could lead to the intensification of the existing built form as desired for the compact city. But it could be done only to a certain extent, because existing networks, particularly of physical infrastructure, would not be able to support a population beyond a certain limit.

Second, the focus of the compact city planning approach will have to be firmly on the urban poor as they form the single largest group, and their needs have been largely neglected. In order to be successful in providing housing and the most basic services to the urban poor, the compact city will have to pass the test of being affordable before being sustainable. Third, the policy of containment at the planning division level should be vigorously pursued and all the commercial district centres should be completed within the next five years. This could greatly curtail the length of journey trips, particularly work, shopping and education trips. But this policy can be realised only if the government was able to attract the large sums of private investment needed for the construction of district centres. Fourth, the Delhi Development Authority should continue with the policy of multi-storey group housing schemes for the future, and private group housing societies should be encouraged to construct more residential developments.

The case of Delhi, with its low-density centre and denser periphery, is unusual. Nevertheless, the attempts to plan its intensification and deal with its problems may give some pointers to other cities in developing countries.

Note

1. According to the Census of India 1991, 'all places with a municipal corporation, cantonment board or notified town area committee' are regarded as census towns. Any other settlement which does not have these local bodies must satisfy the following three criteria to be called a census town. First, the settlement must have a minimum population of 5,000. Second, at least 75% of the male working population should be engaged in non-agricultural pursuits. Third, the settlement must have a density of population of at least 400 persons per km² (Office of the Registrar General and Census Commissioner, 1994, pp.xi–xii).

References

Central Statistical Organisation (1998) *Compendium of Environmental Statistics, 1998,* Ministry of Planning and Programme Implementation, Government of India, New Delhi.

Chakraborty, S. (1999) Delhi: the dark city of the new millennium, *The Sunday Times of India,* **7 (9)**, p.1.

Curtis, S.H. (1998) Housing transformation in the urban villages in Delhi, An unpublished postgraduate thesis, Department of Housing, School of Planning and Architecture, New Delhi.

D'Monte, D. (1999) Flying over Mumbai, 'highwaymen' all at sea, *The Times of India,* **CLXII (231)**, p.14.

Elkin, T., McLaren, D. and Hillman, M. (1991) *Reviving the City: Towards Sustainable Urban Development,* Friends of the Earth, London.

Government of India (1990) Master Plan for Delhi, the *Gazette of India, Part II, Section 3, Sub-section (ii),* Union Ministry of Urban Affairs and Employment, New Delhi.

Government of India (1991) *District Census Handbook: Village and Town-wise Primary Census Abstract,* Part XII A and B, Directorate of Census Operations, Delhi.

Government of the National Capital Territory of Delhi (1995) *Delhi Statistical Handbook,* Directorate of Economics and Statistics, Government of the National Capital Territory of Delhi, Delhi.

Government of the National Capital Territory of Delhi (1996) *Delhi Statistical Handbook 1996,* Directorate of Economics and Statistics, Government of the National Capital Territory of Delhi, Delhi.

Government of the National Capital Territory of Delhi (1997) *Report of Vijay Kumar Malhotra Committee regarding Amendments in the Unified Building Bye-Laws,* Government of the National Capital Territory of Delhi, New Delhi.

Gupta, R.G. (1995) *Shelter for the Poor in the Fourth World, Vol.1,* Shipra Publications, New Delhi.

Hillman, M. (1996) In favour of the compact city, in *The Compact City, A Sustainable Urban Form?* (eds Mike Jenks, Elizabeth Burton and Katie Williams), E & FN Spon, Routledge, London.

Jenks, M., Burton, E. and Williams, K. (eds) (1996) *The Compact City, A Sustainable Urban Form?* E & FN Spon, Routledge, London.

King, A. (1976) *Colonial Urban Development, Culture, Social Power and Environment,* Routledge and Kegan Paul, London.

Kumar, A. (1996) Does the master plan for Delhi have a coherent policy framework? *Urban India,* **16 (1)**, pp.11–45.

Kumar, A. (1999) Organisations and approaches for the development and provision of infrastructure in the national capital territory of Delhi, in *Urban Growth and Development in Asia, Vol.1: Making the Cities* (eds Graham P. Chapman, Ashok K. Dutt and Robert W. Bradnock), Ashgate, Aldershot.

McLaren, D. (1992) Compact or dispersed? Dilution is no solution, *Built Environment*, **18 (4)**, pp.268–284.

Maller, A. (1999) Structured accidentalness: an argument in favour of liveable urban congestion, *Journal of Urban Design*, **4 (2)**, pp.131–154.

Mehra, S. (1999) Delhi, *Outlook*, **5 (25)**, pp.56–57.

Ministry of Urban Affairs and Employment (1999) *The M.N. Buch Report*, Department of Urban Development, Ministry of Urban Affairs, New Delhi.

Narain, S. (1999) Clean air: how can we get it? *The Economic Times*, **39 (58)**, p.9.

National Institute of Urban Affairs (1994) *Urban Environmental Maps – Delhi*, NIUA, New Delhi.

National Institute of Urban Affairs (1997) *Social Sector Service Maps*, NIUA, New Delhi.

National Steering Committee: India (1996) *Second United Nations Conference on Human Settlements Habitat II India, Final National Report*, Society for Development Studies, New Delhi.

Office of the Commissioner of Planning (1992) *Pricing of Land in the Sub-City Projects – a Case Study of Dwarka*, DDA, New Delhi.

Office of the Registrar General and Census Commissioner, India (1994) *Census of India 1991, Series 1, Part II-B (ii), Primary Census Abstract*, Ministry of Home Affairs, New Delhi.

Raj, Y. (1996) Power theft bludgeons DESU reforms, *The Times of India*, **CLIX (113)**, p.1.

Sahoo, M.S. (1995) High speed tram: an appropriate public transport system for metropolitan cities – a case study of Delhi, *Indian Journal of Transport Management*, **19 (6)**, pp.401–413.

Sharma, R. (1998) City witnessed a spurt in crime rates in 1998, *The Times of India*, **CLXI (298)**, p.3.

Singh, R. (1999) Evaluation of public intervention in resettlement of squatter settlements in Delhi, an unpublished postgraduate thesis, Department of Housing, School of Planning and Architecture, New Delhi.

United Nations (1986a) *Population Growth and Policies in Mega Cities: Bombay, Population Policy Paper No.6*, Department of International Economic and Social Affairs, United Nations, New York.

United Nations (1986b) *Population Growth and Policies in Mega Cities: Calcutta, Population Policy Paper No.1*, Department of International Economic and Social Affairs, United Nations, New York.

United Nations (1987) *Population Growth and Policies in Mega Cities: Madras, Population Policy Paper No.12*, Department of International Economic and Social Affairs, United Nations, New York.

Visaria, P. (1997) Urbanization in India: an overview, in *Urbanization in Large Developing Countries, China, Indonesia, Brazil, and India* (eds Gavin W. Jones and Pravin Visaria), Clarendon Press, Oxford.

Giulietta Fadda, Paola Jirón and Adriana Allen

Views from the Urban Fringe:
Habitat, Quality of Life and Gender in Santiago, Chile

Introduction

In recent years, a broad range of contributions has fuelled the debate on the compact city. They have explored its merits and defects from an environmental, economic, social and physical point of view. However, particularly in the South, less attention has been given to the perception women and men have of the different quality of life[1] and livelihood opportunities that are attached to living in the inner or outer city. In this context, the freedom to choose a place to live is often highly dependent on income levels, state policies and, increasingly, on market forces.

Over the past 20 years in Chile, urban planning policies have contributed to a process of urban sprawl and the expansion of Santiago's ecological footprint. Between 1979 and 1995 the city's urban area expanded from 35,000 to 65,000 hectares. During this period, the population increased from approximately 4 million to 4.8 million inhabitants. Thus the urban area increased by 85% and the population by 20%. Simultaneously, Chilean housing policies have managed recently to provide a significant number of housing solutions but this has only been achieved through a rapid expansion of the city's built area. Developments on the urban periphery often cause additional burdens both to local authorities (costs of incorporating amenities, infrastructure and facilities) and to local residents, who now have to spend more time and resources to get access to the city as a place for exchange.

This chapter discusses the impact that an extended city can have on the quality of life of people in low-income sectors. It explores, on the basis of research findings from the District of Pudahuel in Santiago, the different factors that inform people's perception of their living conditions from a gender perspective. The main aim is to draw to the attention of policy makers the diversity of needs, views and realities of those who directly benefit from, or are affected by, the impact of extended cities. This will help to further inform the compact versus dispersed city debate.

The general move towards dispersal and the location of growth on the peripheries or fringes of cities is becoming a world-wide phenomenon. Indeed, the formation of vast and ever-expanding metropolitan regions is often portrayed as an inevitable feature of large cities in the developing world. Within the framework of current discussions on global transition, a new terminology has emerged. It makes reference either to a new kind of urban development (a new landscape of employment and other activity concentrations at some distance from, and independent of, old urban centres), or stresses the processes underpinning new developments (in particular the impact of flexibility in production systems and technology).[2] However, all too often the advantages and disadvantages of suburban sprawl from the viewpoint of the inhabitants living in the urban fringe are overlooked.

The chapter argues that living on the urban periphery of an extended metropolis has important trade-offs that affect the quality of life of men and women, particularly the poor. These often come into play as a direct consequence of coercive government policies that favour peripheral locations despite the externalities they produce.

The chapter starts by examining the relationship between forms of urban development and the quality of life. It then analyses the impact that urban policies and the market have had on the city of Santiago. Finally, it assesses the impact of the urban expansion of Santiago on the quality of life of a group of residents located on the periphery of the city.

The relationship between the compact city and the quality of life

The compact city debate traditionally has focused attention on the crisis in the quality of life in inner-city areas and on the new problems arising from the process of metropolitan decentralisation. The sub-urbanisation and counter-urbanisation of the 1960s and 1970s have been interpreted as being in part a consequence of a collective perception of declining quality of life in the inner city. In late 1980s Britain, this process was associated with NIMBYism[3] – the attempt by those people who have moved out of the city to maintain a higher environmental quality. However, in many European cities a parallel process of gentrification has shown that for some groups in society (particularly young urban professionals), the inner city is still perceived as offering a potentially high quality of life.

These simultaneous trends for residential centralisation and decentralisation indicate that people's perception of their quality of life tends to be informed by complex and sometimes contradictory values. Undoubtedly, quality of life factors shape and reshape different patterns of population movement. The assessment of these factors relates both to the objective conditions and subjective perceptions of urban quality, and the attendant levels of satisfaction or dissatisfaction. An effective assessment of quality of life cannot be arrived at merely in terms of the physical attributes of the living environment. It also demands a consideration of the social, psychological and cultural attributes of that environment, such as a sense of identity, safety, and social representation and inclusion in the wider urban society.

The relationship between the quality of life and the compact city has frequently been understood in terms of the factors shaping satisfaction and dissatisfaction in a post-industrial society. The relationship between quality of life and urban deprivation has, however, been underplayed, and the determinants of quality of life and mobility within the city should not necessarily be identified as the expression of free choice over residential locations.

The principal reasons identified for Latin American urban sprawl include the choice of the upper middle classes for suburban environments, and the displacement of lower income sectors to newly urbanised environments. Indeed, this chapter argues that policies promoting a market-oriented approach to urban development have increased urban sprawl and the polarisation between those mobility trends based on choice, and those based on lack of choice.

Thus it can be argued that an adequate understanding of the recent process of urban sprawl in Latin America demands a thorough consideration of recent changes in the social structure and in people's living habits. Living on the urban fringe for many dwellers means not only living on the geographic edge of the city, but also on the edge of urban society. The conditions under which people choose, or are forced, to live on the periphery can greatly affect their satisfaction and their quality of life.

The assessment of quality of life is a matter of some controversy. Grayson and Young (1994) distinguish four main approaches in the evaluation of quality of life: the personal well-being approach; the liveability comparisons approach; the market/resident approach; and the community trends approach. All are concerned with understanding well-being, but each adopts different assumptions regarding the conceptual definition of quality of life.

This chapter takes up three dimensions from these approaches. The first is the consideration of objective conditions, such as physical environment, services and infrastructure provision, pollution, and social problems. Second is the way in which these objective conditions are experienced and perceived by people. The third involves notions of power and empowerment embodied in people's views and strategies in relation to their capacity to transform their living environments. The last two are critical aspects of the analysis in so far as they situate the assessment of quality of life in the broader political economy of the city, whilst recognising that experiences and responses are shaped by personally and socially constructed conditions such as age and gender.

A gender perspective on the study of quality of life opens a different perspective to understanding the advantages and disadvantages of compact or extended cities. It is clear that the problems and benefits of experiencing large cities affect the different perceptions that men and women, and girls and boys, have on their quality of life.

The evolution of Santiago's extension: the impact of urban and housing policies and the market

Despite official declarations over the past 20 years to deconcentrate the main Chilean public and private activities, Santiago continues to dominate most of the country's activities. Santiago's Metropolitan Region controls over 39% of Chile's GDP. Approximately 35.6% of the population in the country[4] lives in Greater Santiago,[5] at a density of 7,683 persons per km[2] (Schiappacasse, 1998).[6] Although the consolidated urban area of Santiago covers only 41,215 hectares, the 1994 Metropolitan Master Plan assigned two-thirds of the remaining land within the Metropolitan Area as suitable for urbanisation in the near future (MINVU, 1994).

A recent study of the ecological footprint of Greater Santiago revealed that its total footprint was 16 times larger than the Metropolitan Area, and 300 times larger than the built-up area (Wackernagel, 1998). The main determinants of the size of the footprint were energy and food consumption. Approximately 45% of the country's motorised vehicles were concentrated in the Metropolitan Area and food in Santiago is about 20% more expensive than in rural areas. However, Santiago's demand for natural resources was unequally distributed among the different social groups. Breaking down the distribution per capita of the footprint according to income levels, the lowest quintile of the population accounted for an ecological footprint of 0.4 hectares per person, whilst that of the highest quintile accounted for 12 hectares per person.

However, the concentration of capital and income in the Metropolitan Region is an important force attracting residents from elsewhere in the country, who see in it great opportunities for improving their quality of life. Chile's economic restructuring and its incorporation into the global economy have made Santiago an ideal location for the new economic sectors linked to the world economy – e.g. for the headquarters of the main service activities, particularly finance, and for a large proportion of new industry. It is also a main market for global innovations and products and has become a preferred place of residence for the most modern and wealthiest sectors in national society (de Mattos, 1996).

There are numerous explanations for the city's expansion and its physical and social effects. On the one hand a housing-centred approach has determined a pattern of rapid urban expansion. The reliance on the market to regulate land and housing allocation has also contributed to this process. Furthermore, the lack of articulation between the two and the institutions responsible for them has created a number of externalities which cannot be solved without having a broad vision both of the city as well as of the quality of life of those living in it.

Although these externalities have become progressively more evident, their true origins have seldom been identified. Despite some discussion of the issues (Beyer, 1997; de Mattos, 1996; Sabatini, 1998) there is nevertheless a certain inertia limiting the effectiveness of existing mechanisms to improve urban environmental conditions – the overlapping of functions and mandates from different institutions, sectors and territories makes the co-ordination of actions a difficult task.

In order to understand the way public policies have affected urban growth, a historical review is necessary of three periods of time: prior to 1979; between 1979 and 1985; and from 1985 to the present.

The development of Santiago: policies and urban growth

Policies prior to 1979
There were no significant measures for urban planning in Santiago until the early twentieth century. In 1914, the Law for Plans and Urban Limits was promulgated, and in 1929, the Law of Urbanisation and Constructions was created as a reaction to the earthquake that destroyed the city of Talca in 1928.

At that time Santiago had a population of 700,000 inhabitants, and the Austrian urban planner, Karl Brunner, drew up Santiago's Master Plan which was approved in 1934. This Plan contemplated a maximum population growth for a city of 1 million people. By 1958, the city's metropolitan growth was considered as undesirable and an aberration and this had an effect on the quality of housing, infrastructure and transport facilities available. The growth was mainly a result of rapid rural–urban migration over a number of years. The effects of this growth were considered in the 1960 Master Plan for Santiago.

At the end of the 1960s, an unprecedented process of occupation of urban land took place in Santiago in the form squatter settlements – the campamentos or self-provided housing precariously established through land invasions. This phenomenon reached its maximum expression during Allende's presidential period.

Over a three-year period more than 400,000 people settled in campamentos on Santiago's periphery, often exhibiting an unprecedented degree of social and political organisation (Fadda and Ducci, 1993).

This process was abruptly interrupted by the military coup in 1973. During the military regime (1973–1989), neoliberal policies privatising public utilities and stimulating the free market were established. At the urban level, the market displaced the state as the main force driving the expansion of the city. This process was legitimised through legislation, particularly the National Urban Development Policy of 1979 (MINVU, 1979), which adjusted all the instruments and norms of urban planning in Chile to the market economy. Gross (1991) noted that the main guiding principles of this policy were that:

- land was not a scarce resource, and that its apparent scarcity was due to the lack of concordance between the current technical judicial norms and the market conditions of supply and demand,
- it was necessary to apply a flexible planning system, with a minimum of state intervention and the use of generic technical norms,
- procedures should be defined and restrictions eliminated in order to allow for the natural growth of urban areas in line with market trends,
- the state should promote and support an open housing market, leaving the construction process to the market.

The years 1979–1985
The previous plans and 1979 policies had a direct effect on the expansion of Santiago (see Fig. 1). During the five-year period 1979–1985, the size of the Metropolitan Area increased from 36,000 to 55,000 hectares. The Plan, along with the coercive housing relocation methods used, had significant impacts, particularly in the social reorganisation of Santiago. Although one of the main objectives was to reduce land prices, the effects were the opposite and land prices rose rapidly (Gross, 1991).

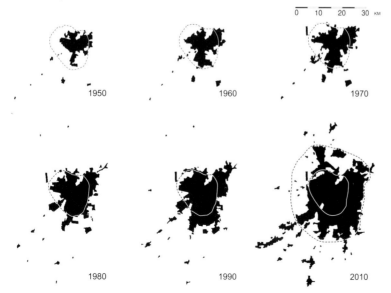

Fig. 1. The projected growth of Santiago, 1950–2010.
Source: Mecsa-Inecon, 1993

Though some land invasions did take place in the 1980s in Santiago, most of them were quickly removed (Gilbert, 1993), and invasion ceased to be a housing option. Land regularisation and slum eradication programmes were initiated in the 1979 Urban Development Policy to promote the harmonious growth of the city and peripheral housing development. The first programme allowed the legalisation of property on occupied sites and the installation of sanitation. The second encouraged the relocation of families from precarious settlements to conventional subsidised multi-storey structures on the outskirts of the metropolitan area (Fig. 2). Between 1980 and 1987, 139 campamentos were regularised, involving the construction of 53,322 units to relocate families away from the affluent northeast of the city towards the peripheral neighbourhoods (de la Puente *et al.*, 1990).

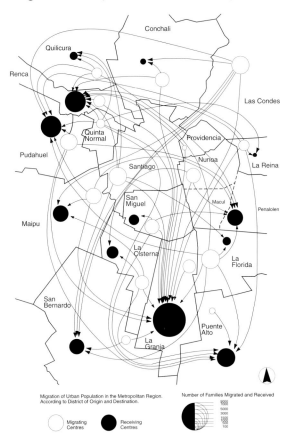

Fig. 2. Residential relocation.
Source: Morales and Rojas, 1986

Approximately 150,000 families were resettled to distant locations, in districts where local government had little capacity to provide infrastructure through this mechanism. This process exacerbated the socio-spatial segregation of the city, increased the distance between rich and poor neighbourhoods, broke social family links, and made travel to centres of employment very difficult (Jirón, 1995).

However, political pressure from those affected, and the negative consequences of these urban policies, forced the military government to modify the 1979 Urban Development Policy. In 1985, it was replaced by the so-called adjusted policy (MINVU, 1985), which reasserted urban planning as an exclusive function of the state, and declared land as a scarce resource which should be allocated according to its most productive use (Torres, 1999). However, the National Law of Urbanism of 1975 has yet to be modified, and the current urban policy can only be considered an ambiguous set of rules which, though theoretically interesting, has proved difficult to implement.

1985 to the present day

Since 1990, the democratically elected governments, far from changing the fundamental elements of the previous economic model, have continued to develop them (Daher, 1993). At the beginning of the democratic transition, there were great expectations about restoring urban planning, co-ordinating housing policies with urban development policies and decreasing urban segregation. However, housing and urban policies have more or less remained the same, providing few concrete responses to these expectations.

One of the main achievements of the democratic government was an impressive increase in rate of housing construction – to an average of 100,000 units per year (MINVU, 1996). This has halted the increase in the housing deficit, and allowed the government to concentrate on diminishing it through leveraging public resources with private ones. However, new developments have mainly been built in those areas of the urban periphery where land costs are the lowest, promoting a rapid process of urban expansion (Fig. 3).

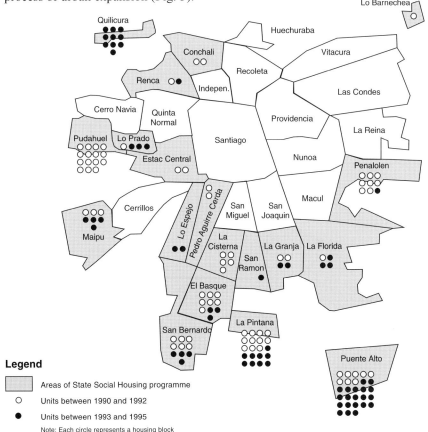

Legend

▨ Areas of State Social Housing programme

○ Units between 1990 and 1992

● Units between 1993 and 1995

Note: Each circle represents a housing block

Fig. 3. Housing construction in Greater Santiago, 1990–1995.
Source: Haramoto et al., 1997

The success of this housing policy has been counter-balanced by some problems. On the one hand a significant number of houses have been built, and a consolidated financial system established that is admired by many Latin American countries. Furthermore, the policy established a complex system that permitted people to wait in a housing queue.[7] But the policy continues to leave few locational options for the urban poor. The peripheral location of these units causes serious problems, both to the residents' quality of life as well as to Santiago's overall quality of life. The high cost of land in the city centre forces the private sector to build in specific areas of the urban periphery where land is cheaper. Social housing is only available in a few very distant areas of Metropolitan Santiago. However, given that the externalities of building on the periphery are never internalised, the allocations for these new developments fail to include the costs of transport, distance, time, equipment, services and infrastructure (Edwards, 1995).

In Chile, urban planning and management continues to be seen in this segregated manner, without a holistic vision or a proposal for the city as a whole. One of the main reasons for this, in Greater Santiago, is the lack of articulation between the policies and practices of its 37 districts, and between the various housing, land and urban policy sectors which remain centralised and controlled by the national government through various ministries and offices.

There have been a few initiatives to curb urban expansion and to revitalise the urban centre. One such initiative was the Municipality of Santiago's Re-population Programme. The basic goal was to convert the District of Santiago into a Modern Metropolitan Centre and to regenerate the business centre and its residential character through a subsidised re-population programme (CORDESAN, 1996). The Municipality of Santiago initiated the programme in 1994, as a strategic management approach to Santiago's development. The three main issues addressed by the programme were poverty, quality of life and competitiveness (IMS, 1994, p.11). The programme can be considered successful in terms of the re-population and revitalisation of a deteriorated downtown area, but a gentrification process has also taken place where few options remain available for the poorer population (Jirón, 1998). The benefits of the inner city were appropriated, in the form of a better quality of life, only by those who could afford it, whilst those who could not were expelled to the periphery.

In general, urban policies and norms in Chile over the last two decades have generated a process of continuous physical expansion. This has resulted in a greater urban and social segregation; an increase in the disparity in access to urban services; a worsening of local living conditions; increased environmental contamination; urban security problems; and the deterioration of urban and historic centres. Because these policies (particularly for housing) are imposed from top to bottom, urban residents, especially the urban poor, have little option but to reside on the outskirts of the city. Their physical and social exclusion is the cause of a continuously deteriorating quality of life.

Impacts of Santiago's urban expansion on the quality of life of the residents of Pudahuel

A research project entitled 'Quality of Life and Gender'[8] was initiated in 1998 in order to examine the conditions relating to a better quality of life for low-income groups in Metropolitan Santiago (Fadda and Jirón, 1999), including two neighbourhoods in the District of Pudahuel on the western periphery of Santiago (see Fig. 4). Both neighbourhoods were built as part of a public housing programme during the first democratic period (1990–1994). The research aimed to assess the quality of life in these neighbourhoods and focused on the residents' perception of their quality of life on the urban periphery. This research is of particular relevance to the quality of life aspects of the compact city debate. It consists of an analysis of a set of objective indicators, residents' subjective perceptions of the quality of life in their neighbourhoods, and the levels of empowerment for residents generated by these objective and subjective conditions.

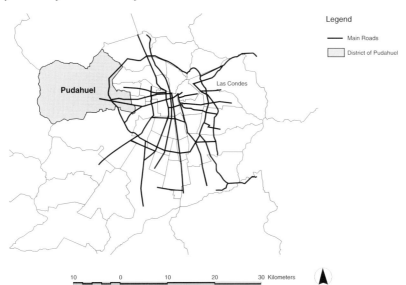

Fig. 4. The location of, and main roads to, the District of Pudahuel in Santiago.
Source: Fadda and Jirón, 2000

Objective and subjective assessment of the quality of life

Objectively, the expansion of Greater Santiago has created marginal environments in peripheral areas such as Pudahuel. The most serious problems created by urban expansion into the District are pollution, poverty and social exclusion.

Santiago is considered the eighth most polluted capital of the world and the Pudahuel District has the most serious pollution problems in the city (de la Paz, 1999). The contamination of its watercourses, the urban impacts, the building of social dwellings on a massive scale, are all part of what has been called a process of 'metropolitan aggression' (Suárez, 1999). The air pollution is partly attributable to the wind patterns that channel the accumulated smog of the city towards this part of the metropolis. Similarly, the watercourses that flow down from the mountain range run through the city before reaching Pudahuel full of wastes that are hazardous for human health. The high levels of pollution concentration are countered by a lack of equipment and services available to counteract it.

Pudahuel is also the third poorest district of the city, with 32.1% of its population living below the poverty line.[9] The District has witnessed a rapid growth in population since 1970, mainly due to the rapid expansion of government housing programmes. Between 1989 and 1994 more than 17,000 low-income housing units were built in the District, attracted by some of the lowest land values in Metropolitan Santiago (see Fig. 5).

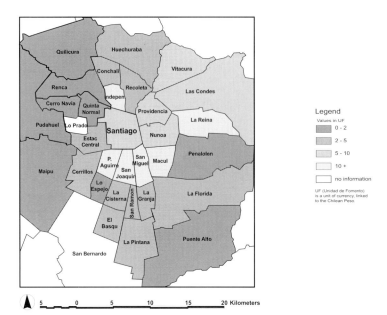

Fig. 5. Land values.
Source: Fadda and Jirón, 2000

Because of the District's peripheral location, access to other areas of the city is difficult, in terms of distance, time and money. Fig. 4 also shows that the distance to high-income neighbourhoods like Las Condes, where many men and women work, demands daily trips of over two hours each way.

Given the different gender roles played by men and women, and their different access to, and control over, social resources, the inaccessibility and lack of facilities in the District are worse for women than for men. Women are responsible for childcare and child rearing and there is a high proportion (61%) of women who stay in the neighbourhood as housewives. Consequently, more women than men perceive the lack of schools, markets, parks, child and healthcare facilities.

Although the residents of these neighbourhoods considered the physical quality of their surroundings as positive, mainly in terms of housing and infrastructure, they nonetheless indicated their intention to leave the neighbourhood if they had the opportunity to do so. In addition to physical factors, the natural, human and socio-cultural dimensions of quality of life in urban areas were also studied. Factors such as a sense of safety, identity, problems of drug addiction, social representation and access to the wider urban society were all rated highly in the subjective determination of quality of life. Here too there were significant gender-based differences in perception. This is certainly true for the problems such as lack of cleanliness, water pollution, flooding and disease that are present in the neighbourhood, which women perceive to be worse and a greater health hazard than do men. This is explicable in terms of their greater contact with issues such as children's health, rubbish collection, water provision and flooding.

A major issue considered detrimental to the quality of life is the problem of drugs and alcohol addiction amongst youth. The District of Pudahuel is ranked 17th out of the 341 districts in the country in terms of its level of drug consumption (CONACE, 1998). The causes of drug addiction and alcoholism are many, but opportunities are lacking and expectations for a better future are minimal in these types of neighbourhoods.

The social housing programmes in the neighbourhoods were targeted at low-income groups and could be accessed either collectively or in most cases individually. Most families on these programmes came from other districts in the city and upon arrival had few links to the neighbourhood. Because of the selection criteria, most beneficiaries presented high levels of poverty, low education levels, few employment skills and, in general, many social problems. The result is problem estates with a high concentration of social problems, feelings of despair and social exclusion, acutely felt by youth. With few opportunities for education, employment or a vision of a better future, drug and alcohol consumption is perceived as a possible escape mechanism.

The situation not only affects youth, but also their families and other residents, as the high drug trafficking and consumption are associated with a high rate of criminality and insecurity on the streets. Women express an unwillingness to leave their houses, they fear public spaces and prefer to remain indoors, especially after dark. Men also perceive the problems related to drugs, crime and theft, but they do not fear the use of public spaces and sense that the possible solution lies in better policing. Both groups think that the neighbourhood is very unsafe, and that the levels of protection are minimal.

In addition, both groups agree that the public transportation available is adequate but women indicate that conditions are not always optimal. Buses are regarded as being overcrowded and dangerous because of driving speeds, and their passage through some areas considered dangerous, particularly at night. Men are more affected by the length of time involved in reaching the city than women, largely, one suspects, because men use transport on a daily basis more than do women. Reasons given to explain problems of access to work are both the distances to the city and, particularly, traffic congestion.

Empowering or disempowering strategies

Empowerment is a long-term social and political process aimed at redressing the imbalance in the power structures of society. It does this by strengthening the powers of civil society, by creating a more transparent state and by making the corporate economy more socially responsible (Friedmann, 1993). The empowerment of civil society is to be achieved through territorially organised communities characterised by autonomy in their decision making, local self-sufficiency, direct (participatory) democracy, and social learning through experience. According to Friedmann (1993), poor households lack social power to improve their conditions. He recognises eight means of acquiring social power, including: a defensible life space; social organisation; social networks; surplus time; appropriate information; knowledge and abilities; instruments of work and livelihood; and financial resources.[10] By identifying some of these means in Pudahuel, it is possible to assess the degree of empowerment or disempowerment involved in the policies being implemented.

In terms of a defensible space, and a physical space to identify with, the residents of the two neighbourhoods stated that ownership of their property was a life-long dream and the main reason for their staying there. Both men and women agreed that their existing living conditions were better than in their previous dwelling. Property ownership can be seen as a form of empowerment. Housing policies aimed at lowering the housing deficit through ownership are a response to felt needs in the population. But the location and type of living space delivered by the policies, and displacement of the beneficiaries, have generally created other problems which inevitably disempower the individuals.

For instance, the way these neighbourhoods were originally formed by beneficiaries from different parts of the city, with no previous knowledge of each other, makes the social organisation and formation of social networks difficult. In the first place, the social capital involved in their prior place of residence can be lost, given the distances to the former neighbourhoods. Moreover, the formation of new networks also becomes difficult, when the different interests, needs and backgrounds of the residents generate an attitude of indifference to each other. Both men and women asserted that improving the quality of life was greatly dependent on the participation of residents. But they also pointed to a strong tendency to inertia in social mobilisation, and the widespread belief that the chances of influencing change were minimal.

In general, men were more optimistic than women towards the possibility of achieving improvement through the municipality and the mayor of the district. Women, on the other hand, felt abandoned by these institutions and the police. They also recognised the reluctance of the majority of neighbours to become involved in the improvement of conditions. Nonetheless, it is the women who organise themselves (albeit in small numbers), whilst male attitudes rested on the belief that someone (an outsider) should reach out to help them. This situation tallies with the idea of women being involved in a community-based role, often voluntarily and without much recognition, whilst men participate in other areas with political or economic rewards, or simply do not get involved.

The priority of maintaining a salary makes it difficult to achieve a surplus of time, especially because of time taken up by long distances to work and domestic chores, and because of the lack of space for recreation and basic services. Some of these difficulties are attributable to the peripheral location of the neighbourhoods, and the shortages of equipment and services to compensate for these distances to the city centre.

Furthermore, the residents also found it difficult to gain access to information necessary for their social empowerment. The distance to the municipality, the city and most institutions had this effect, and these institutions rarely approached them to offer information. In a few cases, when groups have organised themselves, they have been able to access available funds or services to improve their living conditions. However, in general, residents are disempowered in developing strategies that could improve their quality of life. This is not to say that it cannot happen, but that it requires a bigger effort from the community.

Conclusions

From the analysis above, it can be gathered that the different types of urban and housing policies and strategies implemented in Chile throughout different governments have stimulated urban sprawl. This sprawl has generated various impacts on the city's residents, affecting more negatively those living in the lower income peripheral areas. Santiago's urban sprawl has a global impact at the level of the city and its surroundings, and a local level impact on the district and neighbourhood.

Amongst the global impacts affecting the city are: social segregation of metropolitan space, the worsening of local living conditions, an increase in environmental contamination, urban security problems, and the deterioration of historic centres. Local impacts include extreme contamination, high poverty rates, lack of facilities, increased insecurity, high indices of drug addiction, and the lack of access to urban amenities. These externalities affect men and women in a different way. Due to the fact that women spend more time in the neighbourhood, their perception of the problems and their impacts is more acute.

The urban expansion policies implemented have had a disempowering effect on the communities affected. This is due to the relocation element in each programme, as the beneficiaries lose the social networks they previously had and simultaneously find it difficult to articulate new ones. Additionally, the lack of access to citizen participation and other means of social power in daily activities makes the initiation of empowering strategies difficult to achieve. From this research it is clear that policies for, and market forces determining, peripheral urban expansion in large cities such as Santiago lead to problems of social exclusion and increased inequalities. This lends weight to the need to consider the potential benefits of urban containment and compact city policies.

In the context of Latin America, the social and economic disparities between urban centre and urban fringe have tended to limit the debate to 'traditional' terms, all too often assuming that socially homogeneous groups encompassed these changes. The rural–urban migration has virtually ended, the poor classes having contributed, in the large majority of cases, to the creation of a poor class peri-urban fringe around main cities during the 1950s and 1960s. The case study of Santiago shows some of the changes that took place during the 1980s and 1990s in the urban growth pattern. These changes have been related to the segregation of the lower-income sectors of the population in extensive and precarious peripheral areas, where market-oriented policies have allowed them to settle and become 'home owners'.

This spread of the poor to the periphery has been favoured by the way in which metropolitan space has been produced, resulting in the buffering of social conflicts. The three main indicators of these changes are:

- a socio-economic diversification of the peripheral areas, thus reproducing the centre–periphery pattern within themselves;
- the spread of poverty throughout the metropolitan network;
- the emergence of segregation by middle- and upper-class segments of society.

These changes have led to the formation of a more complex urban fringe than the one described in the 1970s. The urban fringe has ceased to be an open space, and in this sense it ceased to be a frontier. Its growth led to the spread of urban land ownership. This trend coexists with a diametrically opposing one: the production of privileged residential neighbourhoods, whose owners belong to higher-income groups, territorially separated from the rest of the city. In the context of the compact/dispersed city debate, this complex and heterogeneous urban structure challenges professional perceptions and knowledge. It raises questions about the adaptation of the conceptual and practical tools of urban and regional planning necessary to cope with the new territorial and social reality.

Notes

1. For a detailed discussion of the concept of quality of life, see Fadda and Jirón, 1999.
2. In Western Europe, the debate on the new spaces in the fringes of the city and the spread of urban functions, lifestyles and ideology across a somewhat unified and common territory has given rise to a set of new concepts, such as *ville éparpillée* (scattered city), *ville archipel* (Viard, 1994; Veltz, 1996), *ville à la carte* in France; or the idea of the dispersed city (Monclús, 1998) in Spain.
3. NIMBY stands for 'not in my back yard'.
4. The total population of Chile is 13,348,401 (INE, 1995).
5. The Metropolitan Region is composed of six provinces. However, the urbanised area, designated as Greater Santiago, is made up of 34 districts (32 from the Province of Santiago and 2 more from two different provinces).
6. Santiago's required gross minimum density is 150 inhabitants per hectare (15,000 inhabitants per km^2) (MINVU, 1994).
7. In Chile, access to housing is a shared effort by the people (via saving), the state (via subsidies) and the financial market (via mortgage credit). The promotion and programming of projects, as well as housing construction, should correspond to the private sector activity (Etchegaray, 1993). The government has set up various subsidised programmes to access housing. The subsidies are offered to the demand in order to fill the affordability gap (Jirón, 1995).
8. FONDECYT-Chile financed Research Project # 1980865/98.
9. Poverty is a per capita income of the household which is lower than twice the value of a basic food basket. Extreme poverty is a per capita income of the household which is lower than the value of one basic food basket (MIDEPLAN, 1999). As of May 2000 the per capita poverty line is equivalent to US$70.00 and per capita extreme poverty to US$35.00 for urban zones (MIDEPLAN, 2000).
10. Because not all the means to access social power were fully studied, only five of them are considered in this analysis.

References

Beyer, H. (1997) *Plan regulador metropolitano de Santiago: el peso del subdesarrollo.* Estudios Publicos (67), pp.147–165.

CONACE (1998) *Estudio nacional de consumo de drogas*, Santiago.

CORDESAN (1996) *Vivir en Santiago*, Corporación para el Desarrollo de Santiago: Santiago.

Daher, A. (1993) Santiago Estatal, Chile Liberal. Revista SIAP, **XXVI**, pp.101–102, Santiago.

de la Paz, P. (1999) Santiago, la 8ª capital mas contaminada del mundo. *La Tercera*, Santiago, 21 April.

de la Puente, Lafoy P., Torres, E. and Muñoz, P. (1990) Satisfacción residencial en soluciones habitacionales de radicación y erradicación para sectores pobres de Santiago. *Revista EURE*, **XVI(49)**, pp.7–22.

de Mattos, C. (1996) Avances de la globalización y nueva dinamica metropolitana: Santiago de Chile, 1975–1995. *Revista EURE*, **XXII(65)**, pp.39–63.

Edwards, G. (1995) Esternalidades e instrumentos de regulación urbana. *Estudios Públicos,* **60**, pp.145–157.

Etchegaray, A. (1993) El Marco Sectorial, in *Primer Seminario Internacional Sobre la Experiencia Chilena en Financiaminto Habitacional*, Seminar held in Santiago from September 28 to October 1, 1993.

Fadda, G. and Ducci, M. E. (1993) Políticas de desarrollo urbano y vivienda en Chile: interrelaciones y efectos, in *Chile: 50 Años de Vivienda Social. 1943–1993*, (eds H. Bravo and C. Martinez), University of Valparaiso, Valparaiso.

Fadda, G. and Jirón, P. (1999) Quality of life: a methodology for urban research. *Environment and Urbanisation* **11(2)**.

Fadda, G. and Jirón, P. (2000) Informe Final, Proyecto FONDECYT N° 1980865-98, Comision Nacional de Ciencia y Tecnologia, Santiago.

Friedmann, J. (1993) *Empowerment – the Politics of Alternative Development*, Blackwell, Oxford.

Gilbert, A. (1993) *In Search of a Home – Rental and Shared Housing in Latin America*, University College London, London.

Grayson, L. and Young, K. (1994) *Quality of Life in Cities – An Overview and Guide to the Literature*, The British Library / London Research Centre, London.

Gross, P. (1991) Santiago de Chile (1925–1990): planificación urbana y modelos politicos. *Revista EURE*, **XVII(52/52)**, pp.27–52.

Haramoto, E., Jadue, D. and Tapia, R. (1997) Programa de viviendas básicas en la Region Metropolitana. *Revista de Arquitectura Facultad de Arquitectura y Urbanismo*, Universidad de Chile, **(9)**, pp.32–37.

IMS (1994) *Memoria de Gestión 1994*, Ilustre Municipalidad de Santiago, Santiago.

INE (1995) *Chile Division Politico – Administrativa Ciudades y Pueblos del Pais*, Instituto Nacional de Estadisticas, Santiago

Jirón, P. (1995) Progressive housing in Chile? An evaluation of the Chilean housing policy and its capacity to reach the Allegados, Master of Science Dissertation, Development Planning Unit, London.

Jirón, P. (1998) Strategic planning and management in Santiago de Chile. Is it the tools or the way of going about them that are inappropriate? Paper presented at the International Congress Shelter and Revitalisation of Old And Historic Urban Centres held in Havana, Cuba, March 30 – April 3.

Mecsa-Inecon (1993) Estudio análisis sobre desarrollo de infraestructura de las Regiones V, VI y Metropolitana. Macro Zona Central, Ministerio de Obras Publicas, Santiago.

MIDEPLAN (1999) Compendio estatistico regionales, *Documentos Regionales*, N° 50, Ministerio de Planificación y Cooperación, Santiago.

MIDEPLAN (2000) *Mediciún Línea de Pobreza*, Ministerio de Planificación y Cooperación, Santiago

MINVU (1979) Política Nacional de Desarrollo Urbano, Division de Desarrollo Urbano, Ministerio de Vivienda y Urbanismo, Santiago.

MINVU (1985) Política Nacional de Desarrollo Urbano, Division de Desarrollo Urbano, Ministerio de Vivienda y Urbanismo, Santiago.

MINVU (1994) Plan Regulador Metropolitano de Santiago, Santiago.

MINVU (1996) Memorias del Ministerio de Vivienda y Urbanismo, Santiago.

Monclús, Francisco Javier (ed.) (1998) La Ciudad Dispersa, Centre de Cultura Contemporania, Barcelona.

Morales, E. and Rojas, S. (1986) Relocalización socio-espacial de la pobreza. Política estatal y presion popular, 1979–1985, Documento de Trabajo No 280, FLACSO, Santiago.

Sabatini, F. (1998) Liberalización de los mercados del suelo y segregación social en las ciudades Latinoamericanas: El caso de Santiago, Chile. *Documentos Serie Azul*, **No.14**, Instituto de Estudios Urbanos, Pontificia Universidad Catolica de Chile, Santiago.

Schiappacasse, P. (1998) Diferenciación del espacio social interurbano en el Gran Santiago. Un analisis a nivel distrital, Tesis para optar al grado de Magister en Geografia, Facultad de Arquitectura y Urbanismo, Universidad de Chile, Santiago.

Suárez, M. (1999) Los límites de la Ciudad. La Encrucijada de Pudahuel. El Mercurio, Santiago, August 1st: F-1.

Torres, M. (1999) Notas docentes. Módulo: Gestión Urbanística, MDI, Facultad de Arquitectura y Urbanismo, Universidad de Chile, Santiago.

Veltz, Pierre (1996) Mondialisation, villes et territoires: l'économie d'archipel, Presses Universitaires de France, Paris.

Viard, Jean (1994) La société d'archipel, Editions de l'Aube, La Tour d'Aigues.

Wackernagel, M. (1998) The ecological footprint of Santiago de Chile, *Local Environment*, **3(1)**, pp.7–25.

Antonio Nelson Rodrigues da Silva, Archimedes Azevedo Raia Jr.
and Antonio Clovis Pinto Ferraz

Minimising the Negative Effects of Urban Sprawl:
Towards a Strategy for Brazil

Introduction

Most large and medium-sized cities in Brazil have undergone a very fast growth process in the last three to four decades. Although there were regional differences, the cities mostly faced the same problem: that urban growth was not matched by the investment to cope with the ever-growing infrastructure demand. The form of urban growth – peripheral leapfrogging development that left behind large vacant areas within the built-up area – also increased the problems. The reasons for this kind of urban growth rate and form can be found in the socio-economic problems that the country experienced during the period.

Massive rural to urban migration after the 1960s was one of the main reasons for the rapid growth of the largest cities in Brazil, and for the pattern of development that occurred in them. First, migrants moved to the city at a faster pace than the capacity of the government to plan for the provision of even the most basic infrastructure. High living costs in the cities forced the new inhabitants away from the old neighbourhoods where land prices were too high, to the urban periphery where land was relatively inexpensive.

Unfortunately, some landowners cunningly took advantage of this situation to increase their profits. They built their new developments as far as possible from the urban area, keeping part of their tract ready for future development. The portions were usually left in-between the existing urban areas and the new development. The reason was quite simple. As the landowners did not build the basic infrastructure in these new developments, sooner or later the municipality would have to do it. Once it happened, this instantly raised the prices of their undeveloped land. Such land valorisation[1] occurs as a result of the provision of all types of infrastructure, but it usually occurs initially through proximity to public transportation routes, which have to be put in place first in order to connect the new developments with the city itself.

This process has left large undeveloped areas within new city limits, extending the urban boundaries well beyond what would have been necessary if speculators had not undertaken a leapfrogging strategy. To make matters worse, the idea of holding land for speculative purposes became widespread, even for small land parcels, in Brazilian cities. For example, in São Paulo and Porto Alegre the proportion of undeveloped land to the total area was 25% and 42% respectively in 1987 (Rolnik *et al.*, 1990; Oliveira *et al.*, 1989). The city of São Paulo alone had around 60 million m² of vacant land already served by an infrastructure capable of accommodating 7. 5 million people (São Paulo, 1991). Medium-sized cities faced the same problem. In 1996 the city of Bauru (circa 300,000 people) had 60% of its land vacant, whilst Araraquara (circa 170,000) and Ribeirao Preto (circa 600,000) both had around 50% of their land vacant (Raia Jr., 1995; Azevedo, 1981).

In summary, one of the main causes of urban sprawl in Brazilian cities is the large amount of vacant land within the urban area. Generally, the developed areas average at least 30 lots per hectare in urban areas, which leads to gross densities of around 100 persons per hectare, even if only one household per lot is assumed. However, due to vacant tracts of land, the gross average density in Brazilian cities is only 40 people per hectare (Sanches, 1988).

Evaluations of compact patterns and urban sprawl
While there is general agreement in Brazil that urban sprawl is undesirable, the implications of alternative development patterns have not been as fully explored as in industrialised countries. There, for example, the energy crisis of the early 1970s led to numerous re-evaluations of urban form as a possible means of minimising energy problems. By the late 1980s, the literature indicated different conclusions about optimal urban forms (e.g. Newman and Kenworthy, 1989; Audirac and Zifou, 1989; Gordon and Richardson, 1989), and more recent papers show that the discussion continues with open and sometimes very passionate debate (e.g. Breheny, 1992; Newman, 1992; Gordon and Richardson, 1997; Ewing, 1997).

The contradictions involved in the debate about the compactness of cities have been pointed out by Jenks *et al.* (1996). The benefits of a compact city include the reduction of travel needs and fuel emissions, a more efficient utility and infrastructure provision, the protection of agricultural land, and social and cultural diversity. On the other hand, they also present problems of pollution, loss of urban quality and the reduction of open space areas.

However, conclusions derived from experiences and observations in developed countries cannot be directly transferred to developing countries. In Brazil some researchers have begun to study the topic. Pampolha (1999), for instance, has conducted one of the few empirical studies in Brazil on the influence of urban spatial characteristics on transport energy consumption, based on the works of Newman and Kenworthy (1989) and Naess (1995). Using satellite images to examine the spatial characteristics of 27 state capitals and their metropolitan areas, Pampolha (1999) found that the urban areas with higher population densities spend less energy on transport than those with lower densities.

Evaluations of urban sprawl in Brazil are usually theoretical and based on the hypothesis of an optimal economic urban density, favouring the compact city design. Mascaró (1979 and 1989) has studied Brazilian medium-sized cities, and explored the possibility of increasing current densities without replacing the infrastructure. He also considered the economically optimal housing pattern, and concluded that the best range was between 100 and 120 dwelling units per hectare (at least 200 people per hectare).

Silva (1993) also found significant savings in urban infrastructure and public transportation associated with an increase in the overall density of medium- sized cities in Brazil. The study arrived at this finding through using two models. The first was the META model (Model for the Estimation of Transportation costs in urban Areas), which was developed to evaluate the transport costs of cities with different characteristics including size, shape, and population densities. The second was called the INFRA model, which was developed to estimate infrastructure costs. More recently, Souza (1996) has analysed the impacts of several factors, including population densities, on urban air temperatures.

An analysis of the impact of more compact patterns of the cities of São Carlos and Araraquara indicated a reduction of both public transportation and infrastructure costs in the more compact scenarios (Souza and Silva, 1998). The results suggest that, in the case of urban public transportation, the cost reductions can sometimes be more effective than operational measures. Furthermore, common to all the Brazilian studies was the point that cities should have higher densities than at present. These stressed that although it was not possible to reach the density value that maximised savings – which seems to start above 100 inhabitants per hectare – neither was it reasonable to maintain the existing densities of around 40 inhabitants per hectare. Densification could promote an optimisation of the existing urban infrastructure, reducing the demand for new infrastructure and the pressure on budgets.

A policy of heavy taxation, based on the additional costs of transportation and infrastructure produced by vacant urban land, may be a way to reduce the problem. A new taxation strategy was proposed in Brazil in 1993, based on the assumption that high urban densities could reduce transportation and infrastructure costs, following recommendations of the Federal Constitution (Brazil, 1988). The amount of tax to be paid would be defined by using mathematical models to calculate the additional cost of transportation and infrastructure produced by the vacant lots that induce city sprawl.

The next section of this chapter describes the assumptions and the specifications of the taxation strategy and is followed by a case study conducted in a real city. The results of this application are discussed in the conclusions of the chapter, along with the merits and limitations of the strategy.

A proposed taxation strategy for transport and infrastructure costs

Models underpinning the strategy
Before introducing the taxation strategy itself, it is interesting to understand how the models that underpin it work. Mathematical models are necessary in developing countries, not only to simulate the complexity of the urban environment, but also because there are strong data limitations. The models have to be efficient and simple, in order to provide good estimates with limited data. One of the first models in Brazil to be developed with these characteristics was created by Silva (1990) for medium-sized cities. However, comparison of the results of that first model with data from a real city (Silva and Ferraz, 1991) showed that it was useful only for observing general trends. The same research team then developed the META model, that once again was based on the characteristics of medium-sized cities (Silva, 1993; Silva and Ferraz, 1993).

The implementation of the META model required four distinct steps: city construction; trip generation; trip production; and estimation of transportation costs. The *city construction* phase consists of dividing the real city into homogeneous traffic analysis zones, taking into account the population distribution and the income levels of the different groups throughout the city. The land uses of these zones are identified, as well as important trip generators in the city. In the *trip generation* phase, given the absence of detailed income data, the estimation of trip production is based mainly on trip rates for three income groups: low, medium and high. Trip attractions were calculated using trip rates based on the number of jobs and students in the traffic zones, as well as on the population numbers in general. The model also included a particular trip generator in the representation of the city – the intercity bus terminal.

The *trip distribution* phase is based on a gravity model, doubly constrained by both trip production and attraction. The measure of impedance[2] used in the trip distribution model was confined to travel distance, in order to simplify the data collection process. There were two impedance functions available in the computer program created for running the META model – exponential and inverse power functions. Travel distances used to measure impedance were not the same for car and bus trips. In the case of bus trips, for example, most were assumed in the model to pass through the city centre. This assumption reflects the way that bus systems operate in medium-sized Brazilian cities – that is, a bus terminal working as a hub. Finally, in the last step of the model, *transportation costs* can be calculated separately for both car and bus trips.

The other model (INFRA), proposed by Silva (1993), was designed to estimate the costs of the infrastructure networks (streets, pavement, drainage, water and power supply and sewerage). INFRA is basically a set of equations representing the findings of Mascaró (1979), who produced graphs showing that total infrastructure network costs do not increase in proportion to population density.

The taxation strategy

The general concept of the taxation strategy can be described briefly, as follows. Implementation and operational costs of both transit and infrastructure networks must be calculated for two different scenarios. The first scenario depicts the existing situation, and the models are used to calculate the costs for the city as it really is (the real city). Next, using the same tools, the costs of the same items are evaluated for a hypothetical city. The latter city is based on the former, but without empty lots. This city serves as a reference for considering both the infrastructure and transportation costs (in a way, it is an 'ideal city' because it has no vacant land). The two cities are displayed in Fig. 1.

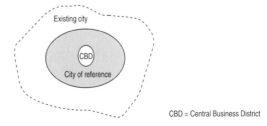

Fig. 1. Sketch of the scenarios considered in the proposed taxation strategy.

Once the costs of both scenarios have been calculated, the areas within the city must be estimated (for either small parcelled lots or large areas), with the vacant areas suitably identified.

Any recipient of these services must pay for the costs relating to the construction expenses for both infrastructure networks and public transportation supply in the city of reference, proportionally to his parcel area. In the case of multistorey buildings, the value must be multiplied by the number of levels of the building, as a way to compensate for the more intensive use of the facilities.

$$I^{land} = \frac{CC_{ref}}{\Sigma A_e^{land}} \times A_e^{land} \times NP \tag{1}$$

Where:
I^{land} = tax to be paid for by the owners of every parcel in the existing city;
A_e^{land} = area of any parcel in the existing city;
CC_{ref} = construction costs in the city of reference;
NP = number of levels of the building.

The operational cost of the facilities in the city of reference must be charged proportionately to the amount of service used. In the case of urban public transportation, it can be charged directly on the buses, at the time of the trip.

$$T = \frac{CO_{ref}}{CoT} \times CoU \tag{2}$$

Where:
T = tax to be paid for by the owners of every parcel served by a specific infrastructure;
CO_{ref} = operational costs in the city of reference;
CoT = the measure of the total infrastructure use (it may be the total area of the parcels served by a particular facility, if it proves impossible to measure the amount of service used);
CoU = measure of the infrastructure utilisation by any parcel.

The difference between the total construction and operational cost of the real city and the city of reference must also be apportioned, not by all property owners, but rather by the owners of vacant urban land, since the latter are responsible for the additional costs for the entire community.

$$I^{vland} = \frac{(CC_e - CO_{ref}) + (CO_e - CO_{ref})}{\Sigma A_e^{vland}} \times A_e^{vland} \tag{3}$$

Where:
I^{vland} = additional tax to be paid for by the owners of every vacant parcel;
CC_e = total construction costs in the existing city;
CC_{ref} = total construction costs in the city of reference;
CO_e = total operational costs in the existing city;
CO_{ref} = total operational costs in the city of reference;
A_e^{vland} = area of any vacant parcel in the existing city.

Application of the strategy

The city of Araraquara has been taken as a case study to exemplify the proposed taxation strategy. Following the steps presented above, the application starts, using equation 1, with that part of the tax that must be paid for by everyone who owns a lot in the city. The sum of all the areas of individual lots used for residential or commercial purposes is equal to 5,463 hectares (5,463 x 104m²). The other element of the equation, CC_{ref}, includes the total costs of infrastructure and public transportation.

The main characteristics of the scenario taken as the city of reference are presented in Table 1, along with the data of the existing city scenario.

Table 1. Construction and operational costs of infrastructure and public transportation in two different scenarios.

Scenario	Area	Population density	Infrastructure costs (US$/day)		Public transportation costs (US$ x 10⁶/year)	
	(km²)	(inhab/ha)	Construction	Operation	Construction	Operation
Existing city	63.81	25	24.35	2.43	13,674	54,696
City of reference	25.83	61	6.74	0.67	8,432	33,728

The transportation costs have to be converted into annual costs, which means US$15,388,389 in the case of the city of reference. Silva (1993) has suggested that the construction costs in this case represent 20% of the total costs. The introduction of these values in equation 1 gives:

$$I^{land} = \frac{6.74 \times 10^6 + 3.08 \times 10^6}{5.463 \times 10^6} \; A_e^{land}.NP = 1.80847.A_e^{land}.NP$$

Where:

I^{land} = tax to be paid for by the owners of every parcel in the existing city, in US$;

A_e^{land} = area of any parcel in the existing city, in m².

The second component of the tax value is related to the operational costs, and must be based on the amount of service effectively used. In the case of public transportation, it is equal to 80% of the total costs already estimated (US$ 12,310,712 per year). The tax could be charged directly on the bus, as it is today. This is not the same, however, as the value per passenger. Given the number of bus riders in Araraquara, the value per passenger would drop to US$ 0.25 instead of the existing US$ 0.40.

For the infrastructure networks, the owners of every parcel served by that particular infrastructure would have to pay their share of the total operational costs (in this case, 10% of the total costs). The value would be added to the first part of the tax already calculated. Considering, for example, that 97% of the streets in Araraquara are paved, the operational costs of the infrastructure would have to be proportional to the area of any parcel. In this example the sum of the individual areas of the lots has to match 1,508 hectares, or 97% of the total area of the 1,550 hectares used for residential and commercial purposes, as follows:

$$T^{pav} = \frac{(26.22 + 9.48) \times 10^6 \times K \times 0.10}{1,550 \times 10^4 \times 0.97} \; A_e^{pav} = 0.29477 \times A_e^{pav}$$

Where:

T^{pav} = tax to be paid for by the owners of every parcel served by paved streets, in US\$;

A_e^{pav} = area of any parcel served by paved streets, in m²;

K = interest rate (in this example, 12% per year).

The procedure is analogous for the other infrastructure networks (e.g., sewerage, water, power supply). While the owners of all lots in the city pay for the first part of the tax and the second part is paid only by those who effectively use a specific infrastructure, a third part is paid only by the owners of vacant land. The total value of this third part has to compensate for the difference between the total construction and operational cost of the existing city and the city of reference.

These are the values estimated for the existing city in the case study:

- Construction costs (infrastructure) – US\$24.35 x 106 per year;
- Operational costs (infrastructure) – US\$2.43 x 106 per year;
- Construction costs (transportation) – US\$19.96 x 106 per year;
- Operational costs (transportation) – US\$3.99 x 106 per year;
- Total construction costs (transportation + infrastructure) – US\$29.34 x 106 per year; and
- Total operational costs (transportation + infrastructure) – US\$22.39 x 106 per year.

These are the values estimated for the city of reference in the case study:

- Construction costs (infrastructure) – US\$6.74 x 106 per year;
- Operational costs (infrastructure) – US\$0.67 x 106 per year;
- Construction costs (transportation) – US\$3.08 x 106 per year;
- Operational costs (transportation) – US\$12.31 x 106 per year;
- Total construction costs (transportation + infrastructure) – US\$9.82 x 106 per year; and
- Total operational costs (transportation + infrastructure) – US\$12.98 x 106 per year.

Assuming an area of 2,872 hectares with vacant land in the city, we have:

$$I^{vland} = \frac{(29.34 - 9.82) \times 10^6 + (22.39 - 12.98) \times 10^6}{2,872 \times 10^4} A_e^{vland}$$

$$I^{vland} = 1.00731.A_e^{vland}$$

Where:

I^{vland} = additional tax to be paid for by the owners of every vacant parcel, in US\$;

A_e^{vland} = area of any vacant parcel in the existing city, in m².

In a first application, the value of this third part of the tax has been estimated by using the sum of all the vacant areas in the city (Raia Jr., 1995). The procedure has been recently refined by Raia Jr. *et al.* (1998), who divided the vacant land in the city of Araraquara into seven different classes, based on the size of the lots. In this way, instead of a flat number valid for any lot of the city, there are now seven different values, one for each group. This would mean, for example, an additional annual tax of US$1.00775 per m^2 for small lots (below 125 m^2) and US$1.86520 per m^2 for large urban properties (above 5,000 m^2).

Conclusions

Despite being an academic exercise, the application makes possible a comparison between the actual tax values and those estimated with the proposed alternative. For example, the owner of a parcel with 300m^2 and a one-level house, which is a quite common in medium-sized Brazilian cities, would pay around US$100 per year. This same parcel would have added to this basic tax value an additional amount of US$133 per year if all basic infrastructure networks served it. However, if the land parcel was vacant, and if the taxation strategy proposed here was applied, there would be an additional tax value of US$302 per year added.

The main strength of the proposed taxation strategy is the fact that it could bring more equity to the urban environment. In the long run, we expect that it could also produce a change in the trend towards urban sprawl by encouraging the occupation of vacant plots. But there are also some serious weaknesses. First of all, it is not easy to apply, and its application requires some expertise which is usually not available in developing country cities. Furthermore, there is always a very strong reaction against any kind of strategy that will reduce the profit of affluent groups. Not only are there many politicians supporting these groups in Brazil, but also the politicians often belong to the group of land speculators.

Although we cannot say that the proposed strategy is easy to understand and to apply in the real world, there is another issue that is even more critical. How are we to define what is really vacant land? Can we charge a property for being vacant just because it is temporarily empty? It is common for someone to have spent all his or her savings on buying a parcel and to have no money left to build anything on it right away. The time span between buying the land and building the house may actually be many years. In other words, not every piece of vacant land is held for speculative reasons. How can the different cases be distinguished? This issue is already on the agenda in many Brazilian municipalities, but so far there has been no adequate solution to this problem. Every initiative to clarify this issue is welcome.

Notes

1. Land valorisation means the enhancement of land prices, values or status.
2. Impedance means resistance to movement.

References

Audirac, I. and Zifou, M. (1989) *Urban Development Issues: What is Controversial in Urban Sprawl? An Annotated Bibliography of Often Overlooked Sources*, CPL Bibliography 247, Council of Planning Librarians, Chicago.

Azevedo, E. A. (1981) Aspectos jurídicos do uso do solo urbano, in *Seminário de Desenvolvimento Urbano*, SEPLAN/JB/Ministerio dos Transportes/BNH/MINTER, Brasilia.

Brazil (1988) *Constitution of the Fedaral Republic of Brazil*, Trabalhista, Rio de Janeiro.

Breheny, M. (1992) The compact city: an introduction. *Built Environment*, **18**(4), pp.241–246.

Ewing, R. (1997) Counterpoint: is Los Angeles-style sprawl desirable? *Journal of the American Planning Association*, **63**(1), pp.107-126.

Gordon, P. and Richardson, H. W. (1989) Gasoline consumption and cities – a reply. *Journal of the American Planning Association*, **55**(3), pp.342–346.

Gordon, P. and Richardson, H. W. (1997) Are compact cities a desirable planning goal? *Journal of the American Planning Association*, **63**(1), pp.95–106.

Jenks, M., Williams, K. and Burton, E. (1996) A sustainable future through the compact city? Urban intensification in the United Kingdom. *Environments by Design*, **1**(1), pp.5–21.

Mascaró, J. L. (1979) *A Study of Infrastructure Costs in Medium Sized Cities*, FAU, University of São Paulo, São Paulo (in Portuguese)

Mascaró, J. L. (1989) *Desenho Urbano e Custos de Urbanizacão*, D. C. Luzzato, Porto Alegre.

Naess, P. (1995) Urban form and energy use for transportation, unpuplished Ph.D. thesis. Trondheim University, Trondheim, Norway.

Newman, P. W. G. (1992) The compact city: an Australian perspective. *Built Environment*, **18**(4), pp.285–300.

Newman, P. W. G. and Kenworthy, J. R. (1989) *Cities and Automobile Dependence: An International Sourcebook*, Gower, England.

Oliveira, N., Barcellos, T. M., Barros, C. and Rabelo, M. M. (1989) *Vazios Urbanos em Porto Alegre: Uso Capitalista do Solo e Implicações Sociais*, Secretaria de Coordenação e Planejamento e Fundação de Economia e Estatística, Porto Alegre.

Pampolha V. M. P. (1999) Urban sprawl and energy use for transportation: the case of state capitals in Brazil, unpublished Ph.D. thesis, São Carlos School of Engineering, University of São Paulo, São Carlos (in Portuguese).

Raia Jr., A. A. (1995) An evaluation of the META model and its application in the taxation of vacant urban land, unpublished M.Sc. thesis, São Carlos School of Engineering, University of São Paulo, São Carlos (in Portuguese).

Raia Jr., A. A., Matsumura, E. M. and Rohm, S. A. (1998) Aplicação de Sistema de Informações Geográficas no planejamento urbano e de transportes, in *IV Congresso e Feira para Usuários de Geoprocessamento da América Latina*, Sagres, Curitiba.

Rolnik, R., Kowarick, L. and Somekh, N. (1990) *São Paulo: Crise e Mudanca*, Brasiliense, São Paulo.

Sanches, S. P. (1988) A contribution to the operational analysis of transit networks in medium sized cities, unpublished Ph.D. thesis, São Carlos School of Engineering, University of Sao Paulo, Sao Carlos (in Portuguese).

São Paulo (1991) *Plano diretor de São Paulo ao alcance de todos, Prefeitura Municipal de São Paulo*, Secretaria Municipal de Planejamento, São Paulo.

Silva, A. N. R. (1990) Economical urban densities: the influence of urban public transportation, unpublished M.Sc. thesis, São Carlos School of Engineering, University of São Paulo, São Carlos (in Portuguese).

Silva, A. N. R. (1993) The costs of idle urban land and a new approach for calculating tax values, unpublished Ph.D. thesis, São Carlos School of Engineering, University of São Paulo, São Carlos (in Portuguese).

Silva, A. N. R. and Ferraz, A. C. P. (1991) Densidades urbanas x custos dos serviços públicos – análise do caso de São Carlos. *Revista de Administração Municipal*, **38**(199), pp.57–65.

Silva, A. N. R. and Ferraz, A. C. P. (1993) Uma nova sistemática de tributação da propriedade urbana. *Revista de Administração Municipal*, **40**(208), pp.51–60.

Souza, L. C. L. (1996) The influence of the urban geometry on the air temperature at the pedestrian level, unpublished Ph.D. thesis, São Carlos School of Engineering, University of São Paulo, São Carlos (in Portuguese).

Souza, L. C. L. and Silva, A. N. R. (1998) Compact city: could this be an option for medium sized Brazilian cities?, in *Environmentally Friendly Cities* (eds E. Maldonado and S. Yannas), James & James, London.

Kerstin Zillmann
Rethinking the Compact City:
Informal Urban Development in Caracas

Introduction

The compact city is often conceived of as having a specific urban form; the important dimensions of compactness are seen as high densities of buildings and mixed uses. The informal city of Caracas shows an unexpectedly compact urban form and a specific urban pattern. It is both densifying and consolidating as a result of the countless individual activities of its inhabitants, involved in a constant process of producing homes, urban space and the city.

This chapter discusses the process of consolidation and densification of two informal settlements, La Montañita and Julián Blanco, in Petare-Norte.[1] Both are the result of three decades of building and development, produced mainly by their inhabitants. The building strategies of the original settlers and their families are examined to illustrate how this dense urban pattern and the compact urban form of clustered building structures have evolved.[2] The positive and negative impact of the compact neighbourhood form on people's lives is explored. The chapter questions how the future urban development of the consolidated parts of the so-called Ciudad de Barrios (City of the Barrios)[3] could be supported, and if the concept of a compact city is a viable option for attaining sustainable urban development.

Compact and informal cities?

According to Jenks *et al.* (1996, p.5) the 'vision of the compact city has been dominated by the model of the densely developed core of many historic European cities', and has led to their interpretation as ideal places to live and experience the vitality and variety of urban life. Often, the compact city is imagined as an option for a more sustainable urban form – a city of mixed uses, short travel distances, with vivid public spaces and a vital urban society. Today, the compact city concept has been revitalised and promoted as an urban form and as a model for counteracting the urban sprawl of European cities.

The compact city concept developed in a European context where urban development has been controlled for most of the time, and managed by a formal set of planning and building regulations. It nevertheless had a certain influence on the foundation of the cities in the New World in colonial times (see Benevolo 1993; Hardoy 1992).

But there was no such direct influence on the building of the informal city. It is therefore interesting to examine how self-managed urban growth, and a set of informal planning and building strategies, could also produce compact urban forms such as the Ciudad de Barrios of Caracas, Venezuela.

Whether the compact city is a sustainable urban form, and whether it can provide a vision for the rapidly growing cities of developing countries, may be answered through research and analysis of the specific realities of different urban agglomerations. This might avoid the dangers of a narrow concept of the compact city, and avoid seeing it as 'a simplistic concept, drawing on particular reified urban forms' (Jenks *et.al.*, 1996, p.5). While large-scale research is needed, this chapter highlights the importance of specific studies of informal solutions and projects as a sustainable answer to urban problems at a time of global urbanisation.

The dynamic growth rate of informal settlements is one of the main elements in the acceleration of global urbanisation. The characteristics and forms of regulation governing this growth are still poorly understood. Although a world-wide phenomena, the focus here is on Latin America. The typical Latin American city is a divided one, with urban patterns and forms relating to the division between its formal and informal parts. In a critical analysis of 2,000 years of Latin American urbanisation, Hardoy (1977) reveals a continuum of formally planned city cores and spontaneously built urban areas throughout history. In pre-Columbian, colonial and post-colonial times, building regulations were mainly used to centralise administrative, economic and religious functions in the city centre. By contrast, the popular housing areas were ignored and neglected by the urban elite in all periods. The evolution of these areas has always been self-directed, and the physical accumulation of countless individual activities has created particular urban patterns and specific urban forms.

The main producers and developers of the Ciudad de Barrios are informal settlers. They act individually as families and households, and collectively as self-organised communities or formally acknowledged neighbourhood organisations. It is the community that has to solve the various problems that appear in different phases of the informal urbanisation process – according to their needs and abilities. Municipal and political actors occasionally support them. In more than 40 years of Venezuela's democracy, the dominant political attitude towards the informal city can be characterised as mainly *laissez-faire*.

The evolution of the informal settlements of Caracas has been a slow process of consolidation and densification involving different actors. This process is not necessarily linear or continuous, but in its course different stages or phases with different qualities can be identified. The phases can also be seen as sub-processes of the informal urbanisation process. The overlapping or mutual enhancement of these dimensions and stages may occur through territorial and physical consolidation, through commodification or market consolidation and through legal consolidation and regularisation of land. Socio-economic and cultural settings have a strong impact on the consolidation activities of the local actors (Harms *et al.*, 1994).

The informal city of Caracas

The metropolitan area of Caracas, currently with a population of at least 4 million, was a late industrialiser and remained a small town until the export of crude oil took off in the 1920s. Venezuela adopted a core region strategy. In the short span of a single generation, Caracas was transformed from a sleepy colonial town into a modern metropolis (Friedman, 1969). This was achieved through the eagerness of central government to make improvements in the city's physical appearance, financed through the expenditure of national oil revenues on the capital city. Between 1920 and 1950 the population of Caracas grew rapidly from 92,000 to 495,000, with 695,000 living in the wider metropolitan area (Wilhelmy, 1958). By this time the modern metropolitan area occupied almost all the flat area of its valley (11,500 hectares). The colonial core of the city was almost completely replaced by large-scale public building projects and apartment blocks.

Over the next 40 years the metropolitan population grew even more rapidly and reached 3.5 million by 1990 (Imbesi and Vila, 1996). The twin processes of physical transformation of the capital city and transformation from an agricultural to an oil-exporting and food-importing economy, had led to widespread rural to urban migration to the capital region.

After the first democratic elections in 1958, the informal city expanded substantially through the mechanism of organised and politically supported land invasions.[4] The settlements researched and reported in this chapter were founded in the early 1960s as precarious *barrios de ranchos* (MINDUR, 1995). Since then, a dynamic process of consolidation and densification of these self-help settlements has taken place without any legal regularisation of the land, which is frequently in the public domain (Zillmann, 1998; 1997a, b, c). An inventory of the barrios in the early 1990s provided a general overview of the phenomenon (FUNDACOMUN, OCEI, 1993). A *Plan Sectorial* was drawn up in an attempt to begin the integration of the settlements into formal urban planning procedures by reviewing and processing city-wide data (MINDUR, 1993). According to official data in 1993, around 40% of the population of the metropolitan area of Caracas lived in informal settlements[5] (FUNDACOMUN, OCEI, 1993).

The informal city of Caracas is now seen reflected in the glass facades of banks and ministries. Numerous barrios lying behind the apartment blocks on the steep slopes that surround the central valley can be seen from the motorways.[6] They are located towards the west along the road to the airport, towards the south along the tributaries of the river Guaire and in Petare in the east of Caracas. Some are embedded in the older neighbourhoods of the city and located close to the boundaries of the Mount Avila National Park (Fig. 1). The further expansion of the Ciudad de Barrios is limited by topography and the time and costs of transport.

The evolution of a compact urban form

Rapid urban growth in the capital city, and on-going population growth, have changed the character of the older barrios from centrally located squatter settlement areas into highly densified settlements with slightly growing commercial activities. They have changed from loosely articulated *ranchos* to compact clusters of solid, multistorey houses, built as concrete frame constructions filled in with red brick.

The consolidation and densification process was further advanced after the construction of the metro which links these housing areas with the city centre.

Legend

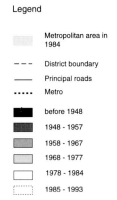

	Metropolitan area in 1984
– – –	District boundary
——	Principal roads
.....	Metro
■	before 1948
▨	1948 - 1957
▨	1958 - 1967
▨	1968 - 1977
☐	1978 - 1984
⬚	1985 - 1993

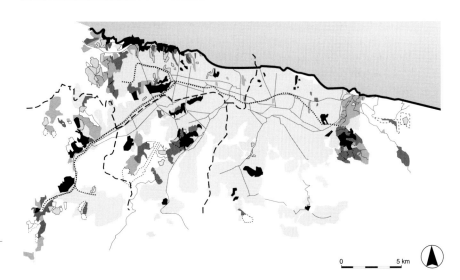

Fig. 1. Evolution of the City of Barrios in Caracas 1948 – 1993.
Source: Zillmann, 1997a

Today, the growth of the older informal settlements is more the result of internal processes than a result of migration into the city. The main reason for the on-going densification is the need for inhabitants to improve their own housing situation, to resolve the lack of housing for their children and grandchildren, and to improve their living and income conditions. This occurs within the constraint of the current economic crisis, and has led to widespread letting of rooms, or even entire floors of houses, and to the use of space for small businesses and workshops.

The two informal settlements of Julián Blanco and La Montañita, studied by the Technical University of Hamburg-Harburg (TUHH) research team, are located in the north of Petare (Fig. 3). Petare was a colonial village that was transformed into one of the biggest areas of low-income settlement in Caracas. Both informal settlements present a level of densification characterised by Bolívar as at a stage where formal intervention and technical support would be most effective (MINDUR, 1994). La Montañita is a sector of José Felix Ribas, one of the largest barrios in the north of Petare. It is located in a narrow valley, scarcely wider than the main street running along it, and climbs up the adjoining hills. It can be reached from a metro station, by foot or by jeep (Fig. 2). Bus or jeep using the Petare–Guarenas motorway can reach the neighbouring barrio, Julián Blanco. Here the main street runs along the top of a 1300m-high hill, and the dwellings descend a gentle western slope and a steeper eastern slope.

The basic physical infrastructure for all of the informal settlements in the north of Petare was provided in the 1970s. According to the studies undertaken in 1990 by FUNDACOMUN, 84% of dwellings of the whole barrio agglomeration were connected to the water supply system, and 88% linked to the electricity and to the sewage system. In 1993 the barrio agglomeration, which includes the settlements studied, covered a total area of 130 hectares (MINDUR, 1993). Through a process of the extension of streets and stairways, informal settlements have developed a more or less functional urban pattern, and specific layouts have evolved in close relationship to the topography. The system of footpaths, steps and streets was expanded and modified several times in the first two decades of the settlement's history to create new pathway connections, or to give more space for the extension

Fig. 2. View of the barrio climbing up a steeply sloping hillside.
Source: Zillmann

of the area covered by buildings.[7] By 1990, around 40% of the total area had been built on, and the path system covered 12% of the area in both settlements (Fig. 4). The remaining green areas were often too steep to be developed.

In three decades since their foundation in the early 1960s, a remarkable physical consolidation of the dwellings took place in Julián Blanco and La Montañita, which can be described as a process of horizontal and vertical densification. La Montañita was founded in 1960 on private land later taken into the public domain. The first settlers built 238 dwellings in the first 16 years of the settlement's existence. By 1990 the number of dwellings had doubled (574), and inhabitants had built new dwellings, reorganised and extended existing buildings and replaced initial dwellings with new buildings.

Top Left: Fig. 3. Location of Julián Blanco and La Montañita in the north of Petare.
Source: TUHH Study Project, 1994

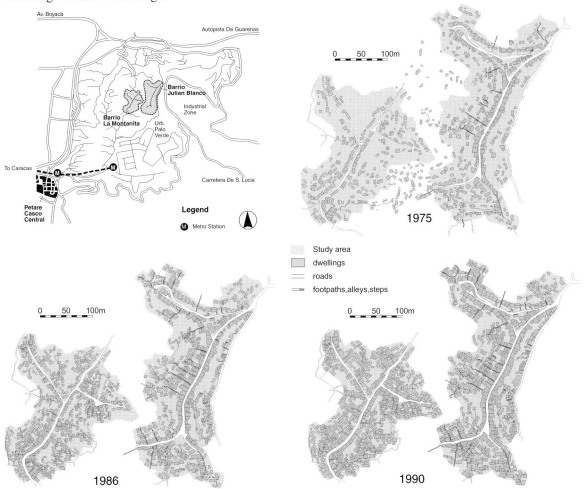

Legend
M Metro Station

Study area
dwellings
roads
footpaths, alleys, steps

1975

1986

1990

Fig. 4. Spatial evolution of Julián Blanco and La Montañita 1976, 1985 and 1990.
Source: Zillmann, 1997a

The barrio Julián Blanco was founded in 1966, and 30 years later it occupied nine hectares. Here too, there has been a continuous process of horizontal densification. In 1976, 22% of the area was covered by 421 buildings, in 1985 30%, and by 1990, 40% had been developed. Not only have new buildings been constructed, but the ground area of existing buildings has also been extended. In 1990 the ground area of buildings which were studied in more detail varied from

$86m^2$ to $140m^2$. The average ground area of the buildings changed in Julián Blanco from $47m^2$ in 1976 to $57m^2$ in 1990, and in La Montañita from $44m^2$ to $48m^2$.

Up to four floors were added to some buildings, and even garages were integrated into the ground floors. By 1994 the total floor area varied from $49m^2$ to $378m^2$ (with the average consisting of $162m^2$ in Julián Blanco and $215m^2$ in La Montañita). Compared to 1985, when floor areas varied from $29m^2$ to $250m^2$, the informal settlers had increased their total floor area by 28% in Julián Blanco and by 56% in La Montañita, over a period of ten years. Vertical densification by adding floors to houses continues, while horizontal densification seems to have slowed down after two decades of self-help activities, with little extension of ground floors.

Building strategies

Who lives in the barrios of north Petare? What strategies did they adopt and how was this kind of compact city achieved?

Who lives there?

The total population of the entire barrio agglomeration in the early 1990s, including La Montañita and Julián Blanco, was 44,726 (MINDUR, 1995).[8] At that time almost 60% of inhabitants had lived in the area for more than 10 years, and most of them were born there. It was a young population: scarcely 7% of the inhabitants were over the age of 50. Around 57% were working, mostly in the formal economy. In 1985, 18% of the population in the two settlements were tenants (Tait, 1993; 1995). The 1990 inventory carried out by the National Foundation of Community Development and Municipal Advancement identified that more than 90% of the dwellings of the entire barrio agglomeration were single-family dwellings, with an average family size of about five persons (FUNDACOMUN, OCEI, 1993).

An analysis of 15 case studies revealed a density of 13.5 persons per building in Julián Blanco and 8.6 persons per building in La Montañita in 1994 (TUHH, 1994). In both barrios, a third of the dwellings were used by more than one family, and another third was used by extended families consisting of more than one household. Only four of fifteen buildings were single-family dwellings. The TUHH study identified 635 such buildings in Julián Blanco and 574 in La Montañita in the year 1990.[9] These figures suggest that around 8,000 persons live in Julián Blanco and around 5,000 persons in La Montañita.[10] From this it was estimated that the total net density in Julián Blanco was 888 inhabitants per hectare, and in La Montañita 757 per hectare in 1994.[11]

What strategies were adopted to achieve compact forms?

Interviews with the first generation of settlers and their families – all of whom owned their houses – showed that they had applied different building strategies according to their abilities, and according to the topography of the lot. An indication of this can be seen from three examples of the houses studied.

Since the physical consolidation of the house was achieved, the owners of building C1 have enlarged the area of each additional floor by using the slope of the land (Figs 5 and 6).[12] In 1976 the family had a small house of $47m^2$. In 1994 the building had four floors and a total floor space of $378m^2$ in relation to a total ground area of $141m^2$. The family rented out $244m^2$ of the total available floor space. The lot was completely built over and even extended, because the family used part of the street to build on. Construction of a fifth floor has already been started. The family who own building C6 have recently started to adopt the same strategy, and the building of additional floors is in the process of completion. Building C3 has been partially extended in a step-by-step process. Because of this building strategy, it has a smaller total floor area (of 164m²) than buildings C1 and C6. The family owning this house left the barrio some years ago and relatives now look after the rented-out apartments and rooms.

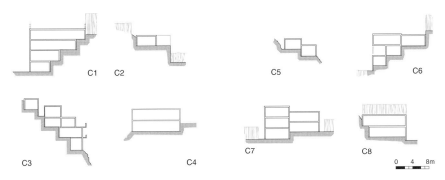

Fig. 5. Sections of the buildings studied in La Montañita in 1994.

Not every family or household can afford to consolidate and densify in the same way. Much depends on various external and internal factors. In 1994 different types of household could be identified. One group of consolidators, who had lived over 30 years in the barrio as owners, had a family structure consisting of three, and sometimes four, generations. They often enlarged their houses extensively, and rented out rooms or apartments.

A second group of owner families succeeded in consolidating their socio-economic and housing situation only in small stages, often with long periods of stagnation. They can be called non-consolidators, or slow consolidators. Some could not improve their situation at all. In this group of settlers, adult children still often live with their parents. Some had returned to their parents' houses when their partnerships failed, or when they lost their jobs, bringing the grandchildren with them. These families now have less space available to house more people. In other words, the occupation rate increased and the per capita floor area decreased. This specific household coping strategy of the urban poor is sometimes called 'nesting' (Moser, 1996). A third group of home-owners, who arrived at a later stage in the barrios' development, purchased their dwellings as completed buildings when they moved into the barrio. Information on the previous owners was not available, but they used their buildings as a source of income by selling them, even if they did not own the lot.

Tenants are a fourth, and increasingly large, group of inhabitants.[13] The renting out of rooms or apartments in the informal settlements is quite common, but illegal, so tenants do not have legal security or protection. However, in some cases the owner's family and tenant families had lived for over 20 years in the same building, and were often relatives. Today, access to the consolidated and older barrios is more difficult. To live in these more or less centrally located barrios means that one has to rent an apartment or a room, or to buy a house there. Buildings are used by their owners as a source of income in several ways. Letting rooms and flats is quite common and a main reason for enlarging the building. Additional space is used for different commercial and productive activities. Garages and workshops have often been built especially for the use of car mechanics. It is notable that buildings in favoured locations, such as street corners, squares, main streets, the entrances of settlements and on less steep lots, have been consolidated and enlarged much more easily than buildings located on steep stairways and in the less accessible zones of the barrios.

Research into survival strategies of the low-income population in different Venezuelan cities revealed several individual household coping strategies as a reaction of poor families to overwhelming economic constraints (Cariola, 1992). These studies confirmed that the barrio has to be seen as a productive site and not only as a place to live. Families try to establish a network of extended informal and formal economic activities that mobilise all household members. In order to satisfy their most urgent needs, they simultaneously reduce their consumption, their reproduction costs and their spatial mobility.

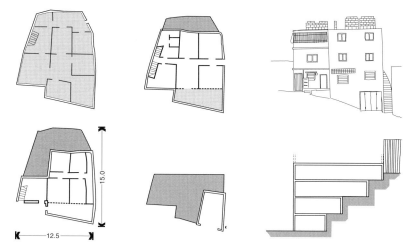

Fig. 6. Plans of the extension of House C1 (1985 – 1994), and elevation and section 1994.
Source: Zillmann, 1997b

The impact of compaction on the barrio population

The informal city of Caracas shows a compact urban form, but its evolution has been quite different from that of the compact cities of Europe. But the same question has to be raised – what have been the positive and the negative impacts of a compact urban form and high densities on people's lives?

The ongoing densification process of the older barrios has a negative impact at settlement level and at household level. To a certain extent this has been the result of uncoordinated individual building activities. What were formerly shacks have been transformed into multi-storey building complexes that present both technical and housing problems (Figs 7–10). Studies of the densification of older informal settlements have documented in detail what happens, step-by-step, over a long period, when people extend their former one- or two-family houses to multi-storey and multi-family building complexes (Bolívar, 1993 and MINDUR, 1994). The research undertaken in Julián Blanco and La Montañita reaffirms these findings.

Frequently households have problems with the design of their apartments, which often include rooms without natural lighting and ventilation. Rooms and apartments can also suffer from drainage problems for different reasons. Often, one wall is formed by the rock of the slope into which the house is built. The sewage system can frequently cause drainage problems. Most barrios were provided with technical

Left: *Fig. 7. House C1 in 1985.*
Photo: Hans Harms

Right: *Fig. 8. House C1 in 1994.*
Photo: Kerstin Zillmann

Left: *Fig. 9. House C3 in 1985*
Photo: Hans Harms

Right: *Fig. 10. House C6 in 1985*
Photo: Hans Harms

infrastructure and urban services in the 1970s, but after three decades these are overloaded, inadequate and often in a deteriorated condition. At the settlement level, a reduction of public and open space has been notable. The public and semi-public space of the stairways has often been reduced by the extension of buildings. But new forms of open space have been created on roofs or terraces, providing the households with exceptional views over the Caracas valley.

Self-helpers and informal builders have developed a specific knowledge of construction through practical experience, and sometimes they come up with quite surprising aesthetic solutions. Nevertheless, structural and landslide problems continuously emerge. Structural problems can occur when a building gets an extra load of two or more storeys, or when single buildings are extended individually and start to form a complex building structure on the slope. Caracas suffers from heavy rainfall, and landslides causing damage to informal buildings happen regularly. In the event of hurricanes and earthquakes, the barrio population is in a highly unsafe situation. However, such is the pressure to settle on empty lots that people continue to build their homes, even if the topography is risky.

The impact of informal consolidation and densification problems could be a question for discussion and regulation by the settlers. But the social cohesion in the barrio communities has changed under the pressures of economic crisis. The initial settler families worked as a core group in the barrio. Neighbours also joined together in smaller areas to protect their homes and streets. But violence, criminal activities and the influence of the drugs trade and drug consumption are increasing, especially among young men. Street gangs are common. There is increasingly strong competition between the use of the street as a public space for leisure activities or sport, and as a traffic zone and parking area. The alternative of travelling from the barrio to enjoy the facilities and public spaces of the formal city has also decreased, because of the high costs of transportation. The chances of older people, women and children enjoying outdoor activities are limited by their lack of income and mobility.

Future perspectives – towards a more sustainable informal city

At the moment the Latin America discourse on sustainable urban development focuses more on urban governance and urban management than on the search for a sustainable urban form, of which the compact city model is one possible option. According to Stren (1995, p.109), during the 1980s a crisis has taken place in urban research, but nevertheless, an important opportunity exists at the conceptual level. Abstract and transcendent ideas such as 'the local state' and 'urban planning' have been replaced by lower-level concerns such as 'local government' and 'urban management' that focus on local and even micro-level case studies. Yet the dynamics of the informal city, and the entity of the divided city, have to be managed effectively, and this includes dealing with serious contradictions and different interest groups. The big challenge of urban planning and management is how to act in a conflictual setting whilst taking into account the mutual dependence of the informal and formal parts of these cities. As Jenks *et al.* have argued: 'Getting the right policies, management and form for cities will be a key factor' in achieving sustainable urban development (1996, p.4). A network of different actors is needed and new partnerships should be established. Regarding the informal city, the different actors should define what is meant by sustainable urban development, and this certainly includes the further development of their built urban form and its qualities.

Marcuse (1998, p.103) has stated that 'sustainability is not enough', reinforcing the principal goal of social justice as a focal point for efforts and as a criterion for long-term political and social viability in the assessment of urban planning and urban design programmes. He argues that it is conceptually unsustainable for the majority of the world's people 'that their present circumstances and their present societal arrangements might be sustained' (ibid.). From the perspective of residents, a more sustainable urban development certainly means, at the least, an improvement in the living, housing and working conditions in the barrios, including a variety of socio-cultural, economic and environmental advances.

A step towards a more sustainable urban development of the barrios of Caracas should be recognition of the informal city as a growing part of the city, with its own specific urban fabric and social space. Planners and politicians should deal with the problems and opportunities of the Ciudad de Barrios, and integrate these dynamic urban areas into urban development and transport policies. Certainly, an analysis and an assessment of the internal potential and the forces producing the informal city are essential for creating strategies to protect the existing positive qualities, as well as to develop new ones. Even if the impact of high densities is similar in all consolidated barrios, those desired features such as improved technical and social services, safe living environments and housing improvements, cannot be expressed in 'town planning standards' that are seen as good for all local realities. Adequate standards seem to depend on many variables, economic, social and local in nature. They can be identified through a dialogue with the producers and users of informal settlements. More effective intervention and support for the Ciudad de Barrios could be elaborated, using their specific expertise. In most cases, the problems associated with the different phases of the informal urbanisation process have to be solved by, or with, the community of the barrio, according to their needs and abilities. This requires more or less collective, or at least organised, activities of the inhabitants. Obviously, the other actors in the consolidation process, such as state, urban and local government agencies and authorities, have to be involved. Technical assistance and organisational support for the informal urbanisation process at the local level is crucial for the future of the fast-growing metropolis and has to be co-ordinated with urban development strategies at the metropolitan level.[14] Meanwhile, in Caracas, the *Plan Sectorial* is being used to select informal settlements for upgrading projects, which are realised in co-operation with barrio organisations (MINDUR, 1993).[15]

Some reflections: rethinking the compact city
The dominance of the European vision of compact cities as 'ideal places to live and experience the vitality and variety of urban life' has been questioned by Jenks *et al.* in relation to its relevance and sustainability in emerging nations 'associated with extremes of growth and size' (1996, pp.4–5). They introduce the terms 'urban intensification' and 'consolidation', which relate to 'the range of processes which make an area more compact', describing a number of strategies by which an area can become more heavily built up or used. Thereby they distinguish between intensification of built form and activities. 'Built form intensification comprises: redevelopment of existing buildings or previously developed sites, at higher densities; sub-division or conversion of buildings; building of extensions to existing structures; and development on previously undeveloped urban land. Activity intensification is defined as: increased use of existing buildings or sites; changes of use which lead to an increase in activity; and increases in the numbers of people living in, working in, or travelling through an area' (Williams *et al.*, 1996, p.84).

In reflecting on the consolidation and densification processes in the barrios studied in Caracas, it seems these fit into this concept of 'urban intensification' in several respects, especially because they show an intensification of both built form and activities. In the barrios, even vertical densification takes place and results in a compact urban form, while in general the densification of squatter settlements happens horizontally. But the reason for the production of this Latin American type of compact city is rooted neither in urban design nor in the vision of a sustainable city. The compact urban form is an expression of a highly competitive situation regarding urban land and central locations, and of the unequal distribution of Venezuela's wealth. It also shows that the barrio inhabitants have gained, as construction workers, special knowledge in the well-developed building industry of Venezuela, which enables them to construct their multi-storey buildings, even in hilly situations.

To understand Latin American cities and their urban development better, different approaches are needed, addressing issues of growing urban segregation and fragmentation, the impact of post-colonialism and modernity on development policies and urban societies, and an understanding of urban conflicts and controversy in times of globalisation. Hardoy (1995, p.33) described Latin American cities as becoming 'agglomerations of fragmented cultures, where even traditional neighbourhood societies seem to have weakened'. He sees that the central challenge for the construction of agendas for urban research and planning is for a new vision of the future for Latin America, and for new ideas for its future cities (ibid., p.27).

This chapter described a process-oriented approach to addressing the phenomenon of the informal city in Latin America. The informal city should not be understood simply as a response by self-helpers to a lack in public housing provision, but rather as a dynamic process in the production of a city. The Ciudad de Barrios of Caracas provides evidence for changing the dominant image of the informal city from one of precarious huts and squatter settlements located on the urban periphery, to one recast as an informal and central part of the city, presenting a compact urban form and high building densities. It is thus a model of a compact city with a very different kind of dynamic from the European model. The case of Caracas suggests that the informal city should be re-conceived as a compact urban form, or, more accurately, a series of compact urban forms. That is, as a variety of compact cities that reflect local knowledge, skills in production and self-regulation, which should be considered as a basis for the comprehensive urban planning and development of fast growing cities.

Notes

1. The research project was undertaken by the author in the Department of Urban Planning and Housing in Developing Countries at the Technical University of Hamburg-Harburg (TUHH) under Prof. Hans Harms in close co-operation with Prof. Teolinda Bolívar, with the Research Group *The Production of Urban Barrios* of the Faculty of Architecture (FAU) at the Central University of Venezuela (UCV). The field work in Julián Blanco was supported by a student group from TUHH, the field work in La Montañita and the documentation of the findings were supported by Jan Scheurer. The digital mapping was done by Frank Rogge.
2. After the original study in 1985, 15 families were revisited in 1992 by members of the research team, to continue documentation of their building activities.
3. Bolívar (1992) first introduced the term 'City of Barrios'. According to MINDUR (1995) a barrio is defined as a growing residential settlement, built on invaded land by inhabitants who do not own the land and have no master plan or urban design project, necessary to meet the formal planning requirements for settlements, neighbourhoods, or towns.
4. In Venezuela, a right exists to build on invaded land. This is called *bienhechuria*.
5. The percentage of the barrio population reported by social organisations and experts was 60 % (El Nacional, 16/6/1993, *El rancho es la vivienda de 60 por ciento de los caraqueños*). In 1996, 40% of the inhabitants of the Municipality of Libertador, which covers the main part of the city of Caracas, lived in barrios (718,000 of 1,823,000 inhabitants). In 1990, 33% of the population of the metropolitan area of Caracas were housed in barrios (1,161,000 of 3,504,000) (Imbesi and Vila, 1996).
6. The average inclination of the hills is 40%.
7. In 1976 the area covered by the system of streets, alleyways and stairs was 7% in Julián Blanco and 4% in La Montañita. These were completed in the second decade of the barrio evolution (1976–1985) and have not been changed significantly since then.
8. In the spatial survey of the metropolitan area of Caracas, MINDUR (1995) defined different units for urban planning (UPF) and smaller units of urban design (UDU). The figures refer to the UDU 4.3 José Felix Ribas and UDU 4.4 Julián Blanco. These do not correspond exactly with the area of the settlements studied by TUHH.
9. These figures are the result of a detailed analysis of an aerial view of the settlements (see Zillmann, 1997a).

10. The exact population is unknown, so it was calculated according to the number of buildings and the average number of persons/building.
11. These figures correspond with the findings of Bolívar's detailed studies of the barrios of Carpintero-Valle Alto in Petare and Santa Cruz in Macarao in the South West of Caracas (Bolívar, 1993). In the barrio Carpintero-Valle Alto, the total net density was 771 inhabitants per hectare. The figures for the barrio Santa Cruz were a total net density of 572 inhabitants per hectare.
12. This type of building, the so-called *torre en pendiente* (tower on the slope), often uses an external stairway as an additional access to the different floors (Bolívar, 1993).
13. See Gilbert's research on rental housing in Caracas, Mexico and Santiago de Chile (Gilbert, 1993).
14. This is a result of a series of *Itinerant Seminars for Participation in Planning and Popular Habitat* organised by an international group of researchers, and carried out in different Latin American cities. The Declaration of Caracas (1991) and the Declaration of Salvador de Bahia (1993) point into the same direction (Bolay *et al.*, 1996).
15. In Julián Blanco and the surrounding barrio agglomeration, a programme for the improvement of basic services was financed by the World Bank (FUNDACOMUN, 1996). The neighbourhood group of the barrio of Julián Blanco, who applied for the programme, had to be well organised in order to act as a partner in the improvement process. At the beginning, the research team of UCV acted as their consultant. The group also acts in the Forum of Inhabitants of the Barrios, exchanging different local experiences across the continent, a seemingly effective and stimulating collective answer to the negative impacts of economic deregulation and globalisation on poor urban neighbourhoods.

References

Benevolo, L. (1993) *The European City*, Blackwell, Oxford.
Bolay, J.-C., Kullock, D., Cruz, M., Meira, M. E. and Bolívar, T. (1996) *New Opportunities: Participating and Planning*, Itinerant Seminar of Participative Planning and Popular Habitat in Latin America, Institut de Recherche sur l'Environnement Construit, Ecole Polytechnique Fédérale de Lausanne/ Fondation pour le Progès de l'Homme, Universidad Central de Caracas, Caracas.
Bolívar, T. (1992) Caracas - Stadt der Barrios. Plaedoyer fuer eine Aufwertung der Armenviertel und ihrer architektonischen Qualitaet. *ila*, **160**, pp.15–17.
Bolívar, T. (1993) *Densificación y Vivienda en los Barrios Caraqueños - Contribución a la determinación de problemas y soluciones*, Facultad de Arquitectura y Urbanismo, Universidad Central de Venezuela, Sector de Estudios Urbanos, Caracas.
Cariola, C. (1992) Sobrevivir en la pobreza: el fin de una ilusión, Editorial, *Nueva Sociedad*, Caracas.
Friedman, J. (1969) The changing pattern of urbanization in Venezuela, in *Planning Urban Growth and Regional Development: The Experience of Guyana*, MIT Press, Cambridge, MA.
FUNDACOMUN (1996) Promueba Caracas. Proyecto de Mejoramiento Urbano, *Boletín informativo*, **1(1)**.
FUNDACOMUN, OCEI (1993) *III. Inventario de los Barrios*, Caracas.
Gilbert, A. (1993) *In Search of a Home*, UCL Press, London.
Gilbert, A. (1998) The urban landscape, in *The Latin American City* (ed. A. Gilbert), Latin American Bureau, London.
Hardoy, J. E. (1977), La construcción de las ciudades de America Latina através del tiempo, in Seminario Interregional Africa-America Latina sobre 'Asentamientos Humanos Marginados', *Revista Interamericana de Planificación*, **42**, pp.9–27
Hardoy, J. E. (1982) The building of Latin American cities, in *Urbanization in Contemporary Latin America, Critical Approaches to the Analysis of Urban Issues* (eds A. Gilbert, J. E. Hardoy and R. Ramirez), John Wiley & Sons, New York.
Hardoy, J. E. (1992) Theory and practice of urban planning in Europe, 1850–1930: its transfer to Latin America, in *Rethinking the Latin American City* (eds R. M. Morse and J. E. Hardoy), Woodrow Wilson Center Press, Washington.

Hardoy, J. (1995) Reflections on Latin American urban research, in Latin America, in *Urban Research in the Developing World, Volume 3* (ed. R. Stren), Centre for Urban Research and Community Studies, University of Toronto, Toronto.

Harms, H. (1993) Aspekte der stadtentwicklung in den metropolen Lateinamerikas, in *Rom – Madrid – Athen – die neue Rolle der staedtischen Peripherie* (eds V. Kreibich *et al.*), Institut fuer Raumplanung, Universitaet Dortmund, Germany.

Harms, H., Tait, J. and Zillmann, K. (1994) Theoretische Annaeherungen an ein Modell der Konsolidierung und Verdichtung informeller Siedlungen – Anotaciones teóricas para un concepto sobre 'consolidación de asentamientos espontanéos', *Arbeitspapier 45/3 – Exposición 45/3*, FSP 1-07, Technische Universitaet Hamburg-Harburg, Germany.

Imbesi, G. and Vila, E. (1996) *Caracas. Memorias para el Futuro*, Gangemi Editore, Rome.

Jenks, M., Burton, E. and Williams, K. (1996) *The Compact City. A Sustainable Urban Form?* E & FN Spon, London.

Marcuse, Peter (1998) Sustainability is not enough. *Environment and Urbanization*, **10(2)**, pp.103–112.

MINDUR, Ministerio del Desarrollo Urbano, Consejo Nacional de la Vivienda (1993) *Plan Sectorial de Incorporación a la Estructura Urbana de las Zonas de los Barrios del Area Metropolitana de Caracas y de la Región Capital*, Caracas.

MINDUR, Ministerio del Desarrollo Urbano, Consejo Nacional de la Vivienda (1994) *Densificacion y Vivienda en los Barrios Caraqueños – Contribución a la determinación de problemas y soluciones, Premio de Investigación en Vivienda 1993*, Caracas.

MINDUR, Ministerio del Desarrollo Urbano, Consejo Nacional de la Vivienda (1995) *Un Plan para los Barrios de Caracas, Premio Nacional de investigación en vivienda 1995*, Caracas.

Moser, C. N. (1996) *Confronting Crisis. A Study of Household Responses to Poverty and Vulnerability in Four Poor Urban Communities*, The World Bank, Washington.

Ramirez, R., Fiori, J., Harms, H. and Mathey, K. (1992) The commodification of self-help housing and state intervention – household experiences in the barrios of Caracas, in *Beyond Self-Help Housing* (ed. K. Mathey), Mansell Publishing Limited, London.

Stren, R. (1995) Towards a research agenda for the 1990's: an introduction, in *Latin America: Urban Research in the Developing World, Volume 3* (ed. R. Stren), Center for Urban Research and Community Studies, University of Toronto, Toronto.

Tait, J. (1993) Statistical analysis of the field survey from the 'Joint research project: self help housing in Latin America', *Part 1: Intermediate Report on San José Alto,* and *Part 2: Intermediate Report on Julián Blanco*, Technische Universitaet Hamburg-Harburg, Germany.

Tait, J. (1995) *José Felix Ribas, Commented Statistical Summary*, Technische Universitaet Hamburg-Harburg, Germany.

TUHH (1994) *Aeltere, ungeplante Siedlungen in Caracas*. Study Project, Urban Planning Programme, Technical University of Hamburg-Harburg, Hamburg.

Wilhelmy, H. (1958) Das moderne Caracas. *Ueberseerundschau*, **10**/1958, pp.18–19.

Williams, K., Burton, E. and Jenks, M. (1996) Achieving the compact city through intensification, in *The Compact City? A Sustainable Urban Form?* (eds M. Jenks, E. Burton and K. Williams), E & FN Spon, London.

Zillmann, K. (1997a) *Cartografía del proceso de consolidación y densificación 1976–1994 en Julián Blanco y en La Montañita (Zona 6 de José Felix Ribas), Petare, Caracas, Informe del trabajo No. 1, Area de investigación 1-07: Urbanismo y Vivienda*, Universidad Técnica de Hamburgo-Harburg, Germany.

Zillmann, K. (1997b) *Documentación de las casas estudiadas en Julián Blanco y la Zona 6 de José Felix Ribas en Petare, Caracas, Informe del trabajo No. 2, Area de investigación 1-07: Urbanismo y Vivienda*, Universidad Técnica de Hamburgo-Harburg, Germany.

Zillmann, K. (1997c) *El proceso de la consolidación territorial y física de los barrios Julián Blanco y en La Montañita, José Felix Ribas, Zona 6 en Petare, Caracas, Presentación en la Universidad Central de Venezuela, Facultad de Arquitectura y Urbanismo, Sector de Estudios Urbanos, Caracas, 10 de junio 1997. Exposición 45/1, Area de investigación 1-07: Urbanismo y Vivienda*, Universidad Técnica de Hamburgo-Harburg, Germany.

Zillmann, K. (1998) Consolidation and densification of informal squatter settlements in Caracas, Venezuela – Consolidacion y densificacion de barrios informales. *TRIALOG 57, A Journal for Planning and Building in the Third World*, **2**/1998, pp.26–35.

Part Three
Responses to Compaction at Low and High Densities
Introduction

Up to now, the book has emphasised the importance of the metropolitan region, processes of rapid urbanisation, concentration and decentralisation, and the meaning and symbolism of some compact city ideas. A number of the key issues of urban compaction have been discussed, particularly urban intensification, the impact of peripheral urban sprawl, and how it might be contained. This part takes a more pragmatic stance. It presents case studies showing responses, plans and policies to achieve compaction or sustainability at two extremes of the spectrum – South Africa (containing some of the world's lowest density urban development) and Hong Kong (arguably the world's highest density city).

The experience of three cities in South Africa is presented – Cape Town, Pretoria and Durban. A different perspective is given on each, although all have the same characteristic of low-density peripheries resulting from apartheid policies. Dewar, an early advocate of compact city concepts, puts forward the case for urban compaction in the South African context. Noting the problems caused by low densities and fragmentation, he argues that problems of employment, and accessibility by foot and public transport could be improved through compaction. He raises an important aim to achieve equity of access to urban opportunities. A structural development plan for Cape Town is analysed in some detail, which sets up a hierarchy of access to urban facilities, from pedestrian access to transport at its lower level, to transport interchanges with associated facilities at its highest.

Drawing on data from Pretoria, Schoonraad, while not opposing the compact city concept, takes issue concerning its feasibility. She raises three key questions: that the urban poor would not be able to afford to live in a compact city; that it might not be possible under current planning frameworks and market forces; and that anti-urban values would be an obstacle to its achievement. However, her conclusions point to possible ways forward. Todes *et al.* provide an analysis of the issues and plans in Durban, and show that compaction can be partly achieved, but that compromises have to be made. In practice, urban sprawl has been curbed, and some coherence and physical compaction achieved. They show that a wider range of policy instruments is needed that includes transport improvements, social provision, and capacity building in the townships and informal sector. Although less idealistic, they demonstrate that working with the existing forces and guiding policy towards more compact forms is potentially effective. The suggestion is that there should be an African view of urban compaction.

Hong Kong is at the other extreme, with densities as high as 116,000 persons/ hectare. The two chapters show the development of the city into its present form, and consider some of its successes and failures. Xing Zhang gives an overview of Hong Kong's development through time, concentrating on the forces that shaped it, of topography and shortage of land, population in-migration, and a cultural acceptance of high-density living. While generally acceptable to residents for many reasons, he raises questions about the environmental sustainability of this density of urban form. Zaman, Lau and Mei give a further dimension to Hong Kong's dense development. They consider the impact of land sales, land reclamation, decentralisation and urban renewal. However, they concentrate on the issue of sustainability, presenting a detailed analysis of its environmental problems such as air quality and transportation, and raise issues of self-sufficiency in decentralised development. The conclusions to both chapters have a different perspective. Xing Zhang questions whether it is possible to generalise from the experience of Hong Kong, especially doubting that it could be transferable to the cities of the West. Zaman, Lau and Mei, however, take the view that, with its compact form, high densities and good public transport, it could be lesson to other cities in Asia. This may be a case of both being right.

Placing these two extremes side by side reveals interesting differences, yet some common concerns, even if for different reasons. Environmental degradation is common to both countries, and so is the issue of transport. It seems particularly apt that, in both cases, there is a view that there should be African and Asian responses to compaction, and that the models from the West, while having some value, are unlikely to be directly transferable.

David Dewar

The Relevance of the Compact City Approach:
The Management of Urban Growth in South African Cities

Introduction

The major social and environmental consequences that stem from the structure and form of South African cities suggest that the current pattern of urban development is entirely unsustainable, and that urban compaction is an essential condition for improved urban performance. However, compaction is not a sufficient condition – it needs to be accompanied by substantial urban restructuring. Furthermore, directed residential infill, which is a primary policy instrument for achieving greater compaction, cannot be applied ubiquitously – it needs to be used to reinforce positive structural change. The case of a recent plan for the City of Cape Town is used to show one way in which this restructuring can be achieved and how infilling can be directed with the greatest benefit. Some of the major obstacles which need to be overcome, if greater urban compaction is to become a reality in South Africa, are identified.

The structure and form of South African cities

Rapid urbanisation is a relatively recent phenomenon in South Africa. The vast majority of urban growth has occurred within the last 50 years. The urbanisation of the majority black population has been much more recent than this. A constant and central theme of the ideology of apartheid was that black people should be viewed as temporary sojourners in towns and cities, to be tolerated only to the extent, and for the period, that their (largely unskilled) labour was required. It is only since the mid-1980s that the relatively unrestricted access of black people into towns and cities has become a reality. Currently, it is estimated that some 54% of the total population is urbanised (Republic of South Africa, 1996a). That figure is increasing rapidly as farm-workers continue to be displaced through increasing mechanisation in the commercial farming areas, and as the fragile economies and resource bases of the overcrowded 'homeland' or communal subsistence farming areas continue to disintegrate. In terms of both in-migration and natural increase, processes of urban growth are contributing to a rapidly growing pool of the urban poor.

Modernism

Above all other forces, the structure and form of South African towns and cities have been shaped historically by two 'ideologies'. The first is the ideology of modernism. Dominant city planning and management systems and policies have been almost entirely imported from the UK, Europe and the US, and have strongly entrenched the urban characteristics of modernism, including:

- A strongly anti-urban or pro-suburban ethos. There has been a focus on the free-standing building surrounded by private space as the basic building block of settlements. The single free-standing house on its own plot is entrenched as the image of the 'good urban life', even in the case of the lowest income communities.
- An emphasis on the separation of the major activities of life (living, working, playing and movement) to avoid 'conflict'.
- An approach to settlement building that is largely quantitatively or programmatically determined. Capacities are calculated, thresholds of different facilities are determined to derive a 'menu' or programme of elements, and planning becomes a more or less efficient assembly of the parts, without particular concern for a framework which holds the whole together. Commonly, different disciplines make decisions about different elements of structure in virtual isolation from each other.
- The promotion of the concept of the neighbourhood unit. Residential dwellings are clustered into discrete 'cells' or neighbourhoods that focus inwardly onto centrally located community facilities in the (naïve) belief that this promotes a sense of community. The cells are not integrated but are simply linked by movement infrastructure.
- The domination of concerns about technological efficiency to the virtual exclusion of social or environmental considerations. A particularly prevalent concern is freedom of vehicular movement. The private vehicle is seen as the primary mode of movement, and settlements are scaled to the motor car, despite the fact that an increasing majority of households will never own a car.

Since most urban development has occurred since the advent of modernism, these characteristics are widely prevalent in South Africa.

Apartheid

The second major form-giving ideology was the policy of apartheid. Spatially, the apartheid model had at its core the separation of racial groups. All racial groups, other than white, were systematically removed beyond the edges of settlements, in the worst cases to distances of over 60km away. Since there is a direct correlation between race and income, the poorest people have been located furthest from agglomerations of urban opportunities.[1] Although the law underpinning this, the Group Areas Act (Republic of South Africa, 1966b), was repealed in 1991, in practice little has changed since. There are a number of reasons for this. First, in terms of existing households, there is considerable inertia within the system. Many households have invested a considerable proportion of their limited resources in making life as comfortable as possible in these remote locations, but there is no active land market there because of the poor location. Second, until 1994, the majority of urban political decision-makers remained white and they had no vested interest in vigorously pursuing change. Third, patterns of in-migration within settlements are strongly based on kinship and social ties, and those social and economic networks which do exist occur around established settlements. Fourth, land prices are considerably cheaper on the periphery of settlements.

While settlements continue to sprawl outwards, urban employment and commercial opportunities have been slow to respond and to follow this pattern of growth. There are two major reasons for this. A lack of investor confidence is one. Environmentally, the low-income environments are sterile and the dominant perception amongst the investor community is that they are high-risk areas. Although a considerable amount of public investment, in the form of social and utility infrastructure, has been flowing into these areas since 1994, it is widely scattered and too thinly spread to change the dominant negative image. Another reason is that patterns of access – the most significant determinant of the spatial distribution of activities – have not significantly changed. Most major transportation decisions are reactive in the sense that they are demand-led and thus destination-based. There is a continuing attempt to make access to existing clusters of urban opportunities easier, but this serves to reinforce existing patterns.

The legacy of modernism and apartheid

Significantly, the precepts of modernism and apartheid were compatible. The emphasis on separation meant that apartheid planners eagerly embraced the concept while grotesquely distorting its scale, and the concept of the neighbourhood unit, with its cell-like form and limited points of access and egress, was seen as efficient in terms of security and of containing unrest. The combination of these forces has resulted in the three spatial characteristics of low density, fragmentation and separation, which fundamentally describe South African towns and cities. The low-density sprawling cities spread further outward daily, in a seemingly formless and random way. With fragmentation, the grain of the urban fabric is coarse, largely because development occurs in relatively discrete parcels or cells of land, frequently bounded by freeways or buffers of open space. Within the cells, environments commonly consist of discrete collections of parts, with no overarching cohesion. The separation of land uses, urban elements, and racial and class groups leads to mono-functionality, rather than a mix of uses.

The human and environmental consequences of these urban structures and forms have been appalling. Agricultural and natural landscapes have been, and are still being, aggressively destroyed. It has been estimated, for example, that the rate of loss of agricultural land to urban development in Greater Cape Town between 1985 and 1995 has been approximately 1.8 hectares per day (Gasson, 1995). The settlements generate enormous amounts of movement, at great and unsustainable cost in terms of energy consumption, infrastructure and pollution. Traffic gridlock is increasingly becoming a fact of urban life. Poverty and inequality are exacerbated, for it is the poor who are most affected. For the majority who cannot afford to own a car, life is cripplingly inconvenient and expensive. Public transport is inefficient and often non-existent, and many households are effectively trapped in remote locations. Limited-access vehicular routes create impenetrable barriers and reduce opportunities for small income-generating businesses because of the diffuse nature of local markets. Access to community facilities is differentiated, as provision depends on whether or not a particular neighbourhood is prioritised. The utilisation of the facilities themselves is tied to the fortunes of the local communities that surround them; some are overcrowded while others are underutilised.

The quality of public space is almost universally poor, despite the fact that large numbers of people spend considerable amounts of time in these spaces because their dwellings are so overcrowded. The dwellings and other buildings fail to define, protect or give a scale to the public spatial environment.

The case for compaction

Given the realities of the structure and form of these cities, there is an overwhelming case for seeking greater compaction in the management of urban growth. Most of the reasons commonly cited in favour of compaction all hold in the case of South African cities. These include, for example, the need to reduce movement, air pollution and dependency on oil imports; to maximise historic investment in utility infrastructure and social facilities; to increase thresholds and thus levels of service; and to increase convenience. Nevertheless, there are three key interrelated factors which make such a policy approach not just 'nice to have', but a necessity.

The first is employment generation. Unemployment in South African cities is high (although there are regional variations, the rate is generally in excess of 30%) and growing. The reality is that a large and increasing number of people have no option but to secure their survival through self-generated income from small businesses. A precondition for small business to thrive, however, is intensive, vibrant local markets. When local markets are intensive, diversification and specialisation – the motors of urban economic growth – are promoted. It becomes cheaper for low-income households to outsource many of the functions that would otherwise be undertaken within the household.

The second factor is that movement on foot is the only mode of travel affordable by a growing majority of urban dwellers. It is therefore necessary to create urban environments that operate efficiently and pleasantly at the pedestrian scale. This demands compaction.

The third factor is the necessity to resolve the current problems of public transport. Because of the static historical pattern of urban opportunities and the sprawling nature of growth, the urban system generates enormous amounts of one-way movement at peak hours, with a dramatic fall-off in non-peak periods. This pattern, and the pattern of low-density sprawl, makes larger capacity fixed-line movement modes such as the train non-viable. The lack of high-capacity, fixed-line public transport has had two major consequences. One is that many households, which would otherwise not choose to do so, are forced to own cars. Since affordability is a problem, the vehicles they purchase are inevitably old. They require on-going maintenance that is a large drain on household income, and they are highly inefficient in terms of emissions. The other has been the birth of a vigorous non-regulated taxi system which, rather than complementing larger capacity carriers such as train and bus, directly competes with them for long-haul routes. This has had the effect of increasing the number of vehicles on the roads, increasing the number of accidents and increasing pollution. It is also a major factor contributing to escalating violence, since vicious taxi 'turf wars' are endemic in almost all major towns and cities.

In order to attempt to alleviate this, the state massively subsidises the train and bus system. In Cape Town, for example, by no means the worst of the major cities in terms of sprawl, the average annual subsidy per bus commuter is a staggering $482.[2] This subsidy further distorts the efficiency of the movement system (for example, it pays bus operators to use buses for short-haul, non-direct trips which would otherwise be more appropriately undertaken by taxi). These subsidies are entirely unproductive and unsustainable. However, any attempts to remove them without a viable alternative would place an intolerable burden on the poorest of the poor and would threaten the very fabric of society.

The government has recently committed itself to achieving an efficient and regulated public transport system, utilising different modes to their best advantage in an integrated way (Republic of South Africa, 1998). This implies three spatial preconditions – compaction, greater intensification along more continuous public transportation routes and a more decentralised pattern of urban opportunities.

While greater urban compaction is clearly necessary, it is not a sufficient condition for improved urban performance. The approach needs to be applied selectively to bring about, simultaneously, greater compaction and a structural manipulation in the patterns of accessibility and urban opportunities. It is little use pursuing compaction passively by defining edges and limits – the areas encompassed within the functional footprints of South African cities are so large as to render this approach invalid. It needs to be actively pursued through a strategy for structural infilling.

Current attitudes to compaction

The first calls for greater urban compaction were made almost 25 years ago (Dewar, 1975) and grew increasingly vociferous from the late 1980s onwards. In 1995 the state formally committed itself to compaction policies with the publication of the Development Facilitation Act (Republic of South Africa, 1995). The first chapter of this Act defines a set of principles that must be considered in all land development decisions. *Inter alia*, these include paragraph [3 (1) (c) (vi)] intended to 'Discourage the phenomenon of sprawl in urban areas and contribute to the development of more compact towns and cities'. In practice, however, little has changed since that time. Analyses undertaken by the National Development and Planning Commission (Department of Land Affairs, 1999) indicate that generally there is little understanding at the level of local government of the meaning of urban compaction and other related principles or about how they can be achieved.

A spatial development framework for the City of Cape Town

Arguably, one of the first systematic attempts to deal with both compaction and spatial structural readjustment in South Africa can be found in the Draft Municipal Spatial Development Framework for the City of Cape Town (City of Cape Town, 1999).

The plan has at its starting point the recognition that the concept of accessibility is central to the making of a more compact, equitable and integrated city (Fig. 1). Equity does not mean that all parts of the city are the same. The achievement of this is neither possible nor desirable. It does mean, however, that all people should have easy access, defined in the first instance in terms of pedestrian movement

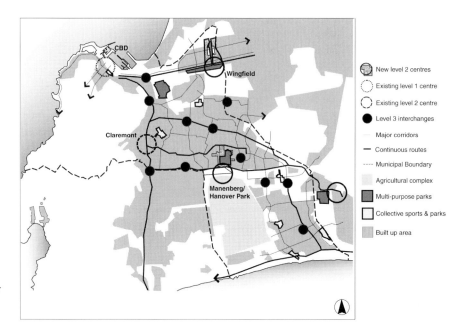

Fig. 1. Integrated framework:
centres and corridors.
Source: City of Cape Town, 1999.

and public transportation, to a broadly similar range of opportunities, facilities, special places and events. The challenge posed by this is two-fold: to make existing opportunities more accessible to the majority, and to create a new hierarchical pattern of agglomerated opportunities and special places. From this starting point, the core concept of the plan can be explained as a logical sequence of steps.

1. Creating a system of urban opportunities required the definition of a hierarchy of zones of relative accessibility. To determine the levels in this hierarchy, it was necessary to balance the two potentially conflicting dynamics of the need to increase convenience, and to maximise the use of limited public resources. In order to activate the system of access, the city was quartered several times to create a three-tiered hierarchy of zones of relative accessibility. At this level of abstraction, the system of access was only notional.

2. Catering for pedestrian movement demanded an area-wide approach, as high-access zones need to be spread relatively evenly across the urban surface. The system, at the lowest level of the hierarchy, adopted an acceptable (but not perfect) walking distance. The average radius around the central point of the accessibility zone in Cape Town was 2.5km. If a walking time of 12 minutes per km is assumed, this gave a maximum walking time of 30 minutes. In the longer term this may be reduced, but the ability to do this will be strongly affected by factors such as disposable income and density.

3. The most equitable public transport-based movement systems are those where people can quickly and easily switch direction and modes of movement. Where possible, the system provides 'access to access', rather than being primarily reactive or destination-determined. The centre points of these higher level zones of access were conceptualised as transportation interchange points (see Fig. 1).

These are places where modes of transport are integrated and where changes of direction are possible. In the case of Cape Town, various combinations of modes are accommodated (taxi, bus/taxi, taxi/train, taxi/bus/train).

4. The notional system of access was then adjusted, while maintaining the original hierarchical logic, to accommodate the realities of the existing movement system. In areas where more than one location had potential as the interchange, preference was consistently given to points of connection with the rail system rather than to purely road-based systems. However, this did not mean that some people would have to walk 30 minutes to access public transport. Access is by walking to the nearest public transport route, which in turn connects with an interchange point.

The hierarchy of access, from pedestrian movement, connection to the transportation routes, through to higher level interchange points, was based on carefully defined spatial policies. The thinking extended to issues of more detailed design. For example, interchange points generate large numbers of people. In every case the interchange point was planned to include a pleasant, landscaped public space which always accommodated a hawkers' market. The concept would generate a city-wide programme of 'people's places' and formal or informal markets. As the interchange points are locations of high accessibility, they are ideal places for government to reach the people with the services they provide. Accordingly, clusters of social services ('kits of public parts') have been linked to the interchange points. The precise make-up of the 'kit' varies with the importance of the interchange; for example, the lowest level interchange points have lower order facilities. The clustering of facilities also promotes a 'one-stop shop' type of service provision that could significantly enhance convenience and open up the possibility of sharing facilities, particularly between schools and the broader community. This would increase the efficiency and sustainability of service delivery.

The activities associated with these places also create ideal opportunities for private-sector retailing, commerce and manufacturing, as well as for high-density housing infill. Where appropriate, publicly funded economic infrastructure would be provided. In these ways the original interchange point was planned to evolve into a 'high activity' urban centre which is also environmentally friendly, and a focus of social activity. Significantly, with investment in urban design and landscaping focused on these centres, they could become 'special places'.

The need to provide equity of access applies not only to urban opportunities, but also equally to nature. Accordingly, a hierarchical system of green spaces was planned, to be associated with a centre. The ordering system was not only related to interchange and other 'points'. The more continuous routes which 'tie' local areas together, particularly those that carry public transport and that allow stopping along their length, are important energy flows in cities. More intensive activities (those which service, and are thus supported by, the public) would be encouraged to locate along these routes, thereby increasing the convenience, efficiency and the sustainability of the activities themselves. These routes were viewed as frameworks of interlinked and continually growing activity systems or corridors. Similarly, a web or interlinked network connecting with the system of parks, promoting habitat biodiversity, productive opportunities and opportunities for recreation, formed an important part of the green concept.

The core concept of the Structural Development Framework therefore provides a clear strategy for compaction through a process of residential infill. Four forms of infilling (or implosion) were suggested.

- *Structural* – the selective insertion of high-density housing to reinforce the pattern of centres and the integrating routes.
- *Economic* – facilitating densification by encouraging people (within certain performance constraints) to sub-divide land parcels they own, giving the potential to create many thousands of 'developers'.
- *Spatial or surgical* – utilising new housing to give definition and enclosure to currently undefined and sterile public spaces. Included in this is the selective infill of unnecessary or excessive road reserves.
- *Social* – many areas suffer from high levels of overcrowding in individual dwelling units but there is considerable residual space around these units. Infill is proposed to decrease the unit overcrowding while maintaining kinship and other forms of social ties.

Obstacles to greater compaction

Achieving greater compaction through the manipulation of urban structure and form is thus both necessary and potentially achievable. In terms of the middle and higher income housing market, there are indications that this is beginning to occur spontaneously. This tendency is fuelled by irritation with increasing travel times and congestion, the increasing impact of the cost of transport on household budgets, and increasing costs associated with holding and maintaining large land parcels. There are also concerns about security, and the housing form of gated townhouse complexes, however undesirable, is becoming increasingly prevalent.

There are, however, a number of obstacles to greater compaction which need to be tackled systematically. The attitude of local planning authorities is important, as their co-operation is required to slow down the rate of lateral spread significantly. However, the revenue of local authorities is entirely based on taxes on land development. This tends to foster an attitude that 'any development is positive', and private-sector developers, continually seeking cheap land, continue to be the central players in determining the urban footprint.

There are obstacles to compaction inherent in the land market as, for example, well-located land is inevitably more expensive. Current housing policy allows for a one-off capital grant of $2,480 per household earning below $117 a month and an income-based declining contribution to households earning less than $220 a month. This amount is a contribution towards land, services and some superstructure. Since the political imperative is to provide as much superstructure as possible, the land price becomes the softest variable and housing schemes continue to be erected on cheaper peripheral land. Central government encouragement to use part of the subsidy to write-down the cost of better-located land is essential to change this, and would in the longer term represent a far more effective form of subsidy. On the more positive side, in most South African towns and cities there are large parcels of strategically located vacant land in public ownership, which can be mobilised towards the ends of greater compaction.

Numerous in-built cultural attitudes to land exist, as many of the immigrants to towns and cities have been displaced from the rural areas. They bring with them a number of new needs that historically have not been accommodated adequately in the urban environment. These may include keeping and slaughtering livestock, initiation rites, the practice of traditional medicine, a desire to work the land – all of which tend to underpin a land-extensive mindset. To change this, it is necessary to meet these needs proactively, on public as opposed to private land.

Investor confidence will need to be raised if urban compaction is to become a reality. A concentration of public and private investments and partnerships, and the conscious generation of high-quality special places, such as that suggested in the plan for Cape Town, represent perhaps the only realistic way to begin to tackle this.

Despite the national rhetoric to the contrary, national housing policy itself promotes diffuse, low-density forms of development. There are two ways in which this is happening. First, the use of the one-off capital grant tied to the free-standing single-storey residential unit as the overwhelmingly dominant policy instrument promotes large, monofunctional mass housing projects. The need for large tracts of land to gain economies of scale in terms of this form of delivery reinforces the use of land on the periphery. Second, the award of subsidies by Provincial Housing Boards in many provinces is tied to large minimum plot sizes (commonly between 300 and 450m^2), a restriction which makes a mockery of legislated calls for compaction. Other national policies provide obstacles. For example, the problems associated with subsidising public transport (described above) suggest that a reversal of policy would lead to a rapid increase in compaction. Such a change is currently mooted widely in political circles.

Conclusion

The current sprawling, fragmented and separated form of South African towns and cities is entirely unsustainable. Greater compaction is essential. There is an increasing national awareness of the need for this and of how it might be achieved technically, but there are a number of entrenched policies and practices which need to be changed if rapid improvement is to happen. The critical variable is political will. What is required, and what has not yet emerged, is a powerful political champion for compaction. Perhaps the greatest single institutional stumbling block is that the distribution of national cabinet portfolios is fractured along sectoral lines: urban issues, for example, are spread over a wide range of government departments such as Housing, Environment, Transport, Economic Affairs. The creation of an integrated urban ministry to consider urban development holistically is arguably the single most effective measure to make rapid progress.

Notes

1. Agglomerations or clusters of urban opportunities refers to the more collective activities of a city including: manufacturing, commerce, retail, recreational activities and major social facilities.
2. At July 2000 rates of conversion, $1 = R6.85. In terms of equivalent purchasing capacity, the value of $1 is approximately equivalent to R2.4.

References

City of Cape Town (1999) *The Draft Municipal Spatial Development Framework*, Planning and Development Directorate of the City of Cape Town, Cape Town.

Department of Land Affairs (1999) *Green Paper on Development and Planning*, National Development and Planning Commission Document DPC 4/99, Pretoria.

Dewar, D. (1975) *Metropolitan Planning and Income Redistribution in Cape Town: The Identification of Some Contextual Realities and Their Implications for Metropolitan Cape Town*, Occasional paper No 1, Department of Urban and Regional Planning, University of Cape Town.

Gasson, B. (1995) Evaluating the environmental performance of cities: the case of the Cape Metropolitan Area. Paper presented at the conference on Structuring the Contemporary City: International Geographical Insights, IGU Commission on Urban Development and Urban Life, Cape Town.

Republic of South Africa (1995) *The Development Facilitation Act (Act No 67)*, Government Printer, Pretoria.

Republic of South Africa (1996a) *Census of the Population of South Africa*, Government Printer, Pretoria.

Republic of South Africa (1996b) *Group Areas Act 36 of 1966*, Government Printer, Pretoria.

Republic of South Africa (1998) *Moving South Africa*, White Paper on Land Based Transportation, Department of Transportation, Government Printer, Pretoria.

Maria D. Schoonraad
Cultural and Institutional Obstacles to Compact Cities in South Africa

Introduction

This chapter seeks to explore some of the reasons behind the increasing sprawl of South African cities and their segregation into monofunctional units. This has occurred despite the importance attached in contemporary policy documents to achieving 'more compact, integrated and mixed-use settlement forms' (DPC, 1999, p.21). This new planning paradigm, introduced in 1994, sought to change radically the structure of South African cities and represents an 'outright rejection of the low density, sprawling, fragmented and largely monofunctional forms of development' that characterised the apartheid city (DPC, 1999, p.22).

The new legislation guiding urban planning is taken up in the Development Facilitation Act (1995) and the Local Government Transition Act Second Amendment (1996) that stipulate that all local authorities must draft Integrated Development Plans and Land Development Objectives. These Acts force all local councils to draw up plans that, amongst others, promote sustainable integrated settlements, higher densities and mixed use.

A brief overview of the type and locality of most new urban developments is sufficient to illustrate that the apartheid city form is being perpetuated and reinforced. The Development and Planning Commission (DPC) even goes so far as to state that 'there are few signs that significant and wide-reaching improvements have been set in place since 1994' and that 'to this extent, the planning system must be judged to be ineffective' (DPC, 1999, p.18).

This chapter argues that reasons for the lack of implementation of the compact city include a clash with preferred lifestyles, popular views of the ideal city, and the role of the private landowner or developer. The chapter is structured around three arguments, that the:

- poor cannot afford to live in a compact city, yet efforts to densify the city have been directed at this group,
- city cannot be restructured into a compact sustainable city within the current planning framework, which is based on the participation of landowners and

the protection of private land-owning interests, at the expense of long-term sustainability,
• anti-urban values of all groups, and the lack of existing medium to high-density mixed-use developments that serve as exemplars of living in a compact city, are powerful elements supporting the low-density, monofunctional sprawl of South African cities.

The chapter first gives a brief overview of the current processes at work in the South African city and then proceeds to address these three arguments. These arguments are underpinned by empirical observation of existing realities rather than by a concept of an ideal city and how it would function. Only this approach can advance the implementation of the ideal. The evidence used to substantiate these arguments is mostly derived from professional experience and from statistics for the Greater Pretoria Metropolitan Area (Fig. 1). Most calculations have been based on new developments that have occurred since 1990 when a major planning shift occurred towards recognising the nature, scale and significance of the urbanisation process. Recognising the shortness of the time span, the aim is to indicate what are the nature and scale of the trends towards compaction and sprawl.

Current dynamics
The most outstanding characteristics of South African cities are their horizontal sprawl and segregation which have made them into some of the most inefficient and dysfunctional cities in the world (Dewar, 1992; Hattingh and Horn, 1991; Van der Merwe, 1993; Watson, 1994). The horizontal extension of South African cities is enormous. The metropolitan area of Pretoria, for example, houses approximately 1.5 million people on an area of 130,000 hectares, and stretches over roughly 100km from north to south, and 75km from east to west (GPMC, 1998). Although it houses, for example, only a tenth of the population of metropolitan São Paolo, it is more than half the area of São Paolo. In Pretoria, only 45% of the total metropolitan area is built up (CCP, 1998b).

These distorted settlements have been created by two forces: first by the obsession of the apartheid governments to separate the different racial groups and to move non-whites progressively further from the core and second, by the obsession of planners to separate even compatible land uses. They have succeeded in creating physical distances between the different groups, but at a high cost in terms of transport subsidies. Apartheid established and entrenched this pattern of segregation and sprawl, but current land market forces and urbanisation processes are reinforcing it.

Both low-income housing programmes and the spatial decentralisation of high- and middle-income groups have perpetuated urban sprawl. The government's low-income housing programme aims to deliver 1 million houses by the year 2000 because of the tremendous housing deficit, which was estimated at 3 million units in 1996 (SAIRR, 1998). Because of the backlog, the housing programme has focused on speed of delivery and affordability. These two factors inevitably lead to peripheral locations for new housing projects, next to existing low-cost areas. Furthermore, the programme adopts a reactive rather than a proactive response towards illegal squatting and squatter upgrading, which is also located on the periphery. All new low-cost housing programmes in Pretoria have been built at a

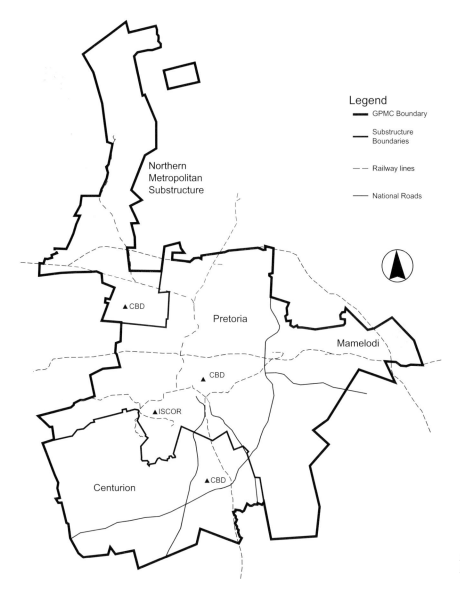

Legend

— GPMC Boundary

— Substructure
Boundaries

– – Railway lines

— National Roads

Northern
Metropolitan
Substructure

▲ CBD

Pretoria

Mamelodi

▲ CBD

▲ ISCOR

Centurion

▲ CBD

*Fig. 1. The Greater Pretoria
Metropolitan Area.*

distance of 20km to 45km from the historic centre. Distances from the new
decentralised centres are even greater and lack direct public transport linkages.
For example, the total area developed for low-cost housing has doubled since
1990 in Mamelodi,[1] an African township founded on Pretoria's urban periphery in
1950, with 1,500 hectares of new land being developed for 19,000 new residential
properties. The spatial impact of subsidised housing schemes on the form of the
city becomes clear when one considers that almost a million housing subsidies
have been approved nationwide, and approximately 750,000 new houses have
already been constructed (Napier, 1999).

   The sprawl caused by low-cost housing projects is matched by the spatial
decentralisation of high-income groups. For these groups, most new developments
take the form of walled enclaves and security villages, also on the periphery. Some

of these developments contain lot sizes ranging from 1,000m² to 4,000m². New medium- to high-income residential development, since 1990, has covered an estimated minimum area of 5,500 hectares. The difference between the high-income and low-income peripheral areas is their accessibility to outlying suburban activity nodes: the high-income areas are well connected to these nodes via private transport routes, i.e. highways, whereas the low-income areas are not connected via public or private transport routes.

The second characteristic of South African cities is that of the very high levels of racial, socio-economic and functional segregation – indeed they are infamous for this. Although the pattern of racial segregation was created by apartheid, the fall of apartheid has done little to change it, as is illustrated by the 1999 election results, which clearly split the city into ANC/PAC[2] supporters and NNP/DP[3] supporters, based on racial groups.

Socio-economic segregation and functional separation are reflected in the absence of diversity in lot sizes and housing types within new neighbourhoods, and their monofunctional character. New residential areas are planned according to the principles of the neighbourhood concept as large, introverted, exclusive, residential areas on discrete consolidated sites (Dewar, 1992). Of the 15 extensions undertaken in and around Mamelodi since 1990, 72% were exclusively for residential use, 24% for non-residential uses and only 4% had a mixed land use. The residential uses were made up entirely of detached houses with a lot size ranging from 150m² to 500m².

The same is true for a traditional white suburban area – Centurion – consisting of 224 neighbourhoods, typical globalised, post-industrial spaces, containing high-technology industries, offices and medium- to high-income residential developments. Of these neighbourhoods in Centurion, only four contain mixed land uses and only 21 have more than two residential typologies, all of which were introduced before 1990. It is clear that exclusive provision is increasingly being made for specific income groups and family types in different areas.

The phenomena of sprawl and segregation generate a tremendous amount of movement, but there is generally a weak articulation of land use to transportation (GPG, 1999). The South African city is a doughnut city, as new developments on the periphery tend to be denser (although still at a low density) than the older more centrally located areas, with smaller lot sizes. They are still not linked to any form of effective public transport. The potential benefits of high densities have been negated by their monofunctionality, and have not led to a decrease in the need to travel by public or private transport. This system tends to aggravate issues of poverty, unemployment, social inequality and polarisation, and fails to create the conditions for a viable, efficient and accessible public transport system (Dewar, 1992).

The poor and the compact city

First argument: the poor cannot afford to live in a compact city, yet efforts to densify the city have been directed at this group.

The debate around low-cost housing has been linked to the debate on the compact city and urban restructuring, and it is frequently argued that the poor cannot continue to live at low densities on the outskirts of the city. The current low-cost housing policy is criticised on two fronts from this viewpoint. First, it is argued that its typology of detached single-family houses, and the size of the stands (often a minimum of 250m^2), creates low densities. Second, it is criticised for its emphasis on peripheral locality and its monofunctionality, which increases the distance as well as the need to travel.

However, this policy holds many advantages for the lifestyles and aspirations of the poor that are often overlooked. Despite appearances to the contrary, low-cost housing areas are actually more sustainable and compact than other parts of the city. The failure to recognise this derives from the attempt to evaluate them in terms of built form and not in terms of actual use. The key difference between the African city and the European city is the lack of correlation between built form and physical appearance, activity and use. Building density and type in African cities has little to do with occupational density and activity because of the informal and temporary character of many of the structures and activities. The initial planning of relatively large lots, accommodating monofunctional single-family units, does not reflect the way they are used nor the densities that develop over time. There is a huge discrepancy between gross layout density, measured in units per hectare, and occupational density, measured in persons per hectare, and there is no correlation between building form and occupational structure. In a study carried out by Senior (1984), the discrepancy is clear. In three different areas developed as detached single-family housing with a floor area ratio of between 0.1 and 0.15, the number of persons per hectare varied from 18 to 92.8 to 120. In two other areas the population density was 700 and 690 persons per hectare respectively, but the floor area ratios were 3.97 and 0.24 respectively.

A survey of the most dense low-cost housing areas in Mamelodi revealed that 80% of all lots had backyard units (CCP, 1998a). There was an average of two additional units per stand, with a maximum of six. The average number of people living in formal houses was seven, with a maximum of 21. Hattingh and Horn (1991) have presented evidence of up to 40 people per lot. The fact that most houses had between two and three bedrooms illustrates the extent of overcrowding. The backyard units accommodated an average of 1.5 persons with a maximum of 5. An examination of the figures on occupational density reveals the difficulty in determining these values: official figures for the Mamelodi area reveal variations between 4.8 persons to 8.6 per unit (CCP, 1998a).

These larger single-family units are not affordable for the majority of South African families, where the average income per family is US$6,000 per annum and where 50% of African households earn less than US$130 per month. Yet an average lot, with basic services and a minimal top structure, costs a minimum of US$2,350, which is the maximum subsidy given by the government. The size of the lot does, however, allow a family to generate an informal income from the site. This becomes more important with growing unemployment amongst the unskilled.

In this survey (CCP, 1998a) it was also revealed that up to 80% of backyard units were rented out, and up to 60% of properties were used to generate an income in the form of shops and services. In this way, residents became part of the housing production process, and satisfied a vital need for rental housing stock not provided in significant quantities by any other sector.

Most families in developing countries have a very low level of mobility, and often live in a single property for their whole lives because of the lack of alternative housing, and the importance of social networks in poor communities (Tipple, 1996). In South Africa, the larger lots also allow for more flexibility in accommodating different life cycles as well as adult children on the same site. In most instances a single lot can accommodate three generations.

In an effort to increase densities, planners have sought to reduce the size of individual lots. This is actually counterproductive, as the actual problem is not the size of the lot, but the difference between gross and net densities caused by unrealistically high service and facility standards (Urban Foundation, 1987). A reduction in lot size, it is argued, will decrease the infrastructure costs and the lack of space can be made up with more public open space. The savings incurred with lower infrastructure costs are, however, often lost in the higher construction costs required to build higher quality units at higher densities. In an exercise carried out in Mamelodi, it was argued that a basic walk-up unit of roughly 60m^2 would be almost three times as expensive as the current 250m^2 lot with a top structure of 30m^2.

Several social housing projects located in central positions have achieved higher density low-cost housing projects. This, however, has happened only with additional funding from donor organisations, and has been available only for higher income groups earning between US$370 and US$510 per month (Adler, 1998).

A survey of public open spaces in Mamelodi has also shown that they are hardly ever maintained because of lack of funding, and frequently become dust bowls and rubbish dumps. Many of these spaces are also taken over by families seeking to increase the size of their lots. In some instances, communities have come together to develop open spaces into community spaces, but this has proved unsustainable and they have largely disappeared, despite much initial enthusiasm and commitment from the residents (CCP, 1997).

As a result of the location of low-income areas on the periphery, the poor have to travel long distances to work and other facilities, and at a high cost because of the lack of public transport. However, there is no other alternative given the operation of the land market, because these are the only areas where land can be made available for low-income groups at affordable prices. People have developed coping mechanisms to address the prohibitive cost of travelling.

A recent survey found that, as a survival mechanism, many people preferred living on the semi-rural outskirts of Pretoria, sending one family member into town to work, whilst the rest relied on informal activities carried out on the lot or in the neighbourhood. Through the reduction in daily living costs, made possible by living in a semi-rural area, they could survive on one formal sector salary. This would not have been possible had they have lived closer to the city (Pienaar, 1999). This confirms Balbo's argument (1993) that the fragmented nature of the African city is both the result and the cause of limited mobility.

There is obviously a need for more creative ways of thinking on reducing travel time and costs, other than simply by increasing density. This does not, however, mean that core housing on the periphery is the solution for the housing problem, as these projects have limited success (Napier, 1998).

Constraints to achieving urban sustainability

> *Second argument*: the city cannot be restructured into a compact sustainable city within the current planning framework, which is based on the participation of landowners and the protection of private landowning interests, at the expense of long-term sustainability.

Urban planning under the apartheid governments was characterised by differential treatment of 'white' and 'non-white' areas through development control; it was distinctly non-participatory and it focused on physical plans enforced through draconian control measures, such as the Group Areas Act. Planners, developers and the government agreed what the ideal city should look like, and were very effective in creating it because their goals overlapped, albeit for different reasons. The character of planning has changed dramatically since then, largely in reaction to apartheid planning and in line with emerging international trends, such as increased competition between regions (Brotchie *et al.*, 1995), communicative planning (Healy, 1992) and urban governance (World Bank, 1999).

Procedurally, planning has shifted from blueprint or master planning towards a strategic development planning process, which integrates social, institutional, economic and physical factors. It has also been influenced by the notion that government is only one of a variety of role players in planning urban areas, and that shrinking government budgets restrict the capacity of government to provide for the needs of all residents. Government thus has to play an enabling role, and work together with a variety of actors, resulting in an emphasis on public participation and consensus (Burgess *et al.*, 1997). There has been an over-reaction on the part of urban planners, leading to excessive participation and the neglect of physical planning. This is ironic, as the creation and reconstruction of compact cities requires strong control measures. South African planners are still suffering from the loss of faith in urban planning first experienced in the 1970s – 'they have become mere pragmatists' (Fishman, cited in Breheny, 1996, p.20).

The result has been a restriction in the means and the ability of both government and urban planners to dictate urban development. According to the Development and Planning Commission (DPC, 1999), the reason behind the lack of implementation of stated principles is the lack of understanding of these principles and wilful recalcitrance, to which must be added the limited use which is made of the various means available to planners.

First, it is clear that implementation is guided more by private developers than by planners. Pickvance's analysis (in Taylor, 1998) found that market forces have had a bigger impact than planners because private developers have powers and initiative to build, whilst planners have mainly negative powers, i.e. powers to refuse permission for development. The role of private developers in creating the distortions associated with the apartheid city has not been properly analysed.

Second, local government development control powers have been eroded by the application of an inappropriate system. Despite the current use of the concept of land-use management, there has been little change in the system of zoning based on the British system of segregation of land uses and minimum densities. This system was only applied in what were white areas and now has been adapted to include all areas. Mabogunje (1990) has pointed out how inappropriate this is for African urban realities. The lack of efficiency of this system has been reinforced by the culture of lawlessness and a focus on private short-term gain, which currently permeate South African society.

The need for areas to compete with one another has further weakened the power of government to enforce certain types of development within its jurisdiction. Government is forced to accommodate development in order to stimulate growth and attract investors, even if it contradicts its own plans. According to Taylor (1998), when an economy is buoyant, developers can be convinced to comply with official plans and to provide for the public good, but when it is weak, as in South Africa, planners cannot dictate the nature of development. But competition has also eroded the scope of planners to control development for the greater good, even in countries with strong economies. Wigmans (1998) has, for example, shown how the focus on attracting foreign investment has led to the disregard of the plight of the poor in Rotterdam in the Netherlands.

Another factor which complicates the enforcement of densification is that strategic plans and policy documents are vague and unprescriptive, but the development control system is based on individual lots. None of the plans have been elaborated into detailed plans that clearly indicate the minimum density and intensity of development. This has resulted in a gap between policy and implementation. Given this fact, it is almost impossible to judge the merit of an application to develop an individual lot. The decision to draw an urban boundary around one of the urban agglomerations (at Gauteng) is a step in the right direction, but this has to be supported by the restructuring of existing areas. Yet there are no effective incentives and measures to promote or enforce the densification and intensification of the existing vast, low-density and monofunctional areas.

Third, the emphasis on public participation has brought the needs of individual communities to the forefront at the expense of the common good. It has also focused on short-term needs as opposed to long-term sustainability goals. In the drafting of integrated development plans for Pretoria, the process of public participation was executed simultaneously at three levels (metropolitan, city-wide and the planning zone) following a similar process. It became clear that people were concerned only with their own areas, and had little concern for effects on the rest of the city (Schoonraad and Van Huysteen, 1997).

A fourth problem is that decision-making powers lie with politicians. This problem originated in an era when planning was the handmaiden of apartheid politicians (Boden, 1989). The Development Planning Commission (1999) has identified the solution for much of the current urban malaise, such as transferring decision-making powers from politicians to technical experts. However, the apartheid legacy, which taints the planning profession today, has discredited planners in the eyes of the public.

Anti-urban values

Third argument: the anti-urban values of all groups, and the lack of medium-to high-density mixed-use developments that can serve as exemplars of compact city lifestyles, are powerful elements supporting the low-density, monofunctional sprawl of South African cities.

Almost without exception South Africans have anti-urban values. Projects carried out with a variety of students from different backgrounds in the University of Pretoria revealed that they view the ideal city as made up of discrete monofunctional low-density areas, separated by green belts. This image is based on their experience of urban life and their inability to imagine a radically different way of life. In recent studies of incremental housing in developing countries, it has also become clear that residents recreate, or reform, their environment until it resembles the rest of the city (Tipple, 1996).

The South African city offers little by way of example in terms of compact city living. Only 19% of the total housing stock in Pretoria can be classified as medium-to high-density units according to South African standards, where a medium-density unit is seen as a stand of between 400m^2 and 250m^2 (GPMC, 1998). In the total Pretoria metropolitan area, the average dwelling size is 96.6m^2, the average population density is 14 persons per hectare and the average building density is three units per hectare (GPMC, 1997).

The aspirations of the poor should not be underestimated in their efforts to create a decent living environment. Not only does the existing low-density life-style of the rich serve as an example, but so too do rural lifestyles. Many residents retain a link with the rural environment and continue rural practices such as tending cattle and planting crops in urban areas. According to Barbir (1998, p.9) 'The tradition of urban living in South Africa is relatively short and much nostalgic feeling for rural or farm lifestyles remains.' In some cases, these rural lifestyles are part of the survival strategies of new arrivals to the city.

The choices that people make are based on these aspirations. In a survey of housing projects carried out by Napier (1998), residents consistently chose a larger lot or house with inferior services rather than a smaller lot with a better quality house. In a survey of squatters on the outskirts of Pretoria, 95% chose detached houses and 5% high-rise flats as the preferred type. This can be expected, especially when no costs are linked to the choice. What is remarkable, however, is that no other typology was chosen. This can only be ascribed to lack of knowledge of other typologies.

Barbir (1998) ascribes this apparently negative attitude towards urban living to the fact that large segments of the urban population do not need, understand or appreciate an urban environment. This is true for the wealthy who can afford to live in suburbia, who are completely dependent on private transport and who are driven into security enclaves by their fear of crime. It is also true for people who have recently arrived from rural areas, seeking only a shelter and basic services and who have yet to accommodate urban behaviour patterns. As Barbir suggests (1998, p.9), 'Both groups are very influential, the former in terms of money and position and the latter in terms of numbers and political pressure. Almost all city planning and development is therefore aimed at meeting the needs of these two groups.'

These views and aspirations will not change spontaneously. Examples are needed of what compact living could be like, as in Crane's (1960) concept of city building, where government was involved in pilot projects to develop alternative typologies which could educate people on the possibilities of compact living. This is highly relevant here.

Conclusion

This chapter has not attempted to refute the idea of the compact city, but has tried to show that there are serious obstacles to achieving it in South Africa. These obstacles are the current survival strategies of the poor that necessitate lower building densities; the freedom and power afforded private landowners and developers within the capitalist market system; the lack of development control measures to ensure that development takes place at higher densities, at central localities and with mixed uses; the lack of exemplars of compact living and the advantages thereof within the existing city; and the anti-urban mindset of both rich and poor. It is not sufficient merely to draft policy documents on the need for a compact city, and then to set out the principles to achieve it. First, the reasons for the persistence of the existing distortions to South African cities must be sought. To lay the blame at the door of apartheid is simply not good enough. The contribution of the different parties that shape cities must be analysed, especially the role of private developers and the social costs of the lifestyles of the rich, for the long-term sustainability of the city.

Second, the differences between the concept of a compact city for Europe and Africa have to be explored. The most appropriate sustainable urban form and its critical elements must be discovered, instead of relying on European examples. Current research on African cities focuses too much on socio-economic and political issues and not enough on their physical implications.

Third, appropriate instruments have to be developed for achieving long-term sustainability instead of the current situation where the wishes of individuals, small groups and the popularity of politicians shape urban development. This has to be accompanied by a change in South African society towards valuing the common good as being equally or more important than the needs of the individual.

Finally, government has to get involved in creating the compact city by means of pilot projects and support for projects that address sustainability, thereby creating a precedent for compact city living.

Notes

1. Mamelodi is a typical African township that was founded under the apartheid government to house Africans removed from 'white' areas. It is a residential area made up of a variety of formal and informal one-storey detached houses, many illegal and of substandard condition. Approximately 300,000 people stay here in overcrowded circumstances. It lacks most social and commercial facilities, such as schools, medical services and shops, forcing people to travel long distances to meet their basic needs. It is also the main reception area for recent migrants to the city.
2. ANC: African National Congress
   PAC: Pan African Congress
3. NNP: New National Party
   DP: Democratic Party

References

Adler, T. (1998) *Social Housing Experience of the Johannesburg Social Housing Foundation*, conference on Social Housing at the University of Leuven, Leuven.

Balbo, M. (1993) Urban planning and the fragmented city of developing countries. *Third World Planning Review*, **15(1)**, pp.24–35.

Barbir, J. (1998) Urban design within local government, paper presented at a Short Course on Urban Design. Spatium, Clarens.

Boden, R. T.(1989) Cultural anthropology in relation to urban design and planning. *Town and Regional Planning*, **35**, pp.11–23.

Breheny, M. (1996) Centrist, decentrists and compromisers: views of the future of urban form, in *The Compact City: A Sustainable Urban Form?* (eds M. Jenks *et al.*), E&FN Spon, London, pp.13–35.

Brotchie, J., Batty, M., Blakely, E., Hall, P. and Newton, P. (eds) (1995) *Cities in Competition: Productive and Sustainable Cities for the Twenty-First Century*, Longman, Melbourne.

Burgess, R., Carmona, M. and Kolstee, T. (1997) *The Challenge of Sustainable Cities*, Zed Books, London.

City Council of Pretoria (CCP) (1997) *Mamelodi Green Plan*, City Council of Pretoria, Pretoria.

City Council of Pretoria (1998a) *Mamelodi Integrated Development Plan*, University of Pretoria, Pretoria.

City Council of Pretoria (1998b) *Pretoria City-wide Integrated Development Plan*, Plan Practice, Pretoria.

Crane, D. A. (1960) Chandigarh reconsidered. *AIA Journal*, May 1960, pp.32-39.

Development and Planning Commission (DPC) (1999) *Green Paper on Development and Planning*, Department of Land Affairs, Pretoria.

Dewar, D. (1992) *Urbanisation and the South African City: A Manifesto for Change*, University of Cape Town, Urban Problems Research Unit, Cape Town.

Gauteng Provincial Government (GPG) (1999) *Gauteng Spatial Development Framework*, APS Africa, Johannesburg.

Greater Pretoria Metropolitan Council (GPMC) (1997) *An Integrated Urban Densification Strategy for the Greater Pretoria Metropolitan Area*, GAPP, Pretoria.

Greater Pretoria Metropolitan Council (GPMC) (1998) *Integrated Development Plan*, Plan Associates, Pretoria.

Hattingh, P. S. and Horn, A. (1991) in *Homes Apart* (ed. A. Lemon), David Phillip Publishers, Cape Town, pp.146-161

Healy, P. (1992) Planning Through Debate: the Communicative Turn in Planning Theory, *Town Planning Review*, **63(2)**, pp.143–162.

Mabogunje, A. K. (1990) Urban planning and the Post-Colonial State in Africa: A Research overview. *African Studies Review*, **33**, pp.121–203.

Napier, M. (1998) Core housing and residents' impacts. *Third World Planning Review*, **10(4)**, pp.391–417.

Napier, M. (1999) Consolidation pathways of households in core housing settlements in South Africa, paper presented at CSIR Workshop on Consolidation of Housing Through Self-Help Extensions.

Pienaar, J. (1999) Quality of Life Survey in the North-West Province, conference on Tenure Security Policies in South Africa, Brazilian, Indian and sub-Saharan African Cities: A Comparative Analysis. Centre for Applied Legal Studies, Johannesburg.

Schoonraad, M. and Van Huysteen, E. (1997) Public participation: the planner's alternative to technical expertise, paper presented to conference, Once upon a Planner's Day, University of Pretoria, Pretoria.

South African Institute for Race Relations (SAIRR) (1998) *South African Survey 1997-1998*, South African Institute for Race Relations, Johannesburg.

Senior, J. B. (1984) Factors affecting residential density – a search for the Zen of density, unpublished Ph.D. thesis, Faculty of Architecture, University of the Witwatersrand, Johannesburg.

Taylor, N. (1998) *Urban Planning Theory since 1945*, Sage Publications, London.

Tipple, A. G. (1996) Housing extensions as sustainable development. *Habitat International*. **20(3)**, pp.367–376.

Urban Foundation (1987) *A Housing Options Assessment Manual – A Decision-Making Framework for Assessing Housing Options and their Density Applications*, Urban Foundation, Johannesburg.

Van der Merwe, I.J. (1993) The South African city in relation to international form. *Development South Africa*, **10(4)**, pp.481–496.

Watson, V. (1994) South African cities: a challenge to planners. *Munivirio*, **11(1)**, p.1.

Wigmans, G. (1998) *De Facilitaire Stad*, Delft University Press, Delft.

World Bank (1999) Urban Development Division. *A Strategic View of Urban and Local Government Issues: Implications for the Bank*. World Bank, Washington, DC.

Alison Todes, Teresa Dominik and Doug Hindson

From Fragmentation to Compaction?
The Case of Durban, South Africa

Introduction

The concept of compact cities has been influential in academic and policy circles in South Africa, and has informed the spatial development frameworks formulated in the 1990s. However, the compact city idea has had to be modified in important ways in the South African context in order to respond to the realities of the inherited urban form (namely, racially divided and spatially fragmented cities), and to emerging social, political and economic forces. As policy has moved towards implementation it has become evident that the vast majority of the black urban poor will remain within the townships and informal settlements on the urban periphery. This acceptance has shifted the focus away from compaction through 'infill' and 'densification' within the urban core, to strategies to upgrade and improve black residential areas internally, and to link and integrate them more effectively to the core.

Such linkages are planned to occur through the development of 'corridors' and 'nodes' – spatial elements built around transport interchanges and routes, where higher density living and mixed land use are to be encouraged. It is assumed that targeted public investment in infrastructure and service provision within nodes and corridors can facilitate compaction over the long term, and promote more spatially and socially integrated, efficient, equitable and sustainable cities.

The chapter examines the application of compact city principles in Durban, a city of 3 million people. It traces their influence and evolution in metropolitan spatial planning, particularly in relation to the current Spatial Development Plan (SDP), and considers the way ideas of compaction have been modified as planning has moved towards implementation. The chapter examines the prospects for compaction and argues that, while these ideas have been helpful in framing thinking about integrated development planning, there are still significant disjunctures between policy and implementation. Furthermore, while greater urban efficiency may be achieved, the aim of social equity remains more elusive. In response, the SDP is evolving to ensure a wider range of approaches that deal with spatial dysfunction.

The legacy of the racial city form

The organising principle informing apartheid planning was spatial segregation according to race.[1] Thus spatial form was racially structured, highly fragmented, sprawling and poorly integrated functionally. The majority of the poor (and largely black) population was located in under-serviced areas on the periphery, while coloured and Indian people were moved to intermediate areas beyond the core (Fig. 1). Development within the largely white urban core also promoted urban fragmentation and sprawl. Planning regulations enforced land-use separation, and encouraged low-density suburban development, oriented to the motor car (Hindson, 1999).

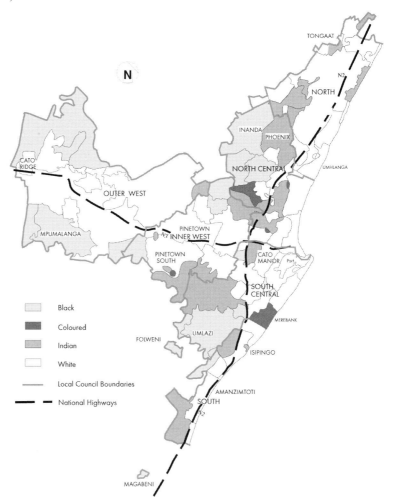

Fig. 1. Historical racial divisions in the Durban Metropolitan Area.

By the late 1970s, however, some of these patterns were beginning to change. Rapid urbanisation of the black population resulted in high levels of overcrowding in townships, while declining controls enabled informal settlements to mushroom within and around them (Hindson *et al.*, 1994). Currently, about 25% of Durban's population lives in informal settlements, sometimes at densities as high as 80–100 households per hectare. Resources, which were always meagre, have been further reduced, with the result that stark poverty has progressively thrown these areas into sharper focus in terms of their relative deprivation.

From the late 1980s, racial segregation began to break down as black, coloured and Indian middle-income groups moved into previously white areas, particularly in the city centre. Poor black people also began to move to locations within the core, establishing informal settlements on open land, or squatting and trading on the pavements within the central business district (CBD) (Morris and Hindson, 1997).

Although some changes have occurred in city form, the apartheid legacy remains a significant challenge for spatial planning. In addition to racial and social inequity, the sustainability of the city form is in question. The poor environmental quality of townships and informal settlements, and the car-dependent, sprawling nature of much higher income development, are key problems of unsustainable settlement form in Durban.

The evolution of the compact city idea in Durban

In the South African context, the idea of compacting the city first emerged within academic planning circles as a critique of the dysfunctionality of the apartheid city, and as an alternative urbanist vision (Dewar *et al.*, 1978; Dewar, 1984). Advocates argued for a dual strategy of concentrating population around existing major core areas (through densification, infill, and the development of well-located land), and creating corridors linking peripheral low-income townships and informal settlements with core areas, while densifying and developing nodes along their routes. From the late 1980s, these ideas became linked to a broader agenda for transformation, as the apartheid state began to crumble.

In Durban, these ideas first entered the public planning realm through Uytenbogaardt *et al.*'s (1989) plan for Southern Pinetown and the Tongaat Hullett Planning Forum (1990) proposal for urban spatial restructuring. In both of these initiatives, the idea of development corridors was emphasised as much as that of concentration around core areas. A major impetus to compaction ideas occurred through their acceptance within the inclusive forum processes that were established during the transitional period in Durban, and in the run up to the 1996 local government elections.

While many of the plans of the early 1990s included both components of compact city strategy, in practice greater emphasis was placed on development around core areas, and on breaking down old forms of exclusion. This was partly a reaction to apartheid state policy, which as late as 1989 proposed to accommodate the black population in large housing projects well beyond city limits. High-density inner-city residential areas were identified as places where the breakdown of urban apartheid was most advanced, offering spaces for exploring urbanist alternatives. Several reports emphasised the costs of subsidising transport to peripheral areas, and argued that employment in Durban was likely to remain centralised in the CBD, and the adjacent Southern Industrial Basin (e.g. World Bank, 1993).

It was assumed that major opportunities for redevelopment existed, arising out of apartheid planning and land zoning restrictions which had kept large tracts of land near city centres vacant (Hindson *et al.*, 1993). A vacant land study conducted by the Durban City Council in 1993 suggested that substantial well-located land (much of it owned by the Council or the state) could be available for low-cost housing (Land Development Working Group, 1993). The Cato Manor area, some 2,000 hectares and 7km from Durban city centre, once the site of mass apartheid forced removals in the 1960s, became a key part of the campaign to restructure the city. Vacant until the 1990s when land invasions began, it was identified as a key priority for low-income housing development.

However, low-cost housing development on strategically located vacant land close to the core has proved to be complex and difficult to achieve in practice. The Cato Manor project, intended to house some 180,000 people, has been highly contested, and has had to draw on substantial political and financial resources to fulfil its mandate. Land invasions, weak and unstable leadership structures within informal settlements, crime and violence, resistance by adjacent higher income white communities, and competing claims to land by past victims of forced removals have all slowed down the rate of development (Foster, 1998).

The amount of well-located vacant land available for low-cost housing development has also been vastly over-estimated. A significant part of this land has turned out to be geologically unstable, or there have been competing claims to it for other uses, such as the open space system. And as in Cato Manor, adjacent communities inevitably contest such developments (Todes, forthcoming). Ironically, political commitment to end land invasions in favour of more ordered settlement has meant that one of the few ways in which densification and integration within the core was beginning to occur by the early 1990s has been curtailed. Currently, only 10% of households in informal settlements are centrally located (Metro Housing Service Unit, 1999).

By the mid-1990s, the emphasis had shifted to improving service conditions in townships and informal areas, and the development of corridors and nodes to integrate these areas into the city. The disappearance of formal apartheid, and the establishment of representative local government in 1996, led to political pressure for 'development where we are' (Baskin, 1998), weakening support for complex and expensive centrally located projects.

The shift away from the emphasis on the core was in many respects inevitable. While those living outside townships and informal settlements might have seen them as marginal and peripheral, this was not necessarily the perception of those who lived there, and who had interests, investments, and social networks and ties there. The state's Reconstruction and Development Programme (RDP), promoting urban renewal, focused on the transformation of these 'areas of need' (see Fig. 2) through integrated development planning exercises based on community participation and capacity building. The spatial components of these plans promoted nodes and corridors, integrating these areas internally and with the core, and providing a focus for the provision of social facilities and for economic activity (Urban Strategy Department, 1998).

The concept of peripherality was also challenged with the ending of the forced separation associated with apartheid, and as these areas became an integral part of local government. There is a growing realisation that many townships and informal settlements in Durban are not so physically distant from its centre, compared with those of other international cities. The problem is more that:

- transport is poor;
- there is little economic activity in these areas;
- they offer undiversified environments, with poor-quality infrastructure, services and facilities;
- there is a legacy of a lack of capacity to engage in development;
- they contain concentrations of poverty and unemployment; and
- they represent the race and class segregation associated with apartheid.

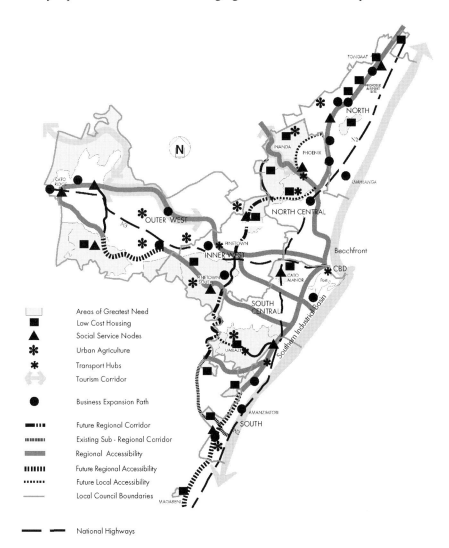

Fig. 2. Durban spatial plan identifying areas of greatest need.

In the late 1990s, as local authorities have attempted to implement compaction ideas, the limitations of a focus on the core have become apparent. The provision of low-cost housing was conceived as a key way in which the city could be restructured, but this aim has proved difficult to achieve. Despite commitment to urban restructuring within the National Urban Development Strategy (Department of Housing, 1997), national housing subsidies based on a capital grant to low-income households are insufficient to cover either the costs of higher density development or higher land costs in well-located areas. Only 50% of the subsidy may be used for land and infrastructure costs, and a minimum of a 30m^2 unit must be built. Under these conditions, Durban's Metropolitan Housing Services Unit (1999) estimates that only 5% of housing subsidies are likely to be used for medium-density infill on well-located land.

These limitations do not imply an abandonment of compaction strategies around the core, but they do imply a weakening emphasis on this element, and a greater acceptance of working with the existing spatial structure of the city. These shifting emphases are reflected in the development of the Spatial Development Plan since 1997.

Durban's Spatial Development Plan

The 1996 elections offered the first opportunity to give political legitimacy to concepts of spatial restructuring. A Spatial Framework Steering Committee (SFSC), representing councillors and officials from the newly created metropolitan council and six local councils, together with representatives from the provincial government and business, was asked to develop a Spatial Development Framework (SDF),[2] and to facilitate its co-ordinated implementation.

The 1997 SDF report argued that compaction should play a prominent role in restructuring the city. It aimed to achieve a sustainable, equitable and efficient city through a focus on:

- nodes and corridors to integrate the city and build on its economic strengths (Fig. 2);
- public transport improvements;
- upgrading and improving the quality of life in the townships and informal settlements;
- densification and infill around nodes, corridors and the core city; and
- the establishment of an open space system.

At the same time, it gave attention to improving management systems, meeting basic needs, and transforming approaches to development within communities.

Local plans provided a means of testing the spatial policy, and translating it into tangible actions. They filled out, added to, and altered the framework, in order to provide a basis for strategies and projects through which the framework would be implemented. The development of local plans shifted the Spatial Framework and highlighted concerns that compaction and integration are contrary to market forces. Plans were developed that embodied the use of nodes and corridors, and densification around them, but which also accepted existing and newly emerging spatial segregation by class.

Although local government is more consolidated than before,[3] remaining fragmentation and a limited revenue base in some of the outer areas has encouraged competitive bidding for projects between areas, and has given greater power to local politics and private developers than might otherwise be the case. Many proposed private developments have been accepted and incorporated into the plans, resulting in some forms of corridor and nodal developments that work with current market trends towards decentralised, car oriented, high-income office, commercial and residential enclaves, distant from low-income areas. The Spatial Framework Committee has little real power to challenge these trends, as metropolitan government (the equivalent to local government) has no overriding land-use controls.

A broadly based metropolitan Spatial Development Plan (SDP) has been produced through a synthesis of the local plans, and interaction with the key metropolitan sectoral departments of economic development, housing, environment and transport. In addition to spatial restructuring, the spatial plan is beginning to play a key role in promoting integrated and co-ordinated development, maximising the impact of public spending, and providing a framework for identifying the role and actions of local government in directing the shape of the city. The resulting SDP (SDFSC, 1999) comprises three interrelated objectives and strategies, within which ideas of compaction and spatial restructuring are still to be found:

- building and protecting vibrant economic areas that lay the foundation for economic growth;
- creating and maintaining viable built environments that support the social and economic needs of the population; and
- sustaining natural environments and resources that provide the basis for both economic prosperity and social well-being.

The SDP is conceived as a flexible framework for managing development, incorporating dynamic concepts of urban form, and framing the actions of a multiplicity of diverse actors. Implementation efforts currently focus on linking key sectoral departments of the Metropolitan Council, and on reform of the land-use management system. Involvement with sectoral departments focused on the development of sectoral strategies linked to the plan will raise contradictions and indicate the limits and possibilities of compaction strategies. The Metropolitan Housing Unit, for instance, is committed to concepts of compaction, but also has a policy of upgrading all informal settlements, some 45% of which fall outside existing nodes and corridors. It nevertheless argues for a shift away from a local demand-based project funding system (which has reinforced the poor location of many housing projects) towards spatial planning. All greenfield projects (which are expected to comprise some 44% of low-cost housing projects over the next 20 years) are to be focused on the SDP's accessibility footprint – 1km on either side of nodes and corridors. About 40% of vacant land within the accessibility footprint will be required for housing (Metro Housing Service Unit, 1999). The suitability of such land remains to be established. Inevitably it will compete with other demands for land, and it requires investigation of ways of financing higher land costs.

The transport sector is also key to the realisation of the strategy. There is considerable commitment at national level to creating economically viable public transport through the development of corridors and nodes which contain substantial employment in or near to current dormitory areas, enabling commuting into and out of these areas. It is argued that tendencies towards decentralisation should be focused on corridors and nodes (Department of Transport, 1999). The feasibility of establishing public transport in this way in Durban is only beginning to be tested, but early results suggest that there are very few routes that can reach the thresholds that make public transport viable.

The reform of the current land-use management system is also critical if compaction ideals are to be realised. Current systems are founded on Garden City concepts, and are based on keeping densities low and preventing mixed use, particularly within suburban areas. Work is currently underway to set in place a new system of land-use management that is more consistent with the aims of the SDP, and with the aims of compaction. Considerable emphasis is placed on the need to encourage densification in both the SDP and the Housing Framework – particularly in view of the fact that densities in central areas have been dropping due to declining household size and suburbanisation (Metro Housing Service Unit, 1999). Although it is recognised that densification in these areas is likely to offer little to low-income households, it is argued that these strategies are necessary for overall densification of the city. Densities directly in nodes and corridors are targeted at 30–70 dwelling units per hectare, while some 20–30 dwelling units per hectare are to be encouraged within the accessibility footprint, and within a range of a 30 minute taxi ride from the CBD (SDFSC, 1998). Current suburban densities are around 10 dwelling units per hectare.

The real prospects for the SDP will be demonstrated over time, as the plan is modified in the light of the imperatives of metropolitan sectoral departments and local dynamics, and as it is tested against market forces. Some comments can nevertheless be made on the prospects for the plan.

Forces and prospects

Housing, densification and integration
A level of integration and densification of the urban core is continuing to occur spontaneously through the private housing market, and through informal settlement. And despite the limitations noted above, Durban has gone further than most South African cities in developing centrally located housing projects.

Beyond the core, Durban's spatial structure offers greater potential for concentrating low-cost housing development close to nodes and corridors than is the case in many other South African cities, although prospects vary across the city. The Pinetown South area (Fig. 2), within a 10km range of the Pinetown commercial and industrial node, has been a major focus for housing development due to a history of organisation focusing on housing in the area, and a highly proactive local authority. There are considerable prospects in areas which were previously group area buffer zones and other areas within the 'middle ring' around the city, in range of the main corridors and routes – although even these developments tend to be contested by adjacent communities. Many of the better located areas within the old townships, which are close to main routes, are already densely settled, offering limited opportunities for further development. Local politics, land markets, and the power of major landholders in the North have influenced the Spatial Framework for the North Local Council. This both limits the extent of low-cost housing in the area, and orients it to the commercial/industrial outer corridor, running through the old Indian towns of Tongaat (Fig. 1) and Verulam, while an inner corridor focuses on office and shopping malls for high-income users. Although current moves to establish a 'Unicity', amalgamating the six local authorities, could limit these tendencies, powerful local interests are likely to remain.

While the tendency to locate low-cost housing projects on or beyond the edge of the city is likely to be curtailed, it could prove difficult to ensure that projects are specifically related to corridors and nodes, and a much looser relationship may have to be accepted. Current migration dynamics may however promote sprawl, and exacerbate core–periphery divides. Cross *et al.* (1996) argue that unserviced peripheral informal settlements within tribal authorities, outside the current boundaries of the Durban Metropolitan Area, have been a target for migration in recent years since they enable households to survive through complex urban–rural linkages and marginal local employment.

The prospects for densification of the order anticipated are also open to debate. At present the main form of densification in low-income housing is provision of small sites, which are largely resented and resisted. Although the built density of black townships is not particularly high, population densities are high, but this has not resulted in the benefits of urban amenity. There is thus little to associate higher density with improvements in people's quality of life, at least outside core areas. Topographical and geological conditions are also likely to limit the density levels that can be achieved (as in Cato Manor), where expected densities are being revised downwards from about 40 to about 35 dwelling units per hectare (CMDA, 1997). Furthermore, as noted previously, the subsidy policy does not support higher density multi-unit housing.

A limited form of densification is occurring through the private housing market, facilitated by the growing popularity of gated housing complexes in the face of rising levels of crime. Housing complexes of this sort are also more accessible to those who are at the lower end of the private housing market. Although these developments are generally at a higher density level than detached housing, densities are usually much lower than the SDP's targets. Developments even at the lower end of the market are oriented to the motor car (although accessible locations are prized by developers), contributing less in terms of sustainability than might be expected. Thus even where developments are consistent with the spatial framework, they do not necessarily support a shift to public transport. Further, the physical form of these developments - separated, inwardly oriented, with large parking areas – do little to contribute to urbanist or sustainability ideals.

Apart from a few high-income complexes in central areas, developments of this sort occur mainly on available vacant or underused land, largely outside the central city. Land costs in central areas are too high, and there is pressure to convert downgraded housing to higher yielding office uses. While some higher density housing complexes are consistent with the spatial framework, and are resulting in a level of racial and class integration, in other cases, they constitute a form of sprawl, serving to densify the edges of the city, and placing pressure on the existing highway system (Todes, forthcoming). The better-located and more integrated projects are more difficult to achieve.

A general revision of the land-use management system might help to facilitate these developments, and could also engender a process of densification through subdivision, development of second dwelling units, and infilling on existing suburban lots. However, it is not clear how much demand there is for these forms of densification given a stagnant economy, a static middle-income housing market, and low population growth amongst the middle classes.

Corridors and nodes

The spontaneous deracialisation of the CBD, although relatively free of racial conflict, has raised questions about the future economic direction of the city centre. The growth of illegal street trading, and increased crime and violence associated with street gangs, has contributed to the flight of white shoppers, accelerating the movement of many commercial and service activities to new suburban malls. By 1998, there were eighteen centres of over 10,000m² outside the CBD (JHI Property Services, 1998). Several corporate head and regional offices have recently decentralised to new office parks to the north and west of the city, marking a shift beyond the previous pattern of decentralisation focused on small offices in neighbourhoods close to the CBD. The proportion of high-quality (A and B grade) space in the CBD dropped from 85% to 76% between 1990 and 1998 (SAPOA, 1990, 1998), while vacancy rates have increased from 2% to 11%.

The decentralisation of shopping and offices is not necessarily inconsistent with the spatial framework, and many of the main decentralised locations are contained within the framework of corridors and nodes. Nevertheless, the movement of shops and offices has largely been towards previously white, and more recently, previously Indian, areas, and is avoiding township and informal areas. Decentralisation is linked, *inter alia*, to growing reliance on the motor car, to a well-developed highway system, and to perceptions of 'crime and grime' in the CBD. Nodes are developed as secure, car-oriented enclaves, sealed off from the world of urban poverty. Furthermore, the physical form of these developments is far from urbanist ideals.

For the most part, private sector economic initiatives are avoiding township and informal areas. Incomes and thresholds are seen as too low to support the development of shopping centres, while high levels of crime and violence undermine all forms of formal development there, even those which would potentially draw on local labour markets. In this context, the major spatial-structural inequalities of the apartheid city are likely to remain, and reliance on commuting will continue, perhaps reduced by declining levels of formal employment, leaving the unemployed isolated on the periphery. It seems unlikely that the transport planners' hope that many people will commute to employment within townships will be realised. In the face of these difficulties, planners are focusing on large nodes on the edge of townships, in part building on market trends towards the location of large wholesalers to service small township shopping areas providing for convenience needs (Watkinson, 1998). Beyond these developments, however, there is still resistance to location close to townships, and anticipated developments have not yet materialised.

Corridors and nodes are nevertheless useful in providing focal points for informal and formal economic activities, which were in part undermined by poor spatial organisation of townships in the past (Harrison *et al.*, 1997). Current planning to give effect to these concepts focuses on the development of nodes, which concentrate public investment (such as police stations, clinics, libraries) at interceptory locations, in order to provide thresholds for other economic activities. Some successes are being achieved, but there are immediate constraints to development. Land close to main routes or existing centres is in short supply, since much open land has been informally settled. In some areas, land ownership questions are difficult to untangle. Furthermore, Durban City Council is still dealing with the history of chaotic administration and dysfunctional servicing inherited from the past (Moonsammy, 1998).

Social, political and environmental issues

A broader set of forces may also reshape the prospects for compaction. The process of change is a slow one, and old policies and institutional arrangements still have to be transformed to meet new challenges. Planning is also occurring in a context of massive social problems such as rising unemployment (estimated at 30%), violence, crime, and AIDS, all of which threaten to dwarf concerns about spatial restructuring. The proposed incorporation of informal settlements on tribal land into the city may also shift the focus back towards basic services (such as water and sanitation). However, where these needs are being addressed in townships and informal settlements, it has led to a demand for higher order community facilities, such as recreation and libraries (Urban Strategy Department, 1999).

The impact of the AIDS crisis on spatial form has still to be confronted. Many of the visions of urban restructuring, including extensive corridors and nodes through currently undeveloped land on the North, were originally based on far higher population projections than now seem realistic. Housing demand projections are based on assumptions of 2.25% pa growth rates over 20 years, while AIDS experts are suggesting figures closer to 0.5% over the same period nationally. As a major city, Durban might expect higher growth rates, but levels of in-migration have been low in recent years as the economy has stagnated. AIDS is likely to slow household formation, and could limit the extent to which housing is used to restructure the city, and reduce opportunities for compaction.

Physical constraints (rivers, steep topography, geology, etc.) influence the shape of development and in the DMA impose major financial constraints on restructuring efforts. Furthermore, while the SDP has embraced concerns about sustainability, and incorporates initiatives such as Local Agenda 21, the Metropolitan Open Space System and environmental policy, in practice there is competition between land for ecological purposes and land for housing.

There are also tensions between social integration and fragmentation, which affect spatial visions. Violence and crime undermine attempts at integration, even within communities. But other forms of integration are occurring. The new democracy has had a tremendous impact upon social processes and institutions. Durban is now a more vibrant and cosmopolitan city than it has ever been, and attempts at integrated social relations manifest themselves in the creative arts such as dance, drama, music, in sport, and in the material artifacts of culture such as craft, cuisine and fashion. There is a gradual acceptance of the reality of integration by higher income groups, and there are some interesting joint initiatives between adjacent high and low-income communities, for example to fight common problems of crime and violence.

Finally, there is a tension between the orientation towards equity and democracy contained in the emphasis on quality of life, lifeline tariffs, capacity building, and community participation, and Durban's attempt to position itself in the context of global competitiveness. This tension manifests itself in terms of debates over expenditure, and over attitudes towards integration, and the extent to which the market continues to structure the spatial form of the city.

Conclusion

The idea of compaction has been useful at a macro-level in framing a spatial strategy for Durban and in raising debates over the distribution of costs and benefits of government interventions spatially across the city. While there has been an acceptance of the concept, and of linked spatial policies,[4] there are still significant disjunctures between policy and implementation. Localised decisions are still taken on grounds that are contrary to the idea of compaction, as are some key national policies, such as housing subsidies. Moreover, local authorities do not have the leeway to engender compaction by reshaping financial instruments in creative ways. Market forces, land markets, 'nimbyism'[5] and lifestyle preferences seem to contradict an integrative and urbanist version of compaction.

The SDP embodies some of the contradictions involved in compaction, and presents a version of a restructured city that, while more spatially coherent, and physically compact, is nevertheless unable to depart entirely from older space–class–race divides, or from newly emerging divisions. Hence, while lateral spread is being curbed by both spontaneous informal settlement and new projects in the middle ring of settlements around the city, and while significant progress has been made in transforming everyday conditions in townships and informal settlement through improvement of services, infrastructure and facilities, the aims of racial and social integration remain more difficult to achieve.

As the spatial framework has evolved, it has moved beyond earlier narrow conceptions of compaction. The form of spatial planning that is emerging is less idealistic in its aims, and works with existing trends and forces. There is a greater focus on more disaggregated concepts of accessibility, and on a wider range of policy instruments, such as the role of improved transport, social service provision and capacity building in altering conditions in townships and informal areas. The emphasis on environmental sustainability and quality of life has shifted the focus to practical physical interventions that can be negotiated and implemented with communities. There is a recognition of the need to explore more participative and qualitative approaches to deal with the causes of spatial dysfunction.

It is still early days for the policy. The SDP is beginning to serve as a basis for integration across sectors, as departments start to recognise its value. The advent of a single local government is likely to improve the potential for restructuring, and will help to generate the necessary long-term commitment. Policy adjustments, particularly in relation to land-use management, are yet to occur. Something of a mind-shift is required to move beyond old rules, regulations, and approaches. Although there are limits to what can be achieved, the value of the SDP lies in the long-term vision that it represents, its role as an integrating mechanism, and its importance in keeping core–periphery imbalances on the agenda.

Notes

1. Some 60% of Durban's population are black, 12% are white, and 28% are coloured or Indian.
2. All documents pertaining to the Spatial Framework and Plan are available on the website, www.durban.gov.za/urbanstrategy/index.html
3. Over 40 local authorities existed prior to the 1996 reorganisation of local government.
4. Such as the Waste Water Plans, and the Durban Metropolitan Open Space System.
5. NIMBY is the acronym for 'Not In My Back Yard'.

References

Baskin, J. (1998) Metro Housing Service Unit, Durban Metro Council. *Interview*.

Cato Manor Development Association (CMDA) (1997) *Cato Manor Structure Plan*, Durban.

Cross, C., Luckin, L., Mzimela, T. and Clark, C. (1996) On the edge: poverty, livelihoods and natural resources in rural KwaZulu-Natal, in *Land, Labour and Livelihoods in Rural South Africa* (eds M. Lipton, F. Ellis and M. Lipton), Indicator Press, Durban.

Department of Housing (1997) *National Urban Development Strategy*, Pretoria.

Department of Transport (1999) *Moving South Africa*, Pretoria.

Dewar, D. (1984) Cities, poverty and development, paper presented to the Second Carnegie Conference on Poverty and Development in South Africa, Cape Town.

Dewar, D., Uytenbogaardt, R., Hutton-Squire, M., Levy, C. and Menidis, P. (1979*) Housing, Urbanism in Cape Town,* David Philip, Cape Town.

Land Development Working Group (1993) *Vacant Land in Durban: A Framework for Strategic Action*, Durban City Council, Durban.

Foster, C. (1998) Cato Manor Development Association. *Interview*.

Harrison, P., Todes, A. and Watson, V. (1997) The economic development of South Africa's urban townships: realities and strategies. *Development Southern Africa*, **14**, pp.43-60.

Hindson, D. (1999) Fragmentation and integration in a post-apartheid city: the case of Durban. *Third World Review.*

Hindson, D., Byerley, M. and Morris, M. (1994) From violence to reconstruction: the making, disintegration and remaking of an apartheid city. *Antipode*, **26**, pp.323–350.

Hindson, D., Mabin, A. and Watson, V. (1993). Restructuring the built environment, unpublished report to the National Housing Forum.

JHI Property Services (1998) *The KwaZulu-Natal Property Market,* JHI, Durban.

Metro Housing Service Unit (1999) *Metro Housing Strategic Framework*, Durban Metro Council, Durban.

Moonsammy, S. (1998). Planning and Development, Durban North/South Central Council. *Interview.*

Morris, M. and Hindson, D. (1997) Class and household restructuring in metropolitan Durban. *Society in Transition*, **1**, pp.101–121.

SAPOA (1990) *Office Vacancy Survey*. South African Property Owners Association, Johannesburg.

SAPOA (1998) *Office Vacancy Survey*. South African Property Owners Association, Johannesburg.

Spatial Development Framework Steering Committee (SDFSC) (1998) *Spatial Development Plan, volume 1*, Durban Metro Council, Durban.

Spatial Development Framework Steering Committee (SDFSC) (1999) *Spatial Development Plan, volume 2*, Durban Metro Council, Durban.

Tongaat-Hullett Planning Forum (1990) *The Durban Functional Region: Planning For the Twenty-First Century*, Tongaat-Hullett Properties, Durban.

Todes, A. (forthcoming) Reintegrating the apartheid city? Urban policy and urban restructuring in Durban, in *Blackwell Companion to Urban Studies* (eds G. Bridge and S. Watson), Blackwell, Oxford.

Urban Strategy Department (1997) *Spatial Development Framework*, Durban Metro Council, Durban.

Urban Strategy Department (1998) *RDP Urban Renewal Report: Areas of Greatest Need*, Durban Metro Council, Durban.

Urban Strategy Department (1999) *Quality of Life Survey May 1999: Summary Results*, Durban Metro Council, Durban.

Uytenbogaardt, R., Rozendal, P. and Dewar, P. (1989) *Greater Marianhill Structure Plan: Report to the Natal Provincial 2Administration*, Pietermaritzburg.

Watkinson, E. (1998). Economic Development Unit, Durban Metropolitan Council. *Interview*.

World Bank (1993) *South Africa: Urban Sector Reconnaissance*. Aide memoire, June 14.

Xing Quan Zhang

High-Rise and High-Density Compact Urban Form:
The Development of Hong Kong

Introduction

Technological development in the twentieth century gave the freedom to create different urban forms and structures. The debate over the concentration or dispersal of urban development has had a long history, and has intensified over the past two decades since the widespread acceptance of the ideas of sustainable development. Urban planners and policy makers increasingly believe that there is a link between the prospects for sustainability and urban form. A powerful argument in favour of urban concentration was made by the Commission of European Communities (CEC, 1990), whose vision for sustainable urban forms is centred on the notion of the compact city. The rationale for the compact city lies in the assumption that high densities can reduce travel demands and energy consumption and pollution and provide more environmental and quality of life benefits (Breheny, 1992; Morrison, 1998).

Although the actual benefits of compact urban form are far from certain, a number of European countries accepted the idea of the compact city as a policy direction in the 1990s (Morrison, 1998). Compared to these latest moves to develop more compact urban forms in Europe, the policy change in urban development from dispersal to compaction in Hong Kong began much earlier, about 40 years ago. This was at a time when western planners, social scientists, architects were stressing the ill effects of high-rise and high-density development such as crime, vandalism, social dysfunction and high vacancy rates. The demolition of St Louis's Pruitt-Igoe housing project and the tragic deterioration of high-rise housing in Chicago, Boston and elsewhere become a symbol of the failure of the high-rise and high-density approach (Fuerst and Petty, 1991). Fear of the ill effects of high densities has also influenced past planning policy in Hong Kong. However, the combination of rapid population growth and limited land resources made dispersed development unsustainable in Hong Kong. As a response, Hong Kong switched to a high-rise and high-density development approach. Now Hong Kong has the highest urban density in the world. It is a good example of the compact city model. This chapter illustrates the forces that caused Hong Kong to adopt the compact city development model and how policies are emerging in favour of high-rise and high-density urban development. It also looks at the advantages and disadvantages of urban compaction in the Hong Kong context.

Forces shaping Hong Kong's urban structure

The forces that shape urban forms are complex (Newman, 1992). This analysis considers two factors to be the dominant forces that have shaped Hong Kong's urban form – the rapid growth of urban population and the scarcity of land resources. Policies for urban compaction have been in response to these forces.

Rapid growth of urban population

Since the end of World War II, Hong Kong has experienced a rapid rate of urban population growth caused both by a high rate of natural increase and large-scale immigration. The population was 600,000 in 1945 and increased by 50% to 900,000 in 1946 alone. In 1947, it reached 1.4 million and had risen to more than 2.5 million by 1957, and to 6.2 million by 1996. The end of World War II in 1945 did not bring peace to China.

The civil war caused a massive wave of immigration from China to Hong Kong. The annual number of immigrants was 486,000 in 1946, 371,000 in 1947, 166,000 in 1948 and 252,000 in 1949. This heavy flow of immigrants had pushed the total population to 2 million in 1949 (Table 1).

Year	Natural Increase	Migration Movement	Total Population
1945			900,000
1946	+14,000	+486,000	1,400,000
1947	+29,000	+371,000	1,800,000
1948	+34,000	+166,000	2,000,000
1949	+38,000	+252,000	2,300,000
1950	+42,000	-242,000	2,100,000
1951	+48,000	+27,000	2,175,000
1952	+53,000	+22,000	2,250,000
1953	+57,000	-57,000	2,250,000
1954	+64,000	+186,000	2,500,000
1955	+71,500	-171,000	2,400,000
1956	+77,500	+57,000	2,535,000
1957	+78,500	+63,500	2,677,000

Table 1. Population growth in Hong Kong 1945–57.
Source: Mok (1959)

The population growth in the decade from 1951 to 1961 continued to be very rapid. This decade saw a 57.5% increase in Hong Kong's population with a net increase of 1,160,000 people. The annual growth rate was 4.7% (ESCAP, 1974). Although population growth has slowed down since 1961, its average annual growth rate remains at 2%. Between 1961 and 1999, the population increase was 3,845,152, which pushed the total population to 6,974,800 in 1999 (HKCSD, 1996; 2000). After the smooth transfer of sovereignty to China in 1997, and the Special Administrative Region government's successful handling of the impact of Asian Financial Crisis in 1998, Hong Kong continues to enjoy its prosperity, attracting early emigrants back to Hong Kong from foreign countries. In 1999, the Hong Kong High Court's interpretation of the right of abode for the mainland-born children of Hong Kong citizens means that an estimated 1.7 million mainland Chinese will qualify for the right of abode in Hong Kong. This may cause another large influx of immigrants from mainland China.

The scarcity of land

The explosive population growth and the scarcity of land in Hong Kong provide a clear illustration of a resource mismatch. Hong Kong is not only small in size, but also physically constrained for human settlement. In 1958, the built area was 57km^2 accounting for 5% of a total land area of 979km^2. However, around 80% of the undeveloped land area was hilly, with slopes mostly ranging from 30 to 45 degrees (Gregory, 1964). Undeveloped flat low land was often swampy, with its coastline dissected by indentations and islands. These areas were not directly suitable for development (Wong, 1975). There is an extreme scarcity of land for urban growth (Table 2).

Land-Use Types	Approximate Area in Square Kilometres[1]	% of the Total Land Area	Remarks
Built-up (urban areas)	57	5	Includes roads and railways
Steep country	287	28	Rocky, precipitous hillsides incapable of plant establishment
Woodlands	34	3	Natural and established woodlands
Grass and scrub lands	448	44	Natural grass and scrub
Eroded lands	59	5	Stripped of cover, granite country, capable of regeneration
Swamp and mangrove	21	2	Capable of reclamation
Arable	132	13	Includes orchards and market gardens
Total	1,038	100	

Table 2. Land-use types and distribution in Hong Kong in 1958.
Source: Gregory, (1964)

Policies in favour of urban compaction

Planning policy: from dispersal to compaction

Massive immigration, rapid population growth, and lack of land, have been overwhelming constraints on Hong Kong's choice of urban development strategies. Its planning policy has been a combination of reality and idealism. In 1947 when the Plan for Hong Kong was being prepared by the newly established Town Planning Office (Abercrombie, 1948; Bristow, 1984), the population was 1.4 million, and the constraints on population growth and land scarcity were not so evident. The 1947 Plan advocated avoidance of New York's high-density approach, and recommended a dispersed urban development strategy, an approach that continued to be adopted in the Outline Plan of the mid-1960s (Bristow, 1984). The Outline Plan estimated that existing urban areas could accommodate a population of up to 3.7 million, and that the additional population should be accommodated in proposed new towns in the New Territories (Chau, 1983). The dispersed urban development strategy led to a fast expansion of urban built-up areas. During the period from 1963 to 1973, the proportion of urban built-up areas doubled from 5.6% to 11.5% of the total land area (Table 3).

Table 3. Urban expansion under the dispersed urban strategy in Hong Kong 1963–1973.
Source: Wong (1975)

	1963	1964	1965	1966	1967	1968	1969	1970	1971	1972	1973
Urban area (% of total land area)	5.6	5.6	7.8	7.8	10.0	10.0	10.0	10.1	11.3	11.3	11.5

The feared ill effects of high-density development and the hilly topography forced urban development onto reclaimed land and limited rural land. By the 1970s, the limitation of the dispersal policies became increasingly obvious, and it was clear that satellite towns did not work in Hong Kong's limited physical area (Prescott, 1971).

Mountains separated the satellite towns from the metropolitan centre. Because of insufficient employment opportunities in the new towns, they mainly remained dormitory areas and it was hard to achieve any real degree of self-sufficiency.

The new towns so far created, at Kwun Tong and Tsuen Wan, were virtual extensions of the enlarged urban area of Kowloon and New Kowloon. The balance of employment in Kwun Tong and Tusen Wan leaned heavily towards industrial with little or no complementary white-collar sector. The non-existence of local government emphasised the lack of any binding community forces. A large percentage of the population sought employment outside the new towns. (Prescott, 1971, p.13)

The rapid encroachment of urban development on limited rural land, and the lack of infrastructure and a viable local economy in the new towns, forced planners to rethink the dispersed urban development strategy. The recognition of the realities and constraints made a high-rise and high-density approach essential, and led to the transformation of Hong Kong's urban strategy from one of dispersal to one of compaction.

Land-use policy

In Hong Kong, all land is owned by the government, which has total control over land supply and land use. The government disposes of land for private residential, commercial and industrial uses by competitive auction or tender, and for public uses through free allocation (Lai, 1993). The sale of land has ensured that scarce land attains its highest value and thus is used as intensively as possible. Most of the land in the metropolitan area is disposed of in this way. The purpose of tendering is when 'the government wishes to examine in advance detailed proposals for the development of a particular lot with an unusual user restriction, to ensure that the best form of development is obtained and that the development meets all the government requirements' (Wu, 1984, p.4). Although the government does not admit to pursuing a high land-price policy, the method of disposal has contributed to high land prices, which further heats up the whole property market and makes Hong Kong's property amongst the most expensive in the world. For example, the average office rent in Hong Kong was US$138.18 per square foot in 1995 (*Asian Business Review*, 1995). High land prices virtually dictate high-rise and high-density compact development in the urban area.

A land-scarce economic policy

Due to the scarcity of land and its hilly topography, Hong Kong cannot adopt a land-rich economic policy based on industry and agriculture. Rather, the economy is based on the accumulation of capital through service sectors such as trade, finance and tourism. The notion that Hong Kong is ruled by banks points to the popular recognition of the banking sector in the local economy (Cartier, 1997). Hong Kong is now the world's third largest financial centre. Unlike traditional industrial cities, Hong Kong directs little of its capital inwards for industrial plant, but instead transfers most of its industrial activities into the neighbouring Chinese provinces. This enables Hong Kong to direct a higher proportion of its wealth into urban infrastructure and to facilitate the provision of quality services and management. The service-orientated economy makes compaction more feasible than in industrial cities, encouraging urban patterns with workplaces and homes in close proximity, shortening travelling time and distances. The high value of property and the development of high-rise office and residential towers in Hong Kong's metropolitan area have made land and property development there one of the world's most profitable businesses (Cartier, 1999). The metropolitan centre has always been the most attractive to new investment, and the property developers' desire for more profits from their limited land lots has raised densities and pushed up the skyline of the urban centre.

Housing policy

Hong Kong did not have a coherent housing policy before the1950s. Its free market economy meant that house prices tended to be determined by location, quality and demand. The closer the housing units to the central business district, the higher their prices. Demand has increased population densities in the urban areas, further raising housing and land prices. The high prices in the metropolitan areas have displaced low-income and lower middle-income households from the urban area to the urban fringe or to rural areas (Tse, 1995). The massive wave of immigrants from mainland China after World War II had to seek shelter in suburban areas in order to reduce their living costs, and this generated a large number of squatters. In 1953, the government estimated that there were about 300,000 squatters. The number of squatters increased to 500,000 in 1959 and to 550,000 by 1964 (Choi and Chan, 1978).

In order to control the spread of squatters, unhealthy conditions and unplanned encroachment on scarce land, the government, at the beginning of the 1950s, intervened by providing affordable housing to low-income and lower middle-income households. The public housing sector expanded very rapidly, and Hong Kong now has the world's second highest proportion of public housing in the market economies. In 1999, the government had a total public housing stock of 985,294 units which included 670,000 public rental housing units and a further 312,294 owner-occupied housing units.[2] 51.7% of the population lived in public housing in 1999 (Hong Kong Housing Authority, 2000). Public sector housing provision is continuing to grow. In 1998, the government's annual housing production of 56,000 flats was more than two and a half times that of the private sector (Hong Kong Government, 1998). It indicates the growing influence of public housing policy on the urban development pattern.

Public housing takes the form of high-rise and high-density development, and it is a form that is acceptable to residents, particularly to those people who are still housed in unhealthy and over-crowded squatter shelters. Furthermore, the rents for public housing are about 20% to 47% of the market value. The growing waiting list for public housing shows the popularity of public housing among low-income households. High-density development has not been accompanied by the problems of social dysfunction and physical deterioration associated with high-rise estates in western countries. This has encouraged policy-makers to continue to produce high-rise and high-density developments.

High-rise and high-density public housing development is also demanded from a financial perspective. The government needs to increase the density and to incorporate commercial facilities in residential blocks to compensate for the financial loss due to the low rent policy of public housing. The pressure for high-density development also intensified with the higher rate of population growth in the 1990s. Furthermore, with family size getting smaller, the number of households is growing at a faster rate than that of the population (Table 4). Residents have also demanded more spacious housing units. Table 5 indicates the increasing trend for additional floor space per unit in the private sector. Public housing faces similar pressures to provide more spacious housing units as household income grows. These pressures combine to strengthen the government's housing policy in favour of high-rise and high-density development, as in the private housing sector. Indeed, housing projects developed by the private sector normally have higher buildings and greater densities than public housing (Lai, 1993). Commercial buildings are even higher still and their density is much greater than that of housing projects. For example, the Bank of China has 72 storeys and the Central Plaza rises 78 storeys and is 374 metres high (Cartier, 1999).

Year	Population	Population Growth Rate (%)	Number of Households	Growth Rate of households (%)
1990	5,704,500	0.32	1,596,656	1.57
1991	5,752,000	0.83	1,622,362	1.61
1992	5,800,500	0.84	1,663,262	2.52
1993	5,901,000	1.73	1,701,857	2.32
1994	6,035,000	2.28	1,756,203	3.19
1995	6,156,100	2.00	1,807,060	2.90
1996	6,311,000	2.52	1,867,254	3.33
1997	6,502,100	3.03	1,955,967	4.75

Table 4. The growth of population and households in Hong Kong in 1990s.
Source: Leung, (1999)

Year	1992	1993	1994	1995	1996	1997
Floor Space per Unit (m²)	53.8	54.2	56.1	63.2	68.8	61.7
Index of Space Change	100	101	104	118	128	115

Table 5. Floor space of newly built housing units in the private sector.
Source: Leung, (1999)

The advantages and disadvantages of high-rise and high-density development

Contrary to conventional Western wisdom and perceptions, high-rise and high-density development is very successful in Hong Kong. It helps meet the urgent housing needs of the fast-growing population. Public housing now accommodates about half of the total population in Hong Kong and there is still a long waiting list for the allocation of public housing. This shows a high degree of satisfaction with high-rise and high-density living. There is a very low turnover. Urban compaction enables residential buildings to be located within, or close to, the central areas and allows residents easy access to the various urban facilities and amenities. The government provides community facilities and commercial centres within the housing estates, making high-rise and high-density public housing very attractive to citizens. Because of the degree of compaction of the city, open space and country are within walking distance on Hong Kong island. A rich array of urban amenities, recreational and natural environments are within easy reach, and contribute greatly to the quality of life.

The positive response to high-rise and high-density living in Hong Kong is not unique. Fuerst and Petty (1991) have observed that people's satisfaction with housing has little connection with height and density – 'It is other features of the housing environment, rather than height, that result in different degrees of satisfaction' (ibid., p.119).

High-rise and high-density developments provide the population thresholds to viably group economic activities together and to provide specialised services, facilities, amenities, recreational and cultural opportunities. The concentration of urban areas brings about the concentration of business, workplace and residence. Excessive daily movement of individuals and goods is reduced to a minimum (Prescott, 1971). For example, 64.5% of the total journeys in Hong Kong are within the urban centre and another 20.8% are between Kowloon and its adjacent areas. Journeys generated from suburban new towns account for only 14.7% of the total daily journeys (Table 6).

Movement	Number of Daily Journeys	Total Daily Journeys (%)
Within the urban centre (i.e. within the harbour area)	6,641,000	64.49
Kowloon to New Territories	2,263,000	20.75
To and from New Towns	1,520,000	14.76
Total daily journeys in the Territory	10,298,000	100.00

Table 6. Patterns of journeys in Hong Kong in 1992.
Source: Hong Kong Transport Department (1993)

However, these high densities are also believed to produce some problems, such as the breakdown of identity, tensions, lack of privacy, lack of communication, and isolation. These problems do not appear to have had much impact on the perception of the quality of life in Hong Kong, nor perhaps by Chinese people in general. Kate Dunham's[3] research on American Chinatowns indicates that the Chinese can adapt extremely well to high-density and crowded living environments. Her view is echoed by many other Western scholars such as Hall and Sommer who argue that 'reaction to spatial invasions might be culturally determined' (cited in Lai, 1993, p.69).

The scarcity of land, high densities and high property values make Hong Kong the world's most expensive city for business in term of office rents. This may deter international business and have a negative effect on the economy. Another major problem, and possible deterrent, is the increasing deterioration of the urban environment. Hong Kong's first large-scale sustainability research initiative (Barron and Steinbrecher, 1999) has revealed the astonishing deterioration of the environment. The main environmental problems are associated with over-concentration due to high-rise and high-density development, and include poor air quality, water depletion, noise, and excessive waste production. The environmental problems are serious enough for the government to put the improvement of the environment at the top of its agenda (Tung, 1999).

Conclusion
Hong Kong's urban form has mainly been driven by the explosive population growth and land scarcity, and the strategy for urban compaction is the response to the physical constraints on its urban growth. As a result, Hong Kong is the most compact city and the highest density city in the world. People are well adapted to high-rise and high-density living and the approach seems very successful. This experience can be used to argue that urban compaction is an acceptable way of development and living.

However, generalisations from the Hong Kong experience may be problematic. Western cities are unlikely to be, nor do they wish to be, as compact and dense as Hong Kong. For example, many large Western cities have experienced population decline in their urban areas during the past few decades, but Hong Kong has always had to face the pressure of population growth. Its people's satisfaction with high-rise and high-density living is also largely culturally determined.

The environmental benefits assumed by Western compact city development models are not upheld in the case of Hong Kong. Its urban environmental deterioration has reached an alarming level. This seems to be caused by the excessive compaction of urban development and leads to a question about the widely accepted assumption of associating urban compaction with environmental benefits. While environmental benefits may be achieved through a reasonable degree of urban compaction, when it goes beyond a certain level, it may be difficult to achieve the claimed benefits, and instead may result in environmental problems. The key lesson to be learnt here is less whether the compact city can achieve its claimed benefits or not, but rather the degree, or extent, of sustainability urban compaction can achieve to maximise the advantages and minimise the disadvantages.

Notes

1. Areas were in square miles in the original data (Gregory, 1964), but these have been converted into square km to enable comparisons to be made with data in other chapters in the book.
2. The figures for total public housing units, and owner-occupied public housing units, have been calculated according to the data provided by the Hong Kong Housing Authority. These indicated that the public rental housing stock was 670,000 units, accounting for 68% of the total public housing stock (i.e. 32% of the total public housing stock are owner-occupied units). See http://www.info.gov.hk/hd/eng/hd/public/index.htm & http://www.info.gov.hk/hd/eng/hd/stat_99/home_f.htm
3. Personal contact.

References

Abercrombie, P. (1948) *Hong Kong Preliminary Planning Report*, Government Printer, Hong Kong.

Asian Business Review (1995) Hong Kong is the world's most expensive city for business, *Asian Business Review*, May 1995, p.54.

Barron, W. and Steinbrecher, N. (1999) *Heading Towards Sustainability?*, The Centre of Urban Planning and Environmental Management, University of Hong Kong, Hong Kong.

Breheny, M. (1992) The compact city: an introduction, *Built Environment*, **18(4)**, pp.241–246.

Bristow, R. (1984) *Land-use Planning in Hong Kong*, Oxford University Press, Hong Kong.

Cartier, C. (1997) Symbolic landscape in high rise Hong Kong, *Focus*, **44(3)**, pp.13–22.

Cartier, C. (1999) The state, property development and symbolic landscape in high-rise Hong Kong, *Landscape Research*, **24(2)**, pp.185–208.

Chau, C. S. (1983) Hong Kong's planners dismiss Western bogeys, *Australian Planner*, **21(2)**, pp.44–47.

Choi, C. Y. and Chan, Y. K. (1978) *Public Housing Development and Population Movement: A Study of Kwun Tong, Hong Kong*, Occasional Paper No. 72, Social Research Centre, The Chinese University of Hong Kong, Hong Kong

Commission of the European Communities (CEC) (1990) *Green Paper on the Urban Environment*, European Commission, Brussels.

ESCAP (Economic and Social Commission for Asia and the Pacific, United Nations) (1974) *The Demographic Situation in Hong Kong*, ESCAP, Bangkok.

Fuerst, J. S. and Petty, R. (1991) High-rise housing for low-income families, *Public Interest*, issue **103**, pp.118–131.

Gregory, W. G. (1964) An architect's comments on land use in Hong Kong, in *Land Use Problems in Hong Kong* (ed. S. G. Davis), Hong Kong University Press, Hong Kong.

HKCSD (Hong Kong Census and Statistics Department) (1996), *1996 Population By-census: Main Report,* Government Printer, Hong Kong.

HKCSD (2000) *Hong Kong Monthly Digest of Statistics*, March 2000, Government Printer, Hong Kong.

Hong Kong Government (1998) *Hong Kong 1998*, Government Printer, Hong Kong.

Hong Kong Housing Authority (1980) *The First Two Million*, Government Printer, Hong Kong.

Hong Kong Housing Authority (2000) *Housing Statistics*, http://www.info.gov.hk/hd/eng/hd/stat_99/mid_f.htm

Hong Kong Transport Department (1993) *Travel Characteristics Survey: Final Report*, MVA Asia Limited, Hong Kong.

Lai, L. W. C. (1993) Hong Kong's density policy towards public housing, *Third World Planning Review,* **15(1)**, pp.63–85.

Leung, C. Y. (1999) Keynote Speech, *Forum on Hong Kong's Environmental Policies*, 10 March 1999, Hong Kong.

Mok, N. H. B. (1959) *A Study of Population of Hong Kong*, Demographic Training and Research Centre, Bombay.

Morrison, N. (1998) The compact city: theory versus practice – the case of Cambridge, *Netherlands Journal of Housing and the Built Environment*, **13(2)**, pp.157–179.

Newman, P. (1992) The compact city: an Australian perspective, *Built Environment*, **18(4)**, pp.285–300.

Prescott, J. A. (1971) Hong Kong: the form and significance of a high-density urban development, in *Asian Urbanization: A Hong Kong Casebook* (ed. D. J. Dwyer), Hong Kong University Press, Hong Kong.

Tse, R. Y. C. (1995) City growth and land policy: special reference to Hong Kong, *Australian Land Economics*, **1(2)**, pp.34–39.

Tung, C. H. (1999) *Policy Address by the Chief Executive the Honourable Tung Chee Hua*, Government Printer, Hong Kong.

Wong, D. O. Y. (1975) *The Future of the Hong Kong Habitat*, University Archive, University of California, Los Angeles.

Wu, C. L. (1984) A high land price policy in Hong Kong?, Discussion Paper 19, Department of Economics, University of Hong Kong, Hong Kong.

Q. M. Mahtab-uz-Zaman, Stephen S. Y. Lau and So Hing Mei

The Compact City of Hong Kong:
A Sustainable Model for Asia?

Introduction

Traditionally, European cities that are dense and fine-grained have been considered efficient (Montgomery, 1998). By contrast, dispersed cities suffer from inefficient transport management and long commuting trips, which leads to a high dependency on automobiles (Wegener, 1995; Newman, 1992; Newman and Kenworthy, 1989). Many Asian cities have developed with little initial infrastructure investment, so they have evolved a 'compact' urban form in which to manage urban activities, and one that seems to enhance the sustainability of the city. However, although urban compaction has become a policy direction in a number of European countries in the 1990s, it is arguable whether 'compact' is a sustainable pattern for a city (Burton *et al.*, 1996; Breheny, 1996 and 1992; Robertson, 1990).

A context of *laissez-faire* policies has determined Hong Kong's past and present economic development, and is shaping its future. Hong Kong has acted as a fulcrum for China's prosperity and as a link to the rest of the world. It has played the role of entrepreneur through successive changes from a primary to a secondary and then a tertiary service provider, both regionally and internationally. Hong Kong's urban form has reflected these successive changes in urban functions. Its urban form has also developed within the constraints of its topography and the shortage of land for development, and has been affected by the high economic and real-estate gains through limited land availability. Today, Hong Kong is a crystallisation of high-density urban forms and developments that are pragmatic and profitable for its economy, reflecting its importance as a world city. The resulting compact form is advantageous for the environment, as almost 70% of Hong Kong's territories have been left green. Hong Kong can be seen as the product of accidental circumstances as well as intentional interventions that have combined to produce an economically and environmentally viable urban model.

This chapter reviews the underlying factors and policies that have influenced the compact city pattern of Hong Kong. The arguments for and against this compactness in Hong Kong are discussed, followed by a discussion about its environmental sustainability. Finally, future sustainable urban development strategies are reviewed.

Hong Kong's urban morphology

The shortage of flat land and the high rate of immigration from Mainland China during the early 1980s have led to the remarkably high densities of both buildings and population in Hong Kong. It is one the most densely populated areas in the world, with an overall population density of 6,160 persons/km^2. Within this figure there are many even more densely populated districts, for example Kwun Tong with 54,030 persons/km^2 (Hong Kong SAR Government, 1998), but the highest density is in the Mong Kok District, with a population density of 116,000 residents/km^2 (Gilchriest, 1994).

Hong Kong's urban developments are constrained along the two sides of Victoria Harbour – Kowloon and Hong Kong Island (Fig. 1). Due to the angular coastline, the developments are highly concentrated at the tip of the Kowloon Peninsula, especially those for commercial use. Another strip of dense development is located along the northern shore of Hong Kong Island, with an area of 22.5km^2 in an area which is 17km long and on average 1.3km wide. This small area, however, houses approximately 1 million people and provides 700,000 jobs (Tong and Wong, 1997). It includes the central business district, shopping complexes, residential buildings, and governmental, institutional and community facilities.

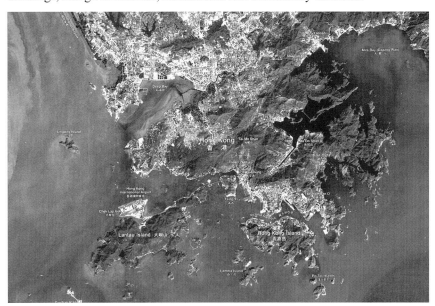

Fig. 1. The satellite image of Hong Kong.
Source: Modified form WorldSat
International Inc., 1997.

Compact urban form in Hong Kong

Topographic constraints to urban development

The compact urban form of Hong Kong has not emerged by design but rather by default. It has a total land area of 1,096km^2, most of which is covered with mountainous terrain. Only 17% of the land area is intensively developed. This topography has induced high-density high-rise design solutions for housing as well as for other developments. To get more land for development near the existing developed areas, large-scale reclamation is taking place: it will produce up to 32% more new land by complementing the existing 1,053 hectares of reclaimed land along the harbour. In old urban areas, large-scale old block renewal is the only option to increase space, with low to medium-rise developments converted into high-density high-rise developments. Reclamation and urban renewal are two of the planning strategies the government is currently implementing in urban development.

Land sales and income revenue for the Hong Kong Government

The government performs a dual role in Hong Kong's urban development. It is the biggest landlord and also an administrator that determines the development agenda in an executive-led policy in the territory. Land is leased, or otherwise held, by the Hong Kong Special Administration Region (HKSAR).[1] Historically, Hong Kong's urban development was regulated by the restricted release of land at a rate of 50 hectares per year, together with the limited buildable land. The demand for housing and urban activities has made land very expensive, and land sales have become a major source of revenue for the government. In the early 1980s, the land-related revenue amounted to more than one-third of the government's total revenue. The HKSAR Government Land Fund Trust[2] gathered 11.5% of the total government revenue (US$93.6 billion or HK$729.7 billion) collected at this time (Hong Kong Government, 1996).

Since land is a scarce resource, efficient land-related development becomes a major concern in the development agenda. The government has given priority to 'economic space' rather than 'life space' (Friedmann, 1988) and this has become the main thrust of land-use planning in Hong Kong (Ng and Cook, 1996). One reason why the formulation of a balanced and comprehensive development strategy for the whole territory may have been hampered is the income raised by land sales. There is always a debate whether the government is practising a 'non-intervention' policy or a 'high land price' policy, since land is leased to the highest bidder through public auction.

Reclamation-based urban development strategy

Since Hong Kong became a British colony, reclamation has been used as a solution to accommodate urban growth. In 1885, a Land Commission was established to find solutions for alleviating the congested living environments. It considered land reclamation to be the principal solution. Reclamation was designated along Victoria Harbour, as it was an important frontier to Mainland China and an economic gateway to the outside world. By 1924, a total of 500 hectares of land had been reclaimed (Ng and Cook, 1996).

In the period from the 1950s to the 1970s, the government shifted the focus towards urban decentralisation through the development of new towns. There was a great demand for land and housing, resulting from the unexpected inflow of immigrants and the 'transfer of industrialisation' from southern China in the 1950s. The government studied the possibilities of building new towns after a review of land demand for industry and housing in the mid-1950s (Bristow, 1989; Territorial Development Department, 1994). Reclamation expanded to New Kowloon and the New Territories. The major new towns, Tsuen Wan; Tuen Mun; Sha Tin; Tai Po; and Tseung Kwan O, are built primarily on reclaimed land. The total reclaimed land for the various new towns now exceeds 3,000 hectares (Territorial Development Department, 1994).

From the 1980s onwards, reclamation has concentrated on the shores of the harbour. China's Open Door Policy has led to the relocation of Hong Kong's manufacturing factories into the Pearl River Delta Region in China, with its cheap land and labour resources. Hong Kong has restructured into a service economy, a process which has reinforced the concentration of jobs and office developments in the urban areas. The government undertook a number of planning studies: the Territorial Development Strategy (TDS), the Study on Harbour Reclamation and Urban Growth and the Metroplan in formulating Hong Kong's urban strategy. The TDS considered the job–housing imbalance in new towns and proposed shifting the strategic development from new towns back to the harbour. A further 23km² of new land was filled in from the harbour, as proposed by these studies. The figures of total reclaimed land (Fig. 2) show that the government recognised the increasing importance of reclamation as a solution for accommodating urban growth between the 1970s and the 1990s.

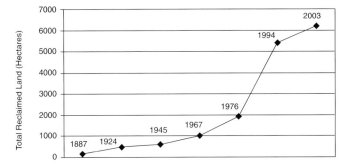

Fig. 2. Total and projected land reclamation in Hong Kong.
Source: Lands Department, Hong Kong.

There remains a question: is the main objective of harbour reclamation to encourage economic growth rather than to improve the quality of life, since the land premium and value of urban areas is higher than in the New Territories? The government asserts that the harbour-based reclamation can best provide the most needed economic space for expanding the hub functions (such as ports) of Hong Kong within Pacific Asia and supporting Hong Kong's status as an international city.

New town development: decentralisation

The new town idea originated in the 'Garden City' proposed by Ebenezer Howard (1898), with his vision that city growth should involve the gradual transformation of existing centrally concentrated cities into decentralised towns. In the 1960s, the Hong Kong Government began to examine the possibilities of a long-term new town programme to decentralise congested development and overcrowded populations into suburban areas.

The Territorial Development Department (TDD) was set up in 1973 to implement the New Town Programme. At that time, the main objective was to provide land for developing public housing in the New Territories. The basic concept of new town development was to create balanced and self-contained communities through the provision of infrastructure, community facilities and basic needs. The first generation new towns were targeted at housing 1.8 million people. To date, about 3 million, more than 40% of the total population of Hong Kong, live in the nine new towns (Fig. 1), with a target of accommodating 4 million people.

The new towns were intended to provide more land at reasonable costs to manufacturing industries, but due to the China's Open Door Policy, they were restructured towards the service economy. Employment in the service sectors[3] increased from 47% (1.26 million) in 1987 to 65.5% (2.1 million) in 1998 (Census and Statistics Department, 1999 and 1991), strengthening the concentration of jobs in the urban core.

Residential density planning policy

Before the Second World War, Hong Kong's buildings were governed by the Building Ordinance Regulations that limited building height to five storeys. Together with site coverage clauses, this resulted in a plot ratio of about 3 (Gilchriest, 1994).[4] In 1963, the concept of density zoning was introduced in Hong Kong and is still in use today (Planning Department, 1996). Table 1 shows the maximum domestic plot ratios and Fig. 3 the density zoning of residential developments in these metropolitan areas. The main objectives of the density zoning are to maximise intensity of people and jobs with close proximity to high-capacity transport systems, and this assists in shaping the Hong Kong's high-density urban form. The new towns, excluding Tsuen Wan, are classified into four density zones for residential developments and the maximum plot ratios range from 8 to 0.4.

Density Zone	Type of Area	Location	Maximum Domestic Plot Ratio
R1	(1) Existing Development Area:	Hong Kong Island	8/9/10 (i)
	i. well served by high capacity public transport systems	Kowloon & New Kowloon	6/7.5
	ii. often incorporate commercial space on the lower one to three floors	Tsuen Wan, Kwai Chung & Tsing Yi	8
	(2) New Development Area and Comprehensive Development Area		6.5
R2	i. less well served by high capacity public transport systems		5
R3	i. with very limited public transport capacity		3
	ii. subject to environmental constraints		

Table 1. Maximum domestic plot ratios: Metroplan area.
Source: Planning Department, 1996.

Note: (i) Maximum domestic plot ratio of 8, 9 and 10 depends on Site Classification.

Urban renewal favouring urban intensification

In the early 1960s, the government carried out a pilot redevelopment scheme with the objectives of redeveloping the old buildings and improving the congested conditions of old residential areas. Sheung Wan was chosen as an 'Urban Renewal District' in 1965. This pilot scheme fulfilled its objectives, but it took more than one decade to complete. Long lead-time is still the main problem of recent redevelopment schemes, because of the difficulties in land acquisition.

The existing private housing stock is ageing rapidly, especially in the urban areas. It is estimated that more than 40% of the public housing stock (about 260,000 units) in urban areas will be over 30 years old by 2005, compared with 20% (about 113,000 units) in 1999 (Planning, Environment and Lands Bureau, 1999). In 1988, the Land Development Corporation (LDC) was established to speed up the pace of urban renewal in order to solve the problem

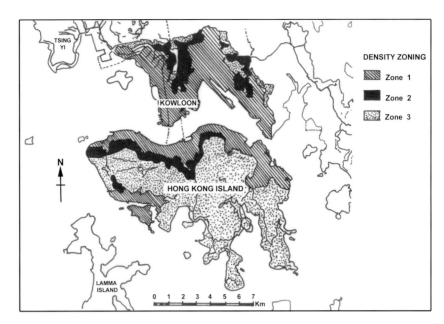

Fig. 3. Density zoning in the Hong Kong Island, Kowloon and New Kowloon.
Source: Planning Department, 1996.

of urban decay and resolve under- or over-utilisation of land. The LDC estimates that over 80 hectares of the urban areas with 46,926 units accommodating 59,235 households merit priority redevelopment (Planning, Environment and Lands Bureau, 1999). In the past decade, the LDC has taken action on 52 urban renewal projects, of which only 15 were completed (Land Development Corporation, 1998). Residential redevelopment was the main component of these 52 projects (Table 2).

Table 2. Land use mix of the 52 redevelopment projects in Hong Kong 1998.
Source: Land Development Corporation, 1998.

Land Use	Area (m²)	Percentage of Total Area (%)
Residential	1,184,183 [1]	54
Office	521,038	24
Commercial	327,760	15
G/IC Facilities	89,420	4
Open Space	76,640	3
Total	2,199,041	100

(1) Comprises 20,000 units

However, the LDC has had to face two basic problems. It is extremely difficult to assemble land lots for redevelopment since they are in multiple ownership, and the process of relocating the affected residents and businesses involves very high financial and social costs.

Urban renewal is heavily dependent on the private sector. Due to high costs, redevelopment projects have to be high-rise, with a high plot ratio, in order to make projects financially viable. Old buildings have been demolished and redeveloped into high-rise and high-density buildings (Figs 4 and 5). One of the typical examples is The Center, an 80-storey skyscraper, which was completed in 1998 (Fig. 5). It has only 8,816 square metres of site area, and at the time of construction was Hong Kong's third tallest building. It offers 122,126m² gross floor area (GFA) for high-quality office space, 4,798m² for commercial space,

3,108m² for government, institutional and community (G/IC) facilities, and 5,927m² for open space (Land Development Corporation, 1998). Urban renewal intensifies development by increasing the plot ratio through the high-rise built form and it achieves an efficient land use.

Left: *Fig. 4. Sheung Wan: old areas (prior to redevelopment).*
Right: *Fig. 5. Sheung Wan: The Center (after redevelopment).*

High-density development: a sustainable urban form?

Some argue that a compact urban form may cause an intermix of incompatible land uses and conditions of overcrowding and congestion. However, the reason that Hong Kong's high-density living environment has not generated many social conflicts is perhaps explained by the high tolerance of the Chinese to congested conditions (Pun, 1994). The compact urban form of Hong Kong has manifold advantages: the economic use of land through vertical space utilisation; the high accessibility enjoyed by residents and short journeys-to-work; few roads and commercially viable public transport (Tong and Wong, 1997). It is thus a highly convenient and efficient city, since the locations of activities and dwellings are close to each other both horizontally and vertically.

High-density development in Hong Kong allows economies of scale for utilities and transport infrastructure. As more people are accommodated through it, the government's per capita expenditure for infrastructure provision is proportionately lower. It helps to make public transport systems such as the Mass Transit Railway (MTR) more efficient and financially viable because more passengers per km reduce the marginal cost of construction and operation. The more the revenue collected, the better the service and the greater its use.

As developable land is such a scarce resource, and the population increases, there is a continuous increase in demand for sites for development. It does not seem physically and financially feasible to provide land in the New Territories and the islands, which would involve large investments because of the physical constraints in developing these areas. Accommodating more people and buildings in the developed urban areas through high-density urban form helps minimise urban encroachment into the countryside. High density, in this case, prevents urban sprawl that would otherwise threaten the recreational and ecological importance of the country parks and rural areas.

Air quality

There has been growing concern over Hong Kong's deteriorating environment, and it is open to question whether or not this is related to its compact urban form. The nitrogen dioxide (NO_2) level has risen 20% in the 5-year period to 1997. The air quality monitoring results for 1997 (Environmental Protection Department, 1998) indicated that six of the nine air quality monitoring stations did not meet the annual average Hong Kong Air Quality Objective for respirable suspended particulates (RSP). The highest annual level at the street site of Mong Kok was almost 36% above the permissible limit. The concentrations of these pollutants are believed to be associated with higher respiratory illness. Some argue that the high concentrations of these pollutants are mainly due to the surrounding tall buildings. But is this true?

The emission of air pollutants within Hong Kong territory is generated by different sectors: residential, commercial, industrial, transport, and the power industry. It is estimated that transport contributed approximately 65% and 75% of the street level emissions of nitrogen oxides and RSP in 1997, respectively (Environmental Protection Department, 1998). Hong Kong's transport sector is dominated by two sub-sectors: road and rail transport. Rail transport is mainly driven by electricity[5] and therefore emissions by rail transport are part of the power sector emissions. Road transport is at present entirely driven by internal combustion engine vehicles and its general trend of emission is rising for the air pollutants: RSP, oxides of nitrogen (NO_X), and hydrocarbons (HC) (Fig. 6). Diesel vehicle emissions were the major cause of the high RSP concentrations.

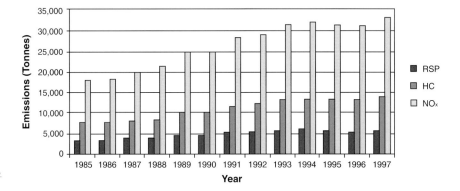

Fig. 6. The major pollutants from the road transport sector.
Source: Barron and Steinbrecher, 1999.

Fig. 7 shows the annual emission level of carbon dioxide (CO_2) in Hong Kong. Although CO_2 does not pose a direct threat to human health, increasing CO_2 emission affects world sustainability as it is one of the greenhouse gases directly contributing to global warming. The overall level of CO_2 emission is now comparatively lower than in the early 1990s. The power sector generates the largest part of CO_2 emission; however, this has fallen from 73.1% in 1990 to 59.4% of the total in 1997. This is mainly due to the partial switching from coal to natural gas for electricity generation. By contrast, the emissions from the transport sector increased from 9.8% in 1990 to 17.5% in 1997.

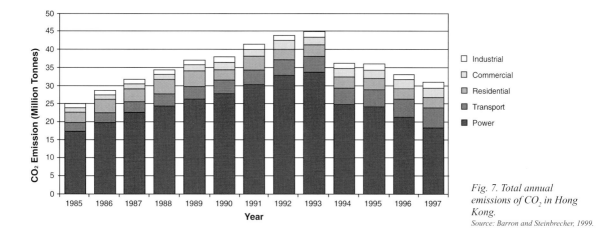

Fig. 7. Total annual emissions of CO_2 in Hong Kong.
Source: Barron and Steinbrecher, 1999.

It is undeniably true that high-rise buildings trap some of the air pollutants produced by the vehicles and the pollutants remain at the street level. However, emphasis should be placed on the sources of these pollutants and the means of reducing them, especially those emitted at the street level. Diesel-fuelled vehicles from the road transport sector produce a large proportion of these pollutants. In Hong Kong, the rail systems are comparatively environmentally friendly since the pollutants are produced from power plants, where it is easier to adopt mitigation measures. The compact urban form favours the use of rail systems because high-density developments ensure passenger flow. Commuters benefit from reliable services that encourage more people to use mass transit. This has resulted in a low dependency on private vehicles because urban form influences transport choices. The following section focuses on two major issues: policies to reduce the physical separation of land uses in both existing urban areas and sub-centres in order to reduce travel needs (polycentric urban growth patterns), and the development of a long-term sustainable transport sector.

The future for Hong Kong's sustainable development

Sustainable development in Hong Kong is targeted to 'balance the social, economic, and environmental needs for the present and future generations to achieve a vibrant economy and better environmental quality locally and internationally' (Hong Kong SAR Government, 1999, p.3). Research on sustainable development for the twenty-first century was commissioned in 1997 with the aim of:

- developing an improved system to incorporate a defined set of sustainability goals into Hong Kong's future developments;
- considering the areas within Hong Kong's sustainability 'footprint'; and
- minimising adverse environmental impacts.

It was argued that urban form, transport, and environmental impacts should be integrated in order to develop a comprehensive planning framework and policies that would achieve an economic–environmental balance.

Improvement of the existing urban areas through redevelopment

The process of redevelopment has been prolonged by the LDC because of difficulties in self-financing, negotiations with property owners, and the shortage of rehousing resources for the affected residents. To overcome these problems, a statutory body, the Urban Renewal Authority (URA) is to be established in 2000 to implement the government's urban renewal strategy in the twenty-first century. The URA will replace the LDC with legal powers, and take over all its assets and liabilities. One of the purposes of the URA will be to achieve better utilisation of land in the old areas and to make land available to meet various development needs. It aims to reduce the lead-time of redevelopment projects and in turn to intensify the urban areas and to maximise the opportunities for improvement to the existing urban areas.

Increasing the level of self-containment of new towns

The Hong Kong Government's decentralisation policy based on new town development has weaknesses. Insufficient job opportunities within the new towns, combined with a lack of rail access to central urban areas, have led to a high dependency on road-based public transport and private automobile use.

Instead of balanced and self-sufficient developments, most of the new towns are housing-led. The mismatch between job availability and housing provision has led to a high travel demand between the new towns and existing urban areas. The Travel Characteristics Survey showed that the percentage of workers who lived and worked in the same area was only 33% for Tuen Mun, and 20% for Sheung Shui and Fanling in 1992, compared to 77% and 67% for the Hong Kong Island and Kowloon respectively[6] (Transport Department, 1993). In 1996, about 50% of the total population lived in the New Territories, but 70% travelled a long distance to their place of work (Census and Statistics Department, 1996).

There is a clear need to diversify land uses and locate mixed-use developments in the new towns in order to create a 'multinucleated' city pattern (concentration decentralisation) with self-sufficiency in terms of job opportunities and supply of basic needs. Decentralising the office and commercial space into the new towns appears one of the workable solutions to reduce commuting trips between urban areas and new towns, and to reduce the pressure on the congested urban areas.

Sustainable transport system

The predominance of public transport

Hong Kong's public transport system is operated both by private operators and by public corporations with a high degree of autonomy. The MTR and the KCR (East Rail), both heavy rail systems, are operated commercially by statutory public bodies. The other transport carriers are operated by private operators, which are driven by market forces. This has resulted in a cost-effective and efficient transport system which is one of the best transport systems in the world. The current system serves around 11 million passengers boarding daily (Transport Department, 1999) and about 90% of the population in Hong Kong depend on public transport. As one of the world's most densely populated cities, Hong Kong faces challenges with rising travel demands which could result in further adverse environmental impacts unless planning policies boost the development of high-capacity and energy-efficient public transport systems.

Shifting the energy base in the transport sector

Reducing negative environmental impacts has given a major direction to the future planning of Hong Kong. The shift from diesel fuel to Liquefied Petroleum Gas (LPG), which produces fewer pollutants, is one of the means used to reduce harmful emissions. Licensed diesel vehicles accounted for only about 30% of the total number of vehicles in Hong Kong in 1996; however, they were responsible for 60% of vehicle kms travelled (VKT) and were the source of a major proportion of the pollutant emissions (Fig. 8).

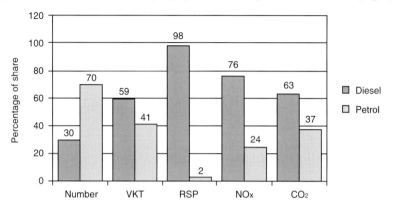

Fig. 8. Comparison of licensed diesel and petrol vehicles of Hong Kong in 1996.
Source: Barron and Steinbrecher, 1999.

Hong Kong's public road transport system at present relies too heavily on diesel-fuelled modes that account for two-thirds of the total, of which 53% are buses and 12% taxis. The Third Comprehensive Transport Study, completed in September 1999, evaluated the environmental benefits and costs of various transport development options in order to identify a comprehensive transport framework which would enhance sustainability in Hong Kong (Transport Department, 1999). Options included the mandatory use of LPG for all new taxis registered from 2001 and possibilities for using alternatively fuelled vehicles such as electric trolley buses.

Higher priority to rail transport

Transportation accounts for 40% of the total energy consumption in Hong Kong (Hung, 1992), and the government has recognised the significant role of railways, specifically of heavy rail systems, amongst all the different transport modes. These can be ranked in a modal hierarchy based on function, efficiency, and carrying capacity, in order to assess how well they serve different types of commuting (Table 3).

Due to their high capacity, low marginal cost, and less polluting service, rail systems are given a high priority in the long-term infrastructure strategy. Heavy rail systems are planned to form the backbone of Hong Kong's passenger transport network since they provide fast, reliable services to commuters, are comparatively friendly to the environment, and at the same time reduce the pressure on roads. The rail network also helps in locating strategic developments along the rail corridors, which will reduce road-based transport. The rail network will be expanded by 40% from 143 kilometres to 200 kilometres over the next five years. There is already extensive planning of the rail network to meet Hong Kong's needs up to 2016. By that time, it is expected that 40 to 50% of all public transport journeys will be made on the railway system compared to 33% now. Five rail projects are expected to be completed between 2002 and 2004, at an approximate cost of HK$ 100 billion (Transport Bureau, 1999).

Mode [1]	Capacity	Usage[2]	% of Total[3]	Costs to Build[4]	Costs to Operate	Flexibility	Use in Hierarchy
Heavy Rail MTR/KCR	Very High	2,923,000	27.18	Very High	Low	Low	Provides major trunk services in corridors with very high demand.
Light Rail (LRT)	High	314,000	2.92	High	Low	Low	Provides trunk services in high demand corridors. May feed heavy rail or ferry.
Bus	Medium	3,912,000	36.38	Low	Medium	High	Provides trunk services in medium demand corridors. May feed heavy rail, light rail or ferry.
Minibus	Low	1,755,000	16.32	Low	High	Very High	Provides services in low demand corridors. May feed heavy rail, light rail or ferry.
Tram	Low	255,000	2.37	Medium	Medium	Low	Provides services for short trips where the low speed is unimportant and the low fare is a major advantage. May feed heavy rail.
Taxi	Low	1,307,000	12.15	Low	Very High	Very High	Provides specialised personal door-to-door services.
Ferry	Medium	171,000	1.59	Low	High	Low	Provides essential services for the outlying islands and supplements other modes in the inner harbour.

Notes:
(1) Non-franchised buses (residential coaches) and the Peak Tram are excluded from the table because of their varying service characteristics.
(2) Average daily boarding in 1998.
(3) The percentage of average daily passenger journeys by each mode of public transport journeys. The figure of total daily passenger journeys (10.754 million) includes the Peak Tram and non-franchised buses.
(4) Costs to build are for new systems; those for existing systems should be considered as sunk.

Table 3. Hierarchy of Hong Kong's public transport modes.
Source: Modified from Transport Department, 1999.

Pedestrianisation

Pedestrianisation can help reduce the number of short motorised trips and the pollutant emissions; however, very few people travel on foot because of the unfriendly walking environment and the busy roads. Consideration is being given to a system of grade-separated walkways to encourage walking for short-distance trips, providing direct access to buildings and transport interchanges. High-density urban forms help fulfil the prerequisite of the provision of pedestrian links, since compact developments reduce the distance between different activities. For example, an escalator and walkway system was constructed in 1993 to link the central business district (Central) and residential areas (Mid-Levels). It is 800 metres in length and rises 135 metres. This system was used by an average of 34,000 people daily in 1997 (Hong Kong SAR Government, 1998) and it has helped to reduce commuting trips by vehicles.

Conclusion

Sustainability and urban form are closely connected in a way that fits the local context. Hong Kong's inherent compact city form supports the current belief in the need to reduce the physical separation of activities. Its high-density mixed-use urban form favours public transport, particularly for less-polluting rail systems. The transit-oriented developments contribute to public transport patronage, which benefits commuters.

Most of the large cities in Asia have experienced the problems of unplanned population growth spreading into suburban areas which then expand outwards, leading to long commuting times, serious traffic congestion, and environmental deterioration. Hong Kong faces challenges to improve its environmental sustainability for its increasing population. In order to accommodate this increasing population and related activities, a concentration/decentralisation strategy is being adopted, to create balanced and self-sufficient sub-centres (multinucleated pattern), linked by energy-efficient and economically viable mass transit systems.

Notes

1. Land lease varied from different periods of time – 999, 99 and 75 years prior to the handover to China. New leases of land are granted for a term of 50 years from the date of grant, at a premium. Government land is usually sold by public auction. Sale by public tender is adopted when the user is strictly defined and the sale is unlikely to attract interests such as petrol filling stations.
2. Land premium income has been split between the Hong Kong Government and the Hong Kong Special Administration Region (HKSAR) Government. The HKSAR Government Land Fund Trust was established on 13 August 1986 to manage the HKSAR's share of revenue obtained from land sales during the period from the entry into force of the Joint Declaration (27 May 1985) until the establishment of the HKSAR. On 1 July 1997, the assets of the Land Fund Trust were vested in the HKSAR Government. When the Land Fund was first established, it had a value of net assets of US$ 99 million (HK$ 772 million). As at 31 December 1997, the total assets of the Land Fund stood at US$ 25 billion (HK$ 196 billion). The Chief Executive of the HKSAR appointed the Financial Secretary as the public officer to receive, hold and manage the fund, as part of the HKSAR Government reserves.
3. Services sectors cover three main groups: (1) wholesale, retail and import and export trades, restaurants and hotels; (2) financing, insurance, real estate and business services; and (3) community, social and personal services.
4. 'Plot ratio is defined as the ratio between the gross floor area [GFA as defined under Building (Planning) Regulations – B(P)R] of a building and the area of the site on which it is erected [the Net Site Area]. Plot ratio controls govern the amount of GFA in buildings but affect population density only indirectly due to the interplay of other factors like, flat size and person per flat ratio' (Hong Kong Planning Department, 1992). A plot ratio of 3 means that the GFA of a residential building is three times the Net Site Area.
5. In Hong Kong, all passenger rails are electrified, while a small level of freight rail is diesel-based.
6. The Travel Characteristics Survey was commissioned by the Transport Department of Hong Kong to study the travel characteristics and establish a database for transport planning in 1992. The study applied a stratified sampling approach for the detailed survey of a 2% sample of total households in Hong Kong, approximately 31,640 households for March 1991, when the total number of households was 1,582,000.

References

Barron, W. and Steinbrecher, N. (eds) (1999) *Heading Towards Sustainability? Practical Indicators of Environmental Sustainability for Hong Kong*, The University of Hong Kong, Hong Kong SAR.

Breheny, M. (ed.) (1992) *Sustainable Development and Urban Form*, Pion, London.

Breheny, M. (1996) Centrists, decentrists and compromisers: views on the future of urban form, in *The Compact City: A Sustainable Urban Form?* (eds M. Jenks, E. Burton and K. Williams), E & FN Spon, London.

Bristow, M. R. (1989) *Hong Kong's New Towns: A Selective Review*, Oxford University Press, Hong Kong.

Burton, E., Williams, K., and Jenks, M. (1996) The compact city and urban sustainability: conflicts and complexities, in *The Compact City: A Sustainable Urban Form?* (eds M. Jenks, E. Burton and K. Williams), E & FN Spon, London.

Census and Statistics Department (1991) *Hong Kong Annual Digest of Statistics*, Hong Kong Government, Hong Kong SAR.

Census and Statistics Department (1996) *Hong Kong By-Census 96*, Hong Kong Government, Hong Kong.

Census and Statistics Department (1999) *Hong Kong Annual Digest of Statistics*, Hong Kong SAR Government, Hong Kong.

Environmental Protection Department (1998) *Air Quality in Hong Kong 1997 – Results from the Air Quality Monitoring Network*, Hong Kong SAR Government, Hong Kong SAR.

Friedmann, J. (1988) Life space and economic space: contradictions in regional development, *Life Space and Economic Space: Essays in Third World Planning*, Transactions Books, Oxford.

Gilchriest, S. (1994) Planning for high density in Hong Kong, in *High Urban Densities: A Solution for Our Cities?* (eds V. Fouchier and O. Merlin), Consulate General of France in Hong Kong, Hong Kong.

Hong Kong Government (1996) *Hong Kong Year Book*, Hong Kong Government, Hong Kong.

Hong Kong Planning Department (1992) *Hong Kong Planning Standards and Guidelines*, Planning Department, Hong Kong Government, Government Printer, Hong Kong.

Hong Kong SAR Government (1998) *Hong Kong: A New Era*, Hong Kong SAR Government, Hong Kong SAR.

Hong Kong SAR Government (1999) *Sustainable Development in Hong Kong for the 21st Century: Second Stage Consultation Document*, Hong Kong SAR Government, Hong Kong SAR.

Howard, E. (1898) *To-morrow: A Peaceful Path to Real Reform*, Swan Sonnenschein, London.

Hung, W. T. (1992) *Transport Energy Policy and Consumption Trends in Hong Kong*, The Centre of Urban Planning and Environmental Management, The University of Hong Kong, Hong Kong.

Land Development Corporation (1998) *10 Years of Urban Renewal*, Land Development Corporation, Hong Kong SAR.

Montgomery, J. (1998) Making a city: urbanity, vitality and urban design, *Journal of Urban Design*, **3(1)**, pp.93–117.

Newman, P. W. G. (1992) The compact city: an Australian perspective, *Built Environment*, **18(4)**, pp.285–300.

Newman, P. W. G. and Kenworthy, J. R. (1989) *Cities and Automobile Dependence: A Sourcebook*, Gower Publishing Company Limited, England.

Ng, M. K. and Cook, A. (1996) *Are There Feasible Alternatives to the Reclamation-led Urban Development Strategy in Hong Kong?*, Occasional Paper No. 12, Centre of Urban Planning and Environmental Management, The University of Hong Kong, Hong Kong.

Planning Department (1996) *Hong Kong Planning Standards and Guidelines*, Hong Kong Government, Hong Kong.

Planning, Environment and Lands Bureau (1999) *Urban Renewal in Hong Kong*, Hong Kong SAR Government, Hong Kong SAR.

Pun, K. S. (1994) Advantages and disadvantages of high-density urban development, in *High Urban Densities: A Solution for Our Cities?* (eds V. Fouchier and O. Merlin), Consulate General of France in Hong Kong, Hong Kong.

Robertson, J. (1990) Alternative futures for cities, in *The Living City: Towards a Sustainable Future* (eds D. Cadman and G. Payne), Routledge, London.

Territorial Development Department (1994) *20 Years of New Town Development*, Hong Kong Government, Hong Kong.

Tong, C. O. and Wong, S. C. (1997) The advantages of a high density, mixed land use, linear urban development, *Transportation*, **24**, pp.295–307.

Transport Bureau (1999) *Hong Kong Moving Ahead: A Transport Strategy for the Future*, Hong Kong SAR Government, Hong Kong SAR.

Transport Department (1993) *Travel Characteristics Survey*, Territory Transport Planning Division, Hong Kong Government, Hong Kong.

Transport Department (1999) *Third Comprehensive Transport Study: Final Report*, Hong Kong SAR Government, Hong Kong SAR.

Wegener, M. (1995) The changing urban hierarchy in Europe, in *Cities in Competition: Productive and Sustainable Cities for the 21st Century* (eds J. Brotchie, M. Batty, E. Blakely, P. Hall and P. Newton), Longman Australia Pty Ltd, Melbourne, Australia.

WorldSat International Inc. (1997) *The Cartographic Satellite Atlas of the World*, Warwick Publishing Inc., Toronto and Los Angeles.

Part Four
Transport, Infrastructure and Environment
Introduction

Part Four considers a number of important factors that affect sustainability. Transport is one of the dominant issues, central to the debate about sustainable urban form. Density, intensification and compaction, discussed in previous parts, are to an extent predicated on the idea that journeys will be reduced, public transport made viable, and thus less fuel burnt and fewer harmful emissions produced. A great deal of research has been carried out in developed countries, but in developing countries, the urban forms, especially where there are very high densities, reveal different dimensions to the problem. For example, high use of public transport may be more related to low income than to the effect of compact urban forms, but congestion, even where there is low car ownership, is related to the built form. Transport provision is one important form of infrastructure, but so too is the provision of services such as water, electricity and sewage disposal, and consideration is given to their costs in this part of the book. Environmental issues are also tackled, including preservation and creation of open space and of an eco-system, and through mapping of sustainability indicators, and through assessing the environmental consequences of domestic fuel use.

Barter presents detailed research of issues related to transport in Asian cities, and makes comparisons with cities in the developed world. He demonstrates that public transport use and non-motorised journeys increase with increases in density. Although desirable, he also shows how density and limited road capacity can lead with alarming rapidity to disastrous congestion. Where public transport is successful in high-density urban forms, it is usually the result of strong government with policies of early car restraint and substantial investment. Moor and Rees show that investment is important, although in the case of Bangkok this could have been too little, too late. They review the plans to create a mass transit system, and show the viability of the concept of densely developed Transit Development Zones (TDZ). It is suggested that if a network of TDZ can be planned and designed well, then it is perhaps safe to leave the intervening development to market forces. Biermann illustrates another aspect of capacity and thresholds with a study of the provision of services infrastructure and the effect this has on development costs and location. Her research studies the relationship between density, capacity thresholds and costs of infrastructure, and questions the assumptions about the necessary connection between compaction and reduced costs.

Downton reviews environmental issues related to the city of Calcutta and its region. Despite being a very dense, compact and crowded city, Calcutta has been developing environmental strategies, with policies to insert open and green space into the city, and linking this to a significant eco-system on the periphery. He suggests that if the policies in Calcutta can be made to work, while by no means perfectly, they may be a lesson for other cities in developing countries. Open space and green, agricultural land is also considered in a range of 31 sustainable indicators developed by Tsou *et al.* for Tainan City in Taiwan. These indicators are mapped across the city and its region to identify significant patterns, and they show how this process has the potential to alert local government to potential sustainability problems. In the final chapter, Reddy provides a detailed analysis of domestic energy use and its impact on the city and region, showing how rich and poor waste energy in different ways. He shows that supplying energy to the city of Bangalore in itself costs energy through the use of transport. The way that energy is used, and how it is used, may, he concludes, have more to do with income inequities than with urban form.

The findings here demonstrate the complexity of attempting to link these factors with urban form. The broad assumptions about the efficacy of compact urban forms are open to question, and the many dimensions raised again point to there being a number of sustainable urban forms.

Paul A. Barter

Transport Dilemmas in Dense Urban Areas:
Examples from Eastern Asia

Introduction

The spatial implications of urban transport patterns have long been an important theme in planning and transport literature (Hansen, 1959; Mumford, 1961; Thomson, 1977). However, most of the debate about connections between transport and the concept of the 'compact city' has focused on cities with relatively low densities. This chapter highlights some results from a study of transport patterns in nine cities in eastern Asia, most of which have high urban densities. It outlines a small number of key urban and transport characteristics and places them in an international context. This sets the scene for discussion of the transport opportunities and challenges that result from high densities. Finally, the implications of high urban densities for transport policies are discussed.

It is widely accepted that low urban densities tend to go together with a high level of reliance on private cars, low use of public transport, and low levels of walking and cycling (Newman and Kenworthy, 1996). In the context of low-density urban areas, arguments have raged over the transport-related pros and cons of encouraging more compact urban development (Bernick and Cervero, 1997). However, at the other end of the urban density spectrum, many aspects of the debate are quite different. High urban densities exist in most large cities in the South, and have profound implications for transport policy in these cities. Scholars and planners who may be attuned to the debates in low-density cities must not overlook these implications, which include both challenges and opportunities.

This chapter examines the issues with reference to a comparative data set on nine major Asian cities with average per capita incomes (in 1990) ranging from lower-middle to high. The cities are Surabaya, Jakarta and Manila (lower-middle income cities), Bangkok, Kuala Lumpur and Seoul (upper-middle income), and Singapore, Hong Kong and Tokyo (high-income). A comparative perspective with other regions is also provided (using eleven high-income cities in Europe, six in Australia, seven in Canada and thirteen in the United States).[1] Most data presented here are from the 1990 update and extension (Kenworthy and Laube *et al.*, 1999) of earlier work by Newman and Kenworthy (1989). Data were collected by a team (which included the author) at the Institute for Sustainability and Technology Policy, Murdoch University, and were primarily from official documents, including transportation studies and vehicle registration data. Great care has been taken to ensure reliability and comparability of the data, especially in cities with less developed data-keeping capacity.

Characteristics of Asian cities in an international perspective

Analysis reveals similar patterns within a region, with the cities of the United States having, on average, among the lowest urban densities, the highest usage of private motor vehicles and the lowest use of public transport. The Asian cities are, on average, at the opposite extreme, with high densities, low vehicle use and high public transport use. The European, Canadian and Australian cities fall between these extremes.

Asian cities, including most of those in this sample, are typically very densely settled (Fig. 1). Only Kuala Lumpur has a medium density similar to typical Western European levels. Six of the Asian cities with high urban densities have above 100 persons per hectare (pph). It should be noted that the population densities quoted here are urban densities, calculated using the urbanised area only (including roads, residential, commercial, industrial and other urban land uses but excluding water bodies, large parks, agriculture and other non-urban land-uses). Although some of these Asian densities may appear unusual when compared with Western cities, high urban densities are common worldwide. Densities above 100 persons per hectare (pph) are typical of large cities in developing countries, especially in Asia. For example, Bombay, Bangalore, Madras, Cairo, Dhaka, Shanghai, Hanoi, and Pusan all have well over 200 persons per hectare (Barter, 1999). Historically, high urban densities existed in the West, but now persist only in the inner areas of the largest cities such as Paris or New York (Newman and Hogan, 1987).

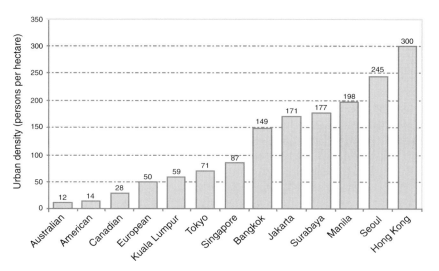

Fig. 1. Urban densities in Asian cities (1990).
Source: Data in Kenworthy and Laube et al., 1999.

Most of the Asian cities have relatively low levels of vehicle use per capita. There is a wide range in the level of private motor vehicle use (vehicle kilometres of travel – VKT) per capita among the cities in this international sample, and even within the Asian group of cities (Fig. 2). Variations in the level of public transport use are just as pronounced (Fig. 3). To a considerable extent, these variations reflect income levels, although at the urban (as opposed to national) level, the connection between income and transport patterns is by no means as direct and simple as is widely believed (Kenworthy *et al.*, 1997). For example, within this sample of nine Asian cities, there is no clear-cut relationship between income and car ownership, nor is there one between income and public transport usage. The least-squares linear regression for car ownership versus Gross Regional Product (GRP) per capita within the Asian sample (r^2=0.2767) is not significant at the 95% confidence level. Rising income is an enabling factor that can unleash the potential for rapidly rising use of private vehicles, but it is not necessarily the primary determining factor (Barter, 1999; Kenworthy and Laube *et al.*, 1999).

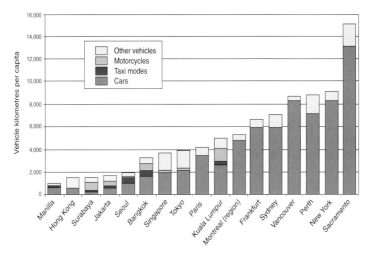

Fig. 2. Private vehicle use in Asian cities (1990).
Source: Data in Kenworthy and Laube et al., 1999.

Note: The 'other vehicles' are primarily goods vehicles. However, in cases where motorcycle VKT figures are not specified separately, then these are included in the 'other vehicles' VKT figure. In cases where taxi VKT are not specified separately, they are generally included under 'car' VKT.

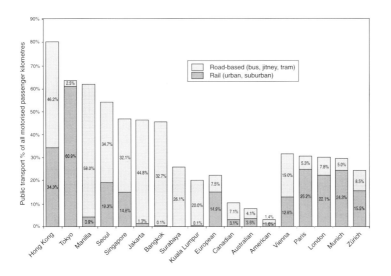

Fig. 3. Percentage of public transport use in relation to total motorised travel (1990).
Source: Data in Kenworthy and Laube et al., 1999.

Transport opportunities for high urban densities

High density presents both opportunities and challenges to transportation. It is the opportunities that have often been emphasised in compact city literature. For example, high density offers the opportunity for average trip lengths to be short and to foster economically viable public transport (Pushkarev and Zupan, 1977). Such high densities also promote a high level of accessibility for non-motorised modes of transport and enable cities to have low levels of energy use per person in transport (Newman and Kenworthy, 1989).

The opportunity that high urban density presents to public transport is exemplified by the case of Hong Kong, where in 1990 public transport carried 82% of all motorised passenger kilometres travelled. Fig. 4 makes clear that a very high use of public transport is possible in high-density cities, even in those with high incomes. However, the examples of Bangkok and Surabaya suggest that high density does not necessarily guarantee the success of public transport.

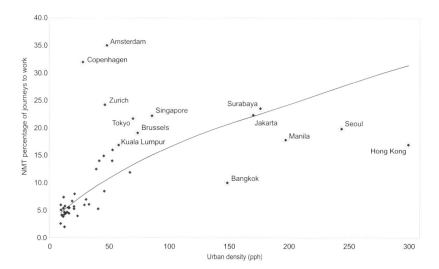

Fig. 4. Urban density and public transport use (1990).
Source: Data in Kenworthy and Laube et al., 1999.

Another opportunity presented by high densities is the possibility that many trips can be short and therefore easily made on foot or by non-motorised vehicles. Fig. 5 demonstrates that a significant role for non-motorised transport is possible even in medium-density cities. In theory, there is considerable potential for non-motorised transport to play a large role in dense Asian cities.

However, Fig. 5 also shows that, although high density provides such an opportunity, it does not guarantee it. For example, Bangkok has remarkably low levels of walking or cycling to work despite its relatively high density. The graph shows that the levels of non-motorised transport for work trips in the high and very high-density cities are no greater than levels found in most medium-density cities. This probably reflects the hostility of the street environments for people on foot or on bicycles in most of these cities.

Thus, some of the high-density Asian cities in this sample do not fully exploit the potential to encourage non-motorised and public transport use. Policies that work with this potential are likely to reap significant rewards for dense cities.

Transport challenges for high urban densities

High urban densities also present formidable transport-related challenges, especially for cities where rising incomes have begun to unleash the potential for higher private vehicle ownership and usage. For example, traffic congestion tends to emerge rapidly as dense cities motorise, even if vehicle use per capita remains relatively low. This is not simply the result of poorly developed road systems, but because road capacities are inherently low. It is physically impossible for dense cities to match the road provision levels of low-density cities. Furthermore, air pollution and other local traffic impacts can become severe problems for dense cities even at low levels of motorisation. The most successful transport policies in dense cities are likely to be those that are compatible with the spatial realities of such urban areas.

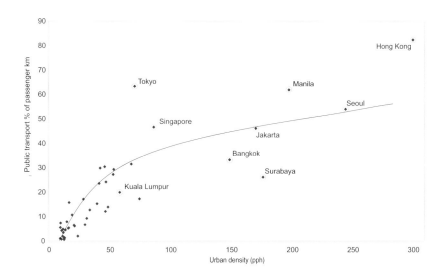

Fig. 5. Urban density and non-motorised transport (NMT) journeys to work (1990).
Source: Data in Kenworthy and Laube et al., 1999.

The voracious space demand for cars has been understood for many years (Mumford, 1961). An influx of cars creates great difficulties for established dense urban areas and generates substantial pressure for activities to spread outwards and be accessible to cars. Research on transport space consumption, using the product of the space occupied by the *time* that it is occupied, shows enormous differences (up to 90 times) in space consumption between cars and public transport for a trip to work in a central business district (Bruun and Schiller, 1995). This approach emphasises the importance of the space consumed for car parking, especially that which is occupied for the entire day in expensive central areas. Unfortunately, the recognition of the inefficiencies of private transport from a spatial perspective has often not penetrated to a policy level.

Congestion and road provision

Severe traffic congestion has rapidly emerged in a number of dense Asian cities, including Bangkok, Manila, Seoul and Jakarta, despite relatively low levels of vehicle ownership and use. The traffic problems of many Asian cities are often cited in terms of a lack of road capacity (Bodell, 1995; Midgley, 1994; Tanaboriboon, 1993; World Bank, 1996). It is true that Asian cities generally have low levels of road length per person relative to cities in the other regions in the international sample. However, it is too simplistic to blame traffic problems solely on a lack of road space. The issue is fundamentally a spatial one: the high-density urban form in Asian cities is the central underlying reason for the low road provision per person. Road space is inherently a scarce commodity and, logically, any measure of road capacity *per person* will necessarily be low in dense cities, unless the space available for roads (road capacity *per hectare*) can be made unusually high.

Figure 6 illustrates these points using data on main road lengths from the international sample. Main road network density varies little across most cities in the sample. In fact, the higher density Asian cities tended to have slightly higher arterial road network densities than others. Yet the Asian cities, especially the highest density ones, had a very low main road length per person.

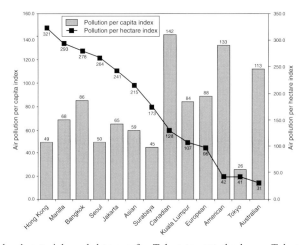

Fig. 6. Road network density compared to road length per person (1990).
Source: Barter, 1999, with data drawn in part from Kenworthy and Laube et al., 1999.

Note: Tokyo's arterial road data are for Tokyo-to, not the larger Tokyo Metropolitan Transportation Area (TMTA).

Could arterial road network density be raised to high enough levels in dense cities to bring road lengths per person up to levels comparable with European or even American cities, and hence allow vehicle use per person also to rise to similar levels? The answer is almost certainly no, unless urban population densities drastically decrease. It would be difficult to increase arterial road network spatial capacity in any city beyond a certain point (Zahavi, 1976).

Expressways provide one way to increase the road network density. However, spatial and financial constraints must inevitably limit this network capacity as well. In any case, some Asian cities in this sample already have quite a high expressway network provision, even by international standards. Data from Barter (1999) show that in 1990 Hong Kong had 4.4m of expressway per hectare of urbanised land. Kuala Lumpur had an expressway network density of 3.6m per hectare (m/hectare) in 1985 and by 1997 it had approximately 4.1m/hectare. Seoul's 1995 figure was about 3.1m/hectare and Singapore's 1990 figure was 3.3m/hectare. These figures can be compared with Los Angeles (County) with 3.9m of expressway per urban hectare in 1990, Paris with 2.8m/hectare in 1990, and New York (Tri-State Region) with 2.7m/hectare in 1980.

It is very difficult, if not impossible, for dense cities to remain dense *and* significantly to increase their road provision per capita, except perhaps by using extraordinary means such as very high-capacity, multi-decked or underground roads, all of which are extremely expensive. Although seemingly obvious, these points have received little emphasis in the literature on urban transport. Indeed, the opposite view has frequently been suggested – that substantially increasing road supply in Asian cities is a viable and desirable policy direction.

Air pollution

Dense cities also tend to be especially prone to suffering acute air pollution from traffic (Fig. 7). Indices of local pollutant emissions per capita and of emissions per hectare for each city were calculated using data on transport emissions of four pollutants of local concern, namely nitrogen oxides (NO_X), carbon monoxide (CO), sulphur dioxide (SO_2) and volatile hydrocarbons (VHC). The emissions-per-person index was derived from the emissions-per-capita figures by multiplying by a coefficient, such that for each of the four pollutants the overall average was 25; then these four figures were added together to produce the overall index. Thus, if a city had average emissions per capita for each of the four pollutants then it would have an index value of 100. The emissions-per-hectare index of each city was then simply proportional to the per-capita index multiplied by the urban density of the city (with the resulting figures adjusted by a common factor so that the mean value within this sample of cities was again 100).

Although the Asian cities had below average pollutant emissions per capita, most of them had much higher than average emissions per urban hectare. This reinforces the many reports of severe air pollution in the Asian cities studied here, especially Bangkok, Manila and, recently, also Hong Kong.

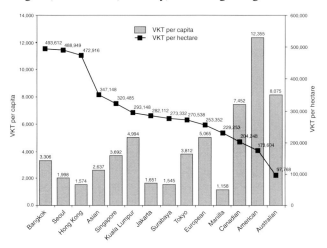

Fig. 7. Transport air pollution emissions per capita for Asian and other cities (1990)
Source: Barter, 1999, based on data from Kenworthy and Laube et al., 1999.

Notes:
a. The American, Australian and European averages cover slightly smaller samples of cities for which emission data were available.
b. For both of the indices, the overall average for all cities in the international sample is 100.
c. The pollutants included are CO, SO_2, NO_X and VHC.

American and Australian cities may be 'villains' with high levels of CO_2 emissions per person from transport and the highest emissions per capita of local pollutants, but this is balanced by relatively low emissions of local pollutants per hectare. At the opposite extreme, transport in Hong Kong, Seoul, Jakarta, Surabaya and Manila contributes low CO_2 emissions per capita and low local air pollutant emissions per capita, but each of these cities has high levels of traffic pollutants per hectare. These cities' high densities are 'unforgiving' in this respect.

Traffic intensity

The parameter 'traffic intensity' (or vehicle kms per year per hectare) helps the understanding of the air pollution conclusions above. In principle, traffic intensity figures provide an indicator of the 'impact' of traffic (all else being equal). It could be expected that cities with high traffic intensity are those likely to have the most severe local air pollution, noise and general traffic nuisance problems (notwithstanding variations from city to city in vehicle fleets, vehicle emissions rates, detailed traffic patterns, city shape and meteorological patterns).

By 1990, most of the Asian cities already had higher vehicle use per hectare than cities in any of the other regions (Fig. 8). This is a striking result, given the low vehicle use per person in most Asian cities.

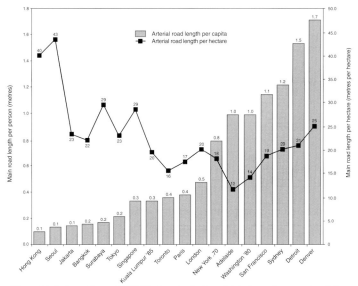

Fig. 8. Traffic per hectare compared with traffic per person for international cities (1990).

Source: Barter, 1999, based on data from Kenworthy and Laube et al., 1999.

Note: The vehicle km of travel (VKT) data include vehicle km of on-road public transport

It is noteworthy that the two highest density cities in the international sample, Hong Kong and Seoul, had very high traffic intensities, despite their low levels of vehicle use per capita. This underlines the strong spatial imperative in Hong Kong and Seoul to restrain private vehicles and to promote the lowest impact modes. Bangkok also had very high traffic levels per hectare, resulting from moderate vehicle use per person combined with moderately high urban density. The American cities had relatively low vehicle use per hectare, despite their very high rates of vehicle use per person. This is related to their low urban densities.

The insights provided by this spatial perspective suggest it will be very difficult for large, dense Asian cities to control vehicle-related air pollution problems without a much greater effort than is made in the West. Many American cities still have air pollution problems despite vehicles with relatively 'clean' technology and lower levels of traffic per hectare. The expectation is that dense Asian cities will face air pollution problems even if their vehicles could be made as clean as those in the US. High traffic intensities in the Asian cities underline the spatial imperative to restrain motorised traffic in dense cities.

Imbalance between transport and land-use patterns

The challenges and opportunities of high densities for transport could be thought unimportant, since land-use patterns will adapt to whatever transport changes occur. However, this overlooks the slow rate of adaptation. In many of the Asian cities, rapid changes in transport over the last decade or two have led to a traumatic imbalance between new levels of mobility, especially private mobility, and many aspects of the existing urban fabric and transport infrastructure. This imbalance has emerged even though levels of private mobility are still relatively low in an international context.

Until recently there was low mobility in Asian cities, which remained compact in order to maintain accessibility and be amenable to non-motorised modes of travel and public transport. The rapid increase in private vehicle ownership has created strong pressure for change to urban form, especially in the design of new development. However, large parts of these cities, housing many millions of people, are already built up to high densities and were never designed to cater for automobiles. Wholesale demolition in such areas, required to adapt them to accommodate mass ownership of automobiles, is virtually unthinkable.

Fig. 9 shows a graphical interpretation of how the imbalance between transport and land-use patterns arises in rapidly motorising cities, such as Bangkok. As average per capita incomes pass through a threshold range of roughly US$3,000 to US$5,000 at 1990 prices, a sudden increase in private motorised mobility becomes possible. Cities with high private vehicle mobility need to have lower densities in order to accommodate the greater spatial demands of private vehicles. However, the urban density of the rapidly motorising middle-income city cannot decrease quickly enough to make space for the new influx of vehicles. Lack of infrastructure is often blamed for the resulting problems, but a more fundamental cause is the fact that high private mobility is inherently incompatible with the pre-existing dense land-use patterns.

The issue of tight spatial constraints in dense cities is also probably a factor in the popularity of motorcycles in many Asian cities (Barter, 1999). Small motorcycles can manoeuvre through stationary traffic and park easily in busy areas where car parking is difficult. Motorcycles are not as space-saving as public transport, but can access congested centres more easily than cars and are in direct competition with public transport. Unfortunately, motorcycles contribute greatly to other problems such as road safety and air and noise pollution, and their popularity is often associated with failing public transport systems.

Policy choices in dense cities

The Asian cities in this sample provide evidence for some of the key transport policy choices. These have varied enormously among the different cities. The most successful policy approaches in the region have been those most sensitive to

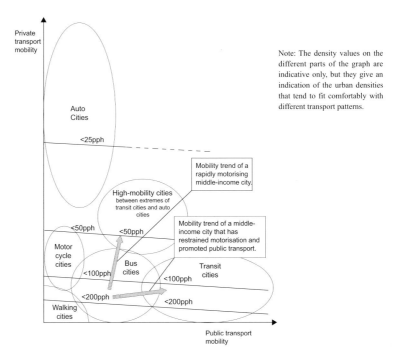

Fig. 9. Motorised mobility trends, city types and urban densities.
Source: Barter, 1999.

the spatial realities of these generally high-density cities. Kuala Lumpur and Bangkok, which have attempted to accommodate private vehicles, contrast strongly with Singapore, Hong Kong, Seoul and Tokyo, which have consistently restrained the ownership and use of private vehicles over several decades. Kuala Lumpur, with its medium density, has faced moderate problems with motorisation, whereas Bangkok, being much denser, has had a 'traffic crisis' since the early 1990s. Jakarta, Manila and Surabaya have not yet adopted either of these two broad strategies.

Private vehicles and private transport infrastructure
The main emphasis of urban transport policy and practice in both Kuala Lumpur and Bangkok has long been on efforts to increase the flow of traffic (Jamilah Mohamed, 1992; Poboon, 1997; Spencer, 1989). Vehicle ownership restraint has been rejected in both places. Proposals for traffic limitation measures for congested central areas were seriously considered then dropped by both cities in the 1980s (Spencer, 1989; Tanaboriboon, 1992; Wilbur Smith and Associates, 1974; Wilbur Smith and Associates *et al.*, 1981). Public transport and non-motorised transport have been relatively neglected in both cities (Barter, 1996). Since the 1970s the Kuala Lumpur metropolitan area has had the highest expressway length per million people among the Asian cities in the sample (Barter, 1999).

By contrast, Hong Kong, Singapore, Seoul and Tokyo have restrained private vehicle ownership and/or use, and have fostered high-quality public transport. Expressway networks in each of these cities are relatively modest relative to their populations. In Japan, government policies in the post-war era restrained private spending on both cars and urban sprawl (Hook, 1994). Except for a spurt in the 1960s, motorisation in Tokyo has been relatively slow, despite Japan's high economic growth rates for several decades. In South Korea, restraint of car use and ownership was imposed over several decades until the mid-1980s through high gasoline prices, a high yearly car-ownership tax, and low availability of credit for private consumption. The motivation for these policies in Japan and Korea was the macro-economic strategy of promoting exports while constraining private consumption (Kim, 1991; World Bank, 1986).

In Hong Kong and Singapore, restraint on private car ownership began in the early 1970s in response to upsurges in traffic (from low base-lines). Usage restraints soon followed, such as increased petrol prices, area licensing (in Singapore), and parking restrictions. In both cities, restraint measures have been strengthened several times since they began (Ang, 1996; Hau, 1995; Pendakur *et al.*, 1989; Phang, 1993). These policies dramatically slowed motorisation in the two 'city-states' despite tremendous increases in per-capita incomes. It is important to note that in each of the four wealthier Asian cities in this group, restraint on cars began early in the motorisation process. All began restraint before car ownership reached 70 cars per 1,000 people.

Lower-middle income cities such as Manila, Jakarta and Surabaya may still be able to follow this example of restraint, although all three were, by 1990, approaching 70 cars per 1,000 persons. A number of reports on these cities have indeed recommended traffic restraint and warned that supply-side approaches are doomed to failure (Dorsch Consult *et al.*, 1996; Freeman Fox and Associates, 1977; Inter-Departmental Working Group, 1993; Jakarta Government, 1987). Jakarta and Manila have taken some tentative steps with traffic restraint (Villoria and Olegario, 1996), but with little effect, although the Asian economic crisis of the late 1990s may have had a greater impact.

Public transport

There are also important contrasts in public transport policies and trends. The restraint of private transport in Hong Kong, Seoul and Singapore, even as incomes have risen, has enabled bus systems to retain viability and encouraged the active improvement of public transport. Until relatively recently, Seoul, Hong Kong and Singapore had bus-dominated public transport, but all now have extensive mass transit systems. Nevertheless, buses remain important and there are now widespread bus priority systems in Hong Kong, Singapore and Seoul. Tokyo's public transport system was already rail-dominated by the 1950s and this was reinforced by further large investments in subsequent decades (Cybriwsky, 1991).

By contrast, in Kuala Lumpur and Bangkok, public transport has been slow to improve. As congestion crises emerged in the early 1990s, public transport failed to offer an attractive alternative to the new cars and motorcycles of the emerging middle class. There was no bus priority in Kuala Lumpur until 1997, contributing to buses becoming the 'mode of last resort'. In the 1980s, Bangkok had some success in giving buses priority (Marler, 1982) but did not persevere (Tanaboriboon, 1992). Significant urban rail investment in Kuala Lumpur and Bangkok began in the 1990s, but only after motorisation had already reached high levels.

Allport (1994) argues that a large part of the importance of mass transit investment is in making traffic restraint politically palatable. Kuala Lumpur and Bangkok rejected traffic restraint in the 1980s with the argument that public transport must improve first (Spencer and Madhaven, 1989). Similar arguments have been used in Jakarta (Forbes, 1990). However, the evidence from this sample does not support the argument that mass transit must precede restraint. In Seoul, Singapore and Hong Kong traffic restraint began many years before mass transit was built (Barter, 1999). In fact, it seems that traffic restraint policies in these cities had the effect of 'buying time' that allowed them later to be able to afford world-class public transport systems, the viability of which was not threatened too soon by rising private vehicle ownership. Public transport in these cities was able to retain the middle class as customers and cater to their rising aspirations for mobility by improving services gradually (eventually with urban rail systems).

Land-use policies

Exploring how developing cities can retain, or reinforce, transit-oriented urban land-use patterns, even as incomes rise, is an important topic for study (Gakenheimer, 1995). Even with the high-density land-use patterns of Asian cities, there is still the potential and need for land-use policies explicitly to favour public transport and non-motorised travel. Explicit policies in Singapore, Hong Kong and Seoul encourage land-use patterns that are increasingly transit-oriented. In Tokyo, the land-use control system is relatively weak but, nevertheless, much new development is transit-oriented in its location and design (Hook, 1994), suggesting that such land-use patterns can develop naturally as a market response.

In the other cities in this group, there is a trend for the design of much new development to be oriented towards access by private vehicles. Bangkok, Kuala Lumpur, Jakarta and Manila had many new housing, office or shopping complexes built during the property boom decade (1986 to 1997), targeted at the newly prosperous middle class with designs giving private vehicular access. Developing Asian cities run the risk of building traffic disasters into their urban fabric. Densities are still too high to cope effectively with high numbers of private cars, and car-friendly design features encourage private transport, making the provision of public transport facilities more difficult.

Conclusion

Public policy on transport needs a keen awareness of the implications of high-density urban land-use patterns. The high densities of many Asian cities provide transport planning with both challenges and opportunities. There are challenges because such cities are vulnerable to traffic saturation and can never provide high levels of road capacity per person. There are opportunities because land-use patterns in Asian cities are potentially highly suited to the non-automobile modes of transport that can provide high accessibility at low cost and in an ecologically sustainable way. Policy settings aimed at exploiting this opportunity are likely to reap rapid and significant benefits, as demonstrated to some extent by the experiences of Tokyo, Singapore, Hong Kong and Seoul. Densities in Seoul and Hong Kong are so high that even with strong restraint of private traffic, they still face problems of very high traffic intensity. Bangkok, by contrast, illustrates that a 'traffic disaster' can arise very quickly as motorisation increases in a dense city with no traffic restraint.

Ever-increasing private vehicle use and unsustainable transport consumption levels are not necessarily the inevitable destiny of Asian cities, even if income levels rise dramatically. In fact, the cities of Asia face a choice, just as do cities everywhere. The choice is between two contrasting approaches towards transport: early restraint of private vehicles with promotion of the alternatives, or a dangerous and unsustainable path of unrestrained growth in private vehicle numbers and lagging public transport development.

Notes

1. The Western cities in the study were Hamburg, Frankfurt, Zurich, Stockholm, Brussels, Paris, London, Munich, Copenhagen, Vienna, Amsterdam, Houston, Phoenix, Detroit, Denver, Los Angeles, San Francisco, Boston, Washington, Chicago, New York, Portland, Sacramento, San Diego, Sydney, Adelaide, Melbourne, Brisbane, Perth, Canberra, Calgary, Edmonton, Montreal, Ottawa, Toronto, Vancouver, and Winnipeg.

Acknowledgements

I gratefully acknowledge the invaluable contributions of Dr Jeff Kenworthy, the team supervisor, and of other students in ISTP at Murdoch University. They are Dr Felix Laube; Dr Chamlong Poboon; Mr Tamim Raad and Mr Benedicto Guia, Jr. Many thanks must also go to the many people in government agencies and other institutions who have given their time to provide much of the vast amount of data behind the analysis presented here. Part of this research on Asian cities was supported with a grant from the Asia Research Centre at Murdoch University and with a travel grant from the School of Social Sciences at Murdoch University, which are gratefully acknowledged. A number of specific data items were collected with the support of a World Bank research contract.

References

Allport, R. (1994) Lessons learnt from worldwide experiences of rail transit systems – implications for future policy. Paper presented at the Mass Transit Asia '94 Conference, Hyatt Regency Singapore, 31 May–1 June.

Ang, B. W. (1996) Urban transportation management and energy savings: the case of Singapore. *International Journal of Vehicle Design,* **17(1)**, pp.1–12.

Barter, P. A. (1996) Prospects for non-motorised transport in rapidly developing Asian cities – implications for a global comparative study of urban transport and land use. Paper presented at the Velo Australis International Bicycle Conference, Fremantle, Australia, 28 October–1 November.

Barter, P. A. (1999) An international comparative perspective on urban transport and urban form in Pacific Asia – the challenge of rapid motorisation in dense cities, unpublished Ph.D. thesis, Murdoch University, Perth, Western Australia.

Bernick, M. S. and Cervero, R. B. (1997) *Transit Villages in the 21st Century.* McGraw-Hill, New York.

Bodell, G. (1995) Bangkok's traffic nightmare – why it happened and the lessons for the rest of Asia. Paper presented at the CityTrans Asia '95 Conference: Urban Planning, Infrastructure and Transportation: Solutions for the Asia Pacific, Singapore, 21–23 September.

Bruun, E. C. and Schiller, P. L. (1995) The time-area concept – development, application and meaning. *Transportation Research Record,* **1499**, pp.95–104.

Cybriwsky, R. (1991) *Tokyo – the Changing Profile of an Urban Giant.* Belhaven Press, London.

Dorsch Consult, PT Pamintori Cipta, Colin Buchanan and Partners, SOFRETU, and IMK Consulting Engineers (1996) *Surabaya Integrated Transport Network Planning Project – Study Report No. 9, Final Study Report.* Government of Indonesia, Ministry of Communications, Directorate General of Land Transport, Urban Transport Improvement Project, Surabaya.

Forbes, D. (1990) Jakarta towards 2005 – planning mechanisms and issues. *Bulletin of Indonesian Economic Studies,* **26(3)**, pp.111–19.

Freeman Fox and Associates (1977) *MMETROPLAN: Metro Manila Transport, Land Use and Development Planning Project, Final Report, Main Volume.* Department of Public Works, Transportation and Communications, Republic of the Philippines, Quezon City.

Gakenheimer, R. (1995) Motorization in the developing world – a draft set of research concepts, MIT, unpublished report for the World Bank, Cambridge, Ma.

Hansen, W. G. (1959) How accessibility shapes land use. *Journal of the American Institute of Planners,* **25**, pp.73–76.

Hau, T. (1995) Transport for Urban Development in Hong Kong. Paper presented at the Habitat II Global Workshop Transport and Communication for Urban Development, Hyatt Regency, Singapore, 3–5 July 1995.

Hook, W. (1994) The role of non-motorized transportation and public transport in Japan's economic success. *Transportation Research Board Paper, 940954.*

Inter-Departmental Working Group (1993) *JABOTABEK Urban Mass Transit Preparation Program – Consolidated Network Proposal.* Government of Indonesia, Ministry of Communications, Jakarta.

Jakarta Government (1987) *Jakarta 2005.* Pemerintah Daerah Khusus Ibukota Jakarta, Jakarta.

Jamilah Mohamed (1992) Whither transport plans for Kuala Lumpur? Progress and challenges in urban transport planning. In *The View from Within: Geographical Essays on Malaysia and Southeast Asia* (eds Voon Phin Keong and Tunku Shamsul Bahrin). Malaysian Journal of Tropical Geography, University of Malaya, Kuala Lumpur.

Kenworthy, J., Laube, F., Newman, P. and Barter, P. (1997) *Indicators of Transport Efficiency in 37 Global Cities,* a report for the World Bank, Sustainable Transport Research Group, Institute for Science and Technology Policy, Murdoch University, Perth, Western Australia.

Kenworthy, J. R. and Laube, F.B. with Peter Newman, Paul Barter, Tamim Raad, Chamlong Poboon and Benedicto Guia (Jr) (1999) *An International Sourcebook of Automobile Dependence in Cities, 1960-1990,* University Press of Colorado, Boulder.

Kim, S. S. (1991) Seoul's transportation dilemma, unpublished draft case study paper, Harvard University, Cambridge, Mass.

Marler, N. W. (1982) *The Performance of High-flow Bus Lanes in Bangkok* (TRRL Supplementary Report 723), Transport and Road Research Laboratory, Overseas Unit, Crowthorne, UK.

Midgley, P. (1994) *Urban Transport in Asia – an Operational Strategy for the 1990s.* Asia Technical Department, Infrastructure Division, World Bank, Washington, DC.

Mumford, L. (1961) *The City in History – its Origins, its Transformations, and its Prospects,* Harcourt Brace Jovanovich, San Diego/New York/London.

Newman, P. W. G. and Hogan, T. L. F. (1987) *Urban Density and Transport: A Simple Model Based on 3 City Types,* Transport Research Paper 1/87, Environmental Science, Murdoch University, Perth, Western Australia.

Newman, P. W. G. and Kenworthy, J. (1989) *Cities and Automobile Dependence – An International Sourcebook,* Gower Publishing, Aldershot, UK.

Newman, P. W. G. and Kenworthy, J. R. (1996) The land use-transport connection – an overview. *Land Use Policy,* **13(1)**, pp.1–22.

Pendakur, V. S., Menon, G. and Yee, J. (1989) TSM innovations in Singapore – lessons from experience: 1974–88. Paper presented at the Transportation Research Board 68th Annual Meeting, Washington, DC, 22–26 January.

Phang, S.Y. (1993) Singapore's motor vehicle policy – review of recent changes and a suggested alternative. *Transportation Research A,* **27A(4)**, pp.329–336.

Poboon, C. (1997) Anatomy of a traffic disaster – towards a sustainable solution to Bangkok's transport problems, unpublished Ph.D. thesis, Murdoch University, Perth, Western Australia.

Pushkarev, B. S. and Zupan, J. F. (1977) *Public Transportation and Land Use Policy.* Indiana University Press, Bloomington.

Spencer, A. H. (1989) Urban transport. In *Southeast Asian Transport – Issues in Development* (eds T. R. Leinbach and Chia Lin Sien), Oxford University Press, Singapore.

Spencer, A. and Madhaven, S. (1989) The car in southeast Asia. *Transportation Research,* **32A(6)**, pp.425–37.

Tanaboriboon, Y. (1992) An overview and future direction of transport demand management in Asian metropolises. *Regional Development Dialogue,* **13(3)**, pp.46–70.

Tanaboriboon, Y. (1993) Bangkok traffic. *IATSS Research,* **17(1)**, pp.14–23.

TEST (1991) *Wrong Side of the Tracks? Impacts of Road and Rail Transport on the Environment.* Transport and Environment Studies, London.

Thomson, J. M. (1977) *Great Cities and Their Traffic.* Victor Gollancz, London.

Villoria, J. and Olegario, G. (1996) Enhancing public transportation in metro-Manila – a key strategy towards sustainable development. *IATSS Research,* **20(1)**, pp.121–130.

Wilbur Smith and Associates (1974) *Urban Transport Policy and Planning Study for Metropolitan Kuala Lumpur.* Ministry of Communications, Malaysia, Kuala Lumpur.

Wilbur Smith and Associates and Jurutera Konsultant (S.E.A.) Sdn. Bhd. (1981). *Kuala Lumpur Master Plan Transportation Study, Final Report.* Prepared for the Datuk Bandar, Kuala Lumpur.

World Bank (1986) *Urban Transport – a World Bank Policy Study.* World Bank, Washington, DC.

World Bank (1996) *Sustainable Transport – Priorities for Policy Reform.* World Bank, Washington, DC.

Zahavi, Y. (1976) *Travel Characteristics in Cities of Developing and Developed Countries* (Staff Working Paper No. 230). World Bank, Washington, DC.

Malcolm Moor and Clarke Rees

Bangkok Mass Transit Development Zones

Introduction

Bangkok has grown at a phenomenal rate, but as a result of weak planning controls the city has no clearly definable centre, with high-rise development arising apparently at random throughout the urban area. Development has followed the arterial roads and the suburbs have spread across flood-prone agricultural land, previously intensively cultivated for rice paddies and shrimp farms. These dispersed car-based developments have led to severe traffic congestion and air pollution threatening the quality of life of its inhabitants, and acting as a disincentive to foreign investment and tourism.

The Thai government, and the Bangkok Municipal Authority (BMA), recognising that roads alone could not keep up with traffic growth, have belatedly introduced new rail mass transit systems into the city, using a privately financed system of procurement. Two elevated metro rail concessions were let and under construction before the Bangkok Public Transport Master Plan was prepared in 1995 (Halcrow/Sofretu, 1995). The plan (Fig. 1) proposed a network of 200km of transit lines and recommended that all lines in the central area should be underground. After much public debate into the environmental consequences of huge elevated structures crossing the city, the two elevated lines, already approved, although still at the design stage, were eventually excluded from this restriction, but the third line was redesigned to be totally underground.

The alignments of the transit lines follow public road and railway rights of way in order to minimise the expense and complications of private land acquisition. As a result, stations predominantly serve existing concentrations of population, rather than opening up new areas for development. The network planning was initially transportation and engineering-led, with the land-use planning implications addressed once station locations had been identified.

The government's Land Transport Agency commissioned a study in 1994 to demonstrate how the benefits of the investment in mass transit could be maximised by encouraging planned developments centred on the new metro stations (Rees and Moor, 1996–97). By creating compact transit zones, the walk-in catchment population of stations would be increased, and better interchange facilities could be planned at stations to increase inter-modal traffic. A more detailed planning study commenced in mid-2000, to prepare local plans for zones around all stations on the Metropolitan Rapid Transit Authority (MRTA) Blue Underground Line, which is under construction (MRTA, 1998).

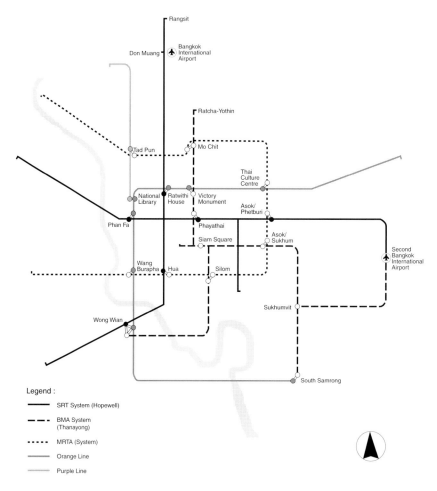

Fig. 1. Bangkok public transport master plan.

A congested city

Bangkok is a relatively new city, having been founded by King Rama the First some two hundred years ago. It was, and remained, a 'compact city' until after World War I, with commerce and housing concentrated along the Chao Phraya riverfront and *khlongs* (canals). The *khlongs* were created to transport produce and materials from rural areas to local docks along the river. The population was about 500,000 in 1900 and grew to 2 million in 1950, to 4 million in 1970, and then rapidly expanded. Today Bangkok has over 11 million people within the conurbation and it contains almost a fifth of Thailand's population (JICA, 1997).

During the nineteenth century the city grew as a densely populated town where people both lived and worked. Densities exceeded 150,000 persons per km² in the commercial parts of the old 'China town' district. These areas continue to have high combined population and employment densities, with some districts still containing over 100,000 persons per km^2, the equivalent of 1,000 per hectare (Rees and Moor, 1996–97). However, most of the population growth has been accommodated by suburban expansion to the north and west. As the core area filled up, new radial roads were built, flanked by medium-density development. Over 60% of the population is now concentrated in the suburban fringes at low densities (BMA, 1998). The suburbs have continued to expand in an unregulated fashion into agricultural land, largely determined by property speculation, government road building programmes and middle-income family housing demand.

Due to the difficulty of acquiring private land for public uses, and in the absence of an enforceable city plan, Bangkok has a very low percentage of area devoted to roads and an absence of a secondary road network. Private landowners build *sois* (small lanes) to access their own strips of land from the main roads, with few cross connections to adjoining plots. This pattern has exacerbated traffic congestion, as even local trips frequently require U-turns on main roads.

The climate and cultural factors do little to encourage people to walk any distance. Utility poles and street hawkers often block narrow, and poorly maintained, footpaths. Vehicles are used for even the shortest journeys. The heavily subsidised bus system can take hours to negotiate traffic, with *tuk-tuks* (three-wheel scooter taxis) and motorcycle taxis being somewhat quicker. Economic prosperity in the last decade (until the economic crisis of 1997) has led to a boom in car ownership, and car use is encouraged by low fuel prices and planning regulations requiring minimum parking provision for new development, even in central areas. Hyper-congestion has become a fact of life for the Bangkok resident. Most people expect to have to spend up to 4 hours per day commuting unless they start their trip before sunrise and return home late at night. The more affluent equip their cars with TV and video and even portable WCs.

By the early 1990s it was finally recognised that this pattern of growth was destructive, and could not be permitted to continue without controls over development, and a better transportation system. It was realised that high rates of population growth in Bangkok were not sustainable. The city was sinking slowly, due to excessive water extraction, power and water had to be imported from other areas, waste was piling up, and most areas of the rest of the country remained poor, because the majority of the new jobs were concentrated in Bangkok.

A new growth policy
For the foreseeable future, economic growth in Thailand means 'industrialisation', but this needs to be undertaken in a sustainable fashion, so that natural resources are exploited without unduly compromising the environment. Bangkok has the jobs and the money but not the infrastructure for it to be a healthy living environment. The Bangkok Metropolitan Administration (BMA) has not been able to keep up with the pace of uncontrolled growth and people are tired of complaining. Help from the huge investment in the road and rail 'megaprojects' and the new Bangkok Development Plan is on the way, but it will not come soon enough.

Sub-regional growth
The current BMA Master Plan (1998), which covers part of the Bangkok core area within its outer ring road, suggests the area could easily accommodate

two to three times the population forecast for the region, as its holding capacity is estimated at over 20 million people. This could create an impossible situation within the urbanised area, yet could still come about, given weak land-use and building-density controls. Indications are that development is not concentrating near the planned district sub-centres around the outer ring road as proposed for the BMA Master Plan by MIT, but is locating wherever the land costs are lowest and the development controls are weakest. This suggests a need for a regional authority for Bangkok, with the legal power to control the location and character of development and funds to implement infrastructure projects, and power to overrule special-interest interference.

Urban growth

A key element for the regional growth strategy will be the restriction of population and employment within the core to prescribed limits, and the gradual redistribution of housing and jobs over time, as older areas are redeveloped and new growth centres become established. This process is called 'Concentrated Growth' (Rees and Moor, 1996–97); in central Bangkok there is a clear need to make living in the city a pleasant and healthy experience again, which can only be done by releasing areas from the problems of extreme congestion. Providing incentives for property developers to concentrate new buildings in designated areas, and securing tax funds to finance utility renewal, new community facilities and infrastructure, may be the key to such a renaissance.

The decision to build the new mass rapid transit systems and feeder systems has stimulated ideas for the concentration of development in the city at locations where the systems meet or are accessed – that is the concept of 'Transit Zones'. Studies prepared for government suggested that if the high capacity mass transit systems were built, the only way that they would be efficiently utilised would be to concentrate population and employment growth in areas near stations (Rees and Moor, 1996–97). Using indices of accessibility, it was suggested that building the transit systems would increase public transport access to stations by an average of 50% over current conditions.

The OCMRT (Office for the Commission of Road Transport) estimated that the master plans for new road and rail infrastructure combined will require 1,000 billion Thai Baht (US$28 billion) of private and public section funds (Rees and Moor, 1996–97). Today, traffic pollutes the environment, and delays cause vast sums of money to be wasted. Tomorrow, were the master plans to be completed, it might be possible to change the balance of use away from private vehicles towards a greater use of public transport.

Present mass transit initiatives

The public transport network comprises a number of separately commissioned fixed track transit systems, some of which are to be built by private investment and others by a combination of both public and private funds (see Fig. 1).

Green Line: Bangkok Transport System Corporation (BTSC)

A privately financed elevated metro system was awarded as a 'Built, Operate, and Transfer' (BOT) concession for 30 years from the BMA in 1992. Initially conceived as an elevated LRT track to be accommodated totally within the right of way of BMA-controlled public roads, the economics of financing the construction solely by ticket sales was found to be viable only if its passenger capacity was significantly increased to a full six-car metro system. This project became operational on 9 December 1999 and there are plans for its extension.

Red Line: Bangkok Elevated Road and Rapid Transit System (BERTS)

A consortium led by the Hopewell Corporation of Hong Kong won the concession from the State Railway of Thailand (SRT) to construct a megastructure along two existing rail rights of way. The project was to elevate and double track the existing main rail line, and to eliminate level crossings that contributed to traffic congestion. As well as the heavy rail tracks for diesel trains, there were parallel nine-car metro double tracks at an upper level, with a six-lane toll expressway above at roof level. Ground-level service roads were to provide access to stations and commercial development within the rail right of way. This ambitious project illustrates well the problems caused by trying to combine too many transport systems with differing characteristics and geometry into one huge structure. The project is currently stalled and is being renegotiated and re-designed by the SRT, probably as a rail-only system, without the elevated expressway, combining the railway and metro functions.

Blue Line: Metropolitan Rapid Transit Authority (MRTA)

This is a fully underground two-line metro system aligned beneath Bangkok's inner ring road. Two radial extensions, partially underground and partially elevated, have also been approved and await a budget from central government. The funding of the project is quite complex, with the government paying for the construction costs of tunnels and stations, and inviting bids from concessionaires to supply electrical equipment, rolling stock and signalling equipment, and then to operate the system on a 30-year concession. Construction began in 1998 and is due for completion in 2003.

Orange and Purple Lines, and light rail projects

Two other transit lines, and extensions of the present lines, are at the planning and preliminary funding stage. The *MRT Feeder System Study* (PADECO, 1998) proposes light rail systems to link in to the heavy rail mass transit network. With these feeder systems in place at MRT stations, it will be important to have good interfaces between the transit systems and good physical integration with surrounding development.

Feeder systems, buses and ferries

Buses and ferries along the river and *khlongs* will remain the main public transport choice for many Bangkok residents, due to the extent of the network and cheapness of fares. Bus-only lanes are provided on many roads, but poor enforcement of private car exclusion renders them ineffectual. The *Bus Network Rationalisation Study* (DCIL, 1998) proposes that the bus system be reorganised and the routes revised to act as feeders to the transit stations. Together with stricter enforcement of bus priority measures, and encouragement of private investment through franchising, bus services could become a more effective part of the transport network.

Transit Development Zones

Proximity to stations along the mass transit lines will be a major factor determining future viability of the location of commercial developments. Financial institutions, lending money for development, are likely to require far more rigorous market research to reassure themselves that projects are soundly based than was the case before the economic crash of July 1997. Given the acute traffic congestion which severely handicaps business development, locations close to stations are likely to be preferred as a guarantee of accessibility, and so be more attractive to potential shop and office tenants. If one accepts that development around stations will eventually occur, the priority is to ensure that these areas are well planned and carefully controlled. The criteria for determining the planning of Transit Development Zones (TDZ) should include:

*   securing good pedestrian access to station entrances within a 500m radius;
*   providing interchange facilities for feeder bus services, taxis, *tuk-tuks* and motorcycle drop-offs;
*   ensuring legibility of station entrances;
*   encouraging mixed land use, and serving local interests and the informal sector; and
*   encouraging land uses which will benefit from improved accessibility and generate increased use of the transit system.

Transit zones incentives

Developers may appreciate the financial benefits of improved accessibility in locating close to transit stations, but may be reluctant to cede valuable land for the improved interchange facilities necessary to make stations operate efficiently. Lacking the planning powers to require the provision of public facilities, the BMA seems to have no alternative but to provide incentives for developers to co-operate. The one incentive potentially within the gift of the BMA planning authority is to grant additional floorspace in exchange for the developer providing public facilities as specified on an approved TDZ plan. This incentive zoning method that has successfully been used in the USA and Australia for building public facilities at no cost to the municipality (Garvin, 1996; City of Sydney, 2000).

New development within designated transit zones could be granted additional built floor area above the maximum permitted 'floor area ratio' (FAR), in strict accordance with agreed guidelines. This would be in addition to the already permitted FAR of 10:1 allowed for Central Area development under present legislation. Benefits may include the site area to be given over to public use, or construction cost of facilities built by the developer as part of the project. Additional, or 'bonus', floorspace could be awarded to property owners for providing benefits such as improved local access roads, wider footpaths, transit interchange facilities, useable open space or other desirable public facilities. The table illustrates what these bonuses could be in terms of percentage increases in built floor space.

Legislative powers would be needed, both to enforce TDZ plans and to grant bonus floorspace, but this is not considered insuperable. The implementation of such a system requires fairness to both parties and transparency to public scrutiny to ensure that guidelines are being rigorously followed.

Facility provided	FAR bonus space allocation (%)
Off-street bus station	20
Off-street taxi or *tuk-tuk* drop-off	10
Weather-protected walkway to station	15
Increased public open space	10
Incorporate station entrance or vent	10
Additional building setback at station	10
Public or community facility	10
Hawker bazaar	5

Table 1. Example of notional FAR bonus allocation for public facilities.

Informal sector

One of the distinctive features of Bangkok streets is the presence of street hawkers, who are a familiar sight in all developing economies. Hawkers are the principal visible manifestation of the informal economy, and employ a large number of people. Hawkers tend to operate two categories of stalls:

- cooked food stalls and fresh food markets, which serve the local working and resident population throughout the city,
- souvenir, clothing and trinket stalls serving the tourist population, which are usually near the tourist hotels.

Stalls locate in areas accessible to their target customers, and where the police tolerate them. They usually set up mobile stalls outside busy shopping centres and offices, and at busy street junctions. They are an essential and colourful element of Bangkok street life, but, unfortunately, create congestion on pavements that are already too narrow for pedestrian flows. This results in pedestrians walking onto the streets to avoid stalls, or even not attempting to walk any distance along city streets, preferring to wait for buses, take *tuk-tuks* or taxis. A number of cooked food stalls also locate in quieter side streets off busy areas, where there is more room for tables and where they create fewer bottlenecks. Some locate in the small number of hawker sites provided by the BMA.

The new mass transit stations will be an obvious magnet for hawker stalls (Fig. 2). One of the major concerns in the success of mass transit is whether people can be encouraged to walk further than they traditionally do to reach station entrances. The weather is hot for most of the year with high humidity in the summer, which, together with poor air quality along busy roads, is a major disincentive to walking. Poorly maintained pavements cluttered with obstacles and potholes are a further handicap. Yet, unless a substantial proportion of the population can be encouraged to walk 500m or so, the use of the transit systems will suffer.

The BTSC elevated stations are normally accessed by six staircases per station, incorporated within the present restricted footpath width (Fig. 3). The MRTA subway system has wider entrances with stairs and escalators occupying space at the back of footpaths. Due to the cost of land acquisition and resistance from landowners, the space provided is only just sufficient for passenger circulation without the addition of hawker stalls and their attendant customers. During summer rainstorms, which often occur during evening rush hours, it may be difficult to enter or exit station entrances, leading to dangerous congestion.

Motorcycle taxis will also wish to have sites close to station entrances to ferry passengers up and down small *sois*. Accepting the inevitability of these informal service providers, and the difficulty of private transport concessionaires enforcing clear pavements, there will be a need to provide convenient off-street facilities. Obviously neither hawkers nor motorcycle taxis could pay for off-street sites in central locations, so the space would have to be a public facility operated by the local authority, or provided by developers through planning gain.

Left: *Fig. 2. BTSC elevated line and station located over a busy street – a likely magnet for hawkers.*

Right: *Fig. 3. A BTSC staircase taking up footpath space and attracting motorcycle taxis to park.*

Scope of TDZ improvements studies

A major study carried out in 1997 (Rees and Moor) examined 18 interchange stations, with the aim of identifying the need for, and a sample of, TDZ studies. One such preliminary study is outlined below (Fig. 4).

Preliminary TDZ study at Ratchayothin Road

The study encompassed an area of 500m radius from the Green Line station at Ratchayothin Road. It is at the fringe of the core area in a transitional zone between urban and suburban development, and mid-way between the town centre and Don Muang Airport. The area's housing is predominantly low to medium-density villas, with shop-houses along main road junctions. The east–west grid of residential *sois* is intersected by Ratchayothin Road, which was built at an angle of 45%, producing irregular triangular shaped plots on each corner. Proximity to the airport and the outer ring road make this a popular location for new offices, with the Siam Commercial Bank headquarters, employing 5,000 workers, recently completed. The idiosyncratically designed Elephant Building and two other office complexes are nearby and an entertainment centre and cinema are under construction.

The viaduct of the elevated Green Line Extension crosses the LRT Feeder along the inner ring road line at right angles. Both stations are 200m from the intersection, as the track has to rise to cross the existing east–west road flyover (Fig. 4). The study recommended bringing the two stations closer to improve the interchange. This entails their being at a higher level, requiring escalator access rather than the standard staircase. The covered interchange walkway was proposed at a higher level, linking the LRT platforms to the Green Line concourse. The additional cost of providing escalators could be offset by incorporating a bus terminus at ground level of a corner commercial building, so that the escalators could serve all three termini as well as pedestrians crossing the main road. Escalators serving a proposed leisure, office and housing complex on the north side could also be used by transit passengers to make optimum use of the expensive infrastructure.

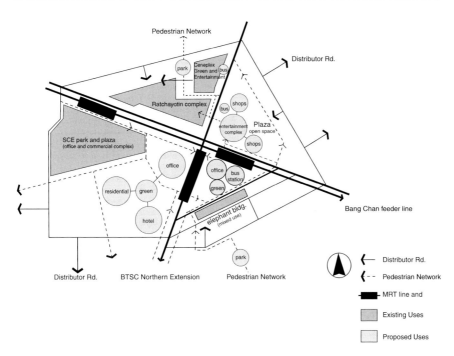

Fig. 4. Ratchayothin TDZ, proposed land uses and circulation.

Conclusions

Cultural characteristics, and the extent to which the market economy is allowed free rein, determine the degree to which the public, and particularly landowners and investors, will accept public direction to influence the pattern and form of development. Planning regulations, which are considered acceptable in Europe, would be considered a flagrant interference of individual rights over private land in many developing countries. This is particularly the case in Thailand, which has both a *laissez-faire* capitalist economy and a democratic government with numerous political parties representing factional interests.

In Bangkok, the best that might be achieved in the short term is probably the tightening of the building regulations to establish, for example, rights to light, bare minimum open space standards and controls on the size of the building envelope. The market will still determine land use, and as permitted plot ratios are already high, there is only limited scope to use this as a planning tool. Rather than trying strictly to enforce a city-wide master plan, adoption of transit development zones offers the opportunity to encourage better planning in specific highly accessible parts of the city, whilst leaving the majority of the space in between to market forces.

The extent to which the private sector can be expected to pay for mass transit systems needs to be weighed against the environmental implications for the city and its residents. To the cash-starved municipal authority of a grid-locked city, the benefits of acquiring a private transit system 'for free' seem irrefutable. With construction costs of building underground three times higher than of elevated, then the private sector will opt for the elevated solution in the hope of a return on the huge investment. The environmental consequences of massive, concrete, elevated structures being shoehorned into busy city streets thus need to be weighed against the drain on scarce public funds of building underground.

Demonstrating to private developers how following the urban design guidelines in a TDZ can be mutually beneficial is a crucial factor in implementing such a policy. Whether financial incentives, in the form of floorspace bonuses to encourage private developers to provide public facilities, is a fair and equitable way of promoting good planning remains to be seen. The result could be overbuilding and a worse environment, especially if TDZ plans were poorly prepared or inadequately implemented. Inevitably the greater the cost of such major projects, the more the decision-making process moves into the sphere of the politicians and financiers. Planners are increasingly likely to be forced into playing a remedial role rather than being proactively involved in optimising the land-use possibilities of transport infrastructure.

The experience of Bangkok has shown a concerted response to some of its major problems. But this leaves much unanswered. In rapidly changing cities like Bangkok, there remains the need, not just to respond to dominant issues of traffic alleviation, but also to bring the issues of sustainability, the appropriate mix of development and the creation of liveable cities, firmly onto the urban agenda.

Note
Only lead consultants are named for referenced Consultants' Reports which all included teams of consultant firms.

References
BMA (1998) *Bangkok Metropolitan Authority Master Plan*, MIT Press, Massachusetts.
City of Sydney (2000) *Central Sydney Heritage Local Environmental Plan*, City of Sydney, New South Wales, Australia.
DCIL Consultants Report (1998) *Bus Network Rationalisation Study,* prepared for OCMLT (Office for the Commission of Land Transport), Kingdom of Thailand.
Garvin, A (1996) *The American City: What Works, What Doesn't,* McGraw-Hill, New York.
Halcrow/Sofretu Consultants Report (1995) *Conceptual Mass Rapid Transit Implementation Master Plan Project*, prepared for OCMRT (Office for the Commission of Road Transport), Kingdom of Thailand.
JICA (Japan International Co-operation Agency) (1997) *The Study on Urban Environmental Improvement Program in Bangkok Metropolitan Area,* for the BMA and Kingdom of Thailand.
MRTA (Metropolitan Rapid Transit Authority) (1998) *Study and Design of Intermodal Transfer Facilities and Station Area Development for the MRTA Blue Line Project,* MRTA, Bangkok.
PADECO Consultants Report (1998) *Mass Transit Feeder System Study,* prepared for OCMLT (Office for the Commission of Land Transport), Kingdom of Thailand.
Rees, M. and Moor, C. (1996–1997) *MRT Transfer Station Development Opportunities* (1996*)* and, *MTS3 Inventory of Mass Transit Transfer Stations Technical Reports*(1997), prepared for OCMLT (Office for the Commission of Land Transport), Kingdom of Thailand.

Sharon Biermann
Bulk Engineering Services:
Costs and Densities

Introduction

In South Africa, national housing, transport and urban development policies all promote the densification and compaction of urban areas and discourage sprawl in the interest of efficient, sustainable and integrated development. This policy accords with the generally accepted view that higher population densities over a smaller land area, as opposed to lower densities over a greater land area, lower the cost of providing public services. This is because shorter distances need to be traversed, and because of savings derived from economies of scale.

Using the results of applying a bulk infrastructure potential cost model in the metropolitan area of Greater Pretoria, it is argued that bulk infrastructure capital costs[1] do not simply decrease with increasing density and compaction of urban form. This is because of the unique interrelationship between infrastructure thresholds, capacities, location and density over time and space. There are three factors contributing to this argument: historically distorted patterns of infrastructure investment, development that has not proceeded according to prediction, and the specific locational differences in environmental and land-use conditions that result in differential infrastructure installation costs.

As a result of the policies of separate development, infrastructure investment was historically allocated in an unbalanced manner, with some areas receiving massive investment and others, very little. Over time, this has resulted in areas, within the consolidated urban fabric, that have spare capacity which could be utilised at a minimal additional cost. Some of these areas are centrally located.

It is not uncommon in South Africa, as elsewhere in developing countries, for actual development not to proceed according to the predictions made at the time of the infrastructure installation. These predictions of demand are based on assumptions of the extent, type and level of service of the development. With changing development pressures and political changes, predicted demand may not be realised, resulting in areas of either under- or over-capacity, unrelated to the distance from the central area, with associated cost implications for accommodating future development. The degree to which an area is either under-

or over-capacity is relevant to the issue of density and cost effectiveness. If an area has spare capacity, it will be more cost effective to develop that area as opposed to others, but only until the infrastructure threshold is reached, at which point additional infrastructure investment is required to accommodate any further development. Thus, such a threshold is critical in influencing the cost of development, although it is largely unrelated to distance from the central area.

Infrastructure costs vary with location, according to local land use and environmental conditions. The same infrastructure installed where excavation is difficult due to factors such as environmental sensitivity, adverse geotechnical conditions or intense levels of existing development, costs more than in other areas. The locations where these adverse conditions exist are largely unrelated to distance from the central areas. In fact, the intensely built-up nature of the more central areas makes it relatively more expensive to install additional engineering services.

It can be argued that all these factors result in differential infrastructure provision costs within a particular study area, largely unrelated to distance from the central area. In addition, these factors also dictate that different urban areas display very different cost patterns for infrastructure provision. It is not possible, therefore, to take the results pertaining to urban form in one particular urban area and apply them directly to another area, in an attempt to generalise conclusions about the cost-benefit of certain urban forms.

The chapter starts by examining the key literature regarding bulk infrastructure costs and urban form. This is followed by a brief description of the 'bulk infrastructure potential cost model' used to generate the potential cost maps and density considerations inherent in the model. The cost maps resulting from the application of the model in the metropolitan area of Greater Pretoria are then analysed in terms of location and density conditions. Some conclusions are drawn concerning the implications for the compact city argument and sustainability.

Bulk infrastructure costing and urban form

By far the most common urban forms investigated and compared are the dense, compact, contained, intense urban form and the sprawling, dispersed urban form. Arguments for and against urban sprawl have been presented from many different angles, yet few are based on empirical evidence, and fewer still include engineering services infrastructure costs. Where engineering services costs are incorporated into the cost analysis, costs are often calculated by applying a constant cost per person rate to hypothetical prototypes (Real Estate Research Corporation, 1974; South African Roads Board, 1992). Costs incurred by the existing capacity conditions, or environmental factors, do not play any role in the costing process. Differential costs between various locations are thus not accounted for in most of the examples considered. The Real Estate Research Corporation (1974) concluded that higher densities result in lower economic and environmental costs, natural resource consumption and some personal costs for a given number of dwellings. The South African Roads Board study concluded that the social costs are less for more central locations than for dispersed peripheral locations, but that costs for the individual are higher in a centralised location than in a dispersed location because of high levels of transportation subsidies for the peripheral location (South African Roads Board, 1992).

Rather than use hypothetical prototypes, Ladd (1992) uses actual statistical data of local government expenditure that relate to gross residential density. He concluded that higher population densities lower the cost of providing public services. The study did not distinguish engineering services costs, but included them in capital outlay costs (Ladd, 1992). Other empirical studies have consistently found that lower operating costs in the suburbs more than offset the higher initial capital costs of installing new infrastructure (O'Toole, 1996).

A number of simulation and optimisation models have been developed to evaluate the impact of alternative urban forms or land-use patterns, but they have not been used to inform the sprawl versus compact city debate. Most of the older models dealt with the interaction of land use and transportation and did not consider bulk engineering services infrastructure costs at all (Stylianides and Gunning, 1990; Chapin, 1965; Reif, 1973; Harvey, 1967; Morrill, 1965; Echenique *et al.*, 1969; Ingram, Cain and Ginn, 1972; Senior, 1973, 1974). More recently, attempts have been made to incorporate infrastructure concerns into GIS-based urban models or planning support systems. The availability of sewer and water services is included as a factor in determining land suitability in the 'what if?' collaborative planning support system (Klosterman, 1999), but infrastructure costs are not considered. In those cases where infrastructure costs have been included in evaluation models of urban form, neither spare capacity nor environmental and land-use conditions, which vary spatially, are accounted for in the cost calculations (Bhattacharyya and Pant, 1996; Birkin *et al.*, 1996; Grigg, 1997; Landis, 1995; Landis and Zhang, 1998; O'Toole, 1996). The one exception is the TOPAZ model which accounts for terrain conditions in the form of slope (Brotchie *et al.*, 1994; CSIRO, 1997). Costs have either been calculated on the basis of static per person rates (Grigg, 1997), as a function of network distance (Bhattacharyya and Pant, 1996), or on operating costs only (Birkin *et al.*, 1996; O'Toole, 1996). Certain models intended for determining optimum engineering design solutions for infrastructure networks, rather than for evaluating alternative urban forms, do include capacity conditions, but do not account for the effect of influencing factors on costs (Wadiso, 1997).

The bulk infrastructure potential cost model

Purpose
The bulk infrastructure potential cost model was developed in order to provide a tool for planners to incorporate bulk infrastructure cost considerations into the early land suitability assessment phase of the integrated development planning process (Biermann, 1999a). Although the model was specifically developed to assist in generating more cost-effective spatial options, it is essentially evaluative in nature and evaluates various density options, and it provides some evidence regarding the cost effectiveness of various urban forms (Biermann *et al.*, 1998).

Potential costs are calculated on the basis of demand for services in terms of density scenarios and the capacity in the existing system, and include additional cost factors such as geotechnical, land-use and environmental conditions to further enhance cost accuracy. The model considers only initial or capital costs, excluding financial, running and maintenance costs, and it emphasises comparative costs but not necessarily actual costs.

The output of the model takes the form of potential cost surfaces which facilitate the relative comparison of infrastructure costs for different density conditions across space. These cost surfaces can be incorporated with other land suitability criteria, using multi-criteria evaluation techniques combined with GIS, to determine development potential (Biermann, 1999b; Biermann and Whisken, 1998), or can be used independently to inform urban form debates.

Theoretical basis
The theory and technique of threshold analysis originated in Poland out of the work of Malisz (1969) and was developed by Kozlowski (1971) and the United Nations (1977), and applied in Scotland (Kozlowski and Hughes, 1967, 1972; Scottish Development Department, 1973). The theory of threshold analysis was based on the observation that towns encounter physical limitations to their spatial growth in the form of natural limitations such as topography, or in the form of man-made limitations such as public utility network systems (United Nations, 1977). These limitations have been called the thresholds of urban development. They are not irremediable, but can be overcome at a high capital investment cost or threshold cost (Kozlowski and Hughes, 1967). Threshold analysis is concerned with those physical characteristics of an area which cause significant differentiation in the unit cost of future urban development, and deals only with costs which vary with location (Lichfield *et al.*, 1975). A threshold occurs when new units of development cannot be constructed and serviced at their previous unit cost levels and significant additional outlays are required. The presence of a threshold is indicated either by a steep rise in the gradient or a discontinuity in the marginal cost curve of urban development. Changes in the unit cost of development can be caused by a variety of physical factors, ranging from the topography to the physical capacity of the public facility (Lichfield *et al.*, 1975).

Pillars
There are three essential elements in the bulk infrastructure cost model – threshold, density and cost (Fig. 1). It is the manner in which these three pillars are incorporated and related to each other which forms the basis of the model.

Engineering services infrastructure is, by its very nature, a utility for people, particularly for urban people, which is necessary for health, mobility and industry. As the number of people increases within an area, so the infrastructure has to expand to accommodate additional requirements. Limits or thresholds, directly proportional to the size of the infrastructure, exist because of the fact that infrastructure has physical dimensions e.g. pipe diameter, reservoir capacity. The relationship between density and threshold dictates whether or not additional infrastructural expenditure is necessary to accommodate additional people.

The manner in which the three pillars are incorporated into the model is largely through capacity analysis (Fig. 1). The density levels set can be converted into the number of additional person units required per sub-area, which in turn can be translated into infrastructure capacity demand figures. The desired level of services influences the resulting capacity demand figures. The lower the level of service, the less the demand for infrastructure. Levels of service are kept constant in order to calculate relative costs. Infrastructure thresholds are equivalent to the design capacities of the various components of the infrastructure system. The existing infrastructure network and facility design capacities are compared with the current utilisation of infrastructure in order to quantify the capacity supply situation. The

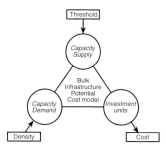

Fig. 1. The three pillars of the 'bulk infrastructure potential cost model' and their interaction mechanisms.

quantitative comparison of capacity demand with capacity supply determines, first, whether or not additional infrastructure is required and second, how much infrastructure is required (or how many infrastructure investment units are required). Investment units can be in the form of metres of conduit or the number of facility modules. Base cost per investment unit is influenced by additional cost factors relating to local environmental conditions (geology, soil type and characteristics, slope and environmental sensitivity) and current land-use conditions (type and intensity) (Biermann and Whisken, 1998; Biermann, 1999a).

Engineering services, including water, sanitation and electricity capital costs (at 1995 prices), are determined and represented spatially, for various population density scenarios. Bulk water costs comprise: link costs (cost of linking the development with the distribution reservoir); distribution reservoir costs (including pressure towers); feeder main costs (pipes linking distribution reservoirs with system mains or bulk supplier mains); system main costs (pipes linking distribution reservoir feeder mains to receiving reservoirs); and receiving reservoir costs. Waste water treatment works costs, bulk outfall sewer network costs and sewer link costs (linking the development with the outfall sewer network) are included in sanitation costs. Electricity costs incorporate 132/11kV substation, cabling and transformer costs.

Densities

Purpose of density scenarios
The establishment of population density scenarios is critical for the modelling process. It is necessary to keep density constant throughout the study area in order to compare potential infrastructure costs spatially across the area. The bulk infrastructure potential cost model is intended for use in the early, informative stages of the planning process when proposals regarding land use and densities have not yet been made. In fact, the intention of the model is to provide precise answers to the question of where it would be most suitable to develop, for what type of land use and at what type of density. The density scenarios set for the model are thus theoretical in nature, with the purpose of facilitating locational comparison of costs across the study area. Different density scenarios are set to enable the assessment of the effect of changes in density on bulk infrastructure costs.

Density scenarios adopted
The existing gross population density for the study area is 14 persons per hectare. Three arbitrary density scenarios were set for this study: a low-density scenario corresponding to 20 persons per hectare, a medium-density scenario of 40 persons per

hectare, and a high-density scenario of 60 persons per hectare. The intention was to show the impact of increasing densities on cost, within reasonable density limits. It was not the intention to set a density scenario corresponding to that of current high-rise development in the study area (98 persons per hectare) throughout the entire area. Rather, without being location-specific, the selected average gross density scenarios were intended to represent a range of housing types and densities which vary with location e.g. high densities along major public transport routes and lower densities, either further away, or to accommodate other land uses, roads and open areas.

The approach in adopting density scenarios was to calculate relative bulk infrastructure costs if all land in the study area was developed to a gross density of 20, 40 or 60 persons per hectare. In instances where current population exceeded the scenario population, the current population was taken as the scenario population. This occurred predominantly in the lower income, previously black, township areas, where densities are between 60 and 100 persons per hectare (GPMC, 1997). In reality, all land in the study area will not be developed. Nature reserves, for example, have been designated for preservation, conservation and recreation activities. The model does not exclude any area from analysis due to current land use, even if it is currently a nature reserve. The model includes all land, developed and undeveloped, and asks the question: if this land were to be developed or redeveloped to a certain density, what would the relative bulk infrastructure potential cost be? It would be the role of the broader land delivery process to include, or exclude, land for development on the basis of a much wider range of issues, including the results of this model.

Density and infrastructure demand
Potential population numbers determine potential infrastructure usage which is utilised in the demand-side analysis of the infrastructure cost model. The residential population is not the only user of bulk infrastructure – industry, agriculture, social and commercial uses also have infrastructure requirements. In the urban context, industrial and commercial activities are the most pertinent. The model does not take into account usage of infrastructure by social facilities, such as schools and libraries, and by business areas, since the usage is relatively minor and does not peak at the same time as the main residential peak (National Housing Board, 1994). It is assumed that for large water and electricity-dependent, high effluent-producing industrial uses, separate infrastructure provision arrangements will be made, and they are not included in the model.

Density and infrastructure supply
The relationship between infrastructure capacity (supply) and density (infrastructure demand) is crucial for the model. Design capacity is compared with the total capacity required (based on total population including existing and potential additional population). Costs are eventually expressed for the additional population on the assumption that the costs incurred by new development are the responsibility of the additional people, and not the responsibility of the people already resident in the area.

Density and over-capacity
A further consideration that relates to density and capacity occurs when the infrastructure is already operating theoretically at over-capacity. This occurs when the existing calculated demand exceeds design capacity. In reality, these

circumstances occur when infrastructure is designed to cater for peak usage, whether that peak occurs daily, seasonally or under emergency circumstances. In periods of non-peak usage, therefore, more users can be accommodated in practice. Operating at over-capacity does not mean the infrastructure ceases to function totally, but rather that certain users, depending on their location in relation to the infrastructure system, will have no service or a limited service, for certain periods, be that daily or seasonally.

The problem created by this phenomenon in the model is that in situations where theoretical over-capacity occurs, as soon as the scenario population exceeds the existing population, the cost of rectifying the current over-capacity problems accrues to the new development. The problem has been solved in the model, in areas where the problem exists, by proportioning the incurred cost to the additional population, defined as the difference between scenario population and infrastructure design population, rather than the difference between the scenario population and the existing population. An element of the theoretical still remains, however, in that the new or additional population figures include some of the existing population. This is preferable to assigning all the cost to the truly new population with the result that the per capita costs for those areas are relatively higher than for other areas where no over-capacity conditions exist.

Application of the model

Study area
The model was applied in the Greater Pretoria Metropolitan Council (GPMC) area (Fig. 2). Pretoria is the administrative capital of South Africa, located in Gauteng Province, about 50km north of Johannesburg. The study area covers 130,000 hectares stretching over a distance of 65km from north to south and over 50km from east to west (GPMC, 1997, p.28). It comprises the three metropolitan substructure areas of the Town Council of Centurion in the south, the City Council of Pretoria in the centre, and the Northern Pretoria substructure in the north (Fig. 2).

Resultant bulk infrastructure potential cost maps
Using the model, 27 base cost maps were generated for the study area, comprising nine cost components (5 water, 3 sanitation and 1 electricity), each for three alternative density scenarios (low, medium and high). An additional four cost maps were generated in the form of composite overlays – one each for water, electricity and sanitation – and a final composite overlay which included all three services (Biermann, 1999a). In this chapter, only some of these cost maps are used to illustrate the argument.

Given the unique interaction between the existing infrastructure capacity, existing and proposed densities, level of service and environmental and land-use conditions across space, our intention is to demonstrate that:

- in terms of location – more compact development in the form of infill, close to the city centre, is not necessarily a sustainable option in terms of cost efficiency as compared to more peripheral, edge development;
- in terms of densities – more compact development in the form of increased residential densities does not necessarily reduce per capita infrastructure costs.

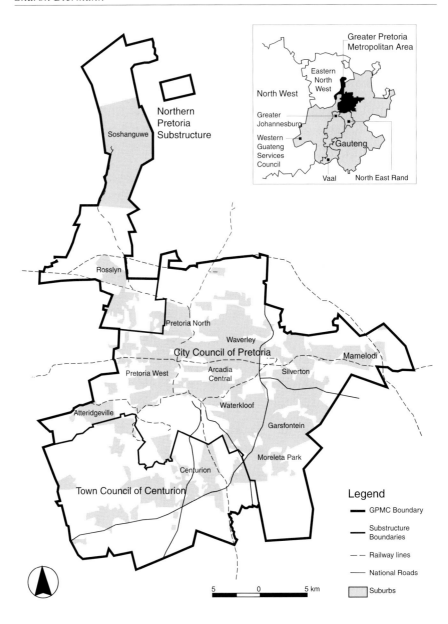

Fig. 2. Locality map of the Greater Pretoria Metropolitan Council area.

Cost effectiveness of central versus peripheral locations

The cost surface for water distribution reservoir costs, using the low-density scenario (Fig. 3), certainly indicates high per capita costs in some peripheral areas. The northern parts of the central area and the south western and south eastern peripheral areas indicate relatively high costs, but a significant part of the non-peripheral, southern portion of the central area displays the highest costs. In comparison, keeping the density scenario constant, the cost surface for outfall sewer network costs (Fig. 4) indicates the highest costs on or near the periphery, in some cases. However, in the case of the far eastern portion of the study area, which is relatively far from the central area, costs are relatively low.

In absolute terms, distribution reservoir per capita cost for the entire study area for the low-density scenario is more than double that of outfall sewers (Table 1). While a consideration of the spatial pattern of the cost of individual infrastructure elements is useful in demonstrating the diversity of spatial cost outcomes, it is essential ultimately to consider total infrastructure costs. The combined cost surface for the low-density scenario (Fig. 5), as expected, strongly reflects the spatial cost pattern of the most costly infrastructure elements, which are water and electricity (Table 1), but it also highlights the effect of environmental conditions, particularly geotechnical conditions (Fig. 5). High costs do occur in the peripheral areas in the north, south west and south east of the study area, but again, high-cost areas also occur in the central areas, while the peripheral far eastern area is a low-cost area (Fig. 5).

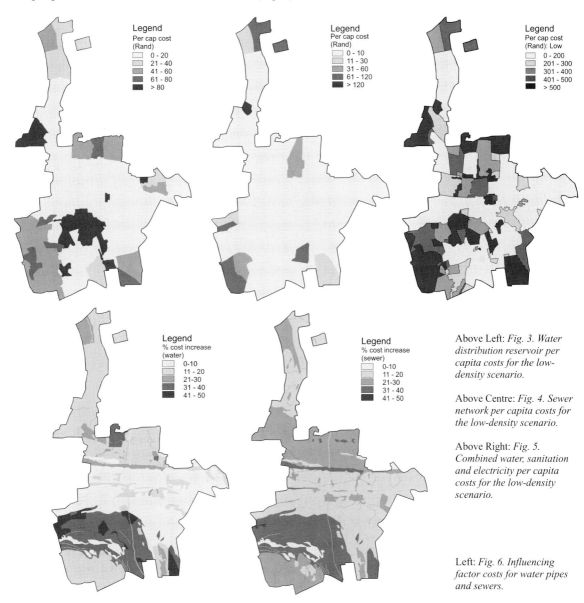

Above Left: *Fig. 3. Water distribution reservoir per capita costs for the low-density scenario.*

Above Centre: *Fig. 4. Sewer network per capita costs for the low-density scenario.*

Above Right: *Fig. 5. Combined water, sanitation and electricity per capita costs for the low-density scenario.*

Left: *Fig. 6. Influencing factor costs for water pipes and sewers.*

Cost effectiveness of increasing residential densities

Because of the increase in the numbers of people requiring additional infrastructure, the total infrastructure costs for the entire study area increase with increasing density for all cost elements, with the high-density scenario costing 200% more than the low-density scenario (Table 1). The cost increase is not proportional to the number of additional people for each scenario. The cost increase from the low to the medium-density scenario is nearly 100%, while the cost increase from the medium to the high-density scenario is just over 50%. This indicates that different thresholds for each different cost element are reached at different times as density increases (Table 1).

Cost element	Total Low	%	Total Medium	%	Total High	%	Per cap. Low	%	Per cap. Medium	%	Per cap. High	%
Water link	58	9	64	5	71	3	43	11	19	5	13	4
Distribution reservoir	59	9	101	8	156	8	47	13	33	9	31	9
Feeder main	11	2	14	1	16	1	10	3	5	1	3	1
System main	18	3	18	1	18	1	25	7	9	3	5	1
Receiving reservoir	6	1	22	2	38	2	16	4	20	6	20	6
Total water	152	24	219	17	299	15	141	38	86	24	72	21
Sewer link	40	6	41	3	42	2	31	8	16	5	11	3
Outfall sewer	28	5	46	4	70	4	22	6	14	4	13	4
Treatment works	19	3	57	5	108	5	18	5	18	5	20	6
Total sanitation	87	14	144	12	220	11	71	19	48	14	44	13
Total electricity	396	62	886	71	1432	74	159	43	222	62	237	67
Total infrastructure	635	100	1249	100	1951	100	371	100	356	100	353	100

Table 1. Total (Millions of Rand) and per capita (Rand) infrastructure costs for each density scenario.

Total infrastructure costs per capita do decrease with increasing density, but very marginally, so as to be almost insignificant (Table 1). This total picture is made up of electricity costs that increase with density, balanced by decreasing sanitation and water costs (Table 1). Most individual cost elements decrease with increasing density, but receiving reservoir, waste water treatment works and electricity costs increase with increasing density (Table 1). Although total per capita costs remain virtually constant with increasing density, per capita cost surfaces obtained for each density scenario indicate that the proportion of the study area associated with costs of greater than US$50 per person increases with increasing density, although the surface area with costs of greater than US$80 per person decreases (Fig. 7).

Again, it is obvious that even in the case of the high-density scenario, some central areas are as costly to develop as some peripheral areas. Higher costs in peripheral areas are usually due to a combination of all services, whereas, in the developed area, there are usually only one or two cost factors, predominantly water factors, responsible for the higher cost (Fig. 7). This can be attributed to the fact that in developed areas not all engineering service thresholds are reached at once, whereas, in newly developing areas, all services need to be provided from scratch at the start of development – there is no condition of existing spare capacity.

Relatively low combined costs in the far northern area and far eastern areas can be attributed to lower levels of service, and the way in which the model

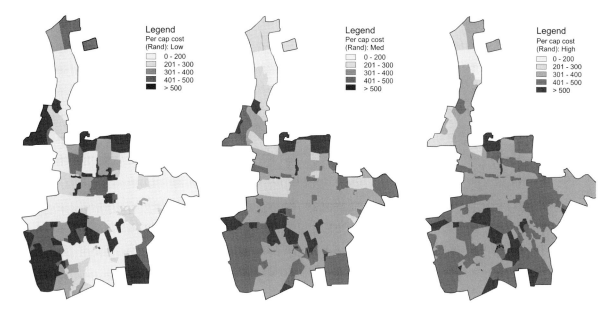

Fig. 7. Combined water, sanitation and electricity per capita costs for low, medium and high density scenarios.

deals with situations where existing density exceeds the scenario density (Fig. 7). Lower service levels exist in these low-income areas, thus per person service usage is lower. Available spare capacity can therefore go much further in meeting the demand than the same available capacity in areas of higher usage. In situations where existing population exceeds the scenario population, the model takes the existing population as the scenario population, and as long as the existing population equals the scenario population, no additional costs are incurred. Due to the fact that these are areas of existing high density, the model generally allocates no additional people to these areas and thus the costs are zero.

Implications for the compact city debate

Density and distance

The results indicate that bulk infrastructure costs do not simply decrease with increasing density and with decreasing distance from the central areas. In all cases, total infrastructure costs increase as density increases, due to the additional demand placed on the system as a whole. Per capita costs, however, do decrease with increasing densities for some cost items but not for all. Electricity per capita costs, for example, increase with increasing density. It has also been demonstrated that for all services considered, the more central areas can be as costly (or more costly) to develop as certain more peripheral areas, as a result of existing spare capacity and environmental and land-use conditions.

The question is posed whether it was worth the effort of including all the costs, and whether it would suffice to consider only the most costly infrastructure elements in future costing exercises. The cost calculations clearly demonstrated that, for the entire study area, certain total costs were much higher than others. However, because of the variation in all the costs with location, it is important to include all the network and facility costs for water, sanitation and electricity. In some areas, a particular cost, which may be the least in terms of total cost for the study area as a whole, may be extremely high for one particular area, and can significantly influence the development potential of that specific location. If that cost were left out of the equation, an incomplete, and thus incorrect, cost pattern would emerge for particular locations in the study area.

Environmental and land-use conditions which are location-specific influence infrastructure costs in a manner unrelated to distance from the central areas. For the study area, the most significant impact of these factors on base costs occurs in the land use-intensive parts of the central areas: in the south western parts, where a geological formation (a dolomite band) influences both central and peripheral areas, and to the north of the study area, where steep slopes and difficult soils also affect both central and peripheral areas.

These results clearly indicate that the existing local infrastructure capacity and environmental and land-use conditions significantly affect the cost at particular locations within the study area. It can be deduced that, as other study areas have very different local circumstances, conclusions relating to sprawl, derived from the application of the model in this particular study area, cannot be generalised or transferred to any other study area.

Policy

National housing, transport and development policies all promote the densification and compaction of urban areas and discourage sprawl in the interest of efficient and integrated development. However, it can be argued that it is not prudent to make generalised categorical statements for densification, or against sprawl, as a policy directive for the following reasons:

• definitions vary,
• there are very few quantitative studies with proven results to back up the statements and position taken,
• differences exist in the range and type of costs included,
• local circumstances differ.

There is not enough evidence in the literature to conclude that densification is the cost-effective alternative in all situations, and under all conditions. The implication for policy making is that such words as 'compact' and 'densify' should be avoided as imperatives. Rather, emphasis should be placed on reducing the negative aspects attributed to both sprawl and densification, and promoting the positive aspects of both. This is in fact advocated in existing housing and development policy to promote the location of residential and employment opportunities in close proximity to each other, and to optimise the use of existing physical and social infrastructure (Republic of South Africa, 1994, p.52; Republic of South Africa, 1995, p.10). Such policy directives unnecessarily complicate interpretation when they include statements like 'discourage sprawl' and 'contribute to the development of more compact settlements' (ibid.). The result of applying polices which emphasise the positive and mitigate the negative aspects of sprawl and densification will be a physical form – sprawling or compact, or some combination of both – but one which is applicable and appropriate to specific local conditions.

A conclusion which can be made in relation to general policy directives concerning sprawl and densification is that development should be promoted in areas of existing spare infrastructure capacity, and in areas where infrastructure would be relatively cheaper to provide. Highly intensive land use, and green-field or infill development, should be avoided on areas of dolomite or slopes of greater than 12°, unless affordability levels are high enough to pay for mitigating costs, as these have the most significant impact on increasing the base cost for both water pipes and sewers.

Implications for sustainability
The development and application of the model has demonstrated the importance of including infrastructure costs in the compact city debate. The model itself is the means by which planning issues such as density, growth and sustainability are integrated with aspects of infrastructure systems, capacity, thresholds and infrastructure costs, in order to ensure a more sustainable urban form.

The model contributes towards sustainable development in that it complies with four of Marrazzo's (1997) sustainability concepts and practices for engineering services provision:

*   Development is promoted in relation to areas of existing spare capacity or cheaper infrastructure provision costs;
*   Bulk infrastructure costs are considered as part of a broader systems approach where it is recognised that many other cost considerations, as well as softer issues, play an important role and should be considered in the development decision;
*   The model promotes the payment of real costs for bulk infrastructure services in that it avoids development in costly areas unless there are commensurate affordability levels; and
*   The model encourages collaboration between disciplines and the use of common data sets, particularly in relation to GIS, so that costly duplication is avoided.

Levying of bulk service contributions
Cost is significant both for housing provided by the state and that provided through private development. In the case of public provision, the lower the engineering services cost, the more is available for other infrastructure such as housing. For private developers, there are often other more important factors than services costs involved in location decision-making. This often means that a locational choice is made which is not the cheapest from the services cost point of view. Local authorities could recover the real bulk infrastructure costs of development by charging the real cost of services. If private developers want to develop in certain areas that are not cost effective for service provision, they can proceed with development as long as they pay the local authority the total costs of the service provision. The way that services contributions are levied in many local authorities (both locally and internationally) is often on an averaged basis. It can be argued that this can encourage sprawl because on

the periphery where land costs are less, infrastructure costs can be high. Yet the services costs to the developer, and eventually to the consumer, will be the same as for infill development in a more central location where land costs are higher. If real costs were levied, this would contribute to development occurring where it is economically sensible to do so, thus reducing the negative impacts of sprawl. The model can assist in determining a differential levy for various locations, which reflects more adequately real costs for that particular location.

Note

1. Bulk infrastructure refers to water, sanitation and electricity reticulation, storage and treatment facilities, operational from the edge of particular settlements or suburbs up to and including storage and treatment facilities for which the particular metropolitan authority is responsible. Capital costs are the initial, once-off costs of providing water, sanitation or electricity infrastructure, but excluding operating costs which refer to routine maintenance and other costs incurred in keeping the service operational.

References

Bhattacharyya, S. and Pant, A. (1996) Infrastructure cost modelling for East St. Louis. http://imlab9.landarch.uiuc.edu/eslarp/durp/UP497-S96/main.html.

Biermann, S. M. (1999a) An infrastructure potential cost model for integrated land use and infrastructure planning, unpublished Ph.D. thesis, University of South Africa, Pretoria.

Biermann, S. M. (1999b) The strategic identification of suitable land for low income housing: a case study from South Africa, in *Spatial Multicriteria Decision Making and Analysis* (ed. J. Thill), Ashgate, Aldershot.

Biermann, S. M., Van Renssen, C. and Fortuin, O. (1998) Bulk infrastructure cost model: integrating engineering services into the strategic planning process, paper presented at the 9th Annual SAICE Congress: Civil engineering and sustainable development, South African Institute of Civil Engineers, East London, 6–8 April 1998.

Biermann, S. M. and Whisken, J. (1998) Bulk infrastructure cost model for integrated land use and infrastructure planning, paper presented at the 4th Seminar on GIS and Developing Countries: GIS tools for effective planning, Department of Town and Regional Planning, University of Pretoria, Pretoria, 1–2 October 1998.

Birkin, M., Clarke, G., Clarke, M. and Wilson, A. (1996) Intelligent GIS: location decisions and strategic planning, *GeoInformation International*, Cambridge.

Brotchie, J., Sharpe, R., Maheepala, S., Marquez, L. and Ueda, T. (1994) TOPAZ-URBAN. Paper presented at the International Seminar on Transportation Planning and Policy in a Network and Price Equilibrium Framework, CSIRO Division of Building Construction and Engineering, 10–11 August 1994.

Chapin, F. S. (1965) A model for simulating residential development. *Journal of the American Institute of Planners*, **31**(2), pp.120–125.

CSIRO (1997) Integrated urban water resource planning and management. http://www.dbce.csiro.au/dbr/topaz.htm.

Echenique, M., Crowther, D. and Lindsay, W. (1969) A spatial model of urban stock and activity. *Regional Studies*, **3**, pp.281–312.

Greater Pretoria Metropolitan Council (GPMC) (1997) Strategic metropolitan development framework: status quo report, The Council, Pretoria.

Grigg, N. S. (1997) Systematic analysis of urban water supply and growth management. *Journal of Urban Planning and Development*, **123**(2), pp.23–33.

Harvey, D. W. (1967) Models of the evolution of spatial patterns in human geography, in *Models in Geography* (eds R. J. Chorley and P. Haggett), Methuen, London.

Ingram, G. K., Kain, J. F. and Ginn, J. R. (1972) The Detroit prototype of the NBER urban simulation model. Columbia University Press, London.

Klosterman, R. E. (1994) Large-scale urban models: twenty years later. *Journal of the American Planning Association*, **60(1)**, pp.3–6.

Klosterman, R. E. (1999) The What if! Collaborative planning support system. *Environment and Planning B: Planning and Design*, **26(3)**, pp.392–408

Kozlowski, J. (1971) The place and role of threshold analysis in the model planning process, *Ekistics*, **192(32)**, pp.348–353.

Kozlowski, J. and Hughes, J. T. (1967) Urban threshold theory and analysis. *Journal of the Town Planning Institute*, February, pp.55–60.

Kozlowski, J. and Hughes, J. T. (1972) *Threshold Analysis*. The Architectural Press, London.

Ladd, H. F. (1992) Population growth, density and the costs of providing public services. *Urban Studies*, **29(2)**, pp.273–295.

Landis, J. D. (1995) Imagining land use futures: applying the California urban futures model. *Journal of the American Planning Association*, **61(4)**, pp.438–457.

Landis, J. D. and Zhang, M. (1998) The second generation of the California urban futures model. Part 1, Model logic and theory. *Environment and Planning A*, **30**, pp.657–666.

Lichfield, N., Kettle, P. and Whitbread, M. (1975) *Evaluation in the Planning Process*, Pergamon, Oxford.

Malisz, B. (1969) Implications of threshold theory for urban and regional planning. *Journal of the Town Planning Institute*, March.

Marazzo, W. J. (1997) The challenge of sustainable infrastructure development. *Forum*, **123(3)**, pp.37–39.

Morrill, R. L. (1965) The negro ghetto: problems and alternatives. *Geographical Review*, **55(3)**, pp.339–361.

National Housing Board (1994) Guidelines for the provision of engineering services and amenities in residential township development, CSIR Division of Building Technology, Pretoria.

O'Toole, R. (1996) The vanishing automobile and other urban myths. *Different Drummer*, The Thoreau Institute, Spring.

Real Estate Research Corporation (1974) *The Cost of Sprawl: Environmental and Economic Costs of Alternative Residential Development Patterns at the Urban Fringe,* Vol. 1, Executive summary, US Government Printers, Washington, DC.

Reif, B. (1973) *Models in Urban and Regional Planning*, Billing & Sons, London.

Republic of South Africa (1994) *White Paper: A New Housing Policy and Strategy for South Africa*, The Department of Housing, Pretoria.

Republic of South Africa (1995) *Development Facilitation Act*, Creda Press, Cape Town.

Scottish Development Department (1973) *Threshold Analysis Manual*, HMSO, Edinburgh.

Senior, M.L. (1973) Approaches to residential location modelling. 1, Urban ecological and spatial interaction models (a review), *Environment and Planning B*, **5**, pp.165–197.

Senior, M. L. (1974) Approaches to residential location modelling. 2, Urban ecological and some recent developments (a review), *Environment and Planning B*, **6**, pp.369–409.

South African Roads Board (1992) Improvement of mobility as a result of land use planning, PR 91/418.

Stylianides, T. and Gunning, D. (1990) The application of a land use simulation model to transport planning in South Africa, paper presented at the Tenth Annual Transportation Convention, Pretoria.

United Nations, Department of Economic and Social Affairs (1977) *Threshold Analysis Handbook*, United Nations Publications, New York.

Wadiso, S. A. (1997) Water distribution system analysis and optimisation with Wadiso S. A, http://www.gls.co.za.

Xiang, W. N., Gross, M., Fabos, J. G. and MacDougall, E. B. (1992) A fuzzy-group multi-criteria decision-making model and its application to land-use planning. *Environment and Planning B*, **19**, pp.61–84.

Xiang, W. N. and Whitley, D. L. (1994) Weighting land suitability factors using the PLUS method. *Environment and Planning B*, **21**, pp.273–304.

Paul F. Downton

Compact City Environmental Strategies:
Calcutta's Urban Ecosystem

Introduction

Calcutta's origins were as a colonial city, the product of an economic and political process imposed from outside the country (Banerjee, 1990). It was established in 1698 on the site of three villages, was formally extended in 1717 when the English purchased 38 villages (Bagchi, 1939, pp.12–13), and by 1793 there were 55 villages immediately outside the town limits of Calcutta (Sinha, 1978). Its growth has been rapid. In 1710 Calcutta had just 12,000 people, and by 1752 it was estimated to have had a population of 409,000 inhabitants. By the eighteenth century Calcutta was larger than any British city except London and held the position of 'Second City of the Empire' (Marshall, 1985). During the nineteenth century its population increased to 700,000, and by 1931 the Census showed its population at nearly 1.2 million (Bagchi, 1939, p.23). By 1960 Calcutta ranked number ten in size as an 'urban agglomeration' with a population of 4.5 million and by 1995 it ranked globally as the ninth largest city with a population of 11.7 million (WRI, 1996).

There can be few places on earth that have transcended their colonial history as completely as Calcutta. It seems that 'excepting two other Indian centres, Bombay and Madras, there is no city where the colonial impact has given birth to a new society and culture so complex, so creative, so stably indigenized' (Chaudhuri, 1990a, Introduction). There are few places that exhibit starker contrasts between wealth and poverty, and power and helplessness, within a legacy of both indigenous and colonial practices. It is a place that has defined itself 'against a background of disorder, deprivation and cynicism exceeding that of most other cities and questioning the very rationale of urban culture' (ibid.). With such a background, how does Calcutta match up to the ideals of compact city theories, and can it achieve environmental sustainability?

Compact, ecological or green?

Compact city theory draws from the same well of ideas as those of the 'green', 'sustainable' and 'eco' city. It is also related to the 'arcological' visions of

Paolo Soleri (1987) and American 'design outlaws' like Pliny Fisk (Zelov and Cousineau, 1997), and to research from the European Union (CEC, 1990), and Australia (e.g. Newman *et al.*, 1990). Models of the ecological city variously stress energy, traffic, and the development of healthy communities (Koskiaho, 1994). The nesting of ideas varies, so that 'green cities' may or may not be compact, and compact cities may or may not be 'green'. Superficial theorists like the UK architect Richard Rogers typically bring together a selection of characteristics to illustrate their preferred model of what a compact city is supposed to encompass. Rogers, for instance, uses 'ecological city' and 'compact city' as subsets of an overall definition of a 'sustainable city' (Rogers and Gumuchdjian, 1997).

The compact city is, emphatically, not about compressing existing cities to make them fit preconceived notions of a proper size. There is no intrinsic value in merely being small – 'if "small is beautiful", the whale is ugly and the mouse is beautiful.... Gigantism is the problem, not size as such' (Soleri, 1987, p.29). In cities that have become dysfunctionally large, the problems and prospects are a consequence of a number of interrelated factors. As Knowles (1996, p.135) points out with respect to architecture, the 'right size, and notably the right size of building' is a relative concept, and his studies in Los Angeles conclude that the best density of building is in a size range that is neither too great nor too small. It is tempting to conclude that the same might apply to cities. As yet we lack the evidence to discern what an 'appropriate' size might be. At this stage of the debate any evidence for compactness or sustainability that 'works' needs to be considered, and the responses to that evidence will need to be specific to the place and circumstance, and allow for a range and scale of proposals from the neighbourhood to the region.

Compact Calcutta?

Calcutta, although not small in area, is very densely populated. Land falls away from high points along the banks of the Hooghly River, so that the best land for building is closest to the river. Part of Calcutta's inheritance from the initial need to build close to the river is a readily distinguishable compact core (Fig. 1). The 'inner city' of the Calcutta Municipal Corporation covers 100km² and contains over 3.5 million people, representing about one-third of the total population living in the surrounding urban agglomeration. Its density of nearly 32,000 people per km² greatly exceeds the World Health Organisation's recommendation of 2,500 per km² (Chakraborti, 1990). The city is still growing and spreading over its hinterland. The underlying compact form of Calcutta has not made any obvious contribution to improved air quality. Whilst the inner city generates garbage at a rate which is less than half that of most industrial cities, air pollution from cars, cooking and diesel generators create some of the worst air quality in the world (Chakraborti, 1990).

According to Chaudhuri, Calcutta has absorbed the biggest mass migration in human history 'with incredibly meagre resources, little attention, and less sympathy' (Chaudhuri, 1990b, Introduction). City boundaries do not remain fixed in time, and the definition of what is or is not within a city's boundaries also changes. Chaudhuri records that acts of exclusion from, and inclusion into, Calcutta's city limits have been very much part of its history. He suggests

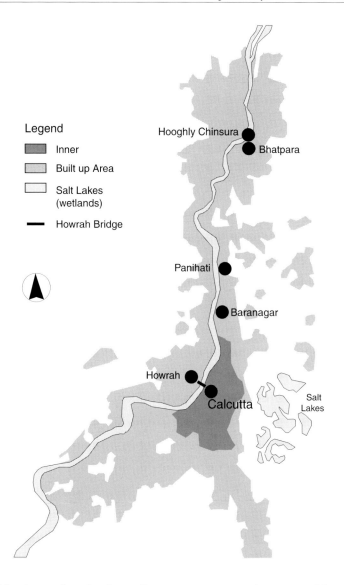

Fig. 1. Calcutta's compact core and surrounding urban agglomeration.

that this shows that the State Government was, quite reasonably, unable to cope with the spread of urbanisation through institutional mechanisms – and that the problem remains unresolved (Chakraborty, 1990). This has had an impact on Calcutta, where the central city density has increased and has remained high over time, and where there are relatively high densities on the periphery, so that the compactness of the city results from high densities overall (Breese, 1966).

If the compact city is about intensive land use, centralised activity and higher densities, then Calcutta is compact. If it is about most people moving around without cars, then Calcutta complies. If quality of life is a key criterion, then the city fails. The compact city model is hard to apply to any spreading metropolis, although in cities like London one can identify a polynucleated structure that possesses some compact city characteristics. While there is no accepted general theory, the compact city idea is strongly linked in current literature to the broad concepts of the sustainable city (Welbank, 1996). Calcutta, although having some relevant characteristics, is neither compact nor sustainable in these terms. However, it does contain aspects of compactness and sustainability that show at least a glimmer of what might be possible in developing countries if sufficient resources and planning were to be mobilised.

Given the characteristics of Calcutta, it is useful to put it in a context within which it can be considered. The city of Curitiba in Brazil is an example that shows how the mobilisation of resources and planning can help improve sustainability. By contrast, Adelaide in South Australia is definitely not a compact city, neither is it remotely sustainable in its present configuration as an energy and resources consumer. These particular examples can be seen to represent an 'urban spectrum' with Calcutta at one end, Curitiba somewhere in the middle, and Adelaide at the other.

Adelaide and the western comfort zone

Although it covers approximately the same physical area as Calcutta, Adelaide could hardly be more different, yet links between Calcutta and Adelaide are not entirely tenuous. Both were founded as intentional colonial interventions for exploiting the resources of their hinterlands. Both successfully extended the reach of the British Empire. In planning for a city of wide streets, Colonel Light, surveyor and founder of Adelaide, was said to have been inspired by the example of Calcutta with the wide streets of its rich colonial urban landscape 'balanced by noble and strategically placed architecture' (Dutton, 1971, p.215). Adelaide was founded a little over 150 years ago. At the time Light visited Calcutta, its history as a British city had already spanned the same number of years.

In Calcutta, slum dwellings may hold a dozen or more people per small room, whereas '25% of households in Adelaide have a single adult living in them either as a single parent or as a lone person – the lone person is 20% of the total households' (Clements, 1992, p.446). This fact is integral to the comfortable, low-density lifestyle that some argue would be disagreeably changed by a move towards compact cities (Stretton, 1996). Such sub-urban apologias, curiously, ignore the real human cost of the transport system on which its 'equitable' low-density form relies. Stretton (1996), for example, whilst praising the Australian auto-dependent lifestyle for its freedom and provision of private space, fails to address the price paid in road deaths. One quarter of a million people worldwide are killed every year by cars and many more are maimed. Even setting individual human and social costs aside, the economic cost of death and disablement is a high price to pay for personal space (Newman *et al.*, 1992). It has also been claimed that more fuel-efficient cars would resolve the problem of transport energy consumption, but more efficient vehicles do not assist in maintaining efficient city morphologies. For example, in the two decades since the Oil Crisis of 1973, vehicles have become more efficient, but whilst California's population increased by 50% in that period, the area of its cities has increased by 100% (Register, 1997). Indeed, Australia's ecological footprint is 10 times greater than that of India – 8.1 hectares per capita versus 0.8. Calcutta thus has approximately the same ecological impact as Adelaide, even though its population is 11 times greater (Wackernagel *et al.*, 1997).

Curitiba

Curitiba is frequently presented as a model for sustainable urban development in a developing country environment. It may not fully qualify as an 'ecological city', but since 1971 progressive city administrations have adopted a development plan that embraces what are often identified as 'ecocity' characteristics. These are 'based on a preference for public transportation over the private automobile, working with the environment rather than against it, appropriate rather than high-technology solutions, and innovation with citizen participation in place of master planning' (Rabinovich and Leitman, 1996, p.27).

Curitiba is also justly famous for its adoption of an above-ground transit system using articulated buses that cost much less than an equivalent subway system. Calcutta is still struggling to complete a subway system whilst ageing trams operate in its crowded streets. The economics of surface transportation versus subways may look good for most urban environments but it can only work if there is sufficient space. Calcutta does not have that option as it is so densely packed with buildings that only 6.5% of the city's area is occupied by roads compared with, for example, 16% for Bombay and 23% for Delhi (Chaudhuri, 1990b, p.148).

Development planning has been on the basis of 'master plans' for at least the last four decades in Calcutta, even though the pattern of the city's development 'was chaotic from the inception of the city' (Chatterjee, 1990, p.133). Nevertheless, 'Calcutta remains one of the least planned cities in the world' (ibid., p.147). It presents an urban environment that does not easily lend itself to 'Curitibanisation' and demonstrates that specific compact or sustainable city issues cannot necessarily be addressed by principles, policies or processes that have been successful elsewhere.

Transferable solutions for Calcutta?

Although, to an extent, the examples of Adelaide and Curitiba are drawn upon arbitrarily to illustrate a spectrum, they indicate that arguments can be made for both compact city and sustainability ideas in very different places with different urban morphologies and contexts. Obviously the low-density forms of Adelaide are entirely inappropriate for the form, density and culture of Calcutta, while Curitiba's transport solutions use more road space than Calcutta can ever provide. At the same time there are some lessons that, at least in principle, could apply. The integrated planning developed within Curitiba, deploying low-technology solutions and involving citizen participation, as will be seen below, has a resonance in Calcutta. Also, even in the suburban context of Adelaide which has ample land to grow food, ideas for urban agriculture and provision of green space within Calcutta have some relevance. Some of these broader ecological issues are thus considered.

Ecological city region?

A city as dense and compact as Calcutta could be seen as having intractable problems if considered in isolation from the context of its immediate region.

Within this context there are a wider range of possibilities that address the major component of its failure as a compact city, that of quality of life. This could be enhanced through ecological or 'green' dimensions that might also contribute to sustainability.

Well-respected, socially aware planners and commentators have drawn attention to those aspects of 'sustainability' that are directly related to technology. Typical is Alexander's view that people are emotionally and spiritually affected by what he calls the 'ecology movement' but that 'people who speak for ecology' have not yet made that clear (Alexander, 1997, p.214). The complex relationships of resource exchange and management between urban centres and their regions has sustained civilisation over centuries. In this process, the natural landscape has become 'artificial' and its remaking has resulted in the creation of an ecology, or 'living fabric' (Alexander, 1997, p.215), that is susceptible to degradation from poor management, or through lack of understanding of its existence and structure. Eco-theorists would probably agree with Aberley (1994, p.127) when he proposes that by 'identifying and protecting ... veins of "natural" habitat, humans would be acknowledging a fundamental change in the definition of progress. We would be accepting that life depends on life, and that the first principle of human survival is to reintegrate bioregional cultures into matrices of native ecological associations'.

Such a perspective may not be articulated explicitly in any regional plan for Calcutta, but it is implicit in planning that recognises the assets of natural systems as integral to human settlements. This is the case in relation to East Calcutta, where 12,500 hectares of 'constructed' wetlands are used for fisheries (Sarkar, 1990). It has been stated that:

> Besides the direct economic benefits offered by the wetlands to the city and its environs, scientific investigations have revealed that wetlands offer a unique ecosystem manifested in nutrient recovery and recycling, releasing excess nitrogen, inactivation of phosphate, removal of heavy metals, chemicals, and toxic and suspended solid matter. Wetlands also play a positive role as a strong reservoir in a drainage basin by recharging aquifers and mitigating floods during the monsoon.
> (Ghosh, 1992, p.7)

These wetlands with sewage-fed fisheries are an example of ecosystem adaptations that have treated human wastewater for millennia (Hill, 1997). The evolution of such ecosystems has produced an environment in which the thirty-odd villages east of Calcutta take its solid waste, liquid sewage and polluted air and produce clean air, fresh water, and fresh fish and vegetables. In addition, income and employment are generated in the rural sector (Sarkar, 1990).

Green Calcutta?
While the region can help to enhance the overall sustainability of a compact city, urban agriculture can also make a valuable contribution to urban sustainability, particularly in developing countries. Smit and Nasr (1992, p.147) note that although agriculture and urbanisation are 'commonly viewed as conflicting activities', it can be seen that 'there are considerable land and water

areas in the urbanized sphere that are available for agricultural use'. The idea of including productive land within the framework of urbanism has been popularised in recent years. There was a surge of interest in localised (and therefore of necessity, urban, or peri-urban) food production in 'western' democracies when environmentalism was boosted by the 'oil crisis' in the early 1970s, evidenced by publications like *Agriculture in the City* (El Mirasol, 1976). Trainer's vision (1996) for transforming Australian cities saw them evolving from suburban street and lawn monocultures to places filled with vegetable gardens and productive landscapes. In many ways these visions recreate the environment of small-scale, localised food production that has been part of pre-industrial cultures. In Calcutta, this diverse and intense approach is repeated at a slightly more extended scale. It may have evolved from the traditional Indian use of ponds as a central feature in village life, and may thus be seen to represent the recasting of rural patterns into an urbanised context.

Santosh Ghosh, as the former Chief Architect for Calcutta and West Bengal, has an intimate knowledge of the city and its planning systems. Undeterred by the scale and scope of Calcutta's problems, he has proposed a 'green' vision for Calcutta. His proposal suggests that 'scattered green space within the compactly built up area will act as an oasis and also a continuous wedge of green, widening at the edge of the city into the green belt and then into a rural landscape, establishing a coherent relationship between urban and rural areas'. The image was focused on the compact urban area but notes that the making of such an ecologically integrated metropolis 'depends on citizens' awareness and a movement to preserve and protect, together with the Government's programme for greenery and wetland projects (Ghosh, 1992, p.18). Calcutta is a case study of environmental improvement in the context of sustainable development. He points out that in planning to cope with the powerful demands of a growing city, concerns for demographic, social, economic and physical imbalances often overshadow concerns for ecological imbalances, but that in Calcutta, these competing concerns have been reconciled in some respects.

Conclusion

Turning Calcutta into an 'ecological metropolis' may be a challenging task. If a city of the population and size of Calcutta is able to sustain its key ecological functions despite the pressures of population growth and development, then it is reasonable to contend that, for compact cities, the challenge may be more easy to achieve than is commonly believed. In recent years the economics of 'constructed ecosystems' have been proved on the compact city scale in Arcata, California, where that city of 15,000 people gained economic benefit and improved fish and wildlife habitat by treating their effluent by developing wetlands and restoring an urban waterfront (Hill, 1997). A similar argument can be advanced for Curitiba, where population and developmental imperatives have also been subsumed within a coherent overall planning framework that accepts the pragmatic realities of its place and time, yet directs both social and economic development towards ecologically sustainable outcomes. Calcutta is planning to meet a number of challenges, including finding creative ways to utilise human, natural and financial resources in the service of the urban poor and their ecosystems (Perlman, 1994, p.82). This has already been established within the region which includes the wetlands, but it may also be achievable through the ideas for greening the city.

While there may be policies and action to improve Calcutta's urban ecosystem, there are still questions about whether, as a 'compact' urban environment, it can achieve a better environment and quality of life. The huge contrasts between poverty and wealth exist, but there is evidence of a more general increase in people's incomes, and with it more concerns over the quality of the urban environment. For example:

> In the 1980s, a middle-class revolution has silently seized Calcutta. There is a new trend towards sporadic beautification, preservation of old monuments, and a certain streamlining, sophistication and even luxury in middle-class homes. With this goes a new concern for the environment. (Bandyopadhyay, 1990, p.78)

Calcutta, with its high overall densities and compact urban form, has made progress in developing environmental strategies, but it cannot yet be held up as a model for compact cities in the developing world. Much remains unresolved. There is a need to review any analysis of ecological functions in terms of social and cultural values, but whose values do we use to establish whether ecological indicators represent a healthy city or simply a pragmatic resource management system? Is the East Calcutta 'created ecosystem' acceptable as a model because it creates employment? In assessing the ecological viability of cities, it would be a mistake not to give social and human health indicators a high weighting, lest mere economic measures become the reductionist rationale for accepting inappropriate conditions. At the same time, people like Ghosh, who know only too well the scope of Calcutta's ecological challenges, see no room for half measures. They suggest that 'Pseudo-environmental approaches are like adding twice the lettuce to a Big Mac and calling it an "eco-burger"' (Polo, 1999, p.15).

References

Aberley, D. (ed.) (1994) *Futures by Design – The Practice of Ecological Planning*, Envirobook Publishing, Sydney.

Alexander, C. (1997) Design for living structures, in *Design Outlaws on the Ecological Frontier*, 3rd edition (eds C. Zelov and P. Cousineau) Knossus Publishing, Philadelphia.

Bagchi, P. C. (1939) *Calcutta Past and Present*, Calcutta University Press, Calcutta.

Bandyopadhyay, R. (1990) The inheritors: slum and pavement life in Calcutta, in *Calcutta – The Living City, Volume II: The Present and Future* (ed. S. Chaudhuri), Oxford University Press, Calcutta.

Banerjee, A. (1990) The city with two pasts, in *Calcutta 1981* (ed. J. Racine), Concept Publishing, New Delhi.

Breese, G. (1966) *Urbanization in Newly Developing Countries*, Prentice-Hall, Englewood Cliffs.

Chakraborti, D. (1990) Calcutta's environment, in *Calcutta – The Living City, Volume II: The Present and Future* (ed. S. Chaudhuri), Oxford University Press, Calcutta.

Chakraborty, S. (1990) The growth of Calcutta in the twentieth century, in *Calcutta – The Living City, Volume II: The Present and Future* (ed. S. Chaudhuri), Oxford University Press, Calcutta.

Chatterjee, M. (1990) Town planning in Calcutta: past, present and future, in *Calcutta – The Living City, Volume II: The Present and Future* (ed. S. Chaudhuri), Oxford University Press, Calcutta.

Chaudhuri, S. (ed.) (1990a) *Calcutta – The Living City, Volume I: The Past*, Oxford University Press, Calcutta.

Chaudhuri, S. (ed.) (1990b) *Calcutta – The Living City, Volume II: The Present and Future*, Oxford University Press, Calcutta.

Clements, P. (1992) The ecocity as an instrument for social change, in *EcoCity 2 – Second International EcoCity Conference Proceedings* (eds P. F. Downton and D. Munn) (published on computer disk), Centre for Urban Ecology, Adelaide.

Commission of the European Communities (CEC) (1990) *Green Paper on the Urban Environment*, European Commission, Brussels.

Dutton, G. (1971) *Founder of a City – The Life of Colonel William Light*, Rigby, Adelaide.

El Mirasol Educational Farm (1976) *Agriculture in the City*, Community Environmental Council Inc., Santa Barbara.

Furedy, C. (1992) Garbage: exploring non-conventional options in Asian cities. *Environment and Urbanization*, **4(2)**, pp.42–61.

Ghosh, S. (1992) The making of Calcutta into an ecological metropolis, in *EcoCity 2* Proceedings (eds P. Downton and D. Munn), Centre for Urban Ecology, Adelaide.

Hill, H. (1997) Natural wastewater treatment systems, in *Village Wisdom – Future Cities*, Ecocity Builders, Oakland.

Knowles, R. (1996) On being the right size, in *Solar Architecture and Planning* (ed. S. Ghosh), Centre for Built Environment, Calcutta.

Koskiaho, B. (1994) *Ecopolis – Conceptual, Methodological and Practical Implementations of Urban Ecology*, Ministry of the Environment, Finland.

Marshall, P. J. (1985) Eighteenth century Calcutta, in *Colonial Cities: Essays on Urbanism in a Colonial Context* (eds R. Ross and G. Telkamp), Martinus Nijhoff Publishers, Dordrecht.

Newman, P., Kenworthy, J. and Lyons, T. (1990) *Transport Energy Conservation Policies for Australian Cities – Strategies for Reducing Automobile Dependence*, Murdoch University, Western Australia.

Newman, P., Kenworthy, J. and Robinson (1992) *Winning Back the Cities*, Pluto Press Australia, Leichhardt.

Perlman, J. (1994) Mega-cities: innovations for sustainable cities of the 21st century, in *Futures by Design – The Practice of Ecological Planning* (ed. D. Aberley) Envirobook Publishing, Sydney.

Polo, M. (1999) Report – environmentally challenged. *Canadian Architect*, **44(1)**, pp.4–15.

Rabinovich, J. and Leitman, J. (1996) Urban planning in Curitiba. *Scientific American*, **274(3)**, pp.26–33.

Register, R. (1997) Ecocity mapping – physical structure and economy in emerging eco-communities, in *Village Wisdom – Future Cities: The Third International Ecocity and Ecovillage Conference* (eds R. Register and B. Peeks), Ecocity Builders, Oakland.

Rogers, R. and Gumuchdjian, P. (eds) (1997) *Cities for a Small Planet*, Faber and Faber, London.

Sarkar, A. (1990) The east Calcutta wetlands, in *Calcutta – The Living City, Volume II: The Present and Future* (ed. S. Chaudhuri), Oxford University Press, Calcutta.

Sinha, P. (1978) *Calcutta in Urban History*, Firma KLM Private Ltd, Calcutta.

Smit, J. and Nasr, J. (1992) Urban agriculture for sustainable cities – using wastes and idle land and water bodies as resources. *Environment and Urbanization*, 4(2), pp.141–152.

Soleri, P. (1987) *Arcosanti – An Urban Laboratory?*, Cosanti Foundation, Scottsdale.

Stretton, H. (1996) Density, efficiency and equality in Australian cities, in *The Compact City* (eds M. Jenks, E. Burton and K. Williams), E & FN Spon, London.

Trainer, T. (1996) *Towards a Sustainable Economy – The Need for Fundamental Change*, Envirobook, Sydney.

Wackernagel, M., Onisto, L., Linares, A. C., Falfan, I. S. L., Garcia, J. M., Guenero, A. I. S. and Guenero, G. S. (1997) *Ecological Footprint of Nations: How much nature do they use? – How much nature do they have?* Universidad Anahuac de Xalpa, Mexico. HYPERLINK http://www.ecouncil.ac.cr/rio/focus/report/english/footprint http://www.ecouncil.ac.cr/rio/focus/report/english/footprint

Welbank, M. (1996) The search for a sustainable urban form, in *The Compact City* (eds M. Jenks, E. Burton and K. Williams), E & FN Spon, London.

World Resources Institute (WRI) (1996) *World Resources 1996–97*, Oxford University Press, Oxford.

Zelov, C. and Cousineau, P. (eds) (1997) *Design Outlaws on the Ecological Frontier,* 3rd edition, Knossus Publishing, Philadelphia.

Ko-Wan Tsou, Yu-Ting Hung and Yao-Lin Chang

Spatial Analysis of Urban Sustainability:
Tainan City, Taiwan

Introduction

The past few decades have seen a large expansion in social and economic activity, and a vast increase in production, consumption and 'disposable' life-styles. These increases have been matched by negative effects on the environment, such as widespread pollution and a sharp decline in non-renewable resources. Accordingly, sustainable development has become a world-wide objective to help achieve benefits for future generations. Cities became a significant aspect of the agenda when the World Commission on Environment and Development (WCED, 1987) declared that health, safety, equity and sustainability should be the target for urban development.

Many countries have started research on sustainable development issues. Although the definitions of these issues vary, they include aspects of the social, economic, technical and natural environments. All explore the relationship between population, resources and environmental development, in the search for balanced human development and co-existence with the environment (e.g. Atkisson,1996; Nijkamp and Pepping, 1998; Sustainable Seattle, 1993; UNCHS, 1997).

Nevertheless, there are gaps in the information produced by this research. Large-scale methods are often used to analyse sustainable development at the urban scale. These allow observation of the general phenomenon of sustainable development, but often do not distinguish the different characteristics of the spaces within urban areas. Other studies concentrate on the community, but are often limited to a single community, ignoring the relationships and the structure between communities. However, distinguishing between various urban spaces is a complicated task. A wholistic understanding of sustainable urban development can best be achieved by basing research on the urban spaces within which human activities take place, across an urban area as a whole.

This chapter presents an analysis of this type to assess their sustainability. Our research developed a number of sustainability indicators and methods for technical analysis, which were then applied to a case study. Tainan was the case study chosen, with the objective of analysing its environmental and spatial structure.

The city of Tainan

Tainan is located on the western plains of Taiwan. The first government was established in 1661, and Tainan is now recognised as the oldest city in Taiwan. Until the late nineteenth century, it served as the political, cultural, and economic centre of Taiwan. Its unique history left it with a heritage of important historic sites and it has a well-established reputation as the country's 'cultural city'.

There have been many different administrative governments in Taiwan's history. When it was a colony of Japan during the middle of the twentieth century, the centre of political and economic power moved to Taipei. After the Japanese occupation, several major urban centres began to expand rapidly. At present, Tainan is divided into seven administrative sections, including 253 communities, and it has a population of about 700,000 people. It is the fourth largest city in Taiwan, and still maintains its cultural and historical role. While Tainan possesses a good quality living environment, its economic development has lagged behind other regions. The city government, along with the central government, has begun a process of planning overall urban space, including the setting up of the 'Tainan Technological Industrial Park', revitalising the railway and planning a waterfront resource, with the aim of improving the economic status of Tainan.

Tainan is facing the challenge of modernisation and globalisation in the twenty-first century. However, the pursuit of economic development will threaten the ecological environment. How to achieve a balance between an ecological environment and economic development while pursuing urban growth is a significant issue.

Indicators and analysis

This chapter seeks to investigate the spatial structure of sustainable urban development. The research established a number of sustainability indicators, and multivariate analysis and GIS were used for the spatial analysis.

Sustainable development indicators

Sustainable development indicators are distinct from economic indices in assessing the effectiveness of economic development. They provide a complete view, evaluating the long-term effectiveness of economic, environmental, and social systems (Atkisson, 1996; OECD, 1994; Sustainable Seattle, 1993; UNCHS, 1995). Five directions are recognised for sustainable urban development. They are to maintain the ecological environment, to promote productive efficiency, to improve the quality of life, to maintain social justice, and to establish intra- and inter-generational equity.

The research concentrates on the region and the community. It aims to reflect the differences between them, to incorporate urban sustainability issues, and to build on existing studies (e.g., Farrell and Hart, 1998; Liverman *et al.*, 1988; Opschoor and Reijnders, 1991). The research identified some principles for establishing sustainability indicators. They had to be appropriate for sustainable urban development, reflect the local character, be acceptable to residents and be operational with collectable data. Using these criteria, 31 sustainability indicators were established (see Table 1).[1]

Cluster analysis

The debate about urban structure frequently concentrates on spatial functional analysis, such as land use and distribution. In this chapter, the sustainable indicators system is used to explore the sustainability of urban spatial structures. To fully

No.	Variable	Definition	Unit
1	Vegetation cover rate	Total area of vertical projection on plant/land) x 100%	%
2	Daily solid waste disposal	Amount of cleaning and transporting wastes/current population/65 days	kg/per person/daily
3	Waste water discharge	Total amount of sewage discharge/ current population	m^3/per person/year
4	Air pollution level	The total discharged amount of air pollution/current population	ha/per person/year
5	Proportion of environmental protection facilities	Environmental protection facilities/ total facilities x 100%	%
6	Agricultural production area	Cultivated lands (including rice paddies and dry fields)	hectare
7	Economic vitality index	Employed population/ current population x 100%	%
8	Employment rate	Employed population/total labour force	%
9	Operational efficiency of enterprises	Total profit / total revenues	%
10	Operational efficiency of manufacturing industries	Total profit / total revenues	%
11	Operational efficiency of commercial enterprises	Total profit / total revenues	%
12	Area used by enterprises	Area used by enterprises	hectare
13	Area used by manufacturing industries	Area used by manufacturing industries	hectare
14	Area used by commercial businesses	Area used by commercial businesses	hectare
15	Capital assets used by enterprises	Resources used by managing enterprises	million
16	Capital assets used by manufacturing industries	Resources used by manufacturing industries	million
17	Capital assets used by commercial businesses	Resources used by commercial businesses	million
18	Public facilities area current population	Total area used for public facilities/ per person	hectare/
19	Natural area	Natural area /current population	hectare/ per person
20	Charities charity groups	Medical care + social service +	group
21	Green land and park area	Green land and park area/ current population	hectare/ per person
22	Population density	Current population/area of lands	per person/ km^2
23	Population growth rate	1990 population/1999 population x 100%	%
24	Dependency rate	(Population above 65 years old +population under 14 years old)/ population between 15 and 64 x 100%	%
25	Ageing index	(Population over 65 years old/ population under 14) x 100%	%
26	Population with educational level beyond junior college	Population with educational level beyond junior college including vocational school	per person
27	Gender composition	Male population/female population x 100%	%
28	Proportion of public facilities	Area of public facilities/ total area of land x 100%	%
29	Proportion of unused land	Area of unused land / total area of land x 100%	%
30	Proportion of old dwellings	Houses over 45 years old/ all houses x 100%	%
31	Proportion of unoccupied dwellings	Unused buildings / all buildings x 100%	%

Table 1. Sustainability indicators.

reflect the sustainability of the urban condition, it was necessary to embark on a complex process of information gathering. The complexity of the data made it difficult to understand their spatial meaning. Hence, cluster analysis was used to assist the research and clarify the meaning of the data.

Cluster analysis groups objects according to their characteristics. Of the two types of cluster analysis – horizontal and non-horizontal – the research adopted the horizontal method because it best described the differences between all clusters and relationships that connect each with the other. Ward's (1963) methodology was used, with a cluster average indicator used to group the clusters. A horizontal icicle plot was used for the cluster gathering procedure, and a dendrogram was used to display the cluster gathering distances.

Empirical research
There are two parts to this case study – the spatial structure analysis of sustainable urban development and the spatial cluster analysis.

Spatial structure analysis of sustainable urban development
The indicators measured from the original data were standardised and then displayed in GIS to view the distribution of each indicator, and to check for the existence of any unknown spatial structure.[2] The results are shown in Figs 1–8. By observing the spatial distribution of each sustainability indicator, the research identified four distinct spatial patterns in Tainan as follows:

Polarisation: The phenomenon of polarisation, identified within urban space, relates to communities which have completely different qualities from each other. Seventeen of the 31 sustainability indicators characterise this spatial pattern. These include: the capital assets of and area used by manufacturing industries and enterprises (see Fig. 1); demographic factors such as gender, age and dependency (see Figs 1 and 2); pollution issues such as air quality, solid and water waste; public facilities and extent of green land, parks and natural areas; environmental protection facilities and condition of dwellings.

Clusters: The spatial analysis revealed several communities with similar characteristics gathering close together in small groups, especially around central points within the urban area. The indicators included: the 'population growth rate' (e.g. an area with a high population growth rate, belonging to a new developing area, see Fig. 3), the 'proportion of public facilities' (e.g. a cluster located in the centre of Tainan City, see Fig. 4), the 'economic vitality index', the 'employment rate', the 'vegetation cover rate', the 'population with an educational level beyond junior college', and the 'proportion of unoccupied dwellings'.

Concentric circles: The analysis showed a dynamic spatial development, represented by an indicator measured at its starting point in a core and then spreading outward on either a declining or increasing gradient. Examples of this included: 'population density' (high population densities centred on the downtown area, and gradually reducing outwards from the centre, see Fig. 5), and 'agricultural production areas' (the gradual increase towards the peripheries, see Fig. 6).

Left: *Fig. 1. Capital assets used by manufacturing industries.*
Right: *Fig. 2. Gender composition.*

Left: *Fig. 3. Population growth rate.*
Right: *Fig. 4. Proportion of public facilities.*

Scatter: While the research indicated clear spatial patterns of polarisation, clusters and concentric circles, it also revealed an irregular scatter of indicators spread over the urban area as a whole. These sustainability indicators included: 'operational efficiency of manufacturing industries' (see Fig. 7), 'operational efficiency of commercial businesses' (see Fig. 8), 'operational efficiency of enterprises', 'area used by commercial businesses', and 'capital assets used by commercial businesses'.

The overall conclusions concerning the development of Tainan included the following:

• Tainan's development is unbalanced because of the priority given to the downtown area. The outward spread is associated with suburban development. However, most of the unoccupied dwellings are concentrated at the periphery of the central downtown area.
• Enterprises are aggregated in specific areas, and these groupings are helpful for their control, and useful in achieving economies of scale and the reduction of external costs.
• The provision of urban public facilities is inequitable, because they are concentrated in the centre, with very little provision elsewhere (see Fig. 4).
• The age distribution, gender composition and dependency rate are polarised, and indicate differences in the structure of Tainan's population.
• The north part of Tainan is the most important ecological environment as both the natural and agricultural production areas are located there.

At the macro-level, a spatial pattern of zoning is to be found in Tainan. The service industry is on the periphery of the downtown area, the locations of natural areas

Left: *Fig. 5. Population density.*
Right: *Fig. 6. Agricultural production area.*

Left: *Fig. 7. Operational efficiency of manufacturing industries.*
Right: *Fig. 8. Operational efficiency of commercial businesses.*

and agriculture are in the north part, and manufacturing industries are distributed throughout the urban area. Nevertheless, there are still some problems with Tainan's socio-spatial structure that affect sustainable urban development.

Spatial cluster analysis

Across the 253 communities of Tainan, the research used Ward's (1963) Semi-Partial R-Squared indicator method to identify 12 clearly defined clusters (Fig. 9). The characteristics and analysis of the clusters are presented below (Table 2).

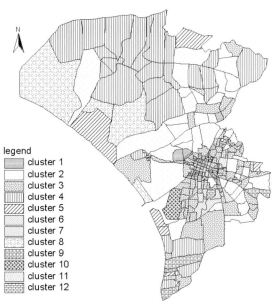

legend
cluster 1
cluster 2
cluster 3
cluster 4
cluster 5
cluster 6
cluster 7
cluster 8
cluster 9
cluster 10
cluster 11
cluster 12

Fig. 9. Spatial distribution of the 12 clusters.

| Cluster | Sustainability indicators | | | | Action to be taken |
	Positive indicators	Neutral indicators	Negative indicators	Overall 'rating'	
Cluster 1	e.g. 6, 18, 28	e.g. 1, 15, 24	e.g. 2, 4, 22	(-)	Policies required to tackle pollution and waste disposal, and provision of public facilities.
Cluster 2	none	e.g. 1, 2, 10	e.g. 3, 22	(-)	Further plans suitable for population and garbage production.
Cluster 3	none	e.g. 3, 19, 40	e.g. 9	(-)	Highlights the need for further research to understand productive developments and the causes of inefficiency, and to draw up schemes in response.
Cluster 4	e.g. 19	e.g. 6, 13, 1	none	(+)	Future policies to protect and promote a good natural environment.
Cluster 5	e.g. 8	e.g. 4, 16, 28	e.g. 5, 26, 27	(-)	Plans to tackle differences in gender structure and educational level.
Cluster 6	e.g. 18, 28	e.g. 7, 14, 22	none	(+)	Municipal administration should allocate the public facility services more appropriately and equitably, to help achieve more sustainable development.
Cluster 7	none	e.g. 5, 16, 28	e.g. 17	(-)	The research indicated those areas that have gradually declined, and pin-pointed the locations where municipal consideration should be given to stimulate the whole area into prosperous and sustainable growth.
Cluster 8	e.g. 1, 6, 7, 8, 19, 30	e.g. 4, 15, 31	none	(+)	Future policies to protect and promote agriculture and the natural environment.
Cluster 9	e.g. 29	e.g. 1, 6, 10	e.g. 11, 23	(-)	The research suggests this is the area is where Tainan can develop its hinterland, but also that corporate plans are needed to take into consideration business efficiency as a prerequisite for sustainable development.
Cluster 10	none	e.g. 7, 28, 29	e.g. 2, 12, 13, 14	(-)	Environmental protection regulations are needed to manage this particular area.
Cluster 11	none	e.g. 13, 25, 30	e.g. 5, 17	(-)	Policies are required to tackle pollution from enterprises.
Cluster 12	e.g. 9, 28	e.g. 18, 26, 27	e.g. 16	(+)	The area is considered rich in resources. In terms of the whole urban area, this is one of the most sustainable areas. Nevertheless, active management planning will still be needed in the future.

Notes:
(-) means tendency for development to be unsustainable, (+) means tendency for development to be sustainable.[3]
The numbers in the 'Sustainability indicator' columns refer to the indicators numbered in Table 1.

Table 2. Assessment of the urban sustainability of Tainan.

Cluster 1: This group includes 55 communities, mainly located in the central and west section. The characteristic of this cluster is the high population density, high levels of daily solid waste disposal and serious air pollution. There is little agriculture, a small proportion of old dwellings and low provision of public and social services facilities. This area has been the most recently developed, and is one that, when assessed by the indicators, deviates from sustainable development objectives.

Cluster 2: There are 41 communities in this cluster, spread over 7 sections of Tainan, mainly in eastern and northern areas. The main characteristics are a high population, with high garbage production. These factors have considerable potential for causing environmental problems, and appropriate policies are needed to pre-empt them.

Cluster 3: This cluster includes 87 communities and is the biggest cluster of all. It is mainly located in the central, eastern and western sections. Generally, most of the sustainability indicators in this cluster are neutral. However, the indicators of operational efficiency are negative, meaning it is an area of poor productive efficiency. There is a need for further research into productive developments and the causes of inefficiency, and for schemes to be drawn up in response.

Cluster 4: This area includes 29 communities, mainly distributed in the northernmost and south sections that surround the urban areas. There are several significant indicators in this cluster, including a lower level of urbanisation, and little industry. This area has a good natural environment. The indicators show this area as Tainan's green zone and it is the area contributing most to sustainable development.

Cluster 5: This area includes 13 communities, spread across different sections. The indicators give a high positive value to the employment rate, but show a small proportion of the population with an educational level beyond junior college and an unbalanced gender structure. In identifying these problems the research indicates the authorities' need to plan for remedial measures.

Cluster 6: This cluster includes seven communities mainly distributed around the areas adjoining the central and south sections. This area is well served by public services facilities, and it has a high-quality living environment. However, its success also puts into focus problems elsewhere, caused by over-centralising public services. The research suggests that the future municipal administration should allocate the public facility services more appropriately and equitably, to help achieve more sustainable development.

Cluster 7: There are six communities in this cluster, mainly located in the central section. Here, capital assets and commercial businesses dominate, along with industrial development. Most of these activities are located in the central business zone of Tainan. This was one of the earliest areas to be developed. The research indicated some areas that had gradually declined, and has pin-pointed those locations where municipal consideration should be given to stimulate the area's growth.

Cluster 8: This cluster includes four communities, scattered along the coast. The indicators show a very high proportion of natural area per person, a high vegetation cover rate, extensive agricultural production, a high level of economic vitality with a good employment rate, and a large proportion of old dwellings. This is mainly an agricultural area and scores well on the sustainability indicators.

Cluster 9: Seven communities are spread over the east, west and south sections in this cluster. The main indicators show the area has considerable development potential. The population is growing rapidly and there are vast tracts of undeveloped land in all the areas. However, the indicator for business operating efficiency is negative. The research suggests this is the area where Tainan can develop its hinterland, but corporate plans are needed to promote business as a prerequisite for sustainable development.

Cluster 10: This area consists of two communities, located in the central and south sections. Manufacturing industries and commercial businesses are the main users of the area, but the indicators identify wastewater discharge problems. This area is the economic base of Tainan, and in order to pursue economic growth and sustainable development simultaneously, environmental protection regulations are needed to manage this particular area.

Cluster 11: Only one community is included in this cluster, which is located in the east section. The main factors influencing this area are the presence of enterprises and problems of environmental pollution. It is different from cluster 10, inasmuch as the indicators show development potential, particularly in relation to commerce. However, it deviates from sustainable development objectives, especially in relation to pollution.

Cluster 12: The cluster also consisted of only one community, located in the section adjoining the southern and central areas. The significant indicators were in relation to the capital assets of manufacturing industries, a good rating for operating efficiency, and the provision of public facilities in the area. The area is rich in resources. From the standpoint of the whole urban area, this is one of the most sustainable areas. Nevertheless, active management planning will be needed in the future.

The overall sustainability of Tainan

The various analyses of sustainability allowed a number of assessments to be made. The understanding gained from the spatial structure and cluster analysis highlighted the problems as well as the successes of sustainable development, and indicated what and where action should be taken. Table 2 summarises some of the measures using the sustainability indicators, and gives a broad assessment of the sustainability of each cluster.

Conclusion

A number of broad conclusions emerge from this research:

- The use of a micro-level concept based on the community helps to deepen the knowledge of the vitality of urban areas through analysis of information on the socio-economic environment and three-dimensional spatial information. The research expounds a spatial structure model and methods to help provide a clearer understanding needed for sustainable urban development.
- By using GIS, the sustainable spatial structure of Tainan reveals patterns of polarisation, clusters, concentric circles, and scattered uses. At a macro-level, there is a prototype spatial pattern for zoning in Tainan, with particular geographic locations for service industry and 'green' areas, and with manufacturing industry spread throughout the whole urban area.
- The use of cluster analysis shows 12 significant groupings in Tainan, that reflect the nature of development within the whole urban area.

This research in Tainan is at an early stage of development. But it has shown the benefit of using sustainability indicators, linked to GIS, to identify particular issues concerning sustainable development. By doing so, it has provided a potential tool for policy makers to identify where action is needed and then to monitor progress. This will help Tainan to achieve urban forms that will be more sustainable both now and in the future.

Notes

1. The selection of sustainability indicators reflects the sources used at the early stages of development of this work. The model does not, at this stage, take into account the complex range of indicators for transport and energy.

2. The categories shown in Figs 1–8 were created using the 'natural breaks' method, which is the default classification in ArcView. This method identifies the break-points between classes using a statistical optimisation method (ESRI, 1996) that minimises the sum of the variance within each of the classes. The tones represent the precise break points, but also give a visual indication of the range from 'best for sustainable development' to 'worst for sustainable development'.

3. The assessments made in Table 2 reflect the measurements made of each indicator as to whether it was positive, neutral or negative. The overall 'rating' is not weighted, but represents the net balance where there are more positive than negative indicators, or vice versa, in each cluster. The 'rating' thus shows a tendency towards either sustainability or unsustainability. Each indicator identified identifies the specific issue that might need to be tackled to help each cluster achieve urban sustainability.

References

Atkisson, A. (1996) Developing indicators of sustainable community – lessons from sustainable Seattle, *Environmental Impact Assessment Review*, **16**, pp.337–350.

ESRI (1996) *Using ArcView GIS*, ESRI, USA.

Farrell, A. and Hart, M. (1998) What does sustainability really mean? The search for useful indicators, *Environment*, **40(9)**, p.12.

Hung, S. L. (1996) *Indicators and Strategy of Sustainable Urban Development for Taipei City*, Taipei City Hall, Taipei.

Liverman, D. M., Hanson, M. E., Brown, B. J. and Merideth, R. W. (1988) Global sustainability: toward measurement, *Environmental Management*, **12(2)**, pp.133–143.

Nijkamp, P. and Pepping, G. (1998) A meta-analytical evaluation of sustainable cities initiatives, *Urban Studies*, **9**, pp.1481–1500.

OECD (Organisation for Economic Cooperation and Development) (1994) *Environmental Indicators: OECD Core Set*, OECD, Paris.

Opschoor, H. and Reijnders, L. (1991) Towards sustainable development indicators, in *In Search of Indicators of Sustainable Development* (eds O. Kuik and H. Verbruggen), Kluwer Academic Publishers, Boston.

Sustainable Seattle (1993) *The Sustainable Seattle 1993 Indicators of Sustainable Community – A Report to Citizens on Long-Term Trends in Our Community*, Seattle, USA.

UNCHS (United Nation Centre for Human Settlements (Habitat)) (1995) Using indicators in policy, *Indicators Newsletter*, **3**, pp.1–8.

UNCHS (United Nation Centre for Human Settlements (Habitat)) (1997) *Global Urban Observatory – Monitoring Human Settlements with Urban Indicators (Draft) Guide*, Nairobi, Kenya.

Ward J. H. (1963) Hierarchical grouping to optimise an objective function, *Journal of the American Statistical Association*, **58**, pp.236–244.

World Commission on Environment and Development (WCED) (1987) *Our Common Future*, Oxford University Press, Oxford.

B. Sudhakara Reddy

Energy Use and Household Income:
A Developing Country Perspective

Introduction

In the twenty-first century, with more than half of the world's population living in urban centres, global problems, particularly concerning energy and the environment, will shift to developing countries. Although most of the world's energy resources are currently utilised by the developed world, it is equally true that a significant portion of these are consumed by urban populations, the majority of whom will, increasingly, live in developing countries. This chapter presents a detailed analysis of different aspects of urbanisation and related energy and environmental systems, using the case of Bangalore City in India as a typical example of a rapidly urbanising centre in a developing country.

Using a 'fuel cycle approach' (Reddy, 1990), the research assesses how a modern urban area consumes energy either directly or indirectly and the impact of energy consumption on forests, environment, transportation, and the economy as a whole. The study throws light on the important question of how the various energy carriers co-exist and are utilised in a highly stratified society. The implications of urban energy consumption are investigated, particularly with regard to the environment, the transport system, and energy and foreign exchange costs. Finally, the research takes a view on whether energy demand in urban areas can be satisfied in a sustainable way and whether there are feasible technological alternatives.

Objectives and methodology

A systematic approach to fuel and energy carriers involves a study of the entire fuel cycle starting from generation/production, through transport/transmission and distribution, to utilisation and consumption. The aims of the research in Bangalore were to understand: who supplied the energy and how much; the modes and quantities of energy transported and distributed; the energy consumed and for what end-use; and the environmental impacts and how they could be minimised.

This study follows a 'fuel cycle approach' that describes the flow of energy from source to end-use. Data were collected pertaining to the sources and supply of energy carriers, their modes of transportation, channels of distribution and patterns of consumption for a period of 10 years between 1986 and 1996 (Anon, 1996). Data came from the agencies concerned, staff interviews, and sample surveys of consumers. For the household sector, a stratified random method was used in selecting the sample of 1,000 households. The sample was assessed for bias, inconsistency and variance in terms of household income. The household survey was based on questionnaires administered by interview. It sought profile data such as household size and income, and included a self-assessed enumeration of the energy used for cooking, water heating, lighting, and other uses. Energy-consumption patterns were studied as a function of income group.

Energy supply, transportation, distribution and consumption

Of the 65,000 TJ (10^{12} joules) of energy consumed in Bangalore (1995–96), 5% came from within a distance of 100 km (in the form of firewood) and 6% from a distance greater than 1,000 km (in the form of coal and LPG). The rest came from between 100 and 1,000 km away, and included petroleum products, firewood, charcoal and electricity. Rail and trucks were the main modes for the transportation, and Fig. 1 shows the flows of energy from source to use in Bangalore (1995–96). Of the 65,000 TJ of energy transported to Bangalore during 1995–96, 54% was transported by rail and 24% by truck; 21% of electrical energy was transmitted through the grid. The channels of distribution included: the Government of India, which distributed 65% of the total supply in the form of coal, LPG and petroleum products, the Government of Karnataka 21%, in the form of firewood and electricity and private contractors 13%, in the form of firewood and charcoal. The remaining 1% was coal, supplied by the Singareni Colleries. Suppliers for each source of energy included: the Oil Co-ordination Committee (petroleum products, 63%), the Karnataka Electricity Board (electricity, 21%), the Coal India Ltd (coal, 3%), and private contractors (firewood and charcoal, 14%). This energy was consumed in various sectors as follows: residential 25,647 TJ (39%), industrial 18,798 TJ (29%), transport 17,292 TJ (27%), and commercial 2,208 TJ (3%).

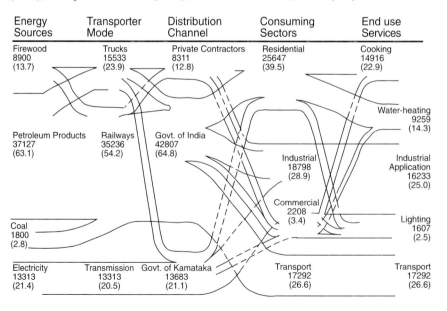

Fig. 1. Flow of energy in Bangalore, 1995–96.
Sources: *Karnataka State, Indian Oil Corporation, Coal India Ltd, Karnataka Electricity Board.*

332

Household energy consumption

The consumption data for various energy carriers indicated that residential energy consumption was the highest, accounting for about 40% of total energy consumption. Therefore it was decided to analyse household energy consumption in depth. There was a significant change in the level of utilisation of various carriers between 1986 and 1996. Wood-based fuels like firewood, which constituted 40% of the total residential energy consumption in 1986, accounted for only 28% in 1996. Over the same 10-year period, the share of kerosene in total energy consumption increased from 28% to 33%. Liquid propane gas (LPG) increased its share from 5% to 11% and electricity increased its share from 21% to 25%. This indicates that many households that used to depend on wood-based fuels have shifted to modern energy carriers like LPG and electricity (Table 1 and Fig. 2).

| Energy carrier | Total energy consumption | | | |
| | Consumption 1986–87 | | Consumption 1995–96 | |
	TJ	%	TJ	%
Firewood	6,015	40	7,120	28
Electricity	3,190	21	6,376	25
LPG	763	5	2,865	11
Kerosene	4,249	28	8,585	33
Other fuels	870	6	700	3
Total	15,087	100	25,646	100

Table 1. Change in energy carrier consumption in Bangalore.

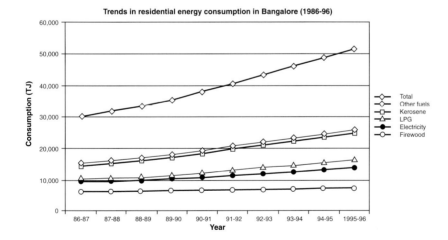

Fig. 2. Trends in residential energy consumption in Bangalore (1986–1996).
Source: Anon (1996), KEB (1996) and ONGC (1996).

Analysis of household survey data

The household survey data indicated that there are variations in the contribution of different energy carriers to the energy mix of different income groups for cooking and water heating. Many types of fuel are used for cooking and water heating, and households tended to use either:

- only one type of fuel for both cooking and water heating, or
- one fuel for cooking and another for water-heating, or
- auxiliary fuels for cooking in addition to one main fuel.

The type of energy carrier chosen for cooking and water-heating depends, as one would expect, on household income and, to a certain extent, profession of the head of the household. The survey households were classified into various categories based on the profession of the head of the household and household income. Tables 2 and 3 show the energy carrier use by various categories of household.

Profession of the head of the household		Households using particular energy carriers (%)					
		Firewood	Kerosene	LPG	Electricity	Other	Total % (no.)
Labourer							
	Casual	81	11	0	0	8	100 (110)
	Skilled	20	48	14	8	9	100 (224)
Service							
	Clerical	9	35	25	13	18	100 (183)
	Higher	4	15	60	15	6	100 (162)
Business							
	Small	5	36	23	16	20	100 (86)
	Higher	0	16	51	22	11	100 (37)
Professional		2	11	50	31	6	100 (54)
Other		3	38	32	17	11	100 (144)

Table 2. Profession of the head of the household and the type of fuel utilisation.
Source: Based on the primary data collected by the author for Bangalore, 1996.

According to Table 2, 81% of households in the casual labour category depended wholly on firewood for both cooking and water heating and only 8% on other fuels, which in their case means dung-cakes, twigs and biomass pickings. In complete contrast is the category of households with a professional background: 98% of this category use fuels such as electricity, kerosene, LPG, for both cooking and water-heating, and only 2% use firewood.

The picture is even clearer if per capita income is considered. Households with the lowest incomes are heavily dependent on the cheaper fuels. For example, 47% of households with monthly per capita incomes of less than Rs 250 (US$5.6) depend on firewood, and 33% on other even cheaper fuels, while only 20% use kerosene. None of this income group use LPG or electricity. These poorer households represent 15% of the survey sample, but account for 42% of the households that depend on firewood. About half of the sample (47%) have monthly per capita incomes of Rs 750 (US$16.8) or less, and almost 90% of these households use firewood. The relationship between energy consumption and per capita income is summarised in Table 3.

Per capita income (Rs/month)	Households using particular energy carriers (%)					
	Firewood	Kerosene	LPG	Electricity	Others	Total % (no.)
<250	47	20	0	0	33	100 (148)
250–500	28	46	0	1	25	100 (167)
500–750	21	49	15	2	13	100 (155)
750–1,000	11	36	34	16	3	100 (138)
1,000–2,500	2	29	42	25	2	100 (150)
>2,500	0	11	62	27	0	100 (242)

Table 3. Per capita income and energy carrier utilisation.
Source: Based on the primary data collected by the author for Bangalore, 1996

Dependency and utilisation indices

The research defined a total energy carrier dependence index (ECDI) related to household income as:

$$\text{ECDI} = \frac{\% \text{ of all households in the income category using a particular fuel}}{\% \text{ of all sample households which belong to the income category}}$$

An ECDI of 'one' means that households within a particular income group are totally dependent on one specific type of fuel (Reddy and Reddy, 1983). Households below a per capita monthly income of Rs 500 (US$11) bear the greatest burden of firewood dependence, whereas those with incomes above Rs 1,000 (US$22.5) depend more on LPG and electricity. This is indicated in Fig. 3 showing the cumulative percentage of various energy carriers used by households divided by the cumulative percentage of households in the various income ranges.

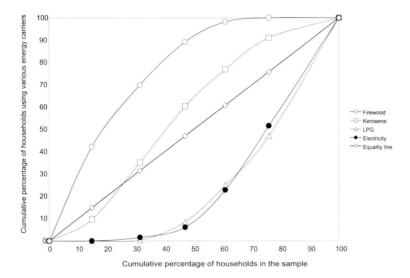

Fig. 3. Energy carrier usage (Lorenz curve).

To interpret the pattern of consumption, a utilisation index (*UI*), which refers to the income group, is defined and calculated. This utilisation index (*UI*) refers to the income group.

$$UI = \frac{X_{ijk}}{\sum\limits_{k} X_{ijk}} = \frac{X_{ijk}}{X_{ij}}$$

where: 'X_i' is the proportion of households, 'k' the income group and 'j' the energy carrier.

The carrier utilisation indices (Table 4) show that there is a variation in the contribution of different energy carriers to the energy mix of different income groups. The low-income groups (up to Rs 500) depend mainly on firewood and agricultural wastes. The middle-income groups (Rs 500–1,000) depend on kerosene and, to a certain extent, on charcoal as well as firewood. The high-income groups (Rs 1,000 and above) depend mainly on LPG and electricity.

Per capita monthly income (Rs)	Energy carrier utilisation index (UI)				
	Firewood	Kerosene	LPG	Electricity	Others
<250	0.47	0.20	0.00	0.00	0.33
250–500	0.28	0.46	0.01	0.01	0.25
500–750	0.21	0.49	0.15	0.04	0.12
750–1,000	0.11	0.36	0.34	0.16	0.03
1,000–2,500	0.02	0.29	0.42	0.25	0.02
>2,500	0.00	0.11	0.62	0.26	0.00

Table 4. Energy carrier utilisation indices.

Energy substitution and the energy-ladder process

The choices in energy consumption reveal a pattern of substitution of one carrier for another, which has been referred to as the 'energy-ladder' process (Reddy and Reddy, 1994). This energy-ladder concept indicates that the pattern of energy use in different households varies with their economic status. Each step of the ladder corresponds to a different and more sophisticated energy carrier, and the step to which the household climbs on the ladder depends mainly on its income. In the present study, with increase in income, solid fuels (charcoal and firewood) tend to be substituted by liquid fuel (kerosene) which in turn is displaced by gas (LPG) and electricity – the most desirable energy carrier for households. The height of the step is determined by economic factors such as the capital cost of the fuel-utilising device, price of the energy carrier, and household energy consumption. An example is the trade-off between a relatively high capital cost for an energy-efficient device such as a stove, with its consequent lower fuel and maintenance costs (or life cycle costs). For poor households, low initial capital cost is the dominant concern. Apart from purely economic factors, other social factors such as size of the family, occupation of the head of household, family tradition, and availability of carrier also play a role in the choice of fuel. Fig. 4 indicates the crossover points from one fuel to another, related to household income.

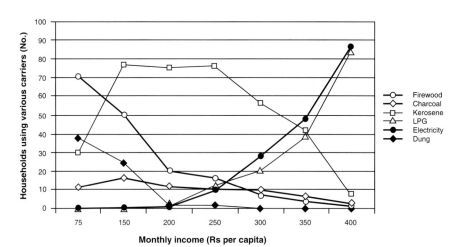

Fig. 4. Fuel use by household income.

Implications of Bangalore's energy supply and consumption
The patterns of energy use over time, and the shifts in use of different fuels with changing incomes, have led to a wide range of impacts on Bangalore and its region. These are discussed below.

Impact on forests
Bangalore consumes significant quantities of energy. The amount of non-commercial fuels consumed, such as firewood, is surprising. Firewood gathering has a serious impact on forests, although there is a difference between urban and rural areas. Rural households depend on the collection of twigs and branches, whereas urban areas use logs that require the felling of trees. Bangalore consumes around 1,200 tonnes of firewood per day, which corresponds to an annual deforestation of about 3,650 hectares, or 10 hectares per day (Parikh and Reddy, 1997). Keeping Bangalore supplied through the non-renewable clearance of forests at this rate is not sustainable. Thus, urban firewood consumption has a much greater negative environmental impact than does rural dependence on firewood as a domestic fuel.

Impact on the transport system
The transport of various fuels into Bangalore involves truck and rail traffic. Weigh-bridge records (for trucks) and railway goods sheds (for railway wagons) for October–November 1995 show that about 12% of the truck and 5 % of rail traffic is committed to transporting firewood, 8% of rail traffic to petroleum products, and 2% of truck traffic to LPG (Anon, 1996). In all, 14% of truck and 13% of rail traffic supplying Bangalore with commodities is tied up in transporting energy. A significant proportion of both road and rail transport is used for the supply of fuel, and in a situation where transport is often in short supply, there is an 'opportunity cost'.[2] Instead of transporting fuel, other essentials could have been supplied.

Impact on transport energy
Transporting various energy carriers from source to destination requires energy in the form of diesel. These energy costs are estimated as follows (Table 5). On an average, about 1,200 tonnes/day of firewood was transported to Bangalore by truck and rail from distances ranging from 35 to 700km. This constituted a total of about 70 million tonnekm which, at an average consumption of 22.04 tonne km/kg diesel for truck and 154 tonnekm/kg of diesel for railway wagons (Anon, 1991), requires 2,250 tonnes of diesel per annum. Bangalore consumed about 618,000 tonnes of petroleum products brought from Madras 350km away by rail, corresponding to about 1,410 tonnes of diesel used per annum. The transport of 18,000 metric tonnes of LPG is by truck from Bombay and Koyali (where the LPG refineries are located) at distances of 1,000 and 1,200km, respectively with diesel consumption of about 910 tonnes. The total diesel consumed to transport energy to Bangalore was about 4,600 tonnes for the year 1995–96.

Impact on foreign exchange
The 4,600 tonnes of diesel/year used to transport Bangalore's energy cost about Rs 15 million[3] or Rs 2.5/litre of diesel (*Commerce Weekly*, 1996). Since about two-thirds of India's oil is imported and paid for in foreign exchange, it can be

argued that Rs 10 million or about US$0.2 million/year is the foreign exchange expenditure on supplying Bangalore with its energy requirements.

Energy carrier	Mode of transport	Quantity supplied (1000 tonnes)	Distance (km)	Tonnekm (1000)	Consumption norm (tonnekg/km)	Diesel consumption (1000 tonnes)	% of total
Firewood	Truck	187	35	6,539	22.04	0.30	
		267	135	36,029	22.04	1.63	
		11	350	3,736	22.04	0.17	
	Sub-total	464		46,304		2.10	
	Rail	25	200	4,982	154	0.03	
		27	700	18,682	154	0.12	
	Sub-total	52		23,663		0.15	
	Total (firewood)	516		69,967		2.25	49.1
LPG	Truck	18	1,100	20,020	22.04	0.91	19.8
Petroleum products	Rail	618	350	21,6373	154	1.41	30.6
Coal	Rail	37	120	4,380	154	0.03	0.6
Total		1,189		310,740		4.60	100.00

Table 5. Energy cost of transporting various carriers (1995–96).
Sources: Karnataka State, Indian Oil Corporation, Coal India Ltd, Karnataka Electricity Board, Karnataka State Road Transportation Dept, Southern Railway - Bangalore, Pundir and Sudhakara (1985).

Impact on the environment

Environmental problems tend to relate to energy use in urban areas. The dominant use of petroleum products in the transport sector with little emission control has contributed significantly to the degradation of air quality. Vehicles emit carbon monoxide (CO), unburnt hydrocarbons (HC), nitrogen oxide (NO_X) and sulphur dioxide which pollute the environment and damage health. Since the environmental implications are dependent on the mode of transport, it is important to look at the various transportation modes and their associated emissions. These were estimated using the emission coefficients for CO, HC and NO_X (Reddy, 1990).

The average emissions and the contribution of various categories of vehicle to air pollution are given in Table 6. An important observation from these figures is that the contribution of two-wheelers to the total emissions is very high for carbon monoxide and hydrocarbons. For 1995–96, the total CO emissions were 33,043 tonnes in which the contribution of two-wheelers was 12,873 tonnes (36%). In the case of HC, the estimated emissions are 14,296 tonnes in which the share of two-wheelers is 54%. Diesel-driven vehicles are the major contributors of NO_X (90% of total). These results suggest that the quantity of emissions, particularly by two-wheelers, is alarming. In the coming years, this will increase further due to increases in the number of vehicles. Unless steps are taken to reduce emissions, there will be a serious damage to the environment. Some fundamental approaches to the fuel economy may lead to emission reductions, e.g. efficient engines, which have lower combustion temperatures, and reduce NO_X formation.

Type of vehicle	Average emissions (g/km)			Vehicle km (million)	Total emissions (tonnes/year)		
	CO	HC	NO$_X$		CO	HC	NO$_X$
Two-wheelers	8	5	-	1,551	12,873	8,034	-
Three-wheelers	16	10	-	382	6,051	3,770	-
Cars	24	4	2	322	7,738	1,150	506
Jeeps	24	4	2	22	529	79	35
Taxis	24	4	2	64	1,538	228	100
Diesel vehicles [1]	0	0	0	189,234 [2]	4,315	1,665	8,156
Total					33,043	14,926	8,797

Table 6. Vehicle emission inventory for Bangalore (1995–96).

(1) gramme emission/gramme of fuel consumed

(2) tonnes of diesel consumed

Implications of energy carrier substitution

The choice of energy carrier in the residential sector of Bangalore is an economic one. Available household income affects the substitution (on the energy-ladder) of a new efficient technology for the old and inefficient. The efficiency of devices varies considerably, with firewood stoves currently only 10% efficient, coal and petroleum product using devices that are 60% efficient, LPG devices that are 65% efficient, and electrical devices operating at 70% efficiency. The rate at which the substitution proceeds depends upon the economic conditions of households (see Fig. 4). This is an evolutionary process, but in a stratified society, where closing the gap between rich and poor may be slow, it can take a long time. Since efficient devices are expensive, reduction in capital costs through subsidies and rebates could induce poorer households to shift to more efficient and energy-conserving devices. Such financial incentives could lower the initial capital cost and make the trade-off toward lower operating cost more appealing. Another possibility would be for the government or electricity boards to install energy-efficient equipment in households and collect the payments in monthly instalments. However, the consumers' knowledge of costs and benefits also plays a significant role in conservation programmes. The government should try to educate consumers to understand the trade-off between the capital cost of the efficient device and the benefits of savings on running costs, and benefits to the environment.

Demand management focused on end-uses

Cooking energy for the urban poor

The research presented here has shown that the vast bulk of firewood used is by the poor who need inexpensive fuel for cooking and water heating. Yet the question of the efficiency of firewood stoves, used by the overwhelming majority of the country's households, was largely ignored by India's scientists and engineers. Over the past few years, however, there has been a growing interest in increasing the efficiency of firewood stoves, leading to ideas for a combination of engineering, heat transfer and furnace design. It now looks as if overall efficiencies as high as 40 % can be achieved in comparison with the present 10%, to deliver the same heat energy to the cooking pot (Johanson *et al.*, 1993). Since about half the firewood used in Bangalore is for cooking, this means that what now requires about 600 tonnes/day can be achieved with 125 tonnes/day.

Further savings can be made where cooking and water heating are carried out in close proximity; it is possible to utilise the waste heat from cooking for heating water. This cascading approach in which the unutilised energy from one task is used for another task is particularly convenient in firewood stoves which can be designed to use waste heat from the chimney. This means that in households using firewood for both cooking and water-heating, efficient stoves can be installed which accomplish both tasks in a single process.

These design improvements can lead to a substantial reduction in, though not elimination of, firewood consumption. A rough estimate indicates that Bangalore's demand for firewood can be brought down to as little as 300 tonnes/day from the present 1,200 tonnes/day (Reddy, 1990). This reduced demand has the potential to be met from managed renewable forests, so that the extraction rate is matched to the growth rate. There are several species of fast-growing firewood crops, which despite varying yields can produce an estimated figure of 10 tonnes/hectare/year (Parikh and Reddy, 1997). This figure implies that a reduced demand of 300 tonnes/day requires a forest of 6,424 hectares or 64.24km² to supply Bangalore with firewood in a sustained and renewable manner. Obviously, if the aim is to reduce diesel consumption for transporting firewood to Bangalore, it would be rational to locate the forest as close to Bangalore as possible. One approach would be to grow a forest belt around Bangalore's circumference. A 1.5km wide belt around Bangalore's proposed metropolitan area would provide its requirements for firewood in a sustainable manner.

Forest belts around urban centres would help eliminate the four negative impacts of the present pattern of firewood consumption – deforestation, reduction of the capacity of the transport system, diesel consumption, and foreign exchange outflow. If firewood from these forest belts was used, one major socio-economic problem would persist: different sections of society would continue to use different fuels, with the rich using LPG for cooking and the poor firewood, albeit with improved stoves. There is a sound technical reason for the preference of the rich – gas cooking is far more convenient to use. If the gap between rich and poor closes, then it might be necessary to replace the direct supply of firewood from the forest belt with the use of the wood to generate gas, which could then be piped to homes. This gas could then be supplemented with methane-rich biogas, obtained from the treatment of the city's sewage.

Efficient appliances and alternative energy sources
Electricity is an important source of energy in the household sector, so its conservation is an issue. For example, a 1% increase in electric water-heaters in Bangalore can increase the electricity consumption by 3,527kWh per day (Reddy, 1990). A large amount of energy could be saved by the substitution of solar water-heaters for electrical water-heaters. Flat-plate solar collectors of 2m² can provide approximately 2.5 litres per minute of hot water at 60°C (Anon, 1991). Since the temperature required to heat water is around 45°C, which can easily be met by solar energy, installation of solar water-heaters is feasible. If hot water for at least 50% of households was provided by solar energy rather than electricity, then 10% of total electricity could be saved.

In the case of lighting appliances, incandescent bulbs are commonly used in domestic and commercial sectors. New compact fluorescent lamps (CFLs) last about eight to ten times longer than incandescents and are four times as efficient. An incandescent lamp with a rating of 60W has an output of 700 lumens, a life of 1,000 hours and is priced at Rs 15. An 11W compact fluorescent has an output of 900 lumens, a life of 8,000 hours and is priced at Rs 250. Similar replacements can be done for ballasts also. Fluorescent tubes are also widely used. Each tubelight fixture has a ballast, which provides a high voltage to initiate the discharge and then limits the current. A conventional magnetic ballast for a 40W rating fixture consumes about 12W of power. Instead of a magnetic ballast, it is possible to opt for an electronic ballast, which draws only 1–3W. The auxiliary consumption of the ballast is 3W. The cost of the ballast is Rs 150, and the life of the ballast is 10 years. With the replacement of incandescent bulbs and magnetic ballasts with CFLs and electronic ballasts respectively, the lighting energy consumption could be reduced by 60% (Parikh and Reddy, 1994).

Conclusions

This study provides an understanding of energy utilisation in a stratified urban society. The energy used in Bangalore is quite substantial, and includes the consumption of significant quantities of non-commercial fuels such as firewood. No policy instrument has been wielded to regulate the flow of these fuels to Bangalore; it is largely left to market forces. Thus, consumers get their supply from retail depots, which in turn obtain firewood from commission agents – creating a predicament for the poor, who are exploited by the private contractor–trucker–retailer nexus. But the major social cost of this private enterprise is environmental degradation in the form of deforestation.

The results of the study have shown an empirical basis for the energy-ladder concept in the household sector. Each step of the ladder corresponds to a different carrier, and the step up to which a household climbs on the energy-ladder depends mainly on its income and the initial costs, energy consumption and carrier prices. It is from this perspective that policy makers should think about encouraging fuel substitution. However, if societies become less stratified and income inequalities reduce (or if inequalities remain but income levels rise above a certain threshold), then this energy-ladder concept, based on income, could disappear. For this to happen, policy intervention needs to be directed towards altering the economic factors. In urban areas, this can be done by reducing prices and increasing availability of LPG and electricity, and by subsidising the initial cost of LPG and electric stoves for poorer sections of society. In rural areas, afforestation programmes and energy-conservation measures through efficient wood-burning stoves would decrease the stress on resources. Thus the energy-ladder concept serves as a useful guide to policy formulation and intervention.

All this constitutes further illustration of a well-known phenomenon: economic inequalities result in negative environmental impacts at both ends of the income spectrum. The rich degrade the environment through a wasteful use of resources, and the poor through the necessity of having to survive at the expense of the environment. The use of energy in Bangalore also illustrates the inefficiency with which energy is used by the poorest sections of society, in contrast to the efficient devices used by the rich.

The highest priority needs to be given to satisfying the energy needs of the poor, in particular their need for inexpensive fuels/devices for cooking and water-heating. Fortunately, the technical means of achieving this objective are available, but political will is needed for implementation. Only then can the environmental degradation, tying-up of transport capacity, unnecessary consumption of high-quality diesel fuel and foreign exchange expenditure be avoided. Energy use in a stratified urban society like Bangalore is therefore one more illustration of the fact that the root cause of society's problems is the existence of grave economic inequalities.

It is clear from the results of the study that urbanisation is a resource-expensive process and the developing countries' aspirations for a 'Western' urban form are likely to increase the burden on the environment. Thus, strategies for resource-conserving urbanisation are warranted. It is suggested here that afforestation programmes and energy conservation measures through efficient technologies will decrease the stress on natural resources such as wood and oil. In the case of electricity conservation, policies should be tailored more to increasing the stock of appliances. Fuel shifts from traditional to modern fuels and from oil to natural gas will decrease the environmental stress. The general approach developed in this chapter can easily be adapted to other urban concentrations, particularly in developing countries. It should be noted that solutions to the energy problems of a metropolitan region are related to those for the rest of the region and vice versa, and cannot function in isolation. It is hoped that an urban energy system can evolve which can sustain an economy and move on to a development path for satisfying basic human needs, yet, at the same time, can ensure sustainability.

Acknowledgement

The author wishes to thank Prof. Amulya K. N. Reddy, President, International Energy Initiative for carefully going through an earlier version of this chapter.

Notes

1. The currency is Indian Rupees (Rs). The exchange rates in June 2000 were $1 = 44.6 Rs.
2. Opportunity cost of a good or a service refers to the cost of forgoing/adopting that good or service and choosing/avoiding another good or service requiring the same resources (*Encyclopedia of Energy*, 1971, McGraw-Hill, New York).
3. Feb. 1996 exchange rate of US$1=Rs 40, at an international rate of US$25 per barrel of crude.

References

Anon (1991) *Encyclopedia of Energy*, McGraw-Hill, New York.
Anon (1996) *Entries of weighing materials (1986–96)*, Bangalore.
Commerce Weekly (1996), **54,** February, pp.19–25.
Johanson, T. B., Kelly, H., Reddy, A. K. N. and Williams, R. H. (1993) *Renewable Energy – Sources for Fuels and Electricity*, Island Press, Washington.
KEB (1996) *Annual Reports (1986–96)*, Karnataka Electricity Board, Bangalore.
KSCST (1995) *Solar Water-Heating Systems - Overview*, Karnataka State Council for Science and Technology, Bangalore.
ONGC (Oil and Natural Gas Committee) (1996)*Annual Reports (1986–96)*, Indian Oil Corporation, Bharat Petroleum Corporation and Hindustan Petroleum Corporation, Bangalore.
Parikh, J. K. and Reddy, B. S. (1994)*, Planning for Demand-Side Management in the Electricity Sector*, Tata McGraw-Hill, New Delhi.
Parikh, J. and Reddy, B.S. (1997) *Sustainable Regeneration of Degraded Lands*, Tata McGraw-Hill, New Delhi.
Pundir, B. P. and Sudhakar, D. (1985) *State of Art – Report on Vehicle Emissions*, Ministry of the Environment, Government of India.
Reddy, A. K. N. and Reddy, B. S. (1983) Energy in a stratified society – a case study of firewood in Bangalore, *Economic and Political Weekly*, **XVII, 41**, pp.1757–1770.
Reddy, A. K. N. and Reddy, B. S. (1994) Substitution of energy carriers for cooking in Bangalore, *Energy - The International Journal*, **19 (5)**, pp.561–572.
Reddy, B.S. (1990) The energy sector of the metropolis of Bangalore, unpublished Ph.D. thesis, Indian Institute of Science, Bangalore.
Reddy, B. S. (1998) Energy efficient options – techno-economic potentials for mitigating GHG emissions, *International Journal of Environment and Pollution*, **9 (2/3)**, pp.253–266.
Train, K. 1985, Discount rates in consumers' energy related decisions – a review of literature, *Energy*, **10, 12**, pp.1243–1253.

Mike Jenks

Conclusion:
The Appropriateness of Compact City Concepts to Developing Countries

> We should be grateful to the poor cities of the South for what they teach us, not
> only about our past, but about the future that awaits us if we do not recognise
> our common fate, and act accordingly.
> (Seabrook, 1996, p.301)

To learn from the experience of developing countries has been one of the
motivations for this third book in the series about sustainable urban form. There is
a great deal of information to draw on. Reviews of data from many countries in
the world, comparative case studies and detailed research from 11 developing
countries form the content of the 26 chapters in the book. Grouping these into four
parts gives first a broad context to the debate about compact cities in developing
countries. Second, key issues are raised about core urban areas, the process of
intensification, and urban sprawl on the periphery. These are then illustrated in the
third part, through case studies. Finally, aspects of transport, infrastructure and
environment are considered in some detail. Within this range of information there
are some common themes, as well as distinct differences. It is clear that there is a
live debate about the compact city in many regions throughout the world. It is
reasonable to ask what issues are most significant, and how appropriate are concepts
so well rehearsed in the West to achieving sustainable urban form in developing
countries?

Urban form
Many complex factors relate to the sustainability of urban form, and include issues
at the regional and city scale, and those of density and peripheral urban sprawl.
These are considered below.

Urban regions and agglomerations
The rapid growth of urbanisation has meant that the world's major cities have
become ever expanding urban agglomerations, making metropolitan regions an
important focus for policy-making and problem solving. The general characteristic

is that, with the exception of many cities in Africa, higher densities are found in the core of cities in developing countries than in developed countries. Yet despite inner-city compactness, there is no evidence of containment as these cities and their metropolitan regions occupy larger land areas than their counterparts in the developed world. The fastest growth is seen in the 'million cities', the secondary cities, and on the urban periphery with extensive low-density urban sprawl and the widespread encroachment on agricultural land. At the same time, there is some evidence of a counter-trend towards urban concentration in some regions and primate cities.

Demographic forces, of migration from rural areas to cities that offer better life chances and health care, and high rates of population growth, fuel urban expansion. So too do global markets, although the spread of capital and income is both uneven and often inequitable. Whether as a result of educated workforces or cheap labour, or as a result of government policies and subsidies, globalisation seeks out and favours some metropolitan regions and neglects others. The global competition for investment is intense, success breeds success, and the potential prize is a city that achieves world status. Inevitably the winners tend to be those developing countries with the strongest economies, and the losers the poorest, struggling in many cases with the highest fertility rates, or in sub-Saharan Africa, with the impact of HIV/AIDS. In the more successful regions, a twin process of both centralisation and decentralisation appears to occur. The city core attracts global headquarters and service industries and acts as a global market place, but the resulting rising prices (and congestion) drive the poor to the periphery. Here the poorer people face social exclusion and inadequate access to facilities and transport, while in close proximity the rich seek protection in gated, luxurious developments. The prospects for the poorer regions and cities are uncontrolled growth, dominated by the informal sector, problems of inadequate infrastructure and services, and environmental degradation.

The research presented here suggests that attempts at containment of this explosive growth have not been particularly successful, either at protecting agriculture or its productivity, or improving the quality of life. Yet the means exist to achieve substantial savings of land and energy used in transport, through more compact development policies. Nevertheless, the certainty is that metropolitan regions will expand, particularly in Asia, to some agglomerations of perhaps 30–40 million people. In this context, Lloyd Jones' argument about the length of time that people are prepared to travel is significant. It implies a self-limiting system that may help to drive policies for development towards denser, polynuclear urban forms, linked by transport – an urban form advocated by many as potentially more sustainable.

Urban form at the city scale

At the macro scale of cities and regions there are clear impacts affecting sustainability through inefficient land use and encroachment, problems of transport, and environmental degradation. But what other issues affect sustainability? Globalisation and ubiquitous modernism also affect urban form. Familiar types of high-rise commercial and residential buildings grouped in blocks within a grid of streets, and the ever-present central business district, are recognisable in most cities in the world. The importance of meaning and image should not be ignored as they can have both positive and negative implications. Brand points to the positive, using the idea of metaphor to give meaning and social purpose to interventions aimed at improving sustainability, in this case in Medellín, one of the world's most violent cities. On the negative side, the rush by cities and regions to win foreign investment and gain world status engenders aspirations for modernity and gigantism, while ignoring the sustainability of such forms. This apparent sameness led de Schiller and Evans to raise the significant issue of climate – which varies from region to region. Urban forms and building designs that pay little regard to climate adversely affect sustainability. They fail to make use of micro-climatic benefits such as shading and air movement, and designs tend to favour buildings that depend on air conditioning that wastes energy and adds to the heat island effect, raising temperatures in cities.

The multitude of factors that can affect sustainability means that policy formulation requires a strategic understanding and good local knowledge. A considerable effort in developed countries has been devoted to the measurement of sustainability indicators, and this has also received attention in developing countries. The example from Taiwan points to the utility of mapping sustainability indicators to alert policy-makers to potential problems, and to point to possible solutions. Very sophisticated models are also powerful. The mapping of the Pearl River delta demonstrates how sustainability can be enhanced through more compact development patterns and through savings on transport use.

Density and urban intensification

The perception is that to achieve a sustainable compact city, denser forms of new development, and the intensification of existing urban areas are needed. However, 'higher density' is not an absolute concept, but a relative one. Densities vary considerably between cities in different countries, and what is considered high density in one country may not be thought as high in another. For example, one of the districts in Hong Kong, Mong Kok, has an exceptionally high density of 116,000 persons per hectare, and even Hong Kong's metropolitan region has a density of 6,160 persons per hectare. This compares with other cities (studied in this book) such as the metropolitan areas of Calcutta and Medellín with 5,696 and 756 persons per hectare, and inner-city densities of 23,500 and 4,212 persons per hectare respectively. But density is often measured in different ways, making comparisons difficult and meaning hard to interpret. It is doubtful whether the high densities in Hong Kong represent, for example, serious overcrowding because development is in the form of high-rise buildings containing large numbers of well-kept dwellings. But overcrowding exists in lower and low-density areas, for example in the Caracas barrios there are between 9 and 13 persons per dwelling and in the townships of Pretoria between 7 and 21 persons per dwelling. Tolerance of different densities is recognised as being, to a great extent, culturally determined.

Achieving higher densities in existing cities can only be through a process of intensification (or densification). This process may be driven by policies through the formal sector, or happen through the efforts of the informal sector. A number of examples stand out. Curitiba, with intensification planned along transport routes aided by the transfer of development rights; the plans of Cape Town and Durban for development along transport corridors and at transport interchanges; and Bangkok with planned transit development zones, potentially enabled by incentives to developers.

Informal and unplanned intensification, by contrast, was found to have virtually no transport benefit. This process occurs through conversions and extensions of residential areas (often illegally), through plot sub-division, and land invasion. Although characterised by congestion, pollution and overstretched (or non-existent) infrastructure, there are benefits of vitality and social interaction. The account of the barrios of Caracas shows not only intensification, but also a process of consolidation over time. This has led to a knowledgeable and skilled construction workforce and impressive examples of community self-organisation. It seems possible that some convergence between the formal and informal sectors could yield benefits, especially in poorer cities where there is a high proportion of the population in the informal sector.

Urban sprawl and the peripheries
The vast and widespread expansion of peripheral development not only takes up valuable land and increases transport problems, but also has other costs and impacts on people's lives. As Fadda *et al.* so aptly point out, living at the physical edge of a city, for many, can mean living at the edge of urban society. Development results from policy in the formal sector, from private developers usually taking advantage of weak controls and low land prices, and from informal and illegal settlement.

Whatever drives its development, the periphery usually suffers from inadequate investment in the infrastructure necessary to integrate it into the city or metropolitan region. Planned peripheral expansion in Dhaka has atrophied through failure to provide adequate transport. In Delhi, the planned peripheral development is at a higher density than the city and is primarily residential, so most of the travel is to the centre, causing congestion, long journeys and extended travel time. Evidence from Brazil shows that developing as far from the city as possible, and leaving vacant land in between, is profitable for developers, as it is the authorities and not the developers that have to provide the infrastructure. Once provided, the value of the vacant land increases and higher private profits can be made. Informal and illegal settlement takes land opportunistically. The form varies, from low-density sprawling squatter settlements to large areas of high-density development constrained by topography. In either extreme, infrastructure, transport, or any other planning consideration will be largely absent.

The few who are rich, and escape to the periphery by choice, achieve a high quality of life, albeit protected by a 'golden cage'. They still face long journeys, but will not be dependent on public transport, and, as reported in Bangkok, may even equip their cars with TV and portable toilets. But for the vast majority of the poor and impoverished middle classes, there is little choice. They often face social segregation in fragmented and disconnected urban areas, poor living conditions including high levels of pollution and environmental degradation, inefficient public transport, and increasing levels of crime.

However, some evidence suggests that urban compaction may not provide all the answers to the reduction of urban sprawl. The costs of more compact development are not affordable by large numbers of those living on the peripheries. Land prices will be higher, and costs of construction greater. Reducing the amount of space available to families also affects their ability to earn income from the plots they occupy. In South Africa, for example, the low-density peripheral forms are deceptive as occupation rates are high, and income can be generated from renting space and from informal business. Income is also gained from plot subdivisions, or by the construction of many extensions to provide space to rent out. Where income inequalities exist, and where the majority of the population earns the least, then the affordable options appear to be either at the periphery or in informal settlements.

Sustainable urban form?

Despite the differences in countries and regions, there is a degree of consensus on a polynucleated urban form as a possible and relatively effective way to achieve sustainable development. This is not surprising given that most city cores are dense and often overcrowded, and that growth is spreading so fast on the periphery. This type of urban form may have a number of different characteristics, such as the intensification (or densification) of low-density areas, particularly around transport interchanges (as transit development zones), dense development along transport corridors (a linear form), and new development linked by efficient public transport (a 'concentrated decentralisation' model). Forms of this type are beginning to find their way into policy and have been implemented in practice. They offer the potential to achieve a network of compact cities within the metropolitan region, and may help to rationalise the emerging megacities. But, of course, this is a very broad generalisation, and although the trend may be in that direction, it is not a universal panacea; many influences and differences need to be considered.

Transport and infrastructure

As in developed countries, high densities and compact development facilitate more viable and effective public transport provision. Excellent mass transit and public transport systems accompany the very high densities in Hong Kong, However, this works because of its strong economy, strong (even authoritarian) government and fairly draconian car restraint policies. Singapore, Seoul and Tokyo provide similar examples. The balance between car restraint and high-quality alternatives means that public transport retains its middle-class custom in these cities. Despite this, the very high densities still lead to traffic problems even though levels of private vehicle ownership are low.

High density alone is not sufficient to assure good public transport and avoid traffic chaos, as evidenced in Bangkok. Here, as in many Asian cities, the road capacity is low, and thus can become saturated with relatively small increases in private vehicle use. The high densities make it impractical to increase road capacity, and possible technical solutions such as multi-decked roads are environmentally undesirable. The problems and benefits of inserting a mass transit system into existing dense urban fabrics are well illustrated in the case study of Bangkok. Creation of transit development zones, built with private finance and enabled through floorspace bonuses, may well be a way forward for those cities that do not have the strong economy of cities like Hong Kong.

Without high-quality public transport systems, the hope of encouraging more sustainable modes of travel is perhaps illusory. High-density cities, such as Dhaka and Calcutta, could be judged sustainable because the majority of traffic is non-motorised, but this is a function of low per capita incomes, rather than of environmental policy. As Zillmann rightly notes, sustainability is not enough – low consumption brought about by low income fails the test of providing an adequate quality of life.

Transport, its costs and benefits, tends to be a dominant issue in the compact city debate. Rather neglected is the provision of infrastructure. Biermann's study provides an important missing perspective. Unlike the clear association of high densities with viability for public transport provision, the relationship between density and infrastructure is not very encouraging. Costs do not decrease with increasing density, and it can be as expensive to provide infrastructure to denser city centres as to developments on the periphery. The crucial issue is one of capacity. The most cost-effective development is where there is spare infrastructure capacity, and least when the threshold is reached, capacity is exceeded and new infrastructure has to be provided. Infrastructure needs to be included as an integral part of the debate about sustainable urban form.

Some aspects of implementation
A considerable range of ideas and examples of good practice that may go some way towards achieving a number of the objectives of sustainable urban form exist. These are considered below.

Political will. The success of the richer cities in public transport and infrastructure provision demonstrates the impact of strong local government, willing to restrain car use and invest in mass transit and other transport networks. However, it is questionable whether such authoritarian forms of government are widely transferable, or even desired by many countries pursuing neoliberal policies. Yet there is a clear understanding of the need for empowered local government if sustainable forms are to come into being. The experience of Curitiba, using its powers to guide development where it is wanted, and link it to public transport corridors, may have wider application.

Fiscal measures. The strength of the private sector in driving development is often the result of weak controls and *laissez-faire* policies. The taxation system has been proposed as one method of achieving a more equitable distribution of costs, and of making development more sustainable. Development taxes are suggested in both South Africa and Brazil, to make developers pay the costs of infrastructure provision, and to encourage development on vacant land within areas of urban sprawl. If taxation is the 'stick', then there are 'carrots' in the form of incentives. The manipulation of permitted floor area ratios to encourage development by giving developers a higher return, or of the transfer of development rights to allow development in planned locations, has been shown to work in practice. Both give incentives to more compact, higher density development. There is a negative side, as global competition to attract foreign investment can lead to granting that loosens controls and gives free rein to market forces that may have little concern for the environment.

The informal sector. A great deal of peripheral development is created within the informal sector and through illegal land invasion. While this development may lack resources and infrastructure, it results from the energy, skill and self-organisational abilities of sometimes a considerable proportion of a city's population. The process of consolidation of informal development turns precariously established shelter into reasonably liveable dwellings. This is a resource that could be empowered and people's efforts integrated into the overall development of the city.

Models and measurement. Knowing what is within the city and metropolitan region is an important precondition of successful policy-making. With the rapid growth in population and development, the advent of remote sensing provides an instrument to identify the extent of development and any potential threats to the environment. The utility of mapping and modelling, whether of sustainability indicators or scenarios for compact development, is shown to be practicable and significant in informing policy direction.

Conclusion

How then does this relate to the developed world and the findings of the other two books in this series? The first point of comparison is in relation to sustainable development – living within environmental means, achieving equity and social justice, and inclusiveness in decision-making processes. It has to be said that in many respects cities in developing countries have a long way to go. Even though the majority of the countries studied in this book (except for Hong Kong) have far smaller ecological footprints than the developed countries, this is more likely to be due to low GNP and poverty rather that to any sustainable development policy. As, or if, economies grow and countries become richer, levels of consumption will rise and increase unsustainability. Clearly, maintaining poverty to keep a measure of sustainability is not an acceptable option. In any case, such global 'sustainability' is bought at a cost of local environmental degradation, poor health and reduced quality of life. Cities in these countries, mostly, do not measure up to the aspirations for equity and social justice expressed in definitions of sustainability, although there are some exceptions. For example, Hong Kong provides high levels of social facilities for its new development along with good public transport provision, and the gap between rich and poor is relatively narrow. Efforts to achieve some equity in access to urban facilities are in evidence in Brazil and South Africa. But on the whole, the wide disparities between rich and poor, the formal and informal sectors, the city centres and disadvantaged periphery, place serious obstacles in the way of achieving sustainable development. The need for inclusiveness in policy-making has been recognised in Latin America and South Africa where the will exists to achieve it. However, in Asia there appears to be little evidence of local participation.

The second point of comparison is in relation to the components of sustainable urban development and questions raised about the 'European' model for the compact city. In the previous two books it was concluded that, rather than a single model, there should be a variety of urban forms and a number of 'pathways' to achieve sustainable urban development. These forms had some common characteristics, including compactness, mixed uses and interconnected streets, good public transport provision, environmental controls and good urban management.

In developing countries, where there is an enormous range of people, cultures and economies, the size of the problem is immense, and growing fast. Nevertheless, there are a number of points of comparison. Compactness appears to be an aspiration and a hoped-for solution to the problems of the explosive growth of urban areas, and it has some meaning when applied to the intensification of many sub-centres within a metropolitan region. Mixed use does not feature as an issue, as the vitality exists in abundance and problems are more likely to arise from there being too much rather than too little of it. Good public transport exists, and in some cases is better than that found in developed countries, although this is the exception rather than the rule. Even so, public transport use is generally much higher in developing countries, but this is more usually the result of low per capita incomes rather than any explicit sustainability policy. The ease with which traffic becomes saturated is a function of dense urban forms, and these in turn become highly polluted. Pollution is a problem even in rich cities like Hong Kong, and while 'clean technology' may help its reduction, it would give no alleviation to congestion. Concerning the other characteristics, neither environmental controls nor urban management measure up to those found in developed countries. In all but a few countries, local government controls are weak.

However, such comparisons may not be very useful; drawing selectively from best practice may be more helpful. For the cities of developing countries the choices are there. The choice exists, for example, to use the most appropriate ideas from the developed world to guide, shape and control the future form of the huge cities in the developing world. The concepts of the compact city, and of sustainable urban forms, have changed and evolved over the past two decades, and, as the research has shown here, a number of them have relevance to developing countries. It is in the cities of these countries, where most growth is taking place, that new theory or new concepts should emerge. The view expressed, that there should be a regional view of the compact city, whether African or Asian or Latin American, is right. It is worth remembering that New York's explosive development at the beginning of the twentieth century took forms not imagined before, and it was seen then as the 'New World'. The same is true of the rapid urbanisation and rise of the megacity in the 'new' developing world today. With 'hyper densities', vast populations, rapid development of the periphery, and a willingness to invest in mass transit provision, change is happening at a breathtaking pace. Developing the theories and ideas that will steer these changes into the 'unimaginable', yet sustainable, urban forms of the future will be a challenge for the policy-makers and designers of these countries. All the ingredients and opportunities are there: it may simply need the confidence (and resources) to meet them.

Reference
Seabrook, J. (1996) *In the Cities of the South: Scenes from a Developing World,* Verso, London

Index

237-8; East Asia, dense urban areas 271-82; Hong Kong 264-6; Santiago, public transport 177; South Africa 211, 212-13, 214-15; Tokyo, public transport 45; congestion 34; and densification 16, 188t; and infrastructure 347-8; travel time, limits to growth 40-1, *see also* infrastructure
Tsai, Te-I Albert, Asia, agricultural consequences 63-70
Tsou, Ko-Wan, Tainan 321-9

Ulam, Stanislaw M. 83
UN Declaration of Human Rights 13
UNCED Agenda 21 proposals 10
urban climate 117-24
urban development: Latin America, new patterns 57; Pearl River Delta, loss of agricultural land 73-88; developing and developed countries 12; implications 11-14
urban farming, effect of containment 68-9
urban form 19-20, 343-7; costs and infrastructure 296-7; Hong Kong 261-4; informal and compact 198-202; spatial form 99-100; sustainable criteria 83
urban management: Brazil 128, 132-8;

Egypt 127-31, 137-8
urban sprawl 346-7; Brazil, minimising effects 183-90; Delhi 162; Dongguan 79-82; Pearl River Delta 76-9; South Africa 209-17, 219-28
USA, growth management 65-6
Uytenbogaardt, R. 233

Vajpayee, Atal Behari 155
Viva o Centro, Sao Paulo 135-6
Von Neumann, John 83

Ward, J.H. 326
waste disposal: Cairo 129; Calcutta 316, see also infrastructure
Wigmans, G. 226
Williams, K. *et al.*, achievability of sustainable urban forms 1
World Bank, urban poverty 13

Yeh, Anthony G., Pearl River Delta 73-88
Young, K. 169

Zhang, Xing Quan, Hong Kong, high-rise development 245-52
Zillmann, Kerstin, Caracas 193-204